SECRETS OF BROKEN POTTERY

SECRETS OF BROKEN POTTERY

Seeing the Great Potter—Being Seen by Him

Heidi McKendrick

Katamerismoú Publishing

The Secrets of Broken Pottery
Copyright @ 2021 by Heidi McKendrick

This title is available as ebook, soft cover, and hard cover.
Requests for information should be addressed to: editor@katamerismou.com
Katamerismoú Publishing
www.katamerismou.com
For the reflections of the book, visit: www.secretsofbrokenpottery.com

Library Congress Cataloging-in-Publication Data

McKendrick, Heidi, 1964-
    The Secrets of Broken Pottery

ISBN: 978-1-7776366-0-9

Scripture quotations marked NIV are taken from THE HOLY BIBLE, NEW INTERNATIONAL VERSION®, NIV® Copyright © 1973, 1978, 1984, 2011 by Biblica, Inc.® Used by permission. All rights reserved worldwide. Scripture quotations marked ESV are taken from the ESV® Bible (The Holy Bible, English Standard Version®), copyright © 2001 by Crossway, a publishing ministry of Good News Publishers. Used by permission. All rights reserved. Scripture quotations marked NASB are taken from the New American Standard Bible®, copyright ©1960, 1995 by The Lockman Foundation. Used by permission. (www.Lockman.org). Scripture quotations marked NKJV are taken from the New King James Version®. Copyright © 1982 by Thomas Nelson. Used by permission. All rights reserved. Scripture quotations marked NLT are taken from the Holy Bible, New Living Translation, copyright ©1996, 2007 by Tyndale House Foundation. Used by permission of Tyndale House Publishers, Inc., Carol Stream, Illinois 60188. All rights reserved. Scripture quotations marked KJV are taken from the King James Version, public domain.

The author has added *italics* to Scripture quotations for emphasis.

Unless noted otherwise, the definitions of original Hebrew and Greek words are taken from Spiros Zodhiates' *Hebrew-Greek Key Word Study Bible. New American Standard Bible.* (Chattanooga, TN: AMG Publishers, 1990). This book consists "The Lexical Aids to the Old and New Testament," "The New American Standard Concordance to the Old and New Testament," "A Concise Dictionary of the Words in The Hebrew Bible; with their renderings in the authorized English version" by James Strong; "Hebrew and Chaldee Dictionary accompanying the exhaustive concordance," and "Dictionary of the Greek Testament."

Any internet addresses (websites, blogs, articles, etc.) referenced in this book are offered as a resource. They are not intended to be or to imply an endorsement by the Author, nor does the Author vouch for the content of these sites for the life of this book.

All rights reserved. No part of this book may be reproduced in any form or by any electronic or mechanical means, including information storage and retrieval systems, without permission in writing from the Author, except by reviewers, who may quote brief passages in a review.

Illustrations and Cover by Marie Muravski
Photos by Eveliina
Interior design by Daiana Marchessi

Printed in the United States of America

So I went down to the potter's house,

and I saw him working at the wheel.

But the pot he was shaping from the clay was marred in his hands;

so the potter formed it into another pot,

shaping it as seemed best to him.

Jeremiah 18:3–4 (NKJV)

Yet you, LORD, are our Father.

We are the clay, you are the potter;

we are all the work of your hand.

Isaiah 64:8 (NKJV)

But indeed, O man, who are you to reply against God?

Will the thing formed say to him who formed it,

"Why have you made me like this?"

Does not the potter have power over the clay,

from the same lump to make one vessel for honor and another for dishonor?

Romans 9:20–21 (NKJV)

Contents

Preface

Part 1: REFLECTIONS OF BROKEN POTTERY

Introduction	3
Chapter 1: When You Accidentally Break Your Clay Pottery	7
Chapter 2: When Someone Accidentally Breaks Your Clay Pottery	13
Chapter 3: When Someone Intentionally Breaks Your Clay Pottery	21
Chapter 4: When You Intentionally Break Your Clay Pottery	31
Chapter 5: When an Unpredictable Force Majeure Breaks Your Clay Pottery	39
Chapter 6: In the Trash Yard of Broken Potteries	45
Chapter 7: In the Great Potter's House	49

Part 2: STORIES OF BROKEN POTTERY

Introduction	61
Chapter 8: Job: The Broken Pottery Who Sees the Great Potter with His Own Eyes	63
Chapter 9: Abraham's Dysfunctional Dynasty	79
Chapter 10: Hagar: Invisible and Voiceless but Seen and Heard by the Great Potter	85
Chapter 11: Leah: Ugly and Unloved	101
Chapter 12: Dinah: Raped and Silenced	109
Chapter 13: Joseph: Broken and Restored	115
Chapter 14: Tamar: The Black Widow	125
Chapter 15: David: The Lusting King	131
Chapter 16: Princess Tamar: The Royal Outcast	141
Chapter 17: Elijah: The Prophet Broken under a Mountain	153

Chapter 18: Jeremiah: The Weeping Prophet — 169

Chapter 19: Mary: The Most Blessed Among Women — 179

Chapter 20: Nameless Women on the Great Potter's Table — 191

Chapter 21: The Bleeding Woman: Healed with New Identity — 193

Chapter 22: The Woman Caught in Adultery and Almost Smashed by Stones — 199

Chapter 23: The Weeping Woman through the Eyes of the Great Potter — 207

Chapter 24: The Samaritan Woman: Predestined to Meet the Great Potter — 217

Chapter 25: Peter: Pitifully Smashed and Reinstated — 227

Chapter 26: Judas Iscariot: Smashed Pottery and Scapegoated — 237

Chapter 27: Paul the Pharisee: Broken but Polished — 249

Part 3: SECRETS OF BROKEN POTTERY

Introduction — 265

Chapter 28: SECRET #1: A Treasure inside Your Clay Pottery — 267

Chapter 29: SECRET #2: You're Loved with the Great Potter's Unfailing and Unconditional Love — 273

Chapter 30: SECRET #3: You're the Recipient of the Great Potter's Never-Ending Grace and Mercy — 277

Chapter 31: SECRET #4: The Great Potter's Grace—Even if You Cannot Feel It — 283

Chapter 32: SECRET #5: The Great Potter Accepts You As-Is — 287

Chapter 33: SECRET #6: The Great Potter's Child— Being an Heir Is Permanent — 291

Chapter 34: SECRET #7: The Great Potter Is Faithful Even When You Are Not — 297

Chapter 35: SECRET #8: The Treasure, Christ in You, Will Not Disappear When Your Pottery Breaks — 301

Chapter 36: SECRET #9: You Are a New Creation, Reconciled and Righteous Even When Broken — 305

Chapter 37: SECRET #10: The Great Potter Is Your Continuous Savior — 309

Chapter 38: SECRET #11: You Are the Great Potter's Most Precious and Beautiful Clay Pottery — 315

Chapter 39: SECRET #12: You Will Learn about the Great Potter When You Surrender — 321

Chapter 40: SECRET #13: No Matter What, the Great Potter Is Always in Control	327
Chapter 41: SECRET #14: The Great Potter's Supernatural Peace Guards You	331
Chapter 42: SECRET #15: Your Empty Pottery Will Be Filled	335
Chapter 43: SECRET #16: You Are Never Damaged Goods for the Great Potter's Service	339
Chapter 44: SECRET #17: Your Broken Pieces Aren't Wasted	347
Chapter 45: SECRET #18: Your Brokenness May Become Your Ministry	351
Chapter 46: SECRET #19: One Day Your Tears Will Be Wiped Away, and Your Pottery Will Be Whole	357
Chapter 47: SECRET #20: There is Blessing in Your Brokenness	361

Part 4: HEALING BROKEN POTTERY

Introduction

Chapter 48: Good News to the Bums	375
Chapter 49: Healing the Brokenhearted	379
Chapter 50: Liberating the Captives	383
Chapter 51: Recovering Macaroni Vision	393
Chapter 52: Liberating the Oppressed	401
Chapter 53: Comforting Those Who Mourn	407
Chapter 54: Healing Through Forgiveness	413
Chapter 55: Tearing Down the False Gods—Distorted Images of the Great Potter	425
Chapter 56: The Mystery Full of Grace—Immanuel—God with us	439
Chapter 57: Broken Vessel in the Great Potter's Service—Building a Healthy Christian Church	447
Chapter 58: Final Words: The Cracked Pottery and Flowers	465
About the Author's Pottery	470
Acknowledgments	472
Notes	474
Bibliography	490

PREFACE

Growing up in a legalistic, performance-focused church community distorted my idea of God, the Great Potter, for three decades. Looking back, it is nothing short of a miracle that I never lost *not only the Potter* but also the broken pieces of my life that scattered when my clay pottery broke. My broken pottery falling into the Great Potter's loving hands is why I wrote this book. I want to share the secrets I've learned about Him and my position as His pottery. No pieces of your brokenness are wasted when the Great Potter collects the fragments and takes them to the Potter's House.

Secrets of Broken Pottery is about broken lives—broken clay pots, and their spiritual healing. Potteries crushed, shattered, cracked, smashed, crumbled, distorted, fractured, and demolished. Ruinations for every imaginable reason. Within these pages you will learn the Great Potter's plan—how He holds all His clay together. You will learn about His characteristics; His unconditional love, never-ending grace, and faithfulness to the generations. He is always in charge of your restoration and reinstation.

The first part of the book introduces broken potteries, reflecting on the reasons for their hurt. Sometimes we break our pottery ourselves, but often, it is by others either accidentally or intentionally. It can also be *a force majeure*, something that can happen to anyone, anytime.

The second part tells stories of broken potteries in the Bible. Stripping away the illusions of embellishment created of Biblical heroes and fashioning them in a realistic light as broken potteries, this book reaffirms that *the Great Potter remains faithful even if we don't.* You will meet Abraham's dysfunctional dynasty—the invisible and voiceless, raped and silenced, the ugly and unloved. A Black Widow, a Lusting King, and a Royal Outcast. There's the Weeping Prophet and another smashed under a mountain. See the apostles revealed in a fashion you may not have encountered before. The nameless women with a divine appointment on the Great Potter's table..., and many others. These stories reflect us, you and me, our life struggles and blessings. The stories celebrate the Great Potter, the One who broke Himself on our behalf so that we could be whole. Every pot is precious, broken or not, the Great Potter never wastes His clay! We all break but our faith in the Great Potter helps us put the pieces back together...

The third part of *The Secrets of Broken Pottery* explores the twenty secrets of broken potteries for all of us broken containers to reflect on—inviting a spiritual discovery, growth, and healing. Had I only known these truths in my youth it would have saved my pottery from holding a distorted view of the Great Potter. But better later than never, I guess... I hope that immersing in these secrets will assist you in ridding yourself of any damaging and false images you may have about the Great Potter.

The final part of *The Healing of Broken Pottery* discusses the process of restoration—or as much as is possible on this side of eternity. As Christians we believe that our tears cannot be completely wiped away until heaven, therefore the healing process continues until then. The final chapter of the book is written for Christian therapists and Pastoral counselors who work with traumatized potteries. This chapter may also be beneficial for those seeking professional therapy.

The main concept of this book conveys the framework of *Christian Pastoral Care*. It is targeted for Christian potteries broken because of life's labours and painful blows—many because of their traumatizing experiences in legalistic and spiritually abusive church communities. The message emphasizes the Great Potter's revulsion of the tarnishing of His name through the abuse perpetrated by so many religious organizations.

This book is not about a prosperity gospel or legalistic performance-focused gospel, and it does not promise that problems and brokenness will disappear if only you have enough faith, or do this and avoid that. Instead, this book is about the Great Potter, our Redeemer, who wants a relationship with His vessels of clay. *Secrets of Broken Pottery—finding the blessings and spiritual growth in our brokenness.*

The book challenges you to reflect and re-consider your image of God, the Great Potter, the way you see Him, and the way you *think* He sees you. As broken pottery you are not only perfectly safe and loved in the Great Potter's hands, but also *cherished*. You *are loved* with the divine love that surrounds your clay pottery inside and out. You *are* His most beautiful and precious pottery!

I hope you will claim for yourself the following truth:
- Even if I am marred or broken and destroyed, the Great Potter will start all over again—He will make something new.
- He will launch a good process, and He will never give up on me—He will see it to the end.
- None of my broken pieces go wasted.
- There is strength in broken pottery…

I wish you the most therapeutic and beautiful process on the Great Potter's table! I hope you will be fully integrated with His unconditional and unfailing love and never-ending grace!

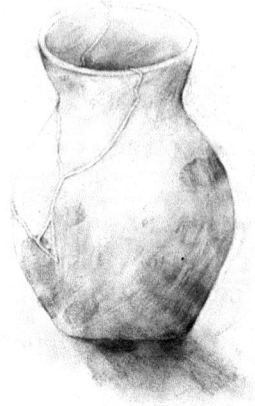

Please, Note

It is important to acknowledge that reading any book about brokenness may be potentially triggering if the reader suffers from past or acute traumatizing experiences. Therefore, I encourage you to be aware of your responses and feelings to the topics in this book. If you read something that triggers painful memories and it becomes difficult to deal with your emotions by yourself, I strongly recommend *finding a trusted friend or professional therapist/counselor* with whom you can discuss and reflect your experiences and emotions. It is often therapeutic to share difficult memories with someone you can trust. Sharing our burdens lightens the load. There is no reason to feel embarrassed to ask for help when you feel you need it! As the Great Potter's potteries, we have been called to share one another's burdens.

PART 1
REFLECTIONS OF BROKEN POTTERY

INTRODUCTION

During Bible times, clay pots were common in daily use. Households had several: water pots, milk pots, food pots… and almost everything was kept in them: oil, spices, herbs, grain, flour. Clay pots were used daily, just like we use stainless-steel pots and pans, which are much more durable. They were inexpensive. Everyone could afford them.

Even though clay potteries were not valuable, they often contained costly items, such as perfumes, papyrus rolls, or even gold or other treasures.

But clay pottery broke easily and often.

Indeed, clay pots broke so frequently that most towns and cities provided trash yards outside the city specifically for disposing of those broken pots. Archeologists have uncovered these areas. I have visited the one outside the historic city of Rome. Perhaps Job was in one of these trash yards as he sat on the ashes scraping his sores with a piece of clay (Job 2:8).

The Bible compares us with clay fashioned by the Great Potter Himself (Isaiah 64:8).

Yes, we are vessels made from dirt and clay (Genesis 2:7)—clay potteries, every one of us. Some of us look shiny, pretty, and embellished while others are a bit rough and plain. Some of us were made like Royal Doulton fine porcelain, and others are as practical as garden pots. Some are used for high tea; others store seeds for the spring. Regardless of how we look or what we are used for, all clay pots are somewhat fragile. We break easily and may become traumatized by experiencing emotional pain,[1] a horrendous amount of helplessness,[2] or a lack of empathy from others. This can happen during daily use, or when merely sitting on a shelf.

Just like Job. Or Joseph. Or Elijah. Or many other Bible heroes.

We shouldn't be surprised to find ourselves broken into pieces, lying smashed on the ground, or back on the Potter's wheel being reshaped. Oh, and there are times when we are undeniably in the hot oven, being refined with fire again. We have times of waiting, when we are sitting on a shelf at the Potter's house, eager to be used. Sometimes we hide in the darkest corner of a storage room, feeling ignored, useless, and sad, or we sit on a ledge, exhausted, and worn out from being used too much and too often without any break or time to rest.

Each of us is in one of these phases of the lifelong process of being a clay pottery. It is only in heaven when we are finally perfect, free of cracks, whole, and restored from our constant brokenness. But no worries! Even if we break, the Great Potter will take care of us. He knows what He is doing. Our process is His responsibility. He never forsakes us nor deserts us, even though we may sometimes feel that way.

The next chapters will explore five reasons why we break before we visit the trash yard of broken potteries and the Potter's House.

Please, pray with me:

Thank You, Jesus, for being my Great Potter

—Thank You for being with me at this moment wherever I am right now.

I affirm that I am clay in a particular phase of the process,

in Your hand on the Great Potter's wheel.

You know me, and You know my name—my name is written on the palm of Your hand.

You know every detail of my life: my past, my present, my feelings, my dreams and my fears.

You also know my wounds and hurts. You know and understand my brokenness.

You know how every crack and fracture came to me and why.

Thank You for Your encompassing empathy toward me—Your unfailing and unconditional love, Your never-ending grace, and Your everlasting faithfulness.

Thank You for giving me a sense of safety in Your hands on the Great Potter's table

… And for starting and completing the good process in me according to Your promise.

Amen

CHAPTER 1

WHEN YOU ACCIDENTALLY BREAK YOUR CLAY POTTERY

It is possible to accidentally break our own clay potteries. You can unintentionally break yourself. Perhaps you are careless or absent-minded. Possibly life has become too busy, and you are under tremendous stress. Or maybe you are so exhausted that you cannot hold anything anymore.

Possibly you don't even take notice of your pottery when you are busy doing the 'important' things of life, even if there is nothing more essential than taking care of *your* pottery. It is sitting on the counter, but you do not even take note. Most of the time, you hardly pay any attention to it. As a result, you accidentally push it with your elbow and it drops off of the counter. When you hear the crashing of the breaking earthenware, you finally stop what you are doing and consider what has just happened.

Standing above the mess, staring at the hundreds of pieces on that floor, you're perplexed and wonder if there is any fast fix, any superglue that could mend the pottery. Instantly because you're busy with other duties and too busy to take these broken pieces seriously. You do a Google search to try to find a miracle glue that would make the obvious scars somewhat invisible as you try to piece yourself back together.

You may also do nothing; you don't pay *any* attention to your pottery. Instead, you may keep taking care of others' potteries thinking your pottery will be fine even if shattered in a thousand pieces.

Does any of this sound familiar?

I know I've been there.

I've filled my schedule with so much work that I've neglected to take care of my basic needs. I did not eat a healthy diet; I did not sleep enough; I did not rest. And the list of ignoring caring for myself goes on. As a result, little by little, my pottery forms cracks. Too much stress, too much cortisol, lack of immunity, several episodes of flu and colds that I never fully recover from, insomnia, a heart attack, a stroke . . .

Sometimes we accidentally break our clay pots because we simply do not take proper care of them or no care at all. Perhaps, we did not even think this pottery is important, wonderfully made, and precious.

If we suffered trauma in childhood, we learned that our needs are not important. Or at least not as important as others' needs. We may have even learned that we do not need to be taken care of or that we need nobody. Or, deeply in our core, we may even feel that we do not deserve good care.

Was there a deeper, unconscious reason you were careless around your clay pottery the day it broke? Was there a deeper reason you felt like you had to please other people? Even to ignore your well-being? Or was it simply an accident? A temporary hurry that caused you to bump your clay pottery because you were not paying attention to it?

And in that pause moment after it shatters, you feel startled:

What was that noise?

What are these pieces on the floor?

What just happened?

It is important to understand that this very moment of this broken pottery could indeed become a turning point, a life-altering moment that I refer to as before and after. Could this be a new beginning? An opportunity for a fresh start? — Well, for sure, it forces you to stop, at least for a moment, to choose what to do with it. Do you allow this crisis to become a new opportunity, or will you take the broom and swipe the ugly pieces under the carpet or straight into the trash can? Whatever you do, you need to ask yourself the following:

Can I tolerate this sudden feeling of an uttermost vulnerability?

Can I not only tolerate it but also embrace it?

Does the Great Potter have something to say on this mess?

He does. This is what He says to you: *"My grace is sufficient for you, for My strength is made perfect in weakness"* (2 Corinthians 12:9 NKJV).

If you choose the way of vulnerability, you will allow the Great Potter to collect your broken pieces from the floor and place them on His table. It means you will need to *reflect* on your past, present, and future while He mixes the new clay with your crumbles, kneading and wedging it all together: Some things to reflect on are:

- *Where did I come from?*
- *Where am I going?*
- *Where am I right now, and why?*
- *Am I allowing my past to determine my future and how I get there?*

- *Am I currently responsible for my actions and my feelings?*
- *Who am I? What is my true self? Do I even know anything but my false self?*
- *What about my needs? Am I true to my real needs, or do I constantly belittle or deny them?*

And then you must reflect on your relationship with the Great Potter Himself:

- *Have I integrated His unfailing and unconditional love and His never-ending grace into myself?*
- *Has it become an integral part of my true self?*
- *Do I even understand what love and grace mean?*

Oh, that idea of unconditional love that never fails. That does not sound like I love you *if . . .* or I love you *but . . .*! What about the concept of grace? The one that will never end? Have you even begun to understand it?

If not, then you are at the right place on the Great Potter's table. You want to integrate with His love, to internalize His grace, and to have the Great Potter launch the healing process of your pottery, reveal your true self, restore your damaged identity. You want Him to change your stone heart into a heart of flesh, despite the pain.

Of course, you may have to deal with some painful memories while on His table or in the firing oven, especially those you have tried to bury. You may have to face difficult feelings, including those you've denied. Even those episodes of your life you insist did not hurt or matter.

Perhaps unresolved anger for something that took place a long time ago turned against you, resulting in "accidentally" breaking your own clay pottery through neglecting to protect it. The anger paralyzed and numbed you so that you ignored your needs and emotions. You may need to face the deep grief and sorrow for something that should have happened but didn't. Maybe you need to deal with guilt, shame, or humiliation.

> *It is my time to feel the feelings that had no voice.*
> *It is my time to finally become visible.*
> *For the first time in my life, it's time to ask myself: What do I need?*

Perhaps in your past you only asked others what *they* needed *you* to need. But now it is safe to become visible and vulnerable on the Great Potter's table. When

Secrets Of Broken Pottery

the new soft clay is mixed with your hard pieces, you suddenly feel safe to feel your feelings. This will be the new beginning.

In the future, when you unintentionally break your pottery, I hope you will remember that you do not have to try to fix it yourself, not with superglues or Band-Aids. You will know the launching pad for your healing; at the Great Potter's table.

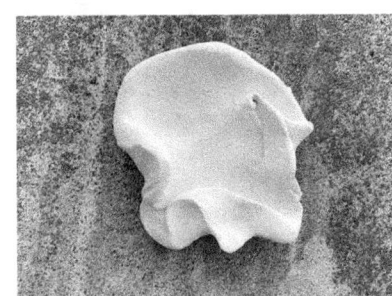

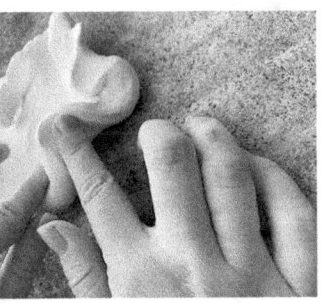
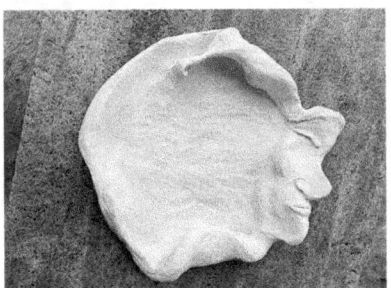
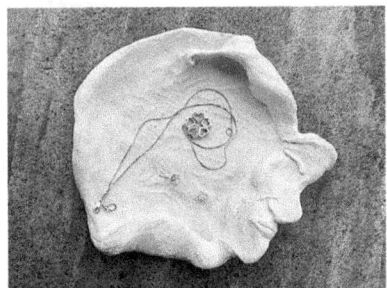

11

CHAPTER 2

WHEN SOMEONE ACCIDENTALLY BREAKS YOUR CLAY POTTERY

It was just an accident. They did not mean anything bad. They did not plot to drop your pottery and break it into a thousand pieces. But there it is. Scattered on the stone floor, some pieces are missing, others splintered beyond recognition. Your precious clay pottery that only a few minutes ago was beautiful is a shattered mess.

Perhaps they were careless, busy, stressed and thus neglected to take care of your clay pottery. Maybe they didn't know it was fragile. Or how they take care of a clay pot was based on how they were treated as a child, and they didn't know that what they were doing could be so damaging. Possibly they did not understand the risk they were taking. And then, there is the possibility that they were just stupid.

They did not mean anything bad. Yet irrespective of their good intentions, these benevolent people demolished your pottery.

A thousand pieces lie shattered on the stone floor, screaming in pain. They scream but silently because they do not believe they have the right to scream out loud, to let others know of their pain. After all, these well-meaning people did not mean anything bad.

And so, you swallow your pain and count to ten—then one hundred and one thousand if nothing else eases the ache. You gulp your pain and anger and try to swallow your sorrow but only a painful clump forms on your throat. You might find relief if you could cry, but nothing comes out. You're broken into a thousand pieces, but you pretend you're okay.

You may even smile. Your self-talk denies what you're feeling:

It was not *so* bad.

I'm *not* traumatized. I'll be fine!

Well, at least they *meant* good…

No, really, it didn't hurt *that* much.

… *Have a nice day, you too!*

Screaming silently. Paralyzed as if moving would increase the pain. Standing still, having no idea where to gather the pieces and how to find all of them. Some dropped inside the stone gaps on the floor, some mixed with the dirt, some smashed as a sandy clay. You have no idea how to ever repair anything.

Restoration feels impossible.

And those folks who broke you can't fix it either. Perhaps they didn't notice what they did. Maybe they never will, as your lips are sealed because you don't want anybody to see you vulnerable and helpless. Their seeing your humiliation would be more horrible than being scattered on the floor in a thousand pieces.

Would it matter if they said they were sorry?

And after a while, anger and rage fill you, followed by sadness then a little bitterness too. *…I want them to pay!* Wouldn't that be the least they could do if they paid for the damage they caused?

…Oh yes, they did not mean it, but whatever! Who cares? They did it, and it is me who is suffering here. I am in this mess not of my own doing.

But they do *not*. At least whatever they do does not make it better. In the end, you are still in bits and pieces. Still scattered over the floor. Whatever you used to do before this took place is now paused. *Done! Kaput!*

It will never be the same.

The sad reality is that the closest relationships can sometimes turn into the most traumatizing in our lives. Even the most kind-hearted parents may *unintentionally* do bad when they try to do what they *think* is best for their children. Often, this well-meaning cycle is passed down from one generation to the next.

Has your pottery experienced this?

Have you ever unintentionally broken *your* child's pottery? Actually—most parents wish they'd done something differently. Words you wish you'd never uttered… Words you wish you'd said… That time you wish you had spent with your children instead of working or cleaning or doing other tasks.

What about your relationship with your parents? Do you think they did *not* intentionally mean to break your pottery when they broke you into bits and pieces with harsh discipline or words and actions that made you feel as though something was seriously wrong with you; that nothing you did was good enough? What about when they led you to believe that *you* were the reason for *their* misery, marital issues, and problems?

If your parents broke you into a thousand pieces, maybe you have not fully recovered twenty, forty, or even sixty years later.

If your main care-giver suffered psychiatric issues, it may not have been easy for you to be beautiful pottery. Uncontrolled mood swings, rage, or paranoia targeted your clay pottery. Perhaps this person threw you against the wall and you smashed onto the floor—then the next morning he or she would walk on that same floor without even being aware of stepping on your broken pieces. Perhaps sometimes this person knelt and comforted you, picking up pieces and trying to fix your pottery. *But why bother?*—You learned that there was always another outburst that smashed you to bits.

Did you learn to prepare your pottery for the blow before it hit?

Perhaps you had a parent with deep depression, and she or he stared at the wall day after day. Your parent did not hear your questions or your crying. They did not compliment your fine Lego train nor your beautiful prom dress. Your neglected, invisible clay pottery sat on a ledge until it began to crack and fracture and finally crumbled to the floor unattended.

Or did your parents abuse alcohol or drugs, filling you with empty promises and pathetic lying? "I will never, ever, ever do this to you again!" But they did. And you broke again. One day, you had no strength to even want to recover because you had lost hope.

Wouldn't it be easier just to stay there on that floor as scattered pieces?
Wouldn't it be easier not to try to fix anything?
At least then, nobody can break it again!

Or did you grow up in foster care or a group home where well-meaning guardians never saw you for who you were? Though you longed to be loved, your need to protect your pottery was stronger, so you fiercely pushed away anybody who got too close.

Perhaps you grew up as a missionary kid, crying yourself sleep in a boarding school somewhere in the world, missing your parents who sacrificed their lives for a bigger purpose. You tried to look joyful and care-free because this was expected from you, but inside you were lonely and abandoned. Did you feel anger toward the Great Potter, who took your parents away from you?

What about being brutally broken pottery in a relationship? Not intentionally, but because your friends lacked relationship skills, or they repeated trauma they had learned and were not able to commit, they tossed you aside. You're left on the floor, thinking that something must be wrong with you for your friends to forsake you. *I am not smart enough. I am too fat. I'm too ugly...* You cried your heart out and decided never to trust anybody again.

Perhaps your spouse broke your pottery. The loving pottery who once promised to love you in good and bad days had a change of heart. It was unintentional, driven by unconsciously triggered past hurts. Your wife meant nothing terrible, but her disappointment that you don't match up with her image and her cutting remarks gradually broke you into pieces. Your husband probably did not realize how hurtful his blunt declarations and sarcastic comments about your looks are. With each remark, a new crack appeared in your pottery. When your relationship with this pottery you used to love breaks, you decided that you will never fall in love again. *Never.* Not with anybody. Neither will you ever allow anybody to love you again. From being broken too many times, you learned that love only hurts and eventually breaks.

Siblings unintentionally broke your pottery when rivalry and innocent competition launched into something more. Vying for your parents' favor became a fierce competition, leaving you a pile of clay crumble. It's no wonder bitterness and the need for revenge grew.

Unintentionally, without meaning anything bad, your children pierced your heart and broke your clay pottery. They treated you as though you were made of iron, flinging harsh words and accusations. In their young self-centeredness, they did not notice that they broke you.

I doubt adult children meant bad when they placed their aging parents in a nursing home and never or rarely visited. Their lives were busy and they had marital and financial problems too. You understand that they never *meant* to forsake your worn-out pottery gathering dust in this nursing home room with only your photo albums and memories for company. However, you needed more than sitting on a shelf. The cracks and fractures began. You missed the human touch, discussions, tender words, your grandchildren's laughter. *"It is what it is."* The cracks deepened and spread. All alone.

Has your clay pottery experienced any of these situations? Have well-meaning potteries—family members, friends, church or club members—broken you?

I am convinced that the preacher of my childhood church had only the best intentions when teaching us kids about the Great Potter dropping hot stones from heaven to smash our clay pottery if we disobeyed. Week after week he told us about hell and brimstones, and the little girl that I was soaked it up. He had no idea that this way of introducing me to the Great Potter destroyed my image of Him for the next thirty years. Rather than see Him as the loving Father He is, who cherishes me, I hid from Him. I avoided Him, fearing His wrath. All the while, unknown to me, I could've asked Him to collect my broken pieces and fix them, and He would've gladly done it.

My Sunday school teacher did not mean anything bad either when she explained to the five-year-old me that the Great Potter reads my every secret thought. If they are not pure enough in every moment, I will undoubtedly be left behind when the heavenly trumpet sounds and the Great Potter comes to take His potteries to heaven. I am pretty sure she did not mean me to nurture within me false guilt and an overly sensitive consciousness. She did not plan for fears and anxiety to grow within me, yet she certainly planted the seeds.

None of these folks who unintentionally broke me meant it. Some might even be horrified if they knew what they did. When they accidentally dropped my clay pottery to the floor, it was *not* out of malice; rather, they were simply rough or held me with unskilled hands. They may have been careless, reckless, or absent-minded, even foolish. I bet some of them were clueless. Regardless, the damage was done, and I remained broken for years.

Actually—maybe many of these well-meaning folks dropped our pottery because somebody had first dropped *theirs*. They treated us the way they had been treated, and they did not see any problems in it. They probably had no idea how to properly demonstrate their love. Maybe they had not been hugged, held, or told that they were loved. Perhaps they were broken too—broken recently or from childhood. Pushed to the floor, smashed to the wall, they did not know any better way but to break our pottery as well—repeating generational trauma. They may have suffered because of war, poverty, injustice, or any number of hardships.

The critical question is, *how do we stop this vicious cycle from repeating* from generation to generation? One way is to reflect on and learn the reasons for our brokenness. If we understand why, we can stop breaking other potteries.

I reflected. —And I understand now how my view of the Great Potter became so distorted. I can see that the incorrect image has interfered with my relationship with Him—I wondered if I could ever understand who He is. I struggled with my fear of Him, thinking He would blame and shame me when He found my broken dirty pieces. I avoided Him because I feared the disdain, dissatisfaction, and coldness that would surely be in His eyes when observing my mess. I questioned that His love would fail me as well, that He also might break my pottery.

But I discovered that the solution was to let the Great Potter collect my broken pieces and put them onto His table, allowing Him, not others, to show me who He is. It was at the Great Potter's table when I began to feel again.

I began to cry.

I began to laugh.

I began to trust.

Even if I wanted to, I could not erase my past trauma. That kind of an eraser does not exist, not even on the Potter's table. However, gradually, by reflecting on and working through each episode that broke my pottery, I gained more insight and a sense of empowerment. When the fresh clay of His unconditional, unfailing love mixed with my hard clay crumble, I began to see everything from a new perspective. Past traumatic episodes no longer defined my clay pottery or triggered painful emotions. The past no longer determined my present, future choices, or the way I use my talents. I learned how to control emotions and reactions that have unconsciously controlled me all of my life. I am learning to see myself through the eyes of the Great Potter. When He looks at me, He sees that I am precious and wonderfully made.

Little by little, I let myself become liberated.

…And I decided to forgive those who broke my pottery.

CHAPTER 3

WHEN SOMEONE INTENTIONALLY BREAKS YOUR CLAY POTTERY

Has someone intentionally broken your clay pottery with rage, maliciousness, or wickedness? Unfortunately, perpetrators inflict such damage. They intend to hurt our pottery. Worse, they feel no sorrow about it.

Most perpetrators have their reasons, of course, all of which point to their own broken potteries, never restored, and never receiving the work of the Great Potter's healing hands. Nevertheless, they *intentionally* damage your pottery. When they saw your precious clay pottery, they formed a plan to break it. Crunch it. Destroy it.

The devil, the great demolisher, does that. He intends to find someone to destroy for good. He particularly enjoys destroying children's lives as early as possible. When the child's sense of safety is damaged and trust is destroyed, he knows that only a miracle can save this child. Indeed, the devil hungers to destroy our image of the Great Potter as early as possible. Wanting us to perceive the Great Potter as malicious, he projects onto us a distorted image that is more like the devil himself: wrathful, angry, looking for reasons to dole out punishment... The devil wishes to hide from us the Great Potter's unconditional, unfailing love and His never-ending grace. If he can make it difficult for us to enter into a healthy relationship with the Great Potter because of our distorted and fearful images of Him, then he is gleeful.

Yes, the devil goes around looking for clay potteries he could smash, crash, crunch, and destroy (1 Peter 5:8), using other broken potteries to do his dirty work as well—very effectively. We see it as child porn, sex trafficking, incest, child abuse, child abduction, terrorist attacks, war crimes, genocide, organized crime, gang-rapes, drug dealing, racial and other type of profiling and discrimination... just to name a very few ways. Working with and visiting refugee camps I've seen countless potteries broken by intentional blows.

Those perpetrators who intentionally break our clay potteries not only smash them to pieces but also destroy our sense of trust, justice, and safety. They kick away our humanity and trample on our broken pieces, stealing our beauty, peace, hope and our future. Their blows not only damage temporarily but also, even when we heal, the scars may remain for a lifetime. Some perpetrators smash to traumatize. They do not do it because they are tired or under stress or stupid. They smash our clay potteries for the sole purpose to destroy them, just like the devil does.

There is something deeply disturbing in realizing that another human being intentionally harmed my loved ones or me.

Has your pottery experienced this?

Your broken pieces are scattered over the floor, screaming in horrendous pain and experiencing total helplessness. You can do nothing to help yourself. Nothing will stop the perpetrator's kicking and smashing the pieces, laughing and dancing at your misery. Even when he leaves, you remain helpless to gather your pieces, your shattered self-esteem. You can only remain in your condition, feeling dissociated and numb.

Is this happening to me? I don't recognize this pile of broken clay.

You may have cried, but after a while, the tears dry like glue on your face, and you cannot cry anymore. From nowhere indifference, meaninglessness, a shiver of coldness invades you. Eventually, you hope to somehow stand up, miraculously, like an unbreakable superhero whose face and body seem to be made of cast iron. Like that indestructible character, you gather your smashed pieces as if the battle was nothing, shrugging it off as if it didn't hurt at all. No way will you let anybody see your humiliation, your vulnerability, your face swollen from the tears you shed when you begged for him to stop.

The humiliation hangs on, making you want to shrink and disappear. You see your loss of dignity in the eyes of your perpetrator, in others' eyes, in your own eyes.

I do not want to look at them.
I don't want to see any empathy in their eyes, assuming there is any.
I do not want to look at myself.
I do not want to be seen.

Indifferent and hoping the earth would open and swallow you, another sensation takes over. You seem to detach from your body. Unreal and in slow motion, you observe your situation as if seeing it from a rooftop looking down. You scan your broken pieces as if they belong to someone else.

Looking in the mirror after a few hours, next week, next year, after fifty years, you still see your raw vulnerability. Just a glimpse, but it is too much to take in. Like a deer in the headlights, you have no place to hide. You grab your makeup and make yourself look good, composed, in control, powerful, strong and unbreakable.

No, I do not want to see that rawness.
I do not want anybody else to see it.
I do not want to remember.
I do not want anybody else to remember.

You tried to fix your broken clay pottery. It took a long time, but you managed to gather the pieces, most of them at least. You got glue and cement and made some mortar and grout. You pieced yourself together. You believe you are better than ever. At least, there are no visible cracks, and your pottery does not look so fragile. *Indeed, you are no longer clay pottery. Your pottery is made of cement and stone. Nobody can break it anymore! Never again!*

They can try, but you will not break again.

They can throw your pottery to the floor, but it will not crack.

They can throw it to the wall, but it will not smash.

They can kick and yell, curse and beat, but it will only bounce back.

It will be all okay in every imaginable situation.

You will never trust, love, or let anybody get too close. *Why should you?* It would only end badly, and you would end up hurt. So, you mastered ways to keep them all away: social and emotional distancing. And you will never, ever let anyone see your vulnerability.

But why do people intentionally want to break another's pottery?

Perhaps because they were not able to feel empathy. Or because of their blind rage and bitterness. Perhaps they were jealous of that clay pottery. It was simply too pretty, too lovely, too beautiful, too original, too excited, or too naïve.

Some clay potteries were broken in early childhood, even before they knew how to speak full sentences. Smashed and abused cruelly or used as an extension of someone's self. Perhaps it was that child's raw helplessness that allowed the abuser to feel power. Sadly, there are numerous instances of parents brutally abusing their children, sometimes even referring to purported Christian parenting books and thinking they were doing it in the name of God.

Some potteries were broken during the school years. Brutally bullied during the recess and on their way to and from school: kicked to the curb, punched, ridiculed, humiliated. Rejected, they found a corner, a wall in the schoolyard where they stood alone, without speaking to anybody. Dissociating. As it was the only way not to be bothered.

Some potteries were broken in romantic relationships. Falling in love only to be rejected. Used pottery forsaken then picked up by someone else only to be again smashed to pieces . . . the cycle running in a seemingly never-ending loop.

Some were broken in marriage by betrayal and cheating. Some were abused until they believed they were good for nothing, sometimes even misguided by well-known Christian marriage authors emphasizing the *false notion* wives have no right to have boundaries and say no. They were left with no strength nor dignity to collect their pieces.

Some potteries were destroyed in the church—a safe haven that was not. Spiritual and religious abuse administered in the name of God although He played no role in it. A facade of religion excusing harassment and humiliation, manipulation and control—power-trips of the power-hungry intentionally misrepresenting the Great Potter to satisfy their selfish reasons and greed. There is something deeply wounding when a cruel abuse is wrapped in the garb of godliness; when the victim is deserted for Satan and for the rest of his existence is made to believe that the Great Potter has forsaken him. To extinguish someone's relationship with their Maker is an abuse beyond comprehension! As therapist, I have encountered many broken potteries who have experienced this.

Maybe in their golden years, the pottery was intentionally smashed onto a corner somewhere it was abandoned and forsaken unable to make it better. They hoped for death to come quickly as every morning is a throbbing agony of paralyzing helplessness.

What of a parent, sitting in the midst of their child's shattered pieces? Destroying their beautiful pottery by running with the wrong crowd, drugs, cruel perpetrators, drug overdoses or dying by suicide. As parents feeling that paralyzing helplessness and throbbing agony—unspeakable pain and anger—they would have done anything to protect their child.

It is terrible when someone intentionally inflicts pain, abuse, and terror on us or our loved ones, breaking and destroying, crushing our pottery into pieces, then scattering our remnants.

How can we survive? How can we collect the pieces? How can we trust again? How can we look in the eyes of those who witnessed our abuse but did not help? How can we, feeling so vulnerable, look into our own eyes without feeling shame and humiliation?

When others destroy our self-value, they break our sense of anything beautiful. It is as if our soul has been murdered. Not knowing how to process our treatment, we freeze the pain and numb our feelings hoping to at least look like we are strong. *…At least they could not take my pride, my composure!* But deep inside, we know they had. Little did we understand that the shame we wore like skin was all projected onto us. *…It did not belong to me but to those who intentionally broke me. It was their shame, their guilt. But they refused to have any, so they projected it onto me.*

Did you grow up with this skin of shame, feeling that you did not have the right to exist, that you had no worth; therefore, it was okay for anybody to treat you badly and not okay for you to establish safe boundaries for your pottery?

… Seriously, of what value does a glued-together, cement-covered ugly pottery have? Who cares how many times it will be smashed, blown, hit? Just add more cement, mortar, and ugly grout…

Paradoxically, as a child growing up in an abusive environment, it is safer to self-diagnose yourself as a "bad child" living with "good adults" than to think you are a "good child" living with "bad adults." A "good adult" would mistreat a child *only* because she or he was so difficult—a bad child. They rebuke or beat that bad child *only* because they had a "good" reason. That child got what it deserved.

Sad, isn't it?

And as an adult, that 'bad child' might still think this of themselves. The false diagnosis can continue for years or more. It is evident in thoughts such as *I don't deserve anything good. At least, I don't deserve anything good that would last.*

This child avoids healthy relationships and has the uncanny ability to join with those who break her a bit more because that is the only language she understands. She finds a skewed comfort in familiar abuse and agony. Any good moments she knows won't last long. When she accidentally develops a relationship with a kind, caring, gentle pottery, she pushes it away, convinced she has no need of it.

Then one day, she has had enough. She can no longer stand her ugly and unlovable pottery. When she throws her nasty-looking pottery into the trash yard, the cement cover breaks.

...Who cares if I am shattered? Nobody sees me as I truly am. Nobody cares. This trash yard is where I belong, with the other good-for-nothing trash and garbage...

Yes, I've been there— my broken pottery scattered on that trash yard.

Oh, that agonizing sense of shame and that humiliation! If you have experienced it, you'll know exactly what I mean. Personally, for years I did not want to see anyone who had witnessed my humiliating mistreatment and failed to rescue me. My humiliation felt like raw skin that needed to be protected and hidden because being vulnerable did not feel safe. In fact, I did not feel safe to be seen. Looking in a mirror I saw eyes staring back at myself there full of pain, which others would see as well. I needed to find a way to hide my vulnerability.

Then one day I hear that the Great Potter was visiting the trash yard. He is planning to make some new potteries there.

It doesn't make sense!

Why would the Great Potter come to the trash yard? Didn't He have enough new clay out there in the fresh air? Or potteries only chipped, not smashed like the hopeless ones scattered about here. It was obvious that all of us were worth nothing. We no longer had any purpose; we had already lost our destiny.

I tried my best to resist Him when He picked up my pieces, one by one. I tried to hide behind the junk, but He found my every piece. I kicked and pushed Him away, showing my sharp edges and nastiest stink I could produce!

Oh, how shameful being lifted into the sunlight by Him!

But then something odd and unexpected happened. It was His touch. His hands were rough and scarred, yet His touch was so tender and warm that I felt a strange kind of melting within. Even though I hardened my defenses, putting on a full force not to surrender to Him.

How can something so scarred be so gentle?

He placed me on His table, and I could not help to notice that the layers of cement softened and fell away, layers of glue peeled off, and chunks of the mortar and ugly grout I'd built around myself when I tried to make myself look strong and unbeatable, dropped away.

Suddenly, all that remained on His table were just my broken clay pieces.

I felt raw, naked, and vulnerable. But I also felt safe. I had never felt that safe before. I still had all of my defenses to cover myself, but I felt no need to do so.

I dared not look at Him. I was sure He would be disappointed with me for being the mess I was. I didn't want to see His frustration or disgust. So, I kept my eyes down, staring at my broken pieces.

As if I had to look first to be seen.

And then He says my name. Quietly. Tenderly. Pronouncing it clearly, and it sounds like music. A sound so beautiful, so precious, one that I had been yearning for years to hear.

How does the Great Potter know my name?

I slowly lifted my face and looked into His eyes, which are locked on me. The tenderness in them astonishes me. I had never experienced such love and acceptance.

Something shakes inside me. It is a warm tingling starting in my spine and spreading to every muscle, nerve, and cell. It reaches into my mind, restoring every memory and gently nailing my being inside out. He saw everything about and in me, all of my pieces: my story, history, trauma, even those parts I never dared face myself.

I felt exposed yet not threatened. Indeed, it felt the way it should have always been: to be seen by the Great Potter.

In His eyes I can see what He thinks about me. It is all clear: love, pride, caring, gentleness, unconditional acceptance. All targeted on me.

You are mine! You are the most precious, beautiful daughter!
You are My very own daughter!

And I melted.

I softened and surrendered to the Great Potter's hands. He gently mixed my broken pieces with the new clay of His unconditional, unfailing love, and never-ending grace. His hands gently molded me into something new. He restored me, healing my wounds and cracks and sharp edges. And no pieces of me were too broken to be wasted or tossed into the trash.

And while the Great Potter worked on my clay, He spoke to me in His tender voice, without hurry. And I told Him everything, He listened, sometimes wiping away tears, His and mine. He explained that sometimes the truth is painful to speak but that it liberates. All of my life I had avoided it because I wanted to avoid the pain. But with Him I was liberated.

While working with my clay on His wheel, the Great Potter promised that He would never forsake me. That nothing would ever be able to separate me from His love. Neither death nor life, angels nor demons. My fears for today and tomorrow couldn't. Even the powers of hell couldn't keep His love away. (Romans 8:31-39.)

As He continued to mix my broken pieces with the new clay, His love filled me, and I could no longer resist it. *I surrendered.* I allowed His love to begin the healing process.

I am still on His table in a process. Sometimes I rest on His shelf, while other times I am on His wheel or fired in His oven. I will be for the rest of my life. And I cherish every moment. I have told Him to make me new and fresh. I have also told Him of my hope that He will use me to tell the other broken clay potteries still lying in the trash yard about Him. I no longer see myself as an outcast about whom no one cares. The Great Potter has restored me (Jeremiah 30:17).

Be assured that neither your broken pottery nor any of your broken pieces will be thrown away. Your brokenness is not wasted. No matter how broken you are, you are precious and valuable to the Great Potter.

Heidi McKendrick

CHAPTER 4

WHEN YOU INTENTIONALLY BREAK YOUR CLAY POTTERY

You can intentionally break your clay pottery, beautiful, precious pottery wonderfully made by the Great Potter. At the beginning of time, He planned and created it. He knit you together in your mother's womb. And He said it was good.

You know there are no excuse for breaking your clay pottery—so you don't bother trying to hide behind any petty defenses or explanations. You know you're guilty.

This confession is not a pang of false guilt or psychobabble to beg others to understand your upbringing or extenuating circumstances. You have no need for patronizing statements or pretending that it was only an accident, you were out of your mind, or not somehow responsible.

It was *not* an accident. You did not mean well. You did not unintentionally screw up everything. You may have been foolish and irresponsible, but you were fully aware when you broke it. You took your clay pottery, your sweet and lovely piece of art designed by the Great Potter, lifted it above your head, and smashed it to the floor. You struck with full force. Your numerous pieces scream accusations against you. They are right, but you wish they'd shut up.

This is all my fault all right. It is my doing.

Oh, how you wish you had not done it. If only you could rewind to these moments before, when you were studying your clay pottery and planning your next move, and choose differently.

But it is too late. What was done was done. The result is thousands of broken pieces all over the floor.

You wonder what others will think when they see the mess. What will the Great Potter think when He sees it? *What a waste of His efforts I am…* And you weep and moan bitterly and pettily. You cry because you are guilty, the mess is your doing, and you can do nothing to undo it.

How should you now react? Shrug your shoulders and say, *Oh well, it's broken. Whatever there was before this is over.* You could collect a few pieces and put them together the best you can. But you are painfully aware it is not even close to what it used to be. You may deny it all and pretend that you don't care.

Whatever! It does not hurt. It's my life. Who cares anyway?

You could glue your pottery together and add glitter, sparkles, and bright colors. But trying to hide your shame like this looks pathetic. But for a moment, you may be able to fool someone, even yourself. However, when you look in the mirror, you see it all. And it is not a pretty look. Deep inside, you have always known the truth. However, you do not let it liberate yourself.

Most likely, you dare not ask anyone for help, least of all the Great Potter. *Wouldn't He strike the last blow from His holy throne?* A pottery must bear the consequences of her actions. Justice does not entail mercy for those who do not deserve it.

But you cannot stop crying because deep down, a tiny shard hopes that the Great Potter *would* hear your cry and care enough to clean up your mess despite the fact you are *not* the victim and can only blame yourself.

Could He fix me?—I don't know how, but somehow?—Would He?

Has your pottery ever been here?

Impulsively, with impatience, frustration, selfishness, and self-destructiveness, you destroyed your clay pottery. In the rash moment, you told yourself that you didn't care what happened to it. It was a moment of choice, and you chose incorrectly. You knew you were putting yourself into a dangerous situation that was damaging to your pottery. For whatever reason, you chose not to protect it.

We *all* have broken our clay potteries in one way or another. According to the Bible, we *all* have sinned (Romans 8:23). We *all* are broken because sin breaks clay potteries. We can blame no one but ourselves. None of us deserves the Great Potter's glory.

But it is the aftermath that matters.

Do we think it is done, finished, and nothing can repair us? Do we dare ask for help? Does our false image of the Great Potter falsely claim that He does not care what happened to us? Do we think He is angry with us and therefore will let us rot where we are? Or do we think that even if He fixes us, we've forfeited our purpose and have no worth as His vessels anymore? After all, did we not show disrespect to our Maker and treat His great grace frivolously when we broke ourselves?

It matters that we do not think He has given up with us.
It matters that we understand He will never give up on us.
He will never give up. He promised.

It is the nature of the Great Potter to restore our pottery—again and again and again because of His faithfulness. He remains faithful even if we don't.

Isn't this something too magnificent to comprehend with our limited clay brain cells?

We may feel done as we lie in the trash yard where we threw the pieces of our broken clay pottery. All hope is so far gone that we do not even hope to someday start over.

Some of us have become quite satisfied with misery. The stoic in us keeps a stiff upper lip while bearing the consequences of our actions. We can't do anything to change what happened, so the trash yard is our home for the rest of our lives. No sense trying to repair our broken pieces. The best we can do is to live a mediocre existence without any real meaning and no reason to wake up each morning. *It is what it is*, and there is no way out from this trash yard. After all, we threw ourselves into the trash, so we cannot expect to be rescued. In fact, we don't deserve to be rescued because we purposely broke our clay potteries.

If only we could quiet that irritatingly gnawing sense of guilt, shame, and self-blame. The never-ending nagging. We would give anything to silence the accuser that keeps repeating and pointing its finger: *You did it! It's your own doing! You can only blame yourself! You have no hope!*

But the Great Potter, He *is* the Hope.

When the Great Potter comes to the trash yard, our first reaction might be to hide because we brought our condition upon ourselves. The last thing we want is Him to witness our self-inflicted shame and humiliation, *the uttermost degradation of a once artistic piece created by His own loving hands.* We certainly hope He passes by without causing a scene; we fear facing His accusing eyes and disappointed look.— We can't expect Him to even want to come close to our broken disarray.

This was my broken pottery at one time.

When I hear the rumors that The Great Potter is indeed looking for the broken clay pieces—the lost ones—and I hear His footsteps, I get a bit startled and resolve to crawl deeper into the junk to hide under the debris until He's gone. Understandable, He came here to collect those of us who had been thrown there by others, intentionally or accidentally—the innocent victims. My pottery is too shattered, I don't think He's here for *my* pieces.

Ever heard of a rescue party organized for the guilty posse? Nope. My cracked clay crumbles are in this trash yard of broken potteries because of my own doing. I am not innocent. The Great Potter owes me nothing, and I don't deserve anything from Him.

But then I hear Him calling my name. His voice becomes louder, as if He is drawing closer to my hiding place; as if He is intentionally moving through the nasty trash and molded garbage to find me. *Maybe it's others with my name He is calling for*, I wonder. If not, a thought freezes me: *What if He came here to rebuke and punish me?* The brimstones of the hellfire! I can feel the heat flicking about me. I do not want to be the target of His wrath or thrown into that fiery lake where the worms never die. I must hide!

Oh, how I want to hide from Him!

I feel Him standing very close. He must know I am here. It feels as though He can see me, which is ridiculous because of the pile of trash and bulky junk covering me.

"Where are you?"

I keep silent, but then He begins to move the trash away, steadily clearing His way, digging deeper into my hiding places, where I think I am invisible.

But I am wrong.

He is gently collecting my broken and miserably smashed pieces one by one. He takes His time as if He has nothing else or more essential to do. He does not finish until He has collected every piece, taking time to locate the tiniest clay crumble of my miserable existence, even those I thought were missing for good. I keep my eyes tightly closed as He carries me away from the trash yard. When placed on His table, I begin to shiver, wondering if punishment is about to fall. Will He beat me with His hammer until nothing but dust remains, making sure no solid piece is left behind? Is it now when He will lash His judgment against me and throw me into that never-ending fire? Or, in case He allows me to live, will He deliver a reprimanding sermon complete with a list of consequences, rules, and to-do duties of my future existence?

None of that happens.

Even though my eyes are closed, I sense Him watching. And then I feel an unexplainable, irresistible tenderness. It is so unexpected that I cry. And I don't care what anybody thinks anymore; I bellow. The tears flow unchecked, because of guilt, shame, humiliation, loneliness, and yearning. It is like Niagara Falls. Tears of regret. Tears of repentance. Tears puddle in His Hands as He holds my pieces.

Though tears blur my vision, I see His Hand, the red scars. And more tears flow. But now I cry because I do not have words to thank Him for His love. I am drenched in His overflowing compassion and lack words to describe experiencing the Great Potter's unconditional, unfailing love and His never-ending grace. His love has nothing to do with anything I do or do not do. It has nothing to do with performance, whether I win or fail. It has nothing to do with my deserving it.

None of us deserve His unconditional love, but we can all *receive* it.

"It's all perfect," the Great Potter says as He gently lays the new clay of His unfailing, unconditional love and His never-ending grace around my aching pieces. "Yes, it is all perfect."

I agree as I stare at the painfully red scars on His hands.

Secrets Of Broken Pottery

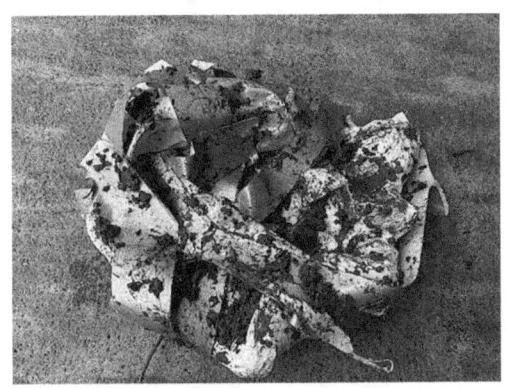

CHAPTER 5

WHEN AN UNPREDICTABLE FORCE MAJEURE BREAKS YOUR CLAY POTTERY

Sometimes your clay pottery being broken has nothing to do with you or anyone else. This time an unknown force of nature, *force majeure*, one that even insurance companies do not cover, hits you.

Like a tornado, earthquake, tsunami, or COVID-19, it strikes unexpectedly, blowing your pottery from its safe and stable shelter. It breaks, smashing so hard that not much is left but a pile of bewilderment among the scattered pieces. You look around and ask, "How can this terrible thing happen to my pottery?"

Wasn't it only yesterday when you believed that the world is a kind and beautiful place, that your life had meaning, and that life made sense? Wasn't it only yesterday when you felt enormous peace and you trusted the Great Potter and His good plans for you? Wasn't it only yesterday when you made great plans for your future? All of that shattered when your pottery flew off the shelf and landed in a million pieces.

You question: "Why am I lying on this floor with my clay pottery broken and scattered? I don't understand what hit me!"

Having naïvely believed in a fair, just, and rational life, you suddenly find yourself in shock over unexpected despair and devastation. It may be

- an accident, an injury,
- the death of a loved one,
- a sudden fatal illness, such as cancer or stroke,
- realization that you are not able to have children even though you have tried everything,
- unexpected job loss or bankruptcy,
- a sudden break of relationship,
- a startling despair that befalls your child,
- a natural disaster, or
- a pandemic that nobody could have predicted much less stopped.

Sitting in the middle of these broken pieces, in pain and feeling total helplessness, bewilderment, perplexity, panic, and unbelief, you have lost control over your life. What happened that changed your perfect life into a shattered life? What took all of your dreams and goals and threw them to the wind—and why? Feeling raw vulnerability, you realize that perhaps your world will never be the same.

Surely, this nightmare cannot be real; this cannot be happening to you. Only a moment ago, your life was full of meaning and purpose. Indeed, you were fulfilling your mission as the Great Potter's vessel. *But where is He now? Why did He allow this?*

As you scream and demand answers, no one seems to even hear you, much less care.

How small and fragile is your clay pottery, helpless because nothing you could have done would have changed the situation.

A force majeure! There isn't one of us protected from its blows!

Living in this fallen world it is not possible to avoid brokenness. Sooner or later something will hit and throw us into crisis, leaving us in the middle of shattered chaos. Along with it, we may experience a faith crisis as well.

- How can I believe in the Great Potter, who seems not to care, not to intervene, and not to hear my prayers when I need Him most?
- *If* He is almighty and if He cares about my pottery, why doesn't He help me?
- *If* He is Sovereign, good, and loving, why doesn't He stop this torment and craziness?
- Why didn't He prevent it?
- Why does He allow it?
- Why don't I feel His presence when I need Him most?

You've asked and asked these questions, demanding answers. You felt that He did not answer, or He answered but you didn't accept it. If you're like me, you've been confused and angry. You've blamed the Great Potter for your crisis, blamed others, and blamed yourself. You've even blamed your lack of faith. *If only* you'd had the amount of faith the size of a mustard seed! You've reflected and blamed your secret sins and confessed even your unconscious thoughts. You've blamed others' lack of faith and suspected their secret sins.

Your friends and family might encourage you to trust Him and say, "Thy will be done."

Sure, you can say it all right. But it sounds like one of those Christian clichés, like praise the Lord; wouldn't it be easier to negotiate and make promises? Wouldn't it be cooler to try to manipulate the Great Potter with your faith, with sacrifices and tricks? Wouldn't it be more sophisticated to barter with Him, trading something you do for something He does in turn?

Thy will be done, whatever that means, although I'm clueless.

Oh, it is so hard to envision your miserably and unfairly broken pieces as being part of the Great Potter's plan! And then you cannot help beginning to wonder:

- Maybe—I don't know how—but is it possible that the Great Potter did not orchestrate this event, but He *allowed* it? And because He allowed it, it has been under His control all the time?
- Is it possible that even though I'm sitting on a pile of broken pieces—some burned to ashes—that the Great Potter, who is in charge of the universe, is *also* in charge of everything that happens to me?

The Great Potter *is* aware of your mess. Whatever happens to you, He *remains* in control. Even though He didn't arrange your brokenness, He is in charge of your recovery.

Sooner or later, at the perfect time, the Great Potter gathers your broken pieces from the floor and places them on His table. He mixes them with the carefully selected new clay of His love, grace, and faithfulness. Once He has finished fashioning you, He will place you in the oven to be fired, specific glaze and color added. In some cases, He may even add gold into your fractures to glorify His name and accent your scars as an evidence of survival and resilience.

You can trust Him because He has good plans for you, plans not to harm you but to give you hope and a future (Jeremiah 29:11), even if it doesn't *feel* like that at the moment.

Despite the circumstances that do not appear to be blessings, we can say with the great songwriter that, "It is well with my soul."[1] You *still* have hope and peace in the middle of agony because your pottery is in the Great Potter's hands.

---

[1] *"It Is Well With My Soul"* -hymn was written by Horatio Spafford after extremely traumatic events, the death of his four-year-old son and financial bankruptcy because of the Great Chicago Fire of 1871 and the economic downturn of 1873. He plans to travel to England to assist with D. L. Moody's revival meetings and sends his family ahead on the SS Ville du Havre-ship. The ship sinks and all four of his daughters die. His wife Anna sends him the telegram, "Saved alone …". When Spafford travels to meet his wife and when the ship passes near the place where his daughters died, he writes this song.

When peace like a river,
attendeth my way,
When sorrows like sea billows roll;
Whatever my lot,
Thou hast taught me to know
It is well, it is well, with my soul.

It is well, (it is well),
With my soul, (with my soul)
It is well, it is well, with my soul. (Horatio Spafford)[3]

You may not understand why things went as they did, but you can still trust the Great Potter. You are safe because He holds your future. Whatever happens to you, it takes place under His all-knowing presence.

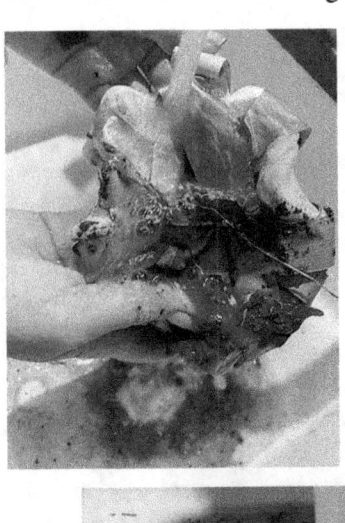

Heidi McKendrick

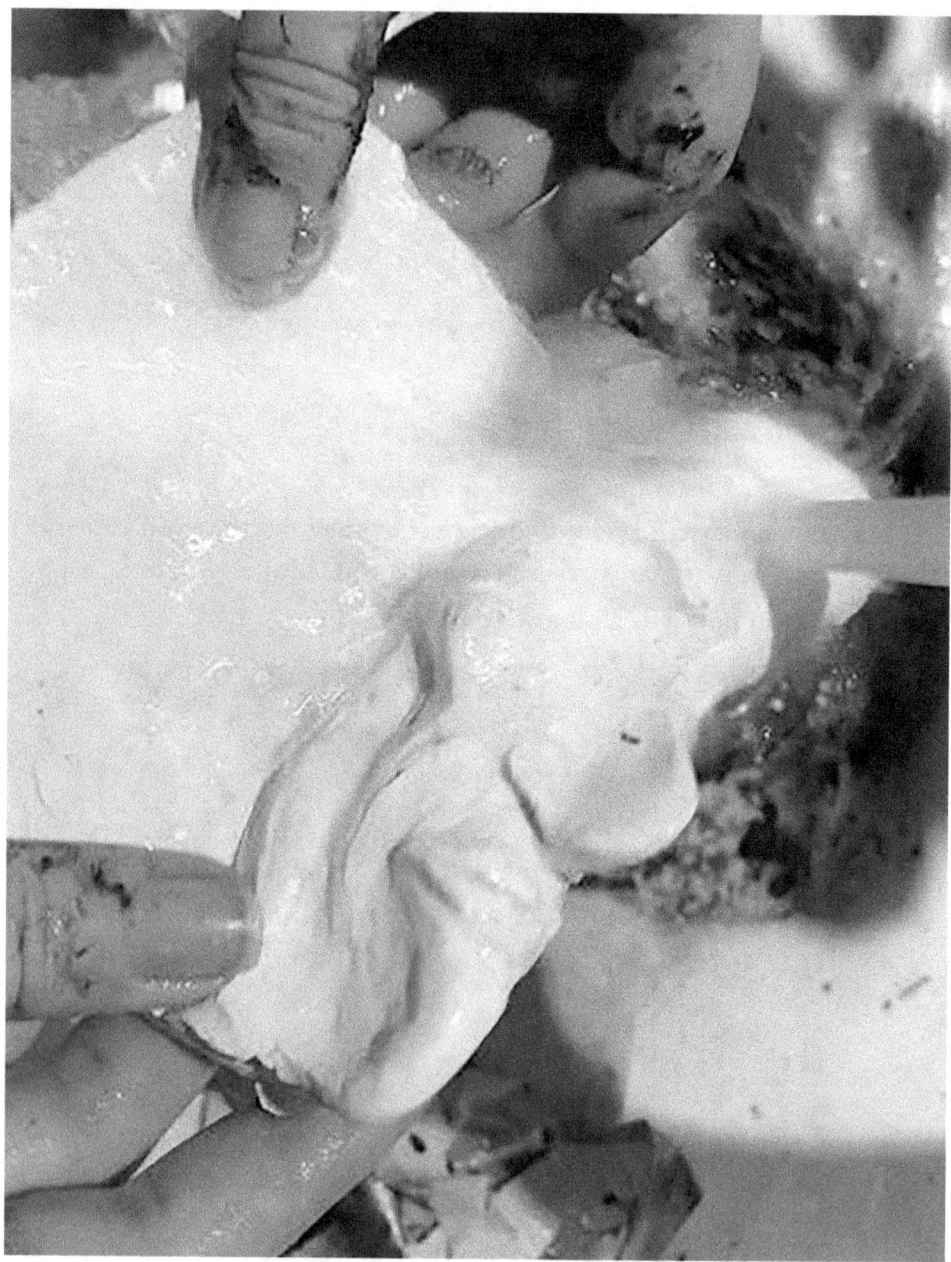

CHAPTER 6

IN THE TRASH YARD OF BROKEN POTTERIES

I am forgotten as though I were dead; I have become like broken pottery.

Psalm 31:12 (NIV)

I am forgotten like a dead man, out of mind; I am like a broken vessel.

Psalm 31:12 (NKJV)

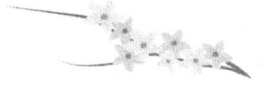

Most towns and cities have a designated landfill area outside the city limits. This is where all of the trash and garbage is tossed, including broken pottery. Outside of ancient Jerusalem, the landfill was located in the Valley of Hinnom.

Lots of us are in the landfill, the trash yard. We lie there, useless. Walking among us one finds assorted styles, shapes, colors, and sizes. Broken differently, some are in two pieces. Others have a big hole in them. A few are in a thousand pieces, and some of the pieces have been ground into a powder and mixed with the dirt and ash.

No matter how the pottery was broken, it was *a trauma*, wounding our souls. All trauma is followed by three elements: emotional pain, a sense of helplessness, and a lack of empathy because nobody was there to help.

Some were thrown into the trash yard recently, still in shock from the unexpected blow. Others have been there for weeks, switching between anger, grief, shame, guilt, regret, and fear. Still others have been there so long that they cannot remember anything before being tossed into the trash yard. Buried in the dirt, they are no longer visible.

Broken potteries are no longer in use. We are a community of numbed emotions, frozen feelings, and murdered souls. Everywhere you look are piles of broken potteries; piles of pain, helplessness, despair; and piles of hopelessness.

And then there's the isolation. The trash yard is outside of town, away from the community where living is in full swing.

Some potteries were broken by accident, some intentionally, and others by our own hands. For some, it was a force majeure; it just happened as if it was our lot of life. Bad stuff happens to good potteries, you know.

All of the broken potteries have a story behind their brokenness, different journeys. But we all ended up here.

For some, one blow was all it took to smash us in bits and pieces in one moment. Just one blow. Some of us were fractured over time. The first knock was not so bad, but after a number of strikes and slaps, we collapsed into pieces. Years of neglect, abandonment, deprivation, and storms did us in…. No one smashed us; rather, a lifetime of adversity crushed us. Or was it simply our destiny? Born at the wrong time, the wrong place. Unfair, yes, but what can we do?

Perhaps it was not allowing ourselves enough time to dry after being repaired and restored. Not waiting for our strength to renew. Maybe we broke the newly repaired clay pottery because of impatience and lack of self-reflection of the previous breakages. By that I mean remaining in the cycle of trauma and reacting the same ways as for the original trauma, treating the flashbacks as if they are real.

Perhaps we had the tendency of ...

- fleeing and running, when we should stay still,
- fighting and attacking when we should simply wait and listen,
- hiding and avoiding when we should have a conversation,
- isolating when we should surround ourselves with others and accept their support,
- burying in shame when we should feel empathy toward ourselves,
- targeting anger at ourselves when we should feel compassion,
- self-destruction instead of self-care,
- feeling guilt when we should forgive ourselves and ask forgiveness from the others,
- being filled with horror when we could check the facts first,
- feeling self-pity when we could take responsibility and the first steps out of the cycle,
- feeling bitterness when we could forgive,
- repeating the original trauma reaction as if not able to choose anything else, or
- shouting "Go away!" when we should surrender.

And now lying on this enormous trash yard of the broken potteries, we could use the time to reflect, to collect some pieces, and try to understand how we got here. At least this would help us to gain some understanding and not repeat the same trauma, not inflict the same pain or choose the same route in the future.

We, the residents of this trash yard of broken potteries share one commonality: We are not forsaken, for the Great Potter has come, not only to the town, but deep into the trash yard to seek for those pieces that are lost. To take us back home.

The trash yard of the broken potteries is not a graveyard of forgotten ones.

Lying in the trash yard need not be the end. There are other phases of the existence of the clay pottery.

One is to be placed on the Great Potter's table.

CHAPTER 7

IN THE GREAT POTTER'S HOUSE

*Then I went down to the potter's house, and there he was,
making something at the wheel.
And the vessel that he made of clay was marred in the hand of the potter;
so he made it again into another vessel, as it seemed good to the potter to make.*

Jeremiah 18:3–4 (NKJV)

Instead of continuing our lives in the trash yard of the broken potteries, we have options. One is to be at the Great Potter's house. Here our broken pieces are gently laid out on the Potters table and mixed with new clay, the type needed to make the pottery, which He fashions according to His vision for it.

Another place to be is on His wheel, being shaped and molded to His plan.

Sitting on the Great Potter's shelf is another phase at the Potter's house. Here we rest, dry, and strengthen. Of course, different potteries require various times for resting. The too-short or too-long resting periods are not suitable for some processes. The Great Potter knows precisely how long each pottery needs to rest. He has an individual plan for all of us.

The Great Potter uses a variety of techniques as He restores each pottery. He chooses the method as unique as the individual.

Then He adds glazing and coloring, sometimes enhancing the pottery by using gold to fill in the fractures, highlighting them in a particularly glorious way.

It all depends on what He has in His mind.

But none of our broken pieces go wasted. None of them will remain lost either. Even if you think you are forsaken and lost, He knows exactly where you are and will find every single broken piece.

While reviewing the different phases and ways of making pottery at the Great Potter's house, perhaps you find yourself in a specific phase, in the midst of a particular process. Maybe this will help you to understand something that has taken place in your past.[4]

1. Finding and Collecting the Broken Pieces

Why does the Great Potter need those broken pieces to make pottery? Wouldn't it better to use new clay that has not been tarnished?

This is one of the Great Potter's secrets: all broken pieces and clay crumble are recyclable and reusable. In fact, the strongest potteries are not made from new clay alone. They also need the finely ground clay powder from the broken pieces. This is good news for all of us broken potteries! None of our pieces are wasted. He turns our most horrible experiences into a beautiful vessel to be used in His service. Our misery is turned into a blessing. Indeed, the more often a clay has been burned and then crushed, it becomes a stronger ingredient for new pottery. The Great Potter's secret to making the most durable vessels for His service is to mix the fine powder of crushed old pottery with the new clay.

It is not difficult for the Great Potter to find the broken pieces. He only needs to visit the trash yard and collect them. And, of course, the broken pieces must be willing to be found and then collected and taken to the Potter's house.

Another secret of the Great Potter is that none of the broken pieces of His potteries are lost. Naturally, the pottery may feel lost or even forsaken, but they are not. The Great Potter knows exactly where each broken piece is; waiting or hiding or even pretending not to be broken at all!

He is waiting for the right moment to come and find them—the moment the broken pieces are willing to be found. "How often I wanted to gather your children together, as a hen gathers her chicks under her wings, and you were not willing" (Matthew 23:37 NKJV).

2. Sourcing Clay

The Great Potter always knows what type of new clay needs to be added with each pottery's broken pieces. He knows our needs! Depending on the purpose, He will add red, or gray clay, or possibly the most delicate white clay, or a lump of specific porcelain clay. The texture is unique to each pottery and its purpose, thus calling for the new clay to be coarse or smooth or something in between.

While He collects our broken pieces, He has a plan for the vessel we will be. He also knows what needs to be done for us to get there. For example, fine porcelain requires extremely fine clay powder, gently crushed from the broken pieces, finely ground, and then mixed with the new clay. "But now, O LORD, You are our Father; *We are the clay*, and *You our potter*; And all we are *the work of Your hand*" (Isaiah 64:8 NKJV).

Without the Great Potter, even clay would be nothing but dust. The Great Potter "formed the man from the dust of the ground and breathed into his nostrils the breath of life, and the man became a living being" (Gen. 2:7 NIV). "Remember now, that You have made me as clay; And would You turn me into dust again?" (Job 10:9 NIV).

3. Washing the Clay

The clay must be washed before the Great Potter can utilize it at His table. Even the newly collected clay must first dissolve in water for a few days. After that, it is washed thoroughly so that all the stones are separated from the powder. Similarly, our broken clay pieces that are extremely dry and dirty must first be liquefied. Some potters set the clay pieces in a water bucket for a few days, thus allowing the clay crumbles to soften and become thoroughly soaked.

Of course, we know the Great Potter washed our broken pieces with His blood. "Though your sins are like scarlet, they shall be as white as snow; though they are red like crimson, they shall be as wool" (Isaiah 1:18 NKJV). The Great Potter gently washes away all of the stones and the coarse dirt from years of abuse, neglect, and pain.

4. Waiting and Drying on the Shelf

The clay is removed from the bucket of water. It is a dripping wet mass that needs to dry a bit before the next phase. The clay can be set outside in the sun for a while so excess moisture can evaporate. Sometimes the clay is wrapped in cloth and set on the Great Potter's drying shelf. During this gradual drying, a phase that is not hurried, the clay adjusts to its new form. While waiting, the lumps of clay are fully immersed in the Great Potter's unconditional, everlasting love and His never-ending grace, both key to the healing process.

Interestingly, the hot, dry, lonely desert was where many Bible heroes were placed to "dry," or to wait, sometimes for years, before their entry into active service. For example, Abraham spent years wandering in the desert before he settled and received the promise of a son. Moses spent years in the desert before he was ready to lead the Hebrew potteries out of slavery. Then they all wandered in the desert for forty years before they entered the Promised Land. John the Baptist also waited and prepared for years on the Jordan side of the desert before he paved the way for the Messiah's coming.

Likewise, our drying time on the Great Potter's shelf has a purpose, and we should never treat it as if we are forgotten or rejected during this phase. Instead, we should let it be a time of soaking in the Great Potter's love and grace. "Being confident of this very thing, that He who has begun a good work in you *will complete it until the day of Jesus Christ*" (Philippians 1:6 NKJV).

5. Kneading and Wedging the Clay on the Potter's Table

The next phase is to knead and wedge the clay and thus compact all the clay particles together. Kneading prepares the clay for shaping, ensuring an even distribution of moisture in the clay. Wedging removes any air pockets and hard spots, ensuring the clay's uniform consistency and making it more pliable. Fresh clay should be wedged at least thirty times, but a combination of new and old clay, which utilizes our broken pieces, should be wedged over a hundred times!

The kneading and wedging make the clay softer and more resilient. This pressing and drawing, mixing and rolling, cutting and layering, allows for learning the particular clay piece's unique characteristics. Any leftover stones and air bubbles must be removed because if left, they would cause breaking on the wheel and even explosion during firing. There is no hurrying this process at the Great Potter's table. Interestingly, He takes His time to *listen to the clay* and meet its particular needs when preparing it for the next phases.

Being at the Great Potter's table is a time for reflection. Here we learn from our past traumas and our self-destructive tendencies. We learn to trust again. It's the time of renewing our relationship with the Great Potter, allowing Him to pour into us His unfailing love.

The Great Potter does not make stone potteries. Having a heart of flesh is much softer than having a stone heart (Ezekiel 11:19). Of course, being soft makes us more vulnerable and exposed; however, it is safe to be vulnerable on the Great Potter's table. In fact, it is the safest place in the entire universe. A place where we do not have to pretend anything, defend ourselves, or hide.

The Great Potter sees everything within us, even our most protected and humiliating experiences. His therapeutic healing process of our wounded hearts launches on the Great Potter's table. Allowing His gentle touch to work through our pain and hurts while adding His love will heal our damaged identities. It allows truth to liberate us. Here is where we learn to trust His process and timing, understanding that we are safe in the Great Potter's hands. He knows what He is doing with us.

6. Resting on the Shelf

After kneading and wedging, the clay piece needs to rest awhile before it is ready to be molded at the Great Potter's wheel. This resting period is necessary so that the clay can peacefully stabilize its new structure so as not to break on the wheel. Sometimes this phase is frustrating for many of us who are soft and warm clay, ready to move on. Sarah asking Abraham to sleep with Hagar is one example of finding it difficult to simply trust and wait for the Great Potter's right timing. Elijah running from place to place in the desert is another example of not allowing enough resting and reflection.

This resting period is crucial for the clay to adjust to its new form and call before being placed on the wheel. The Great Potter does not want to force anyone of us to do His will; therefore, He waits for us to be fully ready.

7. On the Potter's Wheel

On the Great Potter's wheel is a series of changes. He fashions us from a lump of clay to a preview of what we will become as we fulfill our specially designed purpose.

This phase is fast-moving and full of energy, but throughout the process, we are held firmly in His hands.

The Great Potter "throws" us onto the rotating wheel. He molds us with the blades, working His way up, pulling up our vessel. Then the Great Potter opens up the clay, pushing into the clay then gently pulling the clay out to create the base. Then He skillfully pulls the ring of clay surrounding the floor up to create the walls of the pottery.

Throughout this process, He is bringing His plan into reality. What attention for one clay pottery!

When visiting the Middle East, I've seen many potters working on their wheels. It is a fascinating yet speedy transformation of a shapeless clay clump into pottery with its unique size and shape. Whereas during the previous phases of making the pottery, there was no hurry—a lot of sitting on shelves—when on the Potter's wheel, it is all about a speedy transformation.

Once the pottery is ready, the Great Potter, just like many potters in the Middle East, leaves His thumbprint into the pottery. All of His potteries carry His thumbprint. It means that we are not cookie-cutters made in any 'religious factory'— we are the Great Potter's unique designs and we belong to Him forever. "Fear not, for I have redeemed you; I have called *you* by your name; You *are* Mine" (Isaiah 43:1–2 NKJV).

8. Drying on the Shelf

Making clay potteries requires several complicated steps, but one phase repeats. That is resting on the Great Potter's shelf. Our goals are many in this resting phase: waiting, reflecting, adjusting, and drying. Though this phase seems to accomplish nothing, it is a necessary and important phase before the firing.

An interesting characteristic of clay is that it cannot bear its own weight. Therefore, the pottery has to completely dry before firing. "He must become greater; *I must become less*" (John 3:30 NIV).

The largest potteries are molded in several distinct phases for several days, allowing them to carry the weight of the next section of the pottery. If tall pottery were created at once without extra support, it would collapse overnight. This is a beautiful metaphor for Christian life.

The length of the drying time depends on the size and thickness of our pottery. This waiting period is most crucial to protect the newly molded pottery from breaking in the oven. It is also to protect the other potteries because when one pottery explodes in the oven, the flying pieces will easily break all the other potteries in the oven. Doesn't this sound familiar when in a church setting one pottery's blow-up not only destroys itself but also damages the others around them?

Interestingly, it is only after the pottery has completely dried that the Great Potter may want to trim the body on the wheel. He adds colors or decorations to our potteries. However, there needs to be additional drying time after addition and before the firing.

9. Firing Process

Finally, it's time for the much anticipated firing process during which the clay transforms into a durable ceramic. Diverse clay vessels are fired at different temperatures. The potteries that need to become the strongest are fired in the highest temperatures on the lowest shelves. The Great Potter always knows the perfect temperature to fire our clay potteries. "Does not the potter have the right to make out of the same lump of clay some pottery for special purposes and some for common use?" (Romans 9:21 NIV).

Although both ceramic potteries and porcelain are made from a clay mixture, the porcelain is made from highly refined clay and fired at much higher temperatures. The raw materials include new clay, crushed pieces of broken clay, felspar, and silica. These go through a process of thorough crushing and grinding using different types of grinders, crushers, mullers, steel hammers, and ball mills.[5] That does not sound like a pleasant experience! But to achieve the result, this is the only way.

Something special is in these clay potteries who have been fired in the highest temperatures. These are the clay potteries whose faith is sure and strong as a result of enduring extreme hardships, some even being persecuted, for their faith. We admire these people of great faith and wish that we, too, had that depth of faith. But we have to ask ourselves: Am I willing to undergo the similar grinding and firing in the highest temperature that these Christians endured?

Breaking at the Great Potter's House

Sometimes clay pottery may break at the Great Potter's house during one of the making phases, even when it is almost ready. This may be because of our impatience while sitting on His shelf during a resting period, or staying still on His wheel, or moving to a hotter or cooler place in the oven as we are being fired. However, if we break, the Great Potter will simply start our process again. He will faithfully collect our pieces and start the process anew.

Yes, like potteries, we can be marred, but no worries, He makes us into another vessel, as it seemed good to the potter to make. Even if we break, we will not be forsaken or rejected. Our value is not based on failing or succeeding, but it is about our belonging to Him. He will never grow tired of giving us a new beginning.

Even if the pottery breaks a hundred times, it is still precious in the eyes of the Great Potter, and He will not allow its broken pieces to be wasted. It does not matter how many times a clay piece is fired and crushed, after each time, the end result is better and sturdier.

Some stunningly beautiful bowls come from previous brokenness. For example, a Japanese Kintsugi art puts broken pottery pieces back together with gold thus treasuring its marred history. What a lovely idea to embrace flaws, cracks, and imperfections! The Great Potter adding His gold and His glory into our brokenness creates a gorgeous piece of art. The golden scars make your pottery stronger, unique, and even more beautiful. They not only prove you having survived something difficult but also declare His grace and love. Therefore, do not feel embarrassed of your scars!

Every pot is precious—broken or not, the Great Potter never wastes clay.

Our clay potteries will not be finished while on this earth. We are always moving through the different phases at the Great Potter's house. Breaking and being restored—perhaps each time becoming stronger—each time learning something new about ourselves and the Great Potter.

The Great Potter uses broken potteries for His Service.

The next section includes stories of broken clay potteries. All were broken in different ways and for different reasons. And all are in different phases at the Great Potter's house. These are stories of broken potteries, just like you and me.

Some are being collected and washed, others being kneaded and wedged, and still more are resting on the Potter's shelf, waiting and preparing for the next phase. Some are clearly in the oven warmed up or fired in high temperatures. Others are broken and ground at the Potter's hands to become even stronger potteries for a critical calling.

Perhaps you will find your story among them.

PART 2

STORIES OF BROKEN POTTERY

Heidi McKendrick

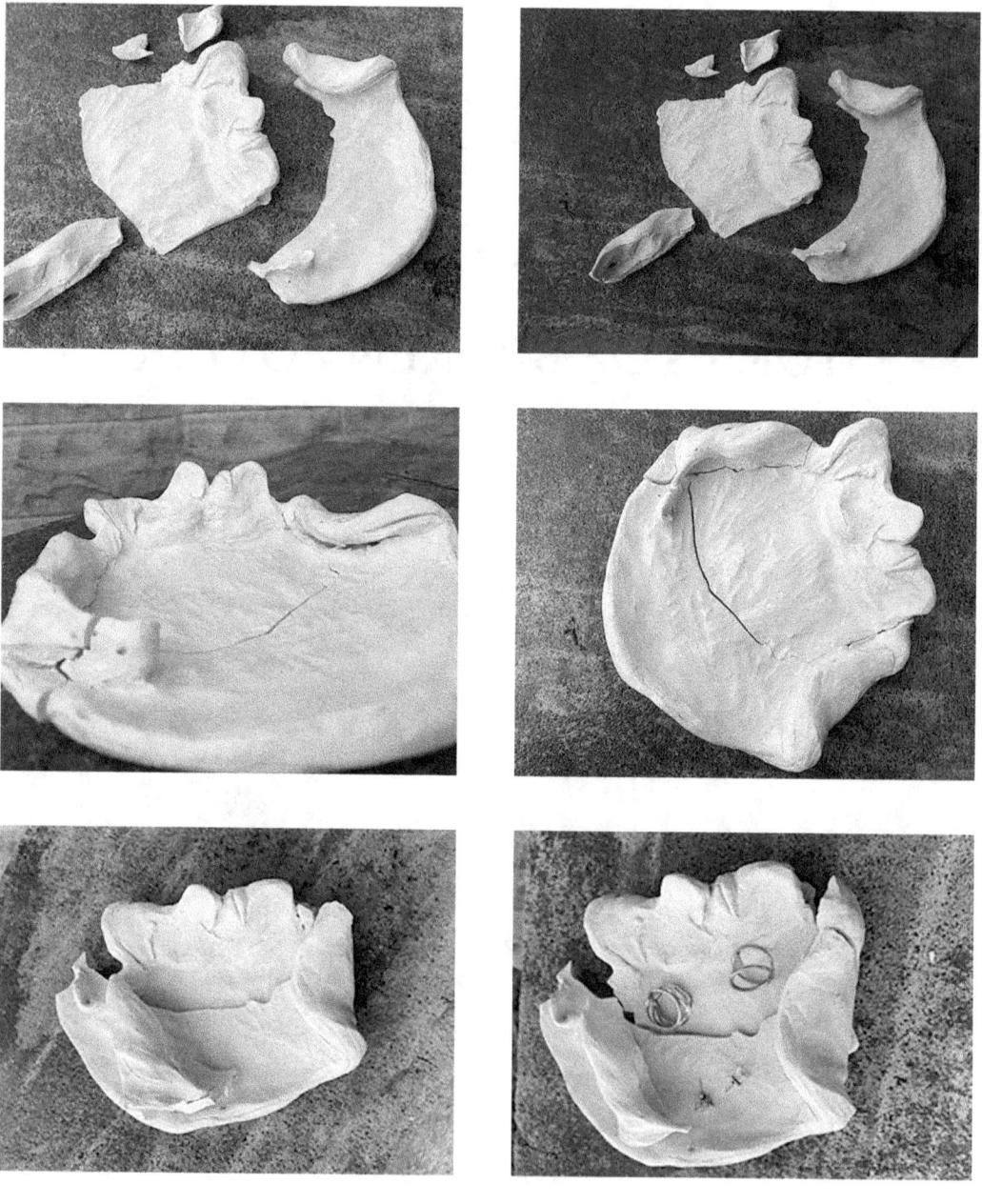

INTRODUCTION

The following stories are about clay vessels living in the Bible times. Some are heroes, mighty servants of the Great Potter, some are less heroic but deeply loved by Him, nonetheless. I chose these stories because I identify with each one of them, maybe you will too. Some of the heroes made many mistakes, either carelessly or intentionally. Others were broken by well-meaning folks or challenging circumstances, some brutally and intentionally. Many even added to their inflictions by repeating their brokenness with unhealthy choices and traumatic reactions. Some broke other potteries. Furthermore, many of the heroes had difficulty understanding what was happening to them. Many had a hard time trusting the Great Potter. Some even tried to escape the Potter's wheel. Others thought they could hide from the Great Potter. All felt devastated.

Remarkably, the Great Potter uses imperfect potteries as His vessels. Of course, this may be because nothing else is available in this broken world. But it can also be that He recognizes that the best vessels are molded and fired from broken potteries. It is good news for us not-so-perfect potteries that even those clay potteries in the Bible were not unlike us.

Although both Noah and Lot were the only ones spared from their worlds' destruction, they were not safe from profound brokenness, such as family relationship issues, even incest. The prophets and kings anointed by the Great Potter certainly had their share of cracks and flaws. The twelve disciples were no better.

The following stories' main characters are women and men found in the Old and New Testaments. The Great Potter called some for specific services, such as the virgin Mary; the prophets, Elijah, and Jeremiah; King David; and the apostles Peter and Paul—He even called Judas Iscariot. In these stories you will read about four nameless women who met the Great Potter, as well as many of Abraham's family members, Hagar, Leah, Joseph, Dinah, and two women both named Tamar. The stories commence with Job, chosen by the Great Potter to experience a variety of force majeure of brokenness in his life.

Each story introduces the meeting point of the Great Potter and the broken pottery. Different scenes, different conversations, different divine interventions, and different results. Each time the Great Potter comes and pours His unconditional, unfailing love and His never-ending grace. His faithfulness never ceases. The Potter's table, His wheel, the waiting shelf, and the oven serve one purpose for each of these characters: to become His vessels to be blessings and be blessed.

While reading their stories, allow yourself to reflect on your own experiences, the similarities and differences. But most of all, allow yourself to meet the Great Potter and challenge your previous ideas of Him.

Maybe— you've had a wrong idea of Him all along?

CHAPTER 8

JOB
THE BROKEN POTTERY WHO SEES
THE GREAT POTTER WITH HIS OWN EYES

Then the LORD said to Satan, "Have you considered my servant Job?
There is no one on earth like him;
he is blameless and upright, a man who fears God and shuns evil."
"Does Job fear God for nothing?" Satan replied.

"Have you not put a hedge around him and his household and everything he has?
You have blessed the work of his hands,
so that his flocks and herds are spread throughout the land.
But now stretch out your hand and strike everything he has,
and he will surely curse you to your face."
The LORD said to Satan, "Very well, then, everything he has is in your power,
but on the man himself do not lay a finger."
Then Satan went out from the presence of the LORD.
One day when Job's sons and daughters were feasting and drinking wine
at the oldest brother's house, a messenger came to Job and said,
"The oxen were plowing and the donkeys were grazing nearby,
and the Sabeans attacked and made off with them.
They put the servants to the sword, and I am the only one who has escaped to tell you!"
While he was still speaking, another messenger came and said,
"The fire of God fell from the heavens and burned up the sheep and the servants,
and I am the only one who has escaped to tell you!"
While he was still speaking, another messenger came and said,
"The Chaldeans formed three raiding parties and swept down on your camels and
made off with them. They put the servants to the sword,
and I am the only one who has escaped to tell you!"
While he was still speaking, yet another messenger came and said,
"Your sons and daughters were feasting and drinking wine at the oldest brother's house,
when suddenly a mighty wind swept in from the desert and struck the four corners
of the house. It collapsed on them and they are dead,
and I am the only one who has escaped to tell you!"

JOB 1:8–19 (NIV)

*So Satan went out from the presence of the LORD
and afflicted Job with painful sores from the soles of his feet to the crown of his head.
Then Job took a piece of broken pottery
and scraped himself with it as he sat among the ashes.*

2:7–8[2]

Job's clay pottery breaks into thousands of pieces of clay crumble without warning. It didn't happen because of something he did or didn't do. Job's clay pottery breaks because the Great Potter allows it. Although He does not orchestrate the misery, He does not prevent it either. Job's story is a stunning example of clay pottery who suddenly loses everything and ends up sitting on a pile of ashes. His story speaks to us today because in his suffering and loss, he does not curse the Great Potter but learns to know Him. By the end of the story, Job will understand that it is the Great Potter who was in charge all the time. It is the Great Potter who will always have the last word regarding the circumstances and destiny of His pottery.

Once upon a time in the land of Uz, there lived an exceptionally good man named Job. Everything is good in Job's life. A content fellow he is—at peace with himself, with other potteries, and with the Great Potter.

A caring and loving father who enjoys his family, wife, and adult children, he manages well and fairly his estate and his enormous wealth. He is respected and a well-known legal advisor. He is a helpful neighbor, nice, fair, and compassionate—so it is no wonder that he is called the greatest man in that area. (1:1–5)

I assume Job felt that the world was quite good, that he had meaning in his life, that everything he was involved in made sense, and that he was worthy enough to expect good stuff to happen to him. Aren't these the basic assumptions of a normal life?[6]

However, Job's good life did not last.

Suddenly, unexpected trauma strikes.

---

[2] *Read also*: Job 1–25.

At first, the terrorists murder his servants and steal his oxen and donkeys. Then all of his sheep and servants burn in a fire. Finally, another group of terrorists rob his camels and slay his remaining servants. In one moment, the wealthiest man of the East loses all of his possessions.

One may think that at least he has his family.

But not for long.

A tornado rips through the estate and kills Job's children, all ten of them. Can you imagine experiencing this? First, you lose all of your property, and now you lose all of your children, the ones most precious to you, whom you loved, cherished, and protected.

Well, at least he still has his health.

But not for long.

Job's physical health plummets. He suddenly finds his entire body riddled with painful sores, from the soles of his feet to the crown of his head.

Well, at least his marriage is intact. He has his wife all right. Isn't that something? Nope!

Even his wife rejects him and, indeed, advises him to kill himself (2:9–10).

Yes, Job experiences accident after accident: terror attacks, natural disasters, disease, rejection . . . everything possible. His clay pottery is not only smashed but also crushed, burned, and exploded, finally mixing with ashes.

And there he sits on a pile of ashes outside of town. Once the greatest pottery of the East, Job is now poor, sick, rejected, and disposed.

Perhaps Job is sitting in one of those trash yards of broken potteries because the Bible tells us that he took a piece of broken pottery and scraped his horrendously painful sores with it.

At least he had his broken clay pieces as his comfort, you might say.

Yes, Job was traumatized according to anyone's definition. Indeed, he experiences all *three elements of traumatization*: *helplessness*, *pain*, and *lack of empathy*.

He feels *enormous helplessness* and has completely lost his sense of security and justice. Job cries: "Do I have any power to help myself, now that success has been driven from me?" (6:13 NIV). However, "Though I cry, 'Violence!' I get no response; though I call for help, *there is no justice*" (19:7).

Job feels *massive physical and emotional pain.* "My spirit is broken, my days are cut short, the grave awaits me! Surely mockers surround me; my eyes must dwell on their hostility" (17:1–2). He sounds frantic: "For sighing has become my daily food; my groans pour out like water. What I feared has come upon me; what I dreaded has happened to me. I have no peace, no quietness; I have no rest, but only turmoil" (3:24–26).

There was no dignity left for Job as he sat on that trash pit of ashes, half-naked and scraping his infected skin. If the ash was a symbol of sorrow, Job's anguish was so enormous that he needed an entire pile to sit on. "I have sewed sackcloth over my skin and buried my brow in the dust. My face is red with weeping, dark shadows ring my eyes" (16:15–16).

Job certainly *lacks the empathy* of others. Those who he used to help and advise now mock him. His business partners reject him. Even kids laugh and spit on him. And, painfully, his wife despises him.

Within a few days, Job loses

- his possessions (1:13–17),
- children (1:18–19),
- health (2:7–8; 17:7; 19:20; 30:16–17,27–28, 30–31),
- wife's respect (2:9; 19:17),
- work (19:9, 15–16),
- family and friends (19:9, 14, 17, 19),
- social status/honor (12:4; Job 29:7–25; 16:10; 17:6; 19:9, 18; 30:1, 9–10),
- sense of safety (17:1; 30:12–15), and
- sense of justice (19:7; 30:20, 24–26).

His story raises several questions:

- How is something *so* horrible possible?
- Why did Job's clay pottery break *this* bad?
- Why Job?

- Whose *fault* is it? — It must be somebody's fault, right?

And yet, Job's calamity was *not* due to anything Job did or did not do.

Other than the nasty assassin attacks, the natural disaster that took the lives of his children and suffering health loss had nothing to do with any other pottery either. Job's clay pottery broke because the Great Potter *allowed* it to break. The Great Potter did not *orchestrate* Job's trauma experiences; rather, it was the devil, the great deceiver who did. —Nevertheless, the Great Potter *allowed* it.

Yes, it's true—while hard to accept—the Great Potter allowed the losses, enormous pain, and devastating suffering. Although it may not have been His original plan for Job, He allowed this trial to take place.

There isn't one who hasn't sat as broken pottery on a pile of ashes of some sort of destruction that hit our life. We were happy and content, planning our future, and then— in a blink of an eye—something struck. Everything crumbled into thousand pieces, leaving in its wake fear, destruction, pain, and questions. Who hasn't questioned, *Why me? Where is the Great Potter when I most need Him?* Who hasn't bellowed in desperation, "Come *quickly*, LORD, and *answer me*, for my depression *deepens*. Don't turn *away* from me, or I will *die*" (Psalm 143:7 NLT).

Visiting with Three Besservissers

And then, of course, Job's friends visit. Eliphaz the Temanite, Bildad the Shuhite, and Zophar the Naamathite. Three friends with good intentions (Job 12:11–13). They leave their homes and meet to sympathize with and comfort their suffering brother. However, when they see Job from a distance, they hardly recognize him. They begin to weep, tear their robes, and sprinkle dust on their heads as a sign of their empathy. Then they sit on the ground with Job for seven days and seven nights. *No one says a word.* They have no words when facing his enormous suffering.

As for their counseling skills, everything goes well during those first seven days and nights as they humbly empathize with Job's suffering while keeping their mouths shut. Perhaps they silently prayed for comfort. Perhaps they were too shocked to speak as they realized their mortality. Maybe they felt tiny before the Great Potter. No doubt they lacked understanding of Job's plight but accepted it. *Thy will be done . . . or not?*

After a week, the well-meaning friends cannot take it anymore. That concept of the Great Potter causing everything to work together for good to those who love Him does not seem to fit *this* particular situation. Not with *this* big a pile of ashes and not with *these* infected sores! They simply cannot see anything divine in it. They do not consider that there *could* be a bigger picture at work in this, or if they *tried* to see the situation in this light, they could not see it from the Great Potter's perspective.

Thy will be done? Nope!— *This* cannot be His will, they decide.

Perhaps the friends feel Job's helplessness. Maybe they become vicariously traumatized while taking in Job's enormous suffering. Or possibly they feel frustrated or uncomfortable facing the unknown. So, they offer their *pottery-made explanations* for Job's suffering. After all, it cannot be that the all-knowing, all-sovereign, all-good Great Potter allows *this much* suffering. It does not occur to them that the reason behind Job's situation is beyond *their* understanding.

When these friends open their mouths and speak, comfort and therapy fly out the window. And it sounds as if these know-it-alls have it all figured out.

What have these friends misunderstood to make their counsel so pathetically wrong?

Certainly, their explanations consist of the reasoning typical for their worldviews and religious doctrines of both legalistic causality and consequences, as well as the prosperity gospel. How they urge Job to repent his obvious secret sins! How they blame him for not having enough faith!

- *First,* Job's friends do not understand the Great Potter's unfailing and unconditional love.

- *Second*, they do not understand His never-ending grace, the deepest and most profound characteristic of the Great Potter.

Instead,

- the friends believe in *the law of causalities*: If you sin, you bear the consequences.
- They also hold to the logic of *the prosperity gospel*: Nothing bad can happen to potteries if they do not sin and have enough faith.

We see this same error at work today. Wherever grace is not understood, the law of causality and consequences becomes the foundation of Christianity.

It was miserably wrong in Job's day, and it is still wrong today.

As a result, Job, a pottery in enormous agony, becomes a victim of spiritual abuse from his buddies. These self-righteous fellows sit next to the pile of ashes, accusing their suffering brother that *he* is to blame for his woes. They rip at his core, pointing to his secret thoughts and unconscious motives, and question the pureness of his heart, which only adds to his over-the-top suffering. Job's friends rationalize that his current state is *proof* that it is his fault because good things happen to good potteries and bad things happen only to bad potteries.

No innocent pottery suffers *this* much.

Oh, how wrong they are! By "helping" Job, they only smash his clay pottery more. It is pretty nasty to take someone's vulnerable position and turn it against them.

As poor counselors, Job's friends simplify the Great Potter's logic to a clay pottery's logic and miss that the Great Potter's rationale and perspective are too big for mere clay potteries to ever understand. Ultimately, they do not acknowledge that the Great Potter's plans are much higher than ours. In fact, we do not always have a clue of what He is doing.

These friend's error is that they cannot understand the Great Potter's sovereign ways, so they try to diminish Him until He fits into their feeble understanding of Him. Trying to mold the Great Potter into their image makes Him something He is not. It's like a clay pot telling the Potter what he *should or should not* be doing with his clay: "Woe to those who quarrel with their Maker, those who are nothing but potsherds among the potsherds on the ground. Does the clay say to the potter, 'What are you making?' Does your work say, 'The potter has no hands'?" (Isaiah 45:9 NIV). We cannot manipulate Him with *our* promises, confessions, or faith—even our faith is nothing but a gift from Him. It is not the task of a clay pottery to advise the Great Potter to make better plans. "But who are you, a human being, to talk back to God? Shall what is formed say to the one who formed it, 'Why did you make me like this?'" (Romans 9:20 NIV)[3].

Furthermore, what these well-meaning but ignorant fellows do not recognize is that *none* of the devastating episodes is Job's fault. When the Great Potter allows His pottery to be smashed into a thousand pieces, it is *not* because the pottery is somehow *bad*. Job's trials occurred because He was *good* (Job 1:8). Indeed, Job's broken pottery becomes an important vessel for the Great Potter through its uttermost brokenness.

Job calls his friends worthless physicians, quacks, and impostors, hoping they would shut up. "You, however, smear me with *lies*; you are *worthless physicians*, all of you! If only you would be altogether *silent*! For *you*, that would be wisdom" (13:4–5 NIV). He deeply disagrees with his friends when they offer him their distorted image of the Great Potter as being vindictive, spiteful, demanding, unforgiving, and small enough to be manipulated by their faith.

Fortunately, Job's image of the Great Potter is healthier, and even though he is in an extremely vulnerable situation, he does not swallow what his friends suggest. Later, the Great Potter rebukes Job's friends for not speaking the truth about Him, as Job did (42:8).

It is profoundly serious when someone does not speak the truth about the Great Potter—or when someone smashes already smashed pottery a bit more.

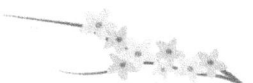

Have you ever heard rumors and whispers blaming a sick pottery for its condition? Rather than comfort and support the sick pottery, accusers plant malicious blame and spew spiteful gossip.

---

[3] See also Isaiah 29:16

- It *must* be *something* he has done or hasn't done.
- Oh, brother, you had better *reflect on* the condition of your heart.
- *If only* you had more faith!

Job's friends' behavior reminds me of a situation I observed in a hospital room when a good friend was dying. One of his friends came into the hospital room and started preaching to his wife and children that they had to confess their secret sins to one another and make sure that they had nothing but faith for his healing, not the tiniest bit of doubt whatsoever. Their faith and pure hearts would be *a defining factor* in their husband's and father's recovery. Instead of humbly praying "Thy will be done," and comforting the family, this "friend" demanded that they *manipulate* the Great Potter with their tricks, works, and rites!

These 'helpers' by Job's pile of ashes and by that hospital bed offer a false image of the Great Potter that has nothing to do with Him; smashing the already broken pottery instead of supporting it.

A cruel image of the Great Potter is planted in this kind of false counseling. Portraying Him as judgemental, meticulous, punitive, and demanding a perfect performance is a reflection of themselves. This false image depicts the Great Potter as weak and easily manipulated, leaving the clay pottery in charge of the situation as it either performs its tricks well or fails.

So when we see some broken potteries smashed in a trash yard, suffering on the pile of ashes, let us not make the same mistakes of Job's friends. When we encounter broken potteries, let us *not* investigate the reason for the suffering or whose fault it is. Instead, let's just *sit* with them, even when there is nothing that can be said; simply showing our empathy and help any concrete way we can. Remember, your mere presence means a lot for someone who is experiencing troubles as Job did. As Christians, we are all called to carry each other's burden (Galatians 6:2) and weep with those who weep (Romans 12:15).

Great Potter's Sovereign Way—It's Not for Me to Manipulate

We live in a broken world. Because of this, we *have* suffering, pain, injustice, turmoil, and death, all of which touch every pottery. Ultimately, the Great Potter will do away with it all but until then, we must conclude, as Job did, that He *is* supreme, and His ways *are* perfect and amazing beyond our comprehension. "I know that you can do all things; no plan of yours can be thwarted. You asked, 'Who is this that obscures my counsel without knowledge?' Surely I spoke of things *I did not understand*, things *too wonderful* for me to know" (Job 42:2–3 NIV).

This realization liberates Job. *He surrenders*, he lets it go— he could never even begin to fathom the Great Potter's reasoning and divine perspective. Just as the Great Potter controls the universe He created, He has full control over His clay pottery. The Great Potter in charge means that *whatever* happens, He has *everything* under control. Nothing happens without His *allowing* it.

And it also means that He's keeping His loving eye on us. We can rest while He does the work.

Job grasps the truth that just as he could never oversee the clouds, stars, or weather, he cannot always comprehend why something happens to his pottery. While still sitting on the pile of ashes, Job realizes that although broken, he is *safe*. He is safe because his Potter has it all under His power. Job also understands that it is not for clay pottery to confront its Maker. Actually, the Great Potter confronts Job: "'Will the one who contends with the Almighty correct him? Let him who accuses God answer him!'" (40:2). "Would you discredit my justice? Would you condemn me to justify yourself?" (v. 8). — And Job realizes: "I am unworthy—how can I reply to you? I put my hand over my mouth. I spoke once, but I have no answer— twice, but I will say no more" (vv. 4–5). Here Job admits that he could never even begin to understand the Great Potter's ways.

Job's friends did not understand this.

They could not comprehend that Job's suffering was completely under the Great Potter's control. The Great Potter—who was not only aware of what was happening but also allowed *all* of it—was in charge *all* the time.

If not even a hair falls from us without Him knowing (Luke 12:7), why would we think that our total breakdown would not be under His care as well?

The Great Potter *could* have stopped Job's misery much sooner than He did. He *could* have healed my friend that day in the hospital. One word from Him would have been enough.

Yes, He could have all right. He always could—but He sometimes does not.

The Great Potter wants us to understand that whatever good happens to us is *not* because of our faith, our achievements or something we could boast about. It is not because *we* successfully manipulated Him with our tricks, rituals, or good deeds. While bad things happen to us, the Great Potter is showing us that He is always in charge. Maybe, in Job's disasters, the Great Potter had faith in Job so that Job would *learn* to have faith in Him!

None of us can fully comprehend why do bad things happen to good potteries; why do beautiful potteries break. We simply must accept the Great Potter sometimes *allows* our clay potteries to break. *And we simply do not know why.* But in heaven we will find out—we will know why and rejoice in the Great Potter's wisdom.

Job Sees the Redeemer with His Very Own Eyes

Job didn't know why this horror had befallen him, but he learned something *new* during his suffering. In the middle of his uttermost torment, when everything had been taken away, when the only thing remained of his life was a pile of trash and burned ashes, Job realizes that the Great Potter indeed oversees his situation. "I *know* that my redeemer lives. And that in the end he *will* stand on the earth" (Job 19:25 NIV).

Job declares this with his last strengths in the middle of an enormous agony as his skin burns as though he were in hell. Then he suddenly grasps something that transforms his perspective forever: "And *after* my skin has been destroyed, yet in my flesh *I will see God*; *I myself* will see him with *my own eyes—I, and not another*" (vv. 26–27).

I myself.

Will see Him.

With my own eyes.

I, and not another!

Through the eyes of his soul while in his most horrendous suffering, Job suddenly *sees* the Great Potter—the Redeemer. He sees Him with his *own* eyes. Not with *somebody else's* eyes. Job not only sees the Great Potter who has his clay pottery on His table and in His hands, but he also gets to *know* Him intimately. He is not a stranger to Job anymore!

Even though none of Job's circumstances had changed, he now knows that he is perfectly safe because the Great Potter, with whom he now has a *personal* relationship, is personally taking care of him. "One day, maybe soon, my Redeemer will say His last word," Job says. "When everything else has collapsed, burned, and destroyed, He is the last One who will be standing on the ashes and ruins. *My Redeemer lives.*"

When everything was good, Job's *ears* had heard of the Great Potter, but now *his eyes* have seen Him as well (42:5)—and Job is *experiencing* Him, learning to *know* Him in a new way. Right now. Right here. For his pottery.

What new did you learn about the Great Potter during your most difficult life situation?

My Redeemer Lives

Interestingly, Job's fourth friend, young Elihu, shows empathy and compassion toward Job, speaking wisdom and the Great Potter's words right to his heart (32:8; 36:2–3). He does not share the false image of the Great Potter with his older three friends. He does not try to instill fear in Job or blame him for his predicament. He does not assume that Job's suffering proves he must be guilty of secret sins or lacking in faith. Instead, Elihu sees himself as another piece of clay, just like Job, astonished by the mysteries the Great Potter has created in the universe. "I am the same as you in God's sight; *I too am a piece of clay*" (33:6). Young Elihu with his servant's heart holds the therapeutic attitude needed for a good counselor.

Though prosperity-gospel preachers mistakenly promise a life free from suffering, the Great Potter allows our potteries to be broken, and we do not always know why. However, we know that He will never leave us. *He will never let us go.* He will not forsake us even if everybody else does. Even if our loved ones, friends, and church turn away from us, even if we forsake ourselves or Him, the Great Potter stays with us and holds us closer.

Job was a clay pottery of pain and sickness. All who saw him turned their faces away. Just as others did with another One thousands of years later. He was despised and rejected by everyone… "A Man of sorrows and acquainted with grief. And we hid, as it were, our faces from Him; He was despised, and we did not esteem Him" (Isaiah 53:3 NKJV). The Great Potter stepped down onto our pile of ashes to ex- perience the same (and more) as we did. He sacrificed Himself for us. He took our sin onto Himself and bore the punishment so that we could personally know the Great Potter. When He proclaimed from the cross, "It is finished!" He was saying that the penalty for sin had been paid, and we could have a relationship with the Great Potter (John 19:30). The Redeemer stood on top of the destructed ruins and the pile of our broken pieces, having gained the victory over the pain and sorrow of life on earth.

There isn't one of us who doesn't have our own pile of ashes—we all need the Redeemer to victoriously stand on the top of the mess of our broken pottery.

Perhaps we come to *know* the Great Potter only when we have entered into an extremely dark corner in our lives—the darkest valley—when nobody else is there for our comfort but the Great Potter. When only Him has not abandoned us…

That is when we may know Him in new ways.

I remember time when my clay pottery had been miserably smashed because of a series of traumatizing and unexpected episodes, I 'saw' the Great Potter as if it was for the first time! Before that, when all was good in my life and I could rely on myself, I had only *heard* about Him, how He loves, how He helps all kinds of *other* potteries, (especially in far-away countries) —how He strengthens *them*. Even how He sometimes does miracles for them. But in the middle of my broken pieces sitting on my ash pile helpless and crushed, for the first time in my life, I *saw* the real nature of the Great Potter with my *own eyes*—I experienced Him personally—I got to know Him in new ways. I saw the sovereign Creator, who holds everything in His hand and under His control. Even though nothing in my circumstances changed or made any more sense, I now *knew* that *I was perfectly safe*. At that moment, I learned that *nothing* can separate me from His love. And I surrendered.

Sometimes, it is only through these darkest experiences that we can know the Great Potter. When we see Him with our own eyes—when we personally experience His presence in our desperation— it is far more clarifying than only *hearing* about Him from others. When we experience Him from the perspective of *our* smashed clay crumble, it is far more real than listening to the rescue experiences of other potteries. The difference is *experiential*. It's like the difference between knowing how to ride a bike in theory because someone explained it and knowing how to ride a bike by getting on it and pumping the pedals as you speed down the road, feeling the wind whip around your hair and tug at your clothes.

Viktor Frankl, a holocaust surviving psychiatrist put it this way: *"Often it is just such an exceptionally difficult situation which gives man the opportunity to grow spiritually beyond himself."* [7]

When we are in a situation in which every thing we had trusted has been taken away from us, that's when we get to know Him. When we are nothing but a clay lump on His table, that is when we get to know Him in new ways. Any false image of Him we had created falls away, and we see Him *as He is*, radiating love, grace, and mercy because that's who He is.

Can we not trust Him in that moment?

Maybe you are in the ruins of your life right now as you sit on the ashes of your broken pottery and burned dreams. You may feel that nothing is left, not a scrap to start over with, no pieces of clay to find much less collect. If you are in the trash yard of broken potteries, the Great Potter has *already* found you. He has already started to collect your pieces, and very soon you will be on His table. Allow Him to start a good process on you, mixing the new clay of His unfailing, unconditional love and His never-ending grace with your burned clay crumbs—perhaps mixing in some pure gold also. He will make you to forever shine His glory over the memories of your broken pottery.

This is your opportunity to see Him with your own eyes, to experience His love, grace, and faithfulness.

CHAPTER 9

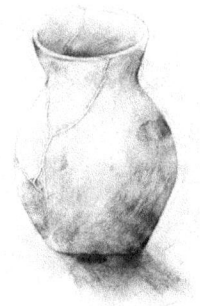

ABRAHAM'S DYSFUNCTIONAL DYNASTY

"Abraham believed God, and it was credited to him as righteousness,"
and he was called God's friend.

JAMES 2:23 NIV

Have you heard of families who hide the shameful actions of their ancestors? What about families in which certain behaviors keep repeating like a curse, and nobody knows why? To keep the secret hidden, any questions are silenced by the elders who swipe away the offending actions as though they never happened. They avoid speaking of it rather than reflecting on it openly and dealing with it in a healthy way. They may even lift their ancestors (or church pioneers) onto a pedestal, forbidding any candid reflection of what really happened.

Interestingly, the family tree of the Great Potter, Jesus, when He came to earth, is full of broken potteries. For example, the dysfunctional drama taking place in Abraham's family could be the basis of any Hollywood soap opera: betrayal, dishonesty, maliciousness, rape, incest, injustice . . . Broken potteries hollering in pain and breaking one another. The sins of the fathers literally playing out as destructive learned behaviours, causing vulnerability to be their children's inheritance (Exodus 20:5).

In Abraham's family, we see the vicious cycle of transgenerational trauma, broken potteries smashed because of unloving and uncaring actions, favoritism, abandonment, sexual assaults, and more. Yet the Great Potter's promise and faithfulness remain despite it all. He keeps His promises to this dysfunctional family, pouring out His blessing even though His chosen ones do not deserve it—this is grace. Despite the pertinent character flaws of Abraham, his son Isaac, and his grandson Jacob, the Great Potter is often identified as the God of Abraham, Isaac, and Jacob. The Great Potter even changed Jacob's name to Israel, confirming His great promises for the family tree for the generations to come.

It's sometimes difficult to understand the Great Potter's faithfulness. It certainly is on a much higher level than what we see and often experience with our fellow clay potteries' vengeful actions toward one another. It is hard to understand the idea that the Great Potter remains faithful simply because He cannot deny His name.

Therefore, it is somewhat comforting to read about Abraham's family's cracks and flaws. If the Great Potter put up with them, then He does with us too.

Take, for example, Abraham's cowardly treatment of Sarah, his wife. You would think that he would have learned from his mistake, but not so with Abraham. Twice, but twenty years apart and with two different kings, Pharaoh of Egypt and Abimelech, King of Gerar (Genesis 12: 10–20; 20:1–18), instead of trusting the Great Potter to keep him and his family safe, Abraham lied about his stunningly gorgeous wife. In fear for his life, as well as being selfish, Abraham said that Sarah was his sister and certainly not his wife. This lie may have saved Abraham, but what about sending Sarah into the kings' bedrooms? Abraham may have thought that living in a harem wasn't so bad. Sarah would have nice clothes, perfumes, cosmetics, and delicious food. From his twisted perspective, this was better than for him to be hanged or tossed into a dungeon. In both instances, once the pagan kings discovered that Sarah was Abraham's wife, they acted godlier than Abraham, a friend of the Great Potter, did.

Isaac, Abraham's son, repeats the generational trauma and similarly lies about his wife, Rebekah. He told King Abimelek of Gerar that Rebekah was his sister (26:1–32). Seriously, what is it with the men in that family? Dazzling women with cowardly husbands!

Abraham's descendants remember him as the friend of the Great Potter. Not only that, he is referred to as a hero of faith, held up as a good example and a role model. This is intriguing (and comforting for us not-so-perfect potteries) because he proved quite a few times that his faith in the Great Potter was not well developed. Had Abraham, Isaac, and Jacob trusted the Great Potter, there would have been fewer games played, fewer heartbreaks, and fewer broken potteries.

Favoritism

In studying this family, we find that favoritism was a generational trauma repetitively ending with broken potteries. Abraham favored his son, Isaac, by Sarah (21:1–14), and abandoned Hagar and Ishmael, his son by Hagar, Sarah's maid. Later, Isaac favored his son Esau, but his wife, Rebekah, favored Jacob, Esau's younger twin brother. Together, Rebekah and Jacob intentionally deceived both

Esau and Isaac (25:19–34; 27; 28). Jacob's life is rife with deception and betrayal as well. Regarding love and wealth, his uncle Laban betrays him for over a decade (29:16–28). Later, Jacob mistreats his first wife, Leah, favoring his second wife, Rachel and her sons.

A tragicomic example of Jacob's open favoritism and unfair love for his children is the episode when the family visits Esau, whom Jacob had betrayed years prior. Esau was known for his strength and violence. Aware of the possible attack against him and his household, Jacob cleverly places his other wives and their sons first on the caravan but puts his favorite wife, Rachel and her two sons in the back. It seems he thought that if someone were to be killed, it will not be anyone he loves (33:1–3).

In Abraham's family, it is obvious that the transgenerational trauma negatively affects the following generations because of unresolved emotions and lack of reflection. His family tree is an example of repeated brokenness and trauma repetition. The widely researched idea is that trauma indeed can leave a chemical mark on genes, which is passed down to the subsequent generations.[8] The children learn these patterns from their parents and grandparents and then develop the same neural networks in the brain.

We see several repeated patterns in Abraham's pedigree: betrayal, poor parent-child relationships, and weak emotional attachment. Reading about this family, we learn about rapes and murders, Reuben, Jacob's son, sleeping with his stepmother (35:22), and Judas, another of Jacob's son, sleeping with a harlot without knowing that she is his daughter-in-law, Tamar. Dinah, Jacob's only daughter, is brutally raped, and in retaliation, her brothers murder all the men in the rapist's city. Further down the lineage is King David, who abuses his authority and orders Bathsheba to sleep with him. After learning of her resulting pregnancy, David has her husband murdered. Later, David's eldest son Amnon rapes his step-sister Tamar, the sister of Absalom, David's favourite son, who murders Amnon and rapes his father's concubines....

We could go on with many other stories of broken potteries in Abraham's line, but the truth is, no matter how much misery contained in the lives of his descendants, the Great Potter chose these broken potteries to be the ancestors in the Messiah's lineage.

Transgenerational Curse

In Abraham's dynasty, the legacy of brokenness is passed down throughout the generations. It is the same for us. Our children and grandchildren are not only shaped by the genes they inherit from us, but also any traumatizing experiences can leave their marks. Of course, we could call it the curse that has been affecting the human race since the fall of Adam and Eve.

It is difficult to cut the generational trauma, to stop the vicious cycle of broken potteries breaking others, to break the cycle of victimization. No broken pottery can do this; however, *it is possible for the Great Potter*. From the beginning of time, He had a plan to break this cycle of evil. He had a plan to break the transgenerational curse of broken potteries.

The plan involved the Great Potter stepping into the trash yard of broken potteries. He had to be broken, thoroughly smashed, so much that He no longer was recog- nizable. He became smashed clay crumbles to rescue His creation, yet the powers of heaven resurrected Him. He fully conquered the rules of death, brokenness, and destruction.

Because He lives, I can face tomorrow.[9]

Matthew 1 and Luke 3 list Christ's genealogy, starting at Abraham. It is a comprehen- sive list of incredibly broken potteries—just like you and me. Interestingly, *we* are part of this lineage: "If you belong to Christ, then *you* are Abraham's *seed*, and *heirs* according to the promise" (Galatians 3:29 NIV). Just as the destructive generational trauma of our forefathers' selfishness, neglect, abuse, and shameful secrets may have overshadowed our upbringing, likewise, the Great Potter's unfailing love on Calvary instituted the Great Reset, a fresh new beginning for whosoever believes in Him (John 3:16). He *is* the way in the desert and the living stream in the wastelands (Isaiah 43:18–19).

The next six chapters will introduce some victims of the vicious cycle of generational trauma pertinent to Abraham's family. The stories expose trauma repetition spiraling from generation to generation. The fathers' sins, unloving and traumatizing actions, are avenged and repeated in the next generation, causing more unloving and traumatizing actions.

Abraham's family members' stories are about potteries broken because of various blows of hurtful situations and transgenerational trauma unconsciously repeating in the family tree. However, that's not all these stories are about. They also tell about the Great Potter, who remains faithful even when we are unfaithful.

CHAPTER 10

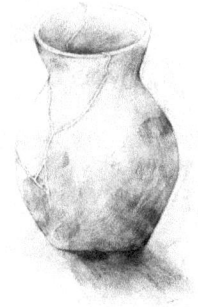

HAGAR, INVISIBLE AND VOICELESS BUT SEEN AND HEARD BY THE GREAT POTTER

Now Sarai, Abram's wife, had borne him no children.
And she had an Egyptian maidservant whose name was Hagar. So Sarai said to Abram,
"See now, the Lord has restrained me from bearing children.
Please, go in to my maid; perhaps I shall obtain children by her."

And Abram heeded the voice of Sarai. Then Sarai, Abram's wife, took Hagar her maid, the Egyptian, and gave her to her husband Abram to be his wife, after Abram had dwelt ten years in the land of Canaan. So he went in to Hagar, and she conceived. And when she saw that she had conceived, her mistress became despised in her eyes. Then Sarai said to Abram, "My wrong be upon you! I gave my maid into your embrace; and when she saw that she had conceived, I became despised in her eyes. The Lord judge between you and me."

So Abram said to Sarai, "Indeed your maid is in your hand; do to her as you please." And when Sarai dealt harshly with her, she fled from her presence.

Now the Angel of the Lord found her by a spring of water in the wilderness, by the spring on the way to Shur. And He said,

"Hagar, Sarai's maid, where have you come from, and where are you going?" She said, "I am fleeing from the presence of my mistress Sarai."

The Angel of the Lord said to her,

"Return to your mistress, and submit yourself under her hand."

Then the Angel of the Lord said to her,

"I will multiply your descendants exceedingly, so that they shall not be counted for multitude." And the Angel of the Lord said to her:

"Behold, you are with child, And you shall bear a son. You shall call his name Ishmael, Because the Lord has heard your affliction.

He shall be a wild man; His hand shall be against every man, And every man's hand against him. And he shall dwell in the presence of all his brethren."

Then she called the name of the Lord who spoke to her, You-Are-the-God-Who-Sees; for she said, "Have I also here seen Him who sees me?"

Therefore the well was called Beer Lahai Roi; observe, it is between Kadesh and Bered. So Hagar bore Abram a son; and Abram named his son, whom Hagar bore, Ishmael.

GENESIS 16:1–15 (NKJV)

Hagar and Ishmael Depart

So the child grew and was weaned.
And Abraham made a great feast on the same day that Isaac was weaned.
And Sarah saw the son of Hagar the Egyptian, whom she had borne to Abraham, scoffing. Therefore she said to Abraham, "Cast out this bondwoman and her son; for the son of this bondwoman shall not be heir with my son, namely with Isaac."
And the matter was very displeasing in Abraham's sight because of his son.
But God said to Abraham,
"Do not let it be displeasing in your sight because of the lad or because of your bondwoman. Whatever Sarah has said to you, listen to her voice;
for in Isaac your seed shall be called.
Yet I will also make a nation of the son of the bondwoman, because he is your seed."
So Abraham rose early in the morning, and took bread and a skin of water; and putting it on her shoulder, he gave it and the boy to Hagar, and sent her away.
Then she departed and wandered in the Wilderness of Beersheba.
And the water in the skin was used up, and she placed the boy under one of the shrubs. Then she went and sat down across from him at a distance of about a bowshot; for she said to herself, "Let me not see the death of the boy."
So she sat opposite him, and lifted her voice and wept.
And God heard the voice of the lad.
Then the angel of God called to Hagar out of heaven, and said to her,
"What ails you, Hagar? Fear not, for God has heard the voice of the lad where he is. Arise, lift up the lad and hold him with your hand, for I will make him a great nation." Then God opened her eyes, and she saw a well of water.
And she went and filled the skin with water, and gave the lad a drink.

21:8–19[4]

---

[4] *Read also*: Genesis 16, 21, 25.

Hagar's clay pottery is broken many times by other potteries. It is as if it is her lot in life to be smashed repeatedly. Rejected, abandoned, betrayed, she feels invisible, a woman without a voice. However, the Great Potter sees her and hears her. Hagar's story is a beautiful encounter with her Creator, who never forsakes. He hears and sees and intervenes.

Hagar, perhaps once a princess of Egypt, is now a slave. She was given as a gift by Pharaoh along with sheep and cattle, donkeys and camels (12:10–20) when Abraham's[5] cowardly games had placed Sarah in Pharaoh's harem. However, as Pharaoh did not want any issues with the Great Potter, he gave all these gifts to Abraham to get rid of him as soon as possible.

Taken away from her home and wandering in the desert with this odd tribe was probably not easy for Hagar. Then in a desperate move to force God's promise, her mistress, Sarah, ordered her to sleep with Abraham. Sarah was so adamant to try to fulfill God's promise that she didn't give her husband a choice either. He seems to not have objected to the plan. He simply takes his mattress and sleeps with Hagar.

Did anybody care about Hagar's needs or feelings?

Sarah didn't. Allthough a role model of faith, all she cared about was her frustration at what she considered a delay in God's promise. Tired of waiting month after month, her biological clock hardly ticking, she grew old and disheartened. Did she think that the Great Potter's promise was fake? Or had she misunderstood it? At some point, wouldn't a woman take matters into her own hands, expecting something to be done properly? ...And she did.

It was all about Sarah's genius planning. It initially sounded like a smart move, but it quickly became apparent that it was anything but, not for anyone involved. Of course, after Hagar got pregnant, it was suddenly as if her fate had changed. Finally, she had something that nobody else had, not even Sarah! Wouldn't it be *her* son who would inherit the ruler of this tribe? Not bad for a slave girl!

---

[5] God changed Abram's name to Abraham to confirm His promise that he would be the father of many. Likewise, God changed Sarai's name to Sarah. I call them Abraham and Sarah in this chapter.

Which came first: Did Hagar begin to despise Sarah before Sarah started to humiliate her, or did Sarah humiliate her then Hagar despised her mistress? It doesn't matter. What does is that the situation deteriorated.

Road Trip #1

What else could Hagar do but run away after Sarah beats and humiliates her? And Abraham does nothing to stop it? It was clear to Hagar that if a fella did not protect his wedded wife from Pharaoh's bedroom, he would not lift a finger to rescue a slave. And even her bearing the master's child seemed not to matter. Nobody cared about her or her unborn child.

Up until now, Hagar's clay pottery had received a few cracks—when she was given as a slave and had to leave her home, family, and country; when she served her mistress, Sarah, and when she was forced into Abraham's bed. Hagar had learned to toughen herself and mind her own business. She kept a stiff upper lip. But she had reached her limit. The harsh treatment at the hand of Sarah, Abraham's refusal to protect her, and believing that nobody cares about her finally breaks Hagar's clay pottery, blowing it into a few sharp pieces in one well-targeted whack.

So, she takes off. I imagine Hagar running away, tears streaming down her face, perhaps screaming in anger. Cursing, kicking the stones away from her. When her strength is spent, she stops running. At an oasis, she drops to the ground. Looking around the desert, she is alone.

In the few times I've explored the various deserts of Israel, Jordan, and Egypt, I thought about Hagar. Even though I drank lots of water and wore a huge hat, I twice suffered heatstroke. How miserable in body and spirit she must've been.

It would have been impossible for Hagar to walk back home to Egypt. There were too many dangers: wild animals, thieves, outlaws, heat, wind, lack of food and water.

The Spring along the Road to Shur

Sitting in the comforting shadows and catching her breath, she drinks from the oasis and washes away the dust and dried tears from her face. Collecting her thoughts, she assesses her situation. What is she to do now? She can't go back—to go back to Sarah would be too much to bear—but where can she go? She can't return home to Egypt because she wouldn't be safe traveling alone. Enough time has passed that if Abraham would've sent someone after her, he would've found her by now. The truth was that she wasn't missed. *No one wanted or needed her.* She remains broken in a thousand pieces.

Have you ever felt like Hagar?

Trauma experience is followed by a trauma reaction, which is triggered by impulsive emotions rather than reasoning or planning. Your choice is to stay and fight or flee the scene— mentally escaping into yourself or physically leaving the scene. If you've been in a situation in which you fled, it is only afterward you stop and consider what happened. You might wonder how you got here. This was not what you had planned for your life, not what you'd prepared for. However, there's no going back. Ask yourself these questions:

- Why did I run away or escape?
- What was my trigger?
- Was I being treated unfairly? Harshly?
- Did I feel insecure?
- Was I afraid?
- Was I disappointed?

In Hagar's case, she could answer yes to the last four questions. The vicious cycle of insecurity began in her youth when she was given away as a slave and grew with repeated instances of no one loving her or even caring about her. We can graph it like this:

Trauma experience → trigger → trauma reaction → re-traumatization → new trigger → new trauma reaction → and re-traumatization . . . and the cycle goes on.

And it is only the devil, the great demolisher, who is happy, for now he can break her pottery even more, hoping to destroy the pottery with one final blow and leaving Hagar desperate and hopeless, primed for self-destruction.

Hagar escaped her situation for the same reasons and in the same ways as many of us have escaped our life situations: when relationships and emotions have become too difficult to bear.

Some of us have fled only symbolically, physically remaining in the wounding situation but building a protective barrier around ourselves: hardened our hearts, numbed our emotions, decided that nobody will hurt us again, vowed never to let anybody too close again.

We learned to smile when we have a black eye.

We learned to smile when our hearts cry.

We learned to smile to hide our raw vulnerability.

We learned to scream inside because we lost our voices a long time ago.

Perhaps Hagar was like this as well as she sat by that spring, desperately trying to figure out her next move while feeling utter helplessness.

Angel Finding Hagar

But then the angel of the Great Potter appears. He finds her. Somebody out there had indeed been looking for her—and seeing her— all the time.

Hagar, servant of Sarah, where have you come from, and where are you going?

Hagar hardly expected anything from the Great Potter. Perhaps she thought of Him as a hypocrite with similar angry outbursts like Sarah's, or as phlegmatic and uncaring as Abraham. Or maybe she felt herself so much an outsider and so low slung that she could not imagine that the Great Potter existed for her types.

But she was wrong.

Actually, the Great Potter came to her dressed as an angel. He sounds like the Great Potter. His question, "Hagar, where have you come from, and where are you going?" reminds us of the question He asked the blind man He was about to heal, "What would you like Me to do for you?" or the paralyzed man, "Do you want to be healed?" What about when He asked the disciples who were panicking in the stormy sea, "Why are you scared?" or when Mary stood crying outside of His grave. "Why are you crying?"

Sounds like the Great Potter, eh?

Of course, He knew the answers to these questions, but He posed them to the broken potteries so that *they* could reflect on what *they* do not know and consider what *they* need.

The Great Potter knows Hagar's heart and her clay pottery's core. He knows her past, her trauma, her trauma reactions, her triggers, as well as her insecurities and pain. By asking this question, He wants her to reflect on her past and learn its impact on her current reactions, to become empowered to make choices rather than unconsciously react.

"Where are you coming from, Hagar?"

"Oh, well, You know… I was first taken away from my family when I was just a girl. And now I'm pregnant with my master's child. I guess I'm coming from this situation that escalated. I'm escaping abuse… I'm running away from my mistress, Sarah."

"Where are you going, Hagar?"

"No idea. Perhaps back to Egypt . . . but it is far away. Not sure how I will make it alone."

Then the Great Potter names Hagar's soon-to-be-born son, *Ishmael*, which means "The Great Potter has heard your misery, your cry of condition." And then Hagar names the Great Potter *El Roi*, which means "You are the God who sees me. I have now seen the One who sees me." (Later, Hagar will learn that these names entail a promise: She will always be seen and heard by the Great Potter.) It is striking how naturally these two new names are given as if the Great Potter and the slave girl both have equal rights to name each other.

Hagar is no longer an invisible woman with no destiny. She has been seen by the Great Potter. She is no longer voiceless because the Great Potter endorsed her voice and sense of dignity.

The Great Potter's encounter with Hagar is such a beautiful example of how He validates those who have become invisible and voiceless because of their continuous trauma experiences and repeated blows against their pottery.

With a new dignity and the Great Potter's promises hidden in her heart, Hagar returns to Abraham's camp. The Great Potter both sees and hears. And He has gently restored Hagar's broken pottery.

As you read this portion of Hagar's story, the Great Potter never blames or runs any guilt trips with Hagar. He does not ask about her role in the episode with Sarah. He does not try to belittle, rationalize, or explain Sarah's behavior. He simply expresses that *He has heard and seen Hagar.*

The ultimate need of any pottery broken into pieces and thrown into a trash yard is to be seen and heard as-is. *To be seen*: isn't this our core's need? The foundation of our mental health? Something we look for all our lives, sometimes in the wrong places? It is with the Great Potter that we can finally be seen and heard and accepted as-is. *We are enough.* We do not need to hide anything or pretend we are someone we are not. Even when everybody else has forsaken us, when nobody is looking for us, He has already seen us. He has already heard us.

It is lovely that the Great Potter always meets us wherever we lie broken. He comes and collects our pieces and restores our pottery. He reinstates our sense of dignity and self-worth.

What do you think He sees when He looks at your pottery?

Road Trip #2

Although clay potteries from diverse cultures have different ideas of what's most important to their communities, we all value justice and want a secure, fair, and rational life. Chaos and violence are not part of that picture, and when they strike, they throw our worlds into a state of shock, confusion, and feelings of powerlessness.10

Hagar experienced this when Abraham woke her and Ishmael early one morning. He swiftly walked them to the edge of the camp and said a brief farewell. Nobody asked Hagar anything. She was not given any opportunity to explain her son's behaviour. They just made these decisions for her and, again, she did not have a voice.

It feels unreal to walk away from the camp, which had been Hagar's home for years. In the beginning she is in a shock, it all feels unreal. She most likely dissociates to protect herself from the sharpness and pain she will certainly experience by the end of that horrendous day.

No, this cannot be happening. It feels like a nightmare. I will soon wake up in my tent and realize it was only a bad dream.

But, no, it is not.

Indeed, just like that, Hagar's life has suddenly turned into a nightmare.

Last night when she went to sleep, it was all good; not perfect, but mostly safe, fair enough, and solid—at least as much as it could be living with the constant relationship drama of Sarah and Abraham and their son.

For sure, Hagar did not expect to find herself wandering in the wilderness of Beersheba, the sun beating down on them as they trudged in the sandy desert.

What am I supposed to do? Our water bottle is empty after giving the last drop to Ishmael over an hour ago. Indeed, is there anything I can do? We will both die by the end of the night. My son and myself! …It feels foggy…

The heat. The thirst. The exhaustion. The tough wilderness. It's excruciatingly real.

And suddenly, mother and son cannot take one more step. Leaving Ishmael under one of the bushes, Hagar collapses nearby, not too close because the pain of watching her son die is too much.

She remains prone under the hot sun and weeps with her last strength as Ishmael moans and sobs. Mother and son hopeless, knowing no one hears them or will rescue them.

No doubt, Hagar recalls the scene from her attempt to run away fourteen years prior.

I should never have returned to the camp that day. That nasty Sarah and her fists. What an idiot I am for trusting them, thinking it all had settled. Oh, that fantasy of "belonging!" That cowardly Abraham—no backbone whatsoever. What kind of a man abandons his son to the wilderness?—A murderer! A godly man, what a joke!

And Hagar weeps, but she does not pray, at least according to the author of Genesis, she doesn't. And why would she? She is bitterly disappointed in the Great Potter because of what Abraham and Sarah did to her. Like so many of us, when so-called Christian potteries treat us badly, we blame the Great Potter.

The heat of the sun continues to suck the life from Hagar and Ishmael, a slow and scary death. *El Roi, the One who is supposed to see me, where is He now? The One who is supposed to hear Ishmael, why doesn't He? What happened to those mighty promises He gave fourteen years ago? Why did He allow us to be treated this way? Why didn't He intervene? All those promises are fake!*

Does any of this sound familiar? There isn't one of us who hasn't asked any of these questions after our clay pottery has been smashed.

Desperate to Destined

Hagar's story ends with the Great Potter intervening again. Not for a moment had the situation been anywhere but under His control. Even though Hagar's pottery is smashed and Abraham abandoned her and Ishmael, the Great Potter never. The Great Potter always acts according to his name. *El Roi* still sees Hagar. He *hears* Ishmael's misery, his cry, just as Ishmael's name promises.

Again He asks a simple question, "What is wrong, Hagar?"

As soon as Hagar hears the question, she immediately knows who is speaking and that her destiny has suddenly changed from desperate to rescued. She realizes that the same Great Potter who saw and heard her fourteen years prior still sees and hears. *The Great Potter still remembers my name. He must also remember the name, El Roi, that I gave Him. —It must mean that He still sees me!*

"Do not be afraid!" Oh, how often the Great Potter starts His message with these comforting words! And He has good news for Hagar; He has heard Ishmael's cry for help. "Now, arise and lift up your boy and give him some water!"

Hagar needed divine intervention to encourage her to arise from that heated ground where her broken pieces had collapsed to die. We too need the Great Potter to collect our broken pieces from the trash yard of broken potteries. When we hear the Great Potter calling, are we ready to listen and react, or do we continue entertaining our misery, self-pity, and bitterness?

It is beautiful to see how the Great Potter knows what Hagar needs. He opens her eyes so that she sees the well only a few meters from where she had collapsed in thirst. How often we find our broken pottery pieces in this situation. Dying of thirst in the dry desert, only steps away from the Living Water. Likewise, we desperately try to fix our broken potteries without realizing that we have indeed fallen into the Great Potter's loving hands who will fully restore us. We are *already* on His table, and He is waiting for our permission to launch the process. He will take care of our needs. The refreshing water will revitalize our dehydrated clay. He adds His unconditional love, never-ending grace, and everlasting faithfulness.

The Great Potter wants to open our eyes to see that everything is possible for Him. He wants us to see that He has it all under His control. He sees our broken pieces.

Hagar chooses to trust the Great Potter. In the middle of a desert wilderness, she decides to simply trust her broken pottery to the Great Potter's table. None of her circumstances changed, but she is no longer desperate because she is with the Prince of Peace. "Do not be afraid," He says, and Hagar is no longer scared but at peace.

Hagar's trauma, being exiled to the desert, was the beginning of something new in her life. There was a blessing for Hagar and Ishmael's lives (Genesis 21:20). Though different from what Hagar had imagined as a young girl, the blessings originated from the Great Potter.

Never did the Great Potter forget or forsake Hagar. Neither are our clay potteries, even if we are forsaken or forgotten by everyone else. The Great Potter is faithful.

Does Hagar's story resonate with you? Have you felt the anger and desperation, thinking this must be the end, and being disappointed, even angry, with the Great Potter? Were you also angry at those who caused your misery by breaking your pottery and abandoning it?

Trauma and Grief Processing Phases

The process, after our pottery is smashed into a thousand pieces, includes a variety of phases yet it is always individual.[11] Difficult emotions tend to come back like a roller coaster.

The Shock Phase is the first response experienced right after our pottery breaks. It usually lasts up to 24 hours but it can also last days or even weeks if the trauma episode continues. The following phases of the process may not launch until we feel safe again. Discussing with many refugee women, they described a prolonged shock phases, *walking for weeks, through a desert or forest…, avoiding the roads because they were scared of the ISIS soldiers. Feeling unreal all the time… Even thinking back only remembering fogginess.* During the Shock our experience feels *dreamlike*—like having a nightmare or watching a horror movie. We may feel numb yet all our senses store all the detailed images of the event. Later, those same sensations may trigger flashback, disturbing images and nightmares.[12] However, the Shock Phase protects against pain that would be too much for the mind to receive and process.

The Reaction Phase or ***Outcry Phase*** is a carousel of extreme emotions and yearning. It lasts 2-4 days or longer, even weeks. This is when our broken potteries become painfully conscious of the incidence and its consequences; its devastating meaning for our lives. Both body and mind scream in pain—anger, sorrow, anxiety, fear, guilt, shame, hopelessness, and other feelings will escalate and recede, like in a rollercoaster. Denying the permanence of the loss may also take place. During this phase, it is important to acknowledge that something horrible took place, i.e. violence, and it was all wrong. Gradually, it will be essential to *accept* the reality of the loss and acknowledge, express, and work through the painful emotions. Trauma and grief processing use an enormous amount of our energy so no wonder if it feels exhausting. There may also be various physiological symptoms, such as headaches, nausea, heart issues, muscle tension, dizziness, fatigue, insomnia, stomach aches, difficulty to breath, lump in a throat, choking feeling, muscle weakness, shaking, no appetite… The body may remain in an alarmed stage which may impact a weakened immune-system.[13]

Remembrance and Mourning Phase usually lasts from one month to one year. However, this phase will not launch before the immediate danger has faded. Typical feelings are emptiness, despair, and hopelessness, as well as difficulty to concentrate and focus, to 'be present,' or plan the future. It will be crucial to learn to distinguish between an outside danger and inside danger, *'I am safe even though I may not feel safe.'* As around this time many broken potteries may be on a danger zone to develop depression, other potteries are needed to help them to reach Hope instead of despair and have connections instead of withdrawal.

Processing, Renewal and Reconnecting with Ordinary Life, may continue the rest of our lives. It includes forming a new identity as a survivor rather than a victim and finding *new meanings* within the trauma episode and for our broken potteries; the proverbial silver lining. Although the pain may never go away, nor can our broken pottery experience be erased from our memory, little by little we learn to cope; the trauma-episode no longer controls our life; it does not need to be our destiny. Like Hagar, we will arise and begin to move towards our new future.

The grief process is never easy but it is part of life. After reflecting our trauma-episode, gaining understanding of it, and working through our emotions, at some point we often naturally find ourselves turning a new page and beginning to plan a different future. Like Hagar, we may allow ourselves to arise above the hurtful and unfair circumstances that we simply cannot change. The Great Potter has something else already planned for our pottery.

Are you ready to launch into reflecting on your past, present, and future? Are you ready to investigate: *Where am I coming from? How did I end up in this trash yard of broken potteries? What am I doing here? Where will I go from here?*

What phases of the grief process and trauma recovery have you experienced; where are you now in your process? How do you *know* when you have reached the next phase; what will be different?

To arise and take the first step towards future means that we…

- accept that there is no going back because trauma permanently changed something,

- realize that although we cannot change our traumatized past or erase anything that took place there, our past trauma experiences need not define our present or future,
- acknowledge that we cannot change anybody else—much less their feelings toward us,
- take responsibility for our emotions—as we cannot change anybody else's emotions,
- leave the ground surrounded by our smashed pottery pieces, bitterness, and self-pity,
- take responsibility for the choices we make today and in the future, and
- surrender our life to the Great Potter and ask Him to lead us out of the desert of desperation and hopelessness.

Looking back on your life-road, the journey that took you where you are right now, perhaps you see different landscapes, dark valleys, wilderness, deserted areas, green pastures, mountains, caves, refreshing waters, rivers, wells, gates… the Great Potter's divine interventions that led your path from one point into another. Maybe you can recognize His protection—perhaps beginning to see a new meaning or even blessing.

Trying to visualize from the Great Potter's perspective, perhaps you are also able to see that your life has always been in His hands—you have always been seen and heard by the *El Roi*.

He never forsakes you!

CHAPTER 11

LEAH
UGLY AND UNLOVED

Now Laban had two daughters:
the name of the elder was Leah, and the name of the younger was Rachel.
Leah's eyes were delicate,
but Rachel was beautiful of form and appearance.
Now Jacob loved Rachel; so he said,

"I will serve you seven years for Rachel your younger daughter."
And Laban said, "It is better that I give her to you than that I should give her to another man. Stay with me." So Jacob served seven years for Rachel,
and they seemed only a few days to him because of the love he had for her.
Then Jacob said to Laban,
"Give me my wife, for my days are fulfilled, that I may go in to her."
And Laban gathered together all the men of the place and made a feast.
Now it came to pass in the evening, that he took Leah his daughter and brought her to Jacob; and he went in to her. And Laban gave his maid Zilpah to his daughter Leah as a maid.
So it came to pass in the morning, that behold, it was Leah. And he said to Laban,
"What is this you have done to me? Was it not for Rachel that I served you?
Why then have you deceived me?"
And Laban said, "It must not be done so in our country, to give the younger before the firstborn. Fulfill her week, and we will give you this one also for the service
which you will serve with me still another seven years."
Then Jacob did so and fulfilled her week. So he gave him his daughter Rachel as wife also.
And Laban gave his maid Bilhah to his daughter Rachel as a maid.
Then Jacob also went in to Rachel, and he also loved Rachel more than Leah.
And he served with Laban still another seven years.

The Children of Jacob

When the Lord saw that Leah was unloved, He opened her womb; but Rachel was barren.
So Leah conceived and bore a son, and she called his name Reuben; for she said,
"The Lord has surely looked on my affliction. Now therefore, my husband will love me."
Then she conceived again and bore a son, and said,
"Because the Lord has heard that I am unloved, He has therefore given me this son also."
And she called his name Simeon. She conceived again and bore a son, and said,
"Now this time my husband will become attached to me, because I have borne him three sons." Therefore his name was called Levi. And she conceived again and bore a son, and said,
"Now I will praise the Lord." Therefore she called his name Judah. Then she stopped bearing.

GENESIS 29:16–35 (NKJV)

And God listened to Leah, and she conceived and bore Jacob a fifth son. Leah said, "God has given me my wages, because I have given my maid to my husband." So she called his name Issachar. Then Leah conceived again and bore Jacob a sixth son. And Leah said, "God has endowed me with a good endowment; now my husband will dwell with me, because I have borne him six sons." So she called his name Zebulun. Afterward she bore a daughter, and called her name Dinah.

30:17–21[6]

No matter who inflicted the first blow on Leah's pottery, the morning after smashed it for good. Leah's clay pottery was broken by betrayal and humiliation. The situation was unfair, rife with political games, betrayal—typical transgenerational trauma repeating in Jacob's family. Her smashed pottery feels the raw pain of humiliation daily because she is the unloved wife despite her trying her best to earn her husband's love. Her pottery is further ground into the ground as she watches her husband and her sister's relationship as a continuous honeymoon. Adding further stinging pain is seeing her sons treated unequally compared with her sister's sons.

Leah will never forget that morning, the day after the wedding. That raw sensation of pure humiliation and stinging pain after Jacob suddenly realizes she is not the one he wanted. He discovers the game her father had played, deceiving him into marrying her instead of Rachel, the one he loved, the one with beautiful eyes!

We do not know for sure what happened the night before. Did Laban intentionally blow Leah's pottery to pieces? Or did he simply want to blow Jacob's and unintentionally broke Leah's also? Or did Leah break her pottery herself by willingly taking part in the deceit? Maybe she hoped that after a night of lovemaking, he would not see her as an ugly duckling but a swan. Perhaps because of the custom of the time, Leah had no voice. All she could do was obey her father as her maids

---

[6] *Read also*: Genesis 29–33, 35.

dressed her in her wedding attire before being taken to the tent to wait for her newlywed husband to arrive. Did she honestly think that Jacob had agreed to marry the elder sister?

The wedding night would not change Jacob's feelings toward her. Making love with her thinking it was Rachel did not make him want *her* more. Imagine the first sunlight suddenly uncovering the sleeping Leah's face and Jacob realizing the bitter betrayal and deceit.

Wrong girl! Leah acutely aware He had not made love to *her*. He had made love to Rachel!

Jacob likely stormed from the marriage tent to his uncle's tent that morning, ripping aside the flap, and letting loose a tirade of anger. "What is this you have done to me? It was for Rachel that I served you? Why have you deceived me?" Even though Leah tries not to think about it, she cannot help but hear Jacob's hurtful screeching. The way he recoiled when he realized it was *her*, not Rachel holding him in her sleep—pushing her away from himself in repulsion. Then blaming her for taking part in this nasty betrayal. Marching to Laban's tent yelling in the early morning.

Not only did Laban hear what Jacob thought about this betrayal and the woman with whom he slept, but the entire camp got an earful. Imagine the humiliation Leah suffered for it to be public knowledge that her husband didn't want her. *He never, not for a moment, had wanted her.* He wanted only her younger sister. It was bad enough that she will be remembered as the woman who got a husband via deceit and manipulation. Worse, she could not keep him. What kind of woman causes her newlywed husband hollering on the camp on the dawn about his bitter disappointment with his new wife?

Leah stopped breathing when she learned of the new deal between Laban and Jacob. As soon as the "festivity" week of the forced marriage ended, Jacob would take his beloved Rachel as his wife. *How hurtful is this?* He doesn't even try to fake it. On that first night when he thought he was with Rachel there was no rush, only tenderness and gentle whispers. But now there is no making love as there is no love. Sex, yes— but not making *love*. Yes, she tries her best to please him, but her heart is broken. And, after the week, he continues the honeymoon in her sister's tent. And an extra week perhaps, and a third one. Oh, those gossiping glances on the camp and blathering whispers when the other women look at her.

Everyone in the camp knows that Jacob loves Rachel. So much so that he is willing to give Laban seven more years of service after the wedding. For Leah, Jacob wouldn't have worked one hour, but for Rachel, he gladly worked fourteen years.

But how could she not have known that this would happen? When her father told her about the marriage and that it was to be kept a secret, she probably suspected that something was not right. The looks of the women helping her to dress likely signaled that something was amiss. How could she miss the coy and loving looks that passed between Jacob and Rachel, their secret whispers?

Had she heard the rumors in the camp, murmured pities behind her back of course? She was the butter face, kind and hard-working… Invisible rather than a beauty queen, especially when compared with Rachel. Nobody could hold a candle to her dazzling sister, who had always been referred to as "the pretty one" while of Leah it was said, "Oh, but she has an inner beauty" as though the old ladies could convince her that this was more important than good looks. "A husband wanted a good cook and reliable mother for his children," they said. Her current situation blew apart that reasoning.

No matter who, Laban, Jacob, or Leah herself, inflicted the first blow on Leah's pottery, her morning-after experience strikes the breaking blow. That Jacob doesn't want her grounds Leah's broken pottery pieces into smaller crumbles. That the en- tire camp knows it humiliates her, and her crumbles become dust.

How do you even begin to collect such smashed fine pieces, clay crumbles cruelly ground into the dirt? What do you do when you love your husband, but he feels he is stuck with you?

A few women in this situation murder their husbands, while others try seductions of various sorts. But most keep trying to win his love through various means, hoping their husbands see them in a new light. But it's like trying to light a fire with a wet match.

In her desperation to earn Jacob's love, Leah tried love spells and tricks, seducing and manipulation as well (30:14–16). Day after day. Month after month. Year after year. Leah's entire life is a painful, unsuccessful effort to win her husband's love, trying to force him to love her. Jacob performs his husbandly duties in her tent during the certain time of the month, and Leah births seven sons. Laboring love. Laboring births. *Laboring but not loved.*

However, the Great Potter has compassion on Leah.

Leah's first son is born nine months after the wedding. She names him Reuben, meaning, "See a son." *Because the Great Potter has seen my suffering and now, because of this son, my husband can't help falling in love with me.*

But Jacob did not love her despite the son. So, Leah kept trying. Her second son's name, Simeon, means "to hear." *Because the Great Potter has heard that I am unloved and hated, He has given me this son so that my husband would fall in love with me because of him.* Leah and her great-grand-stepmother-in-law, Hagar, could have shared a story or two about being unloved by their husbands yet being seen, heard, and loved by the Great Potter Himself, who saw Leah's pain and gave her many sons. He knew that at least this way, the community respected her. But how Leah hoped her husband would love her!

The third son Leah names Levi, meaning "attached." The name reveals that she had not yet lost hope but that she was being more pragmatic. She kept hoping that her sons would force Jacob to feel, if not love, at least *some* connection with her. *Now my husband will finally become closer and attached to me because I have given him three healthy sons.*

But nothing changes between Jacob and Leah. He has room in his heart for only Rachel. Maybe the best compliment Jacob could pay to Leah, the mother of his sons, was, "You may not be attractive, but you've served me well."

Leah names their fourth son, Judah, meaning "praise." *Now I will simply praise the Great Potter.* Despite her still being unloved and neglected by her husband, it is touching that Leah has found solid joy in the Great Potter. She praises the Great Potter for the blessings of four healthy sons and is not asking for something she cannot have, which reveals the peace she has and where she is in her grief process:

accepting what she cannot change, adjusting. Bittersweet, yes, but she accepts the reality that she cannot trust her spouse or her father, but she can trust the Great Potter. Her sons love her—that is a blessing.

After a break of a few years, and after Leah's maid, Zilpah, had borne two sons to Jacob, Leah bears her fifth son, naming him Issachar, meaning "wages" or "hire." *The Great Potter has given me my wages because I allowed my maid to bear two sons to Jacob.* Leah is content in her circumstances.

She names her sixth son, Zebulun, meaning "dwelling." *God has awarded me with a good gift; finally, my husband will live with me as I have given him six sons.* —Or so she hopes, but Jacob does not. Not in decades, not until his beloved Rachel dies. In the end, Leah is buried next to Jacob. But that's all.

Leah's pottery remains partially broken for the rest of her life. The crack, sore and hurtful, is visible every day of her life. No matter how much she hopes and wishes, she receives nothing from Jacob; she gives everything but he gives it all to Rachel and Rachel's sons. Such a cruel and brutal transgenerational trauma of favoritism.

However, Leah is right. The Great Potter had endowed her with the blessing that in her son's, Judah, lineage would come the Messiah, a blessing for the entire world. It is also the combined twelve sons from Leah, Rachel, and their two maids that the house of Israel is built. At the Great Potter's table, the imperfect clay potteries with not so good intentions or motives turn according to His great plan.

Can you relate to Leah's brokenness? Can you empathize with her many efforts and yearning to be loved? Has similar trauma pierced your heart? Just as blessings were found in Leah's brokenness, so too can blessings come out of your broken clay pottery. The Great Potter's presence in your brokenness *is* a blessing. Experiencing contentment and peace despite your circumstances comes from knowing that the Great Potter loves you and has your pottery in His hands.

Just as Leah named her sons, the Great Potter has named you.

Your name is "Beloved."

CHAPTER 12

DINAH
RAPED AND SILENCED

*Now Dinah, the daughter Leah had borne to Jacob, went out to visit the women of the land.
When Shechem son of Hamor the Hivite, the ruler of that area, saw her,
he took her and raped her.
His heart was drawn to Dinah daughter of Jacob;
he loved the young woman and spoke tenderly to her.*

And Shechem said to his father Hamor, "Get me this girl as my wife."
When Jacob heard that his daughter Dinah had been defiled,
his sons were in the fields with his livestock; so he did nothing about it until they came home.
Then Shechem's father Hamor went out to talk with Jacob.
Meanwhile, Jacob's sons had come in from the fields as soon as they heard
what had happened. They were shocked and furious,
because Shechem had done an outrageous thing in Israel by sleeping with Jacob's daughter
—a thing that should not be done.
But Hamor said to them, "My son Shechem has his heart set on your daughter.
Please give her to him as his wife. Intermarry with us; give us your daughters and take our
daughters for yourselves. You can settle among us; the land is open to you.
Live in it, trade in it, and acquire property in it."
Then Shechem said to Dinah's father and brothers,
"Let me find favor in your eyes, and I will give you whatever you ask.
Make the price for the bride and the gift I am to bring as great as you like,
and I'll pay whatever you ask me. Only give me the young woman as my wife."
Because their sister Dinah had been defiled,
Jacob's sons replied deceitfully as they spoke to Shechem and his father Hamor.
They said to them, "We can't do such a thing; we can't give our sister to a man who is not
circumcised. That would be a disgrace to us. We will enter into an agreement with you on one
condition only: that you become like us by circumcising all your males.
Then we will give you our daughters and take your daughters for ourselves.
We'll settle among you and become one people with you.
But if you will not agree to be circumcised, we'll take our sister and go."
Their proposal seemed good to Hamor and his son Shechem.
The young man, who was the most honored of all his father's family, lost no time in doing
what they said, because he was delighted with Jacob's daughter.
So Hamor and his son Shechem went to the gate of their city to speak to the men of their city.
"These men are friendly toward us," they said. "Let them live in our land and trade in it; the
land has plenty of room for them. We can marry their daughters and they can marry ours. But
the men will agree to live with us as one people only on the condition that our males be

circumcised, as they themselves are. Won't their livestock, their property and all their other animals become ours? So let us agree to their terms, and they will settle among us." All the men who went out of the city gate agreed with Hamor and his son Shechem, and every male in the city was circumcised.

Three days later, while all of them were still in pain, two of Jacob's sons, Simeon and Levi, Dinah's brothers, took their swords and attacked the unsuspecting city, killing every male. They put Hamor and his son Shechem to the sword and took Dinah from Shechem's house and left. The sons of Jacob came upon the dead bodies and looted the city where their sister had been defiled. They seized their flocks and herds and donkeys and everything else of theirs in the city and out in the fields. They carried off all their wealth and all their women and children, taking as plunder everything in the houses.

GENESIS 34:1–29 (NIV)[7]

A rapist intentionally smashed Dinah's clay pottery. But her brokenness didn't stop there. Further destruction came by the lack of action of her phlegmatic father and her brothers' murderous revenge and acting-out. Dinah's voice was never recorded, and possibly she suffered additional trauma of being blamed for and stigmatized by her rape.

It started as an innocent visit to her girlfriends in the town. After all, any teenage girl living with rough brothers needs a break and quality time with other girls—a little shopping, mani/pedi, maybe even a new henna tattoo with her friends. Who would have thought that a day that started so well would end with a rape and total disaster?

It is heartbreaking that Dinah's clay pottery smashes into pieces from unexpected trauma. Because her abuser is a big Mr. Somebody, Dinah is even more helpless. Shechem, the prince of the region, always got what he wanted. And now he wanted Dinah, and he would have her.

---

[7] *Read also*: Genesis 34; 35:1–7.

He raped Dinah, breaking her clay pottery into a thousand pieces through chaos and violence, throwing her world into a state of shock, confusion, and powerlessness. It is a disturbing episode, but more disturbing is that Dinah's family ignores her needs in favor of their own interests. Imagine her increasing helplessness when she hears that her father and brothers are planning to marry her to her rapist for a price, a large dowry, thus trying to twist the rape into legalized sex. This deal would benefit the tribe enormously, giving them safety and position. Dinah has no say; her destiny is in the hands of her father and brothers. Her fuming brothers focused on *their* feelings and humiliation of their sister being made a whore (34:31) rather than Dinah's feelings and horror. Their attitude serves to further destroy Dinah's clay pottery.

Dinah was abducted and raped, yet nobody thinks to ask how she is doing, or tend to her. Even when her brothers, Simeon and Levi, negotiate her marriage, a destiny she does not want, she remains in the role of an outsider of her own life. Would it have mattered if she wanted to marry someone else? Dinah is helpless to stop her brothers slaughtering all the men in that town. They murder her girlfriends' fathers, brothers, and boyfriends. They even take her friends as their captives!—What fate awaited them?

What about Jacob remaining passive during the marriage negotiations? Present but silent. Jacob did not portray a loving and caring father for his daughter. Only Joseph and Benjamin, sons of his beloved Rachel, matter to him. Throughout the negotiations, he resembles his grandfather Abraham and father, Isaac, and seems interested only in the dowry. What is with these men and their sacrificing their women for their own safety? Jacob selfishly rants: "You have brought trouble on *me*, making *me* odious among the inhabitants of the land, the Canaanites and the Perizzites; *my* men are few in number so that if they unite against *me* and attack *me*, I and *my* house will be destroyed" (v. 30).

It seems that because Jacob loved only Rachel, he did not have any emotional ties with Leah's children, not even his only daughter. Transgenerational trauma of favoritism and phlegmatic reactions are repeating in situations where protection is needed. It is deeply disturbing why Jacob is not actively negotiating himself and, instead, allowing his sons to plot their murderous plans. I cannot imagine it was the Great Potter's will or that it was necessary to break every innocent pottery in the town when only one man was guilty.

This is doing bad in the name of the Great Potter, who had nothing to do with the act. Holy wars without holiness. Godly revenge without God. Self-righteous murders without righteousness. Good intentions without goodness. Much evil has been attributed to the Great Potter's name over the last thousand years, and much abuse has been conducted in His name, ending in countless potteries smashed though He had no part in the atrocities.

This is the great demolisher's work, breaking potteries in the Great Potter's name. The deceiver convinces the broken potteries to blame the Great Potter instead of seeking His comfort and help.

Back to the Great Potter's Table

Soon after Dinah's rape and the nasty massacre of the town, the Great Potter tells Jacob to move away from the area and go back to Bethel. There he is to rebuild the same altar he had built a long time ago when he first fled from Esau (35:1–7).

Decades before, Jacob fled his home after deceiving his brother and father. I'm sure he felt guilt at what he had down. Now feeling guilt, he must again flee his home. So much bad had happened—so much brokenness and pain inflicted. Another pile of broken potteries is piled at his feet. Broken because of their actions, but Dinah was an innocent victim whose pottery was intentionally broken by others.

Time to go back to Bethel, the Potter's House. Time to rebuild the broken altar as well as the altar of broken potteries. But before that, all the foreign gods in the possession of his household had to be left behind. Interestingly, Jacob buried them under a big oak, at that miserable place of rape, murders, and betrayals. Jacob's family left them when they returned to the house and table of the Great Potter.

For sure, that dirty clay needed cleansing. In fact, it needed to be dissolved in water before it could be taken back to the Potter's table. The sharp stones and the dirt needed to be washed away. It needed a clean start, which could come only after the Great Potter renews His calling and promise. Here again we see that the Great Potter is faithful even when His potteries are not.

Sadly, once Jacob and his family move back to Canaan, his father's land, we hear no more about Dinah's pottery. Did she recover, heal from her attack? There is no mention of her getting married or having children. Was she socially disgraced, shamed, isolated? Was she blamed and stigmatized as so many rape victims are in our times? Did gossip follow her to Bethel? Hopefully, it was at Canaan that Dinah also found restoration and peace from her trauma.

We don't know what happened to the innocent women and children who were taken captive by Dinah's brothers after their husbands, fathers, and sons were killed. This story is filled with disturbing images and so many broken potteries. The number of clay potteries of girls and women worldwide who are broken every day because of violence, sexual assault, and rape is nothing short of distressing. With every violent act these potteries are silenced. Too many of them are forced to bear the shame and blame that belongs to their perpetrators.

"There is no 'happy ever after'; wounds may perhaps heal, but scars remain. How to make sense of the inhumanity of abuse …? How to stay human amidst such inhumanity?"[14]

Can you relate with Dinah's broken pottery first being abused and then silenced? Have you suffered from being stigmatized, blamed and shamed for what your perpetrator did? Have you been the victim of someone doing bad in the name of God?

Let the Great Potter gather you to Himself and restore you into something unique and beautiful. He is with you, waiting for you to give Him permission.

Say yes!

CHAPTER 13

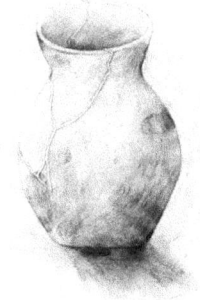

JOSEPH
BROKEN AND RESTORED

Now Israel loved Joseph more than all his children, because he was the son of his old age.
Also he made him a tunic of many colors.
But when his brothers saw that their father loved him more than all his brothers,
they hated him and could not speak peaceably to him.
Now Joseph had a dream, and he told it to his brothers; and they hated him even more.

So he said to them, "Please hear this dream which I have dreamed:
There we were, binding sheaves in the field.
Then behold, my sheaf arose and also stood upright;
and indeed your sheaves stood all around and bowed down to my sheaf."
And his brothers said to him,
"Shall you indeed reign over us? Or shall you indeed have dominion over us?"
So they hated him even more for his dreams and for his words.
Then he dreamed still another dream and told it to his brothers, and said,
"Look, I have dreamed another dream.
And this time, the sun, the moon, and the eleven stars bowed down to me."

Genesis 37:3–9 (NKJV)

So Joseph went after his brothers and found them in Dotan.
Now when they saw him afar off, even before he came near them,
they conspired against him to kill him. Then they said to one another,
"Look, this dreamer is coming! Come therefore, let us now kill him and cast him into some
pit; and we shall say, 'Some wild beast has devoured him.'
We shall see what will become of his dreams!"
But Reuben heard it, and he delivered him out of their hands, and said,
"Let us not kill him." And Reuben said to them,
"Shed no blood, but cast him into this pit which is in the wilderness,
and do not lay a hand on him"
—that he might deliver him out of their hands, and bring him back to his father.
So it came to pass, when Joseph had come to his brothers,
that they stripped Joseph of his tunic, the tunic of many colors that was on him.
Then they took him and cast him into a pit. And the pit was empty; there was no water in it.
And they sat down to eat a meal.
Then they lifted their eyes and looked, and there was a company of Ishmaelites,
coming from Gilead with their camels,
bearing spices, balm, and myrrh, on their way to carry them down to Egypt.

So Judah said to his brothers,
"What profit is there if we kill our brother and conceal his blood?
Come and let us sell him to the Ishmaelites, and let not our hand be upon him,
for he is our brother and our flesh." And his brothers listened.
Then Midianite traders passed by; so the brothers pulled Joseph up and lifted him out of the pit,
and sold him to the Ishmaelites for twenty shekels of silver. And they took Joseph to Egypt.
Then Reuben returned to the pit, and indeed Joseph was not in the pit;
and he tore his clothes. And he returned to his brothers and said,
"The lad is no more; and I, where shall I go?"
So they took Joseph's tunic, killed a kid of the goats, and dipped the tunic in the blood.
Then they sent the tunic of many colors, and they brought it to their father and said,
"We have found this. Do you know whether it is your son's tunic or not?"
And he recognized it and said, "It is my son's tunic. A wild beast has devoured him.
Without doubt Joseph is torn to pieces."
Then Jacob tore his clothes, put sackcloth on his waist, and mourned for his son many days.
And all his sons and all his daughters arose to comfort him;
but he refused to be comforted, and he said,
"For I shall go down into the grave to my son in mourning." Thus his father wept for him.
Now the Midianites had sold him in Egypt to Potiphar,
an officer of Pharaoh and captain of the guard.

vv. 17–36[8]

Joseph's pottery is intentionally broken by his older brothers, but other situations occur in which his actions add a few blows, putting his pottery on the edge. Jacob's favoritism and unfair treatment of Joseph's brothers add further complications. In the end, the Great Potter proves that He has everything under control and eventually restores the family's famine-broken potteries.

---

[8] *Read also*: Genesis 37, 39, 40–48.

Meet seventeen-year-old Joseph, his father's favorite. His clay pottery is about to be smashed into pieces, but right now, it's still pretty solid. His older brothers played a nasty prank by throwing him into an empty well, but his clay pottery remained in fairly good shape. At least there is nothing wrong with his lungs as his shouts and yells echo from the walls of the abandoned well.

Let me out! How dare you treat me like this! Just wait until I tell my father!

He is perhaps a bit scared, and he is cold and uncomfortable sitting on the rough moist bottom of the well. His brothers had stripped him of the new multicolored coat his father had made for him. Why had they bullied him so harshly in this manner? His bragging wasn't so bad, nothing out of the ordinary.

What Joseph didn't know was that the multicolored jacket, the precious present from the father to his favorite son, is sitting on the ground by the firepit as his nine older brothers eat their hearty meal during their lunch break. They hear his cries, begging them to let him out. It sounds as if his clay pottery is starting to crack. This prank has gone too far. It is no longer funny.

Let me out, please! I'm cold and thirsty!

The older brothers who despise Joseph ignore his screams and pleadings. Soon they will give him their final blow. Should they kill him quickly or slowly? That seems a bit extreme even to them. Selling him as a slave to a caravan passing nearby is a heartless decision, but it keeps them from being murderers.

They will need to explain Joseph's sudden absence, so they devise a story of wild animals killing their father's favorite son. But deception and betrayal are the way in this family. They are repeating the dysfunctional family's generational trauma: dishonesty, betrayal, deception, and abandonment.

Joseph's clay pottery is one victim of many within this family tree. His current abuse by his brothers is a result of his father not treating his wives and sons fairly. Remember, Jacob loved and favored Joseph and Benjamin's mother, Rachel, over their brothers' mother, Leah. Of course, Joseph's brothers were not blind or unaffected. They daily saw their mother's agony and despair over the lack of love from her husband.

This favoritism and unfairness make his sons emotionally unstable. It was long ago when the older sons had learned the painful fact that no matter how hard they worked or how much they tried, their father would never love them.

And now these broken clay potteries revenge and smash Joseph's pottery in their blind rage and jealousy. They do not care what will happen to Joseph. They want him gone. Once Joseph is on his way into slavery and Jacob has been fed the lie of what happened to his son, Jacob's clay pottery is a pile of broken pieces from which it seems impossible that he could recover.

Chained and Broken

Joseph chained, looking back with his horrified eyes wide open, crying, and begging in anguish, *Please, let me go! I won't tell my father. Please, don't do this! I'm your brother...*

The brothers calmly watch as Joseph is led off in the caravan—disappearing to the horizon. That is the last they see of him, so they think. They have no clue about the Great Potter's plan for Joseph, which includes them.

No doubt as Joseph trudged alongside the camel caravan traveling to Egypt, he questioned his circumstances. *Why me? How can this happen to me?*

When the familiar fields are left behind, and every new day repeats the same misery, the new normal begins to hit Joseph. Soon his clay pottery will be nothing but dry clay crumble in chains, slowly rambling under the hot sun toward a foreign land and an unknown destiny.

Possibly Joseph reflected on what had hit his pottery so violently. Perhaps he realized that he had been the favorite son since birth, born with a silver spoon in his mouth, growing up loved and cherished by his parents but hated and detested by his not-so-fortunate siblings.

Perhaps it was not Joseph's personality that made him brag like a brat. Perhaps he was just clueless about his status of being the worshipped prince by his unfair father. Or maybe no one had ever taught him empathy for others' feelings.

For months, before the final blow by his brothers, Joseph had placed his pretty little decorated clay pottery on the edge of the counter for any brother to "accidentally" drop it. As Joseph goes on and on about his magnificent dreams, interpreted as his brothers and father bowing down to him, Joseph nearly pushes his pottery off the edge. He almost pushes it over the edge when he hid in the fields, spying on his brothers and tattling to their father. A bit risky for his clay pottery is to show off his new multicolored coat his father had made just for him. Surely one of the initiators smashing his clay pottery was himself.

Clueless, perhaps, but guilty.

Ultimately, was it the transgenerational trauma going back decades that smashed Joseph's clay pottery?

The brothers did not mean well toward Joseph, a sad fact. They were full of rage and malice that day they threw him into the pit, sold him as a slave, and then deceived their father with a lie. They delivered blow after blow until Joseph's pottery flew off the shelf and shattered.

Did they regret their actions? Reuben did, as he had planned to rescue Joseph from the well and was not part of the brother-mob who sold Joseph into slavery. There is also an indication that over the years, the brothers felt guilt about what they did. However, if they truly repented, they could have tried to find and rescue Joseph from the Ishmaelites, but they didn't. And they never told their father the true story of Joseph's disappearance.

But for Joseph, this event is just the beginning of the blows that are to come. At first he was thinking this cannot really be happening. He fully expected his brothers riding their camels and coming for his rescue. Later on, waiting for his father's army to surround their camp site and take him home. But none of this happens, and the shock begins to wear off.

It's not certain when Joseph's clay pottery finally breaks. Perhaps it is a moment during the long walk behind the caravan that the reality hits him. Perhaps it is at the slave market or once he is sold.

The Great Potter is in Control

The Great Potter is in control of Joseph's clay pottery. Even later, when he is thrown into prison because Potiphar's, his master, wife unfairly and falsely accuses him. While in prison, he helps his fellow inmates. But when one is released, he forgets about Joseph for years. Even then, the Great Potter has not forgotten about Joseph, and is in charge. None of the broken pieces are missing or go wasted during the process of rescue and restoration.

And surprisingly, during his time on the Potter's table, on His wheel, and in His firing oven, Joseph learns to trust Him. He is being prepared for a special task. He is a vessel made for a magnificent position as the ruler of Egypt. He is the one chosen to rescue the nation from widespread famine.

The brothers intended to harm him, but the Great Potter "intended it for good to accomplish what is now being done, the saving of many lives" (50:20 NIV). The Great Potter turns Joseph's broken clay crumbles into something pretty amazing!

Restoration and Forgiveness

The restoration of Joseph's clay pottery is not finished until forgiveness changes his brothers and father's life.

Forgiveness, not revenge. Grace, not justice.

Have you been in a similar situation of knowing you ought to forgive, yearning to reconcile, but realizing how difficult it is?

Forgiveness is *not* simple for Joseph when his brothers stand before him, asking to buy food. They don't recognize him. And they had no reason to think that the ruler before them, dressed in royal robes, was their younger brother. Then they did the unthinkable: they bowed before him, kneeling, just like his childhood dreams had predicted.

We wonder if throughout the years Joseph recalled his dreams and imagined how they would play out, what he would say or do if he ever saw his brothers and father again. When his brothers enter his royal room, Joseph doesn't reveal himself to them. What he puts his brothers through could suggest that he's going to play some games with them. Is it out of revenge? What Joseph does to his brothers seems to be a reversal of roles because it involves blackmail, imprisonment, and false accusation.

Interestingly, it seems that Joseph never tried to contact his family. This should have been easy to do for a ruler of Egypt. Was he angry with his father for not coming to his rescue? Was it too painful or risky to contact his family? Or maybe he did secretly find about them and anonymously sent them news that food was available in Egypt.

Did he numb his emotions, freeze his grief, and deny his loss? Even in the Great Potter's hottest oven temperatures, it takes time for the hardened stone heart to soften. It takes time, but little by little, as the Great Potter helps Joseph work through his trauma and emotions, his heart is suddenly ready to let it go. And when the process of melting starts, nothing can stop it.

Joseph weeps. He cannot help it.

And then he forgives his brothers. He truly does, although this is hard for the brothers to internalize even years after (vv. 15–21).

However, this forgiveness process does not mean that Joseph belittles what was done to him: "It's okay. It was nothing. I'm over it." He does not rationalize his pain. He does not excuse his brothers' actions. Instead, he says, "Yeah, you *meant* evil for me. You smashed my pottery into tiny crumbles and I thought I would not survive. You smashed my clay, but the Great Potter turned it into a beautiful vessel for His service."

Joseph *chooses* to forgive even though he painfully understands every detail and every hurtful impact of the episode. Forgiveness means to let mercy go before justice, to administer the ever-unfair grace in which nobody gets what they deserve.

Forgiving allows Joseph to recognize that he *also* is capable of breaking others. He *also* needs forgiveness from the Great Potter.

Knowing their dysfunctional tendencies, it is intriguing that the Great Potter continues choosing Abraham's family tree for the Redeemer and Messiah to be born. Isn't it astounding that He did not regret His calling? He did not regret His promises. He did not take back His words. He did not give up and find a more sophisticated family-tree.

The Great Potter remains faithful even if we do not. He is faithful because He cannot deny Himself.

Yet dysfunctional and full of broken potteries for any reasons, Joseph's ancestors and brothers were vessels in the Great Potter's service, for His bigger picture and as a blessing to the entire world.

From this less than perfect family tree, the lineage of Judah, a Son would be born. The Great Potter stepped down to the earth and deep into our trash yards of broken potteries to be broken Himself so that whosoever believes in Him will have eternal life and hope.

When you think about your life, can you recall situations in which the Great Potter turned something that was evil into good and to serve His purposes?

Maybe you can already begin to see His big picture and plan.

CHAPTER 14

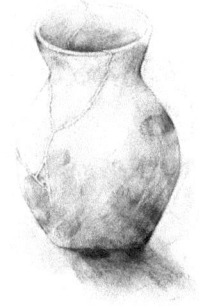

TAMAR
THE BLACK WIDOW

*Judah got a wife for Er, his firstborn, and her name was Tamar.
But Er, Judah's firstborn, was wicked in the Lord's sight; so the LORD put him to death.
Then Judah said to Onan, "Sleep with your brother's wife and fulfill your duty to her as a
brother-in-law to raise up offspring for your brother."
But Onan knew that the child would not be his; so whenever he slept with his brother's wife,*

*he spilled his semen on the ground to keep from providing offspring for his brother.
What he did was wicked in the Lord's sight;so the LORD put him to death also.
Judah then said to his daughter-in-law Tamar,
"Live as a widow in your father's household until my son Shelah grows up."
For he thought, "He may die too, just like his brothers."
So Tamar went to live in her father's household.
After a long time Judah's wife, the daughter of Shua, died.
When Judah had recovered from his grief, he went up to Timnah, to the men who were
shearing his sheep, and his friend Hirah the Adullamite went with him.
When Tamar was told, "Your father-in-law is on his way to Timnah to shear his sheep,"
she took off her widow's clothes, covered herself with a veil to disguise herself,
and then sat down at the entrance to Enaim, which is on the road to Timnah.
For she saw that, though Shelah had now grown up, she had not been given to him as his wife.
When Judah saw her, he thought she was a prostitute, for she had covered her face.
Not realizing that she was his daughter-in-law, he went over to her by the roadside
and said, "Come now, let me sleep with you."
"And what will you give me to sleep with you?" she asked.
"I'll send you a young goat from my flock," he said.
"Will you give me something as a pledge until you send it?" she asked.
He said, "What pledge should I give you?"
"Your seal and its cord, and the staff in your hand," she answered.
So he gave them to her and slept with her, and she became pregnant by him.
After she left, she took off her veil and put on her widow's clothes again.
Meanwhile Judah sent the young goat by his friend the Adullamite in order to get his
pledge back from the woman, but he did not find her. He asked the men who lived there,
"Where is the shrine prostitute who was beside the road at Enaim?"
"There hasn't been any shrine prostitute here," they said.
So he went back to Judah and said, "I didn't find her. Besides, the men who lived there
said, 'There hasn't been any shrine prostitute here.'"
Then Judah said, "Let her keep what she has, or we will become a laughingstock.
After all, I did send her this young goat, but you didn't find her."*

Secrets Of Broken Pottery

About three months later Judah was told, "Your daughter-in-law Tamar is guilty of prostitution, and as a result she is now pregnant." Judah said, "Bring her out and have her burned to death!"

As she was being brought out, she sent a message to her father-in-law.

"I am pregnant by the man who owns these," she said. And she added, "See if you recognize whose seal and cord and staff these are." Judah recognized them and said, "She is more righteous than I, since I wouldn't give her to my son Shelah."

Genesis 38:6–26 (NIV)[9]

Tamar's clay pottery was intentionally broken by two wicked husbands. Then her father-in-law's betrayal was a swipe to her pottery. Her plan to get what she believes she is due is another blow to her pottery that almost does it in for good. However, her story has a happy ending because the Great Potter restores her pottery. **The Great Potter's faithfulness remains no matter the mess we make in our lives.**

It was not a fairy tale Tamar imagined. No safe houses to flee to. No princes riding white horses to her rescue. No caring relatives intervening to protect her.

It is the humiliation that breaks what the abusive blows did not.

Perhaps the daily black eye only ignites a new round of gossip at the well in the morning. Perhaps wounds not visible to the naked eye. Internalized wounds that cut her very soul. In the end, there's no dignity left from once so beautiful a clay pottery.

Sadly, Tamar's clay pottery is brutally smashed shortly after her wedding. There is no honeymoon as she soon realizes her husband is nothing less than evil. We're not told which action was the final straw before the Great Potter took Er's life, leaving Tamar a young widow.

---

[9] *Read also*: Genesis 38.

According to the law, her husband's brother must marry her and produce a child, who bears the deceased brother's name (Deuteronomy 25:5). But something is terribly wrong with Judah's sons. They are wicked. We can guess that this is the legacy of transgenerational trauma, spiralling from Judah and his brothers selling Joseph into slavery and orchestrating the massacre of Shechem.

Wretchedly, Tamar's second marriage with Onan is no better, possibly worse. During sex, Oman withdraws, spilling his sperm on the ground. Continuing to refuse to bear a child under his brother's name, he disgraces Tamar by using her body but not allowing her to become pregnant because the baby would be considered his brother's heir.

According to the Great Potter's divine intervention, Onan also dies, and now Tamar receives the questionable stamp of a Black Widow for whom Judah dares not marry his third and only remaining son.

So, Tamar ends up back in her father's home. The rumors fly. Whispers. Malicious looks from the other women. The once pretty and beautiful clay pottery cracks. A widow without a son. Dubious deaths of two husbands. Shame and humiliation break her pottery.

But Tamar is not meekly submissive, silently claiming the trash yard of the broken potteries as her new dwelling. She devises a plan to get what she is legally due. Veiled as a prostitute, Tamar deceives Judah to sleep with her and thus perform the duties his sons should have done. She orchestrates him to leave her a receipt of his action, something that would identify him. This smart move saves Tamar's life in the very near future.

Remember my saying that this family tree rivaled Hollywood soap operas!

Crushing. Intimidating. Full of brutality and cruelness! When Judah learns that Tamar is pregnant, he insists she be brutally killed as her punishment for her sin: burned alive. I'm sure we all agree that Judah was a hypocrite, a ruthless and merciless scoundrel.

No wonder his sons were wicked—transgenerational trauma repeating.

However, when Tamar is being dragged to the execution place, a woodpile ready to be lit with her atop it, Tamar produces the evidence: Judah is the father of her unborn baby.

At least Judah has some honor as he does not deny the truth. He reflects and realizes what he did and immediately releases Tamar. And then the family moves back to his family, back to Canaan, where Jacob was living.

So Tamar's clay pottery has a happy ending: restoration and healing.

A few months later, Tamar bears twin sons, Perez and Zerah, and it is from Perez's line that both King David and later the Messiah is born. This is evidence of the Great Potter's never-ending mercy and faithfulness.

No pottery is too broken not to be a vessel in His service. No pottery is too smashed not to be used and blessed by Him. Not because of the potteries' merit but because of His faithfulness.

CHAPTER 15

DAVID
THE LUSTING KING

*One evening David got up from his bed and walked around on the roof of the palace.
From the roof he saw a woman bathing.
The woman was very beautiful, and David sent someone to find out about her.
The man said, "She is Bathsheba, the daughter of Eliam and the wife of Uriah the Hittite."
Then David sent messengers to get her. She came to him, and he slept with her.
(Now she was purifying herself from her monthly uncleanness.)*

Heidi McKendrick

Then she went back home.
The woman conceived and sent word to David, saying,
"I am pregnant."
So David sent this word to Joab: "Send me Uriah the Hittite."
And Joab sent him to David. When Uriah came to him, David asked him how Joab was,
how the soldiers were and how the war was going.
Then David said to Uriah, "Go down to your house and wash your feet."
So Uriah left the palace, and a gift from the king was sent after him.
But Uriah slept at the entrance to the palace with all his master's servants
and did not go down to his house.
David was told, "Uriah did not go home." So he asked Uriah,
"Haven't you just come from a military campaign?
Why didn't you go home?"
Uriah said to David, "The ark and Israel and Judah are staying in tents,
and my commander Joab and my lord's men are camped in the open country.
How could I go to my house to eat and drink and make love to my wife?
As surely as you live, I will not do such a thing!"
Then David said to him, "Stay here one more day, and tomorrow I will send you back."
So Uriah remained in Jerusalem that day and the next.
At David's invitation, he ate and drank with him, and David made him drunk.
But in the evening Uriah went out to sleep on his mat among his master's servants;
he did not go home.
In the morning David wrote a letter to Joab and sent it with Uriah.
In it he wrote, "Put Uriah out in front where the fighting is fiercest.
Then withdraw from him so he will be struck down and die."
So while Joab had the city under siege,
he put Uriah at a place where he knew the strongest defenders were.
When the men of the city came out and fought against Joab,
some of the men in David's army fell; moreover, Uriah the Hittite died.

2 SAMUEL 11:2–17 (NIV)

When Uriah's wife heard that her husband was dead, she mourned for him. After the time of mourning was over, David had her brought to his house, and she became his wife and bore him a son. But the thing David had done displeased the LORD.

vv. 26–27[10]

King David becomes an adulterer and murderer, bitterly breaking others' clay potteries as he smashes his own. Trying to hide his mess, he creates destruction and breaks others' innocent potteries into smaller bits. In the end, he calls for the Great Potter's grace and faithfulness.

A sledgehammer still in his hand standing in the middle of the broken pieces of his very own pottery—the man's first natural reaction is trying to hide the mess and covering up before anybody notices. Then trying to fix whatever possible as quickly as possible.

Nobody else needs to know who is guilty.

King David was a specialist in disasters. This time he pretty much acted as his own worst enemy. Lusting after beautiful Bathsheba, he forces her from the safety of her home into his bed. She has no voice in the matter. He is the king. His word is the law. Bathsheba is not in a position to consent.

David not only rapes and sexually exploits a vulnerable woman, he also commits adultery, stealing another man's wife. When he learns that his deed has resulted in pregnancy, he tries to cover it up. He brings Bathsheba's husband Uriah home from the war and encourages him to go home and sleep with his wife. Uriah, a loyal and honorable man, denies such comfort while his men are in battle. So, David, desperate to hide his offence, abuses his power again and orders Uriah's murder by placing him in the heat of battle where he is sure to die.

---

[10] *Read also*: 1 Samuel 16–31; 2 Samuel 1–12, 20–24; 1 Chronicles 3, 11–23, 25, 28–29; 1 Kings 1–2; Luke 2:4; Matthew 1:1–17; Psalms 2–32, 34–41, 51–65, 68–70, 86, 95, 101, 103, 105–106, 108–110, 122, 124, 131, 138–145.

David—Man After the Great Potter's Heart

Not only was he a murderer, David with his large harem of many wives, concubines, captive women, and young virgins to keep him warm in the night was obviously a regular womanizer (2 Samuel 5:13; 1 Chronicles 14:3-5; 1 King 1:2). It seems that status was critical for David as he went to extremes to protect his reputation and cover up his actions. Yet the Great Potter calls him "a man after his own heart" (1 Samuel 13:14 NIV). Despite his miserable brokenness, David *remains* as the Great Potter's *chosen* one.

How do we reconcile David's actions with the Great Potter's declaration?

It is only after the Prophet Nathan disclosed to David that the Great Potter was aware of what he had done, David finally drops the charade (2 Samuel 12). Without Nathan's confrontation, would he have ever confessed? For over a year he continued his life as if nothing had happened.

However, now, being confronted, the reality hits him, and he drops his tangled web of illusion. He sees himself as he is. He cannot fix his pottery with superglue or cover his cracks with a concealing paint. He no longer pretends to be more polished than he is. Better later than never, I suppose.

It is the aftermath that matters. What we do with our broken pieces?

David was *not* a man after the Great Potter's heart because of his hurtful actions but because *he knew the Great Potter's heart*. In the end, He *trusted* the Great Potter enough to turn to Him for delivery. David's pottery was pitifully smashed but the situation was not as hopeless as it *could* have been because he knew where to turn for restoration of his broken pottery.

Psalms 32, 38, 51, and 86 most likely describe his sense of anguish during this episode.

Have Mercy on Me—I'm Poor and Needy!

David knows he would not survive without the Great Potter's grace and mercy. Although he knows that he doesn't deserve any of it, he knows he can *receive* it—because it is a gift. "Hear me, LORD, and answer me, for *I am poor and needy ... Have mercy on me*, LORD, for I call to you all day long" (Psalm 86:1, 3 NIV).[11]

David no longer tries to conceal his broken pottery.

He is realistic. He recognizes that he is poor, wretched, and needy. A king, yes, but spiritually a beggar not deserving the Great Potter's favor. David feels that his offences had overtaken him and were more than the hairs on his head (40:12). After realizing what he has done, David reflects and confesses: "For I know my transgressions, and my sin is always before me" (51:3).

David Holds a Healthy Image of the Great Potter

David is neither self-righteous nor self-sufficient at this point. He knows his pottery needs a miracle—but He also knows the miracle maker, his Redeemer.

David *trusts* that the Great Potter will not forsake Him. He knows that He is *already* there at his trash yard of broken potteries collecting his lost pieces. David is ready, waiting and asking to be restored (v. 12). He also knows his dirty clay pieces must be thoroughly washed first. "*Wash away* all my iniquity and *cleanse me* from my sin ... *Cleanse me* with hyssop, and I will be clean; *wash me*, and I will be whiter than snow ... Create in me a *pure heart*..." (vv. 2,7,10).

Just as David now has a realistic image of himself, he also has, since his childhood, held a healthy image of the Great Potter's love, faithfulness, and mercy. All through his youth he had seen and experienced Him as loving father and caring protector, Good Shepard. When fighting against Goliath and during his years of exile being hunted by King Saul, David learned to trust the Great Potter, seeing Him as his deliverer, rock, fortress, refugee, shield, horn, salvation, and stronghold (Psalm. 18:2). His psalms prove that he felt he can share his true feelings with the Great Potter.

Therefore, with his pottery and his sharade pitifully smashed, David is *not* scared to approach the Great Potter and ask for His grace. Had his childhood teaching and experiences *distorted* his idea of the Great Potter, who knows what might have hap-

---

[11] *See also* Psalm 40:17.

pened. Perhaps he would have lived the rest of his life avoiding the Great Potter in the trash yard of broken potteries, scared of Him and not understanding that He wanted to pour His mercy over him. Isn't this what many of broken potteries do with their broken pieces?

Good for David; he holds a true image of His Redeemer!

Therefore, he is fully restored.

In contrast to the countless broken potteries immersed in legalistic teaching, David knew the Great Potter's heart—he trusted His true characteristics. That's why he did not bury his broken pieces deeper in the trash yard but simply asked for the Great Potter's help.

And *this* pleased the Great Potter.

David messed up his life and broke his pottery, but because he knows the Great Potter he knows *the Hope*. He knows that he could never mess enough to have the Great Potter forsaking his shattered pieces! He knows that he could do *nothing* to make Him love him less or love him more.[15]

The Great Potter would not despise David's broken heart and broken spirit—David *relies* on this fact. Although he knows he is guilty not only for breaking his pottery but also for breaking Uriah's and Bathsheba's, he *trusts* on the Great Potter's faithfulness and great compassion that will *always* protect him. The Great Potter would not cast David's broken pottery away. Instead, He is always close to the broken hearted—He always *saves those who* have crushed spirit (34:18). David's appeal reiterates and echoes his knowledge of the Great Potter's true characteristics: loving, merciful, and faithful.

"Teach me your way, LORD, that I may rely on *your faithfulness*" (86:11).

"For You, LORD, are *good*, and *ready to forgive*, And *abundant in mercy* to all those who call upon You" (v. 5 NKJV).

"Have mercy on me, O God, *according to your unfailing love; according to your great compassion* blot out my transgressions" (51:1 NIV).

"Do not withhold *your mercy* from me, LORD; may *your love and faithfulness* always protect me" (40:11).

While David is sitting among his broken pottery pieces, he knows the Great Potter is pleased to save him: "Be pleased to save me, LORD; come quickly, LORD, to help me ... You are my help and my deliverer; you are my God, do not delay" (vv. 13, 17). He has no doubts that the Great Potter has *already* prepared his restoration: "When I am in distress, I call to you, because you answer me" (86:7).

David dares to pray to the Great Potter because he knows He will not forsake him no matter how messed up David is. He knows the Great Potter "is trustworthy in all he promises and faithful in all he does" (145:13). He knows that the Great Potter wants him to have a fresh start. No matter that he orchestrated his mess!

Though I Have Fallen, I Will Rise…

So, David's broken pottery has a happy end.

The Great Potter collects the broken pieces, half-sunken into the trash yard of broken potteries. He collects each piece and places them on His table, solid because of His love and grace. David declares: "For great is your love toward me; you have delivered me from the depths, from the realm of the dead" (86:13). The Great Potter turned to David's broken pieces and heard his cry. "He lifted me out of the slimy pit, out of the mud and mire; he set my feet on a rock and gave me a firm place to stand" (40:2).

The devil did not have the final say in David's case. "Do not gloat over me, my enemy! Though I have fallen, I will rise" (Micah 7:7 NIV). Not only David, all of us can rely on this: "for though the righteous fall seven times, they rise again" (Proverbs 14:16 NIV). No wonder David praises the Great Potter's faithfulness with his harp and psalms (Psalm 71:22). He declares: "As for me, I will always have hope; I will praise you more and more" (v.14 NIV). "He put a new song in my mouth, a hymn of praise to our God" (40:2).

Later, David and Bathsheba's sons, Nathan and Solomon are both in the Messiah's line of ancestors (Luke 3:32, Matthew 1:6–7). Solomon was anointed Israel's next king even though Bathsheba was David's 7th or 8th wife (depending on who you ask), and Salomon was not in line for the throne. Once again, the Great Potter brings blessings out of evil to serve His good purpose.

Do you think that David had the nerve to approach the Great Potter after his horrible crimes? Do you think there should be some limit for the Great Potter's grace; that His love should have *some* conditions, and that He should remain faithful *only* if we do?

If you said yes to any or all of these, you think the way most clay potteries do who do not understand the Great Potter's faithfulness, love, and grace. Granted, with our clay brains it can be hard to grasp that this is who the Great Potter *is*. It would be easier to think the Great Potter treats us the way we treat one another, and that everyone gets what they deserve. It is easy to have a false image of the Great Potter. But this is trying to squeeze Him into our clay pottery–size boxes. We so quickly "turn things upside down, *as if the potter were thought to be like the clay!*" (Isaiah 29:16 NIV). He is not!

The Great Potter's grace has nothing to do with fairness, nothing to do with any of us deserving it. Nothing to do with justice of some potteries receiving it more than some others—or more often. His compassion is on all potteries He has made (Psalm 145:9). He has so much compassion that He stepped down into our trash yards to restore the most miserably broken and forsaken potteries. He came because we have no idea how to fix our messes. He came to find all of our missing pieces. "For the Son of Man came to seek and to save the lost" (Luke 19:10 NIV).

The Great Potter came into our trash yard of broken potteries to redeem His relationship with His lost and broken potteries who were miserable and destroyed. He did not come for the self-sufficient shiny potteries who believe they do not need any help or healing. He came for the spiritually poor and needy, those of us who are lost without Him (6:20). He came to wash our dirty potteries whiter than a snow.

What does David's broken pottery speak to you? What is your image of the Great Potter? Is it something you've devised, or is it the image of who He says He is? When you pitifully break your pottery, do you trust, as David did, the Great Potter to collect your pieces, forgive you, take you back home, and restore your pottery?

Or, perhaps instead you have difficulties to trust that you will remain as the Great Potter's chosen one if you intentionally broke your pottery. After the Great Potter has washed your pottery, you may *still* see it as stained and dirty… If so, you have a distorted vision of Him and need to fix it. You are loved unconditionally and His grace is never-ending. He not only forgives, but *chooses* to forget.

He remains faithful even if you don't.

CHAPTER 16

PRINCESS TAMAR
THE ROYAL OUTCAST

*In the course of time, Amnon son of David fell in love with Tamar,
the beautiful sister of Absalom son of David.
Amnon became so obsessed with his sister Tamar that he made himself ill.
She was a virgin, and it seemed impossible for him to do anything to her.
Now Amnon had an adviser named Jonadab son of Shimeah, David's brother.*

Jonadab was a very shrewd man. He asked Amnon, "Why do you, the king's son, look so haggard morning after morning? Won't you tell me?" Amnon said to him, "I'm in love with Tamar, my brother Absalom's sister."

"Go to bed and pretend to be ill," Jonadab said. "When your father comes to see you, say to him, 'I would like my sister Tamar to come and give me something to eat. Let her prepare the food in my sight so I may watch her and then eat it from her hand.'"

So Amnon lay down and pretended to be ill. When the king came to see him, Amnon said to him, "I would like my sister Tamar to come and make some special bread in my sight, so I may eat from her hand."

David sent word to Tamar at the palace: "Go to the house of your brother Amnon and prepare some food for him." So Tamar went to the house of her brother Amnon, who was lying down.

She took some dough, kneaded it, made the bread in his sight and baked it. Then she took the pan and served him the bread, but he refused to eat. "Send everyone out of here," Amnon said. So everyone left him. Then Amnon said to Tamar, "Bring the food here into my bedroom so I may eat from your hand." And Tamar took the bread she had prepared and brought it to her brother Amnon in his bedroom. But when she took it to him to eat, he grabbed her and said, "Come to bed with me, my sister." "No, my brother!" she said to him. "Don't force me! Such a thing should not be done in Israel! Don't do this wicked thing. What about me? Where could I get rid of my disgrace? And what about you? You would be like one of the wicked fools in Israel. Please speak to the king; he will not keep me from being married to you."

But he refused to listen to her, and since he was stronger than she, he raped her. Then Amnon hated her with intense hatred. In fact, he hated her more than he had loved her. Amnon said to her, "Get up and get out!" "No!" she said to him. "Sending me away would be a greater wrong than what you have already done to me." But he refused to listen to her. He called his personal servant and said, "Get this woman out of my sight and bolt the door after her." So his servant put her out and bolted the door after her.

She was wearing an ornate robe, for this was the kind of garment the virgin daughters of the king wore. Tamar put ashes on her head and tore the ornate robe she was wearing.

She put her hands on her head and went away, weeping aloud as she went. Her brother Absalom said to her, "Has that Amnon, your brother, been with you? Be quiet for now, my sister; he is your brother. Don't take this thing to heart." And Tamar lived in her brother Absalom's house, a desolate woman. When King David heard all this, he was furious. And Absalom never said a word to Amnon, either good or bad; he hated Amnon because he had disgraced his sister Tamar.

2 Samuel 13:1–22 (NIV)[12]

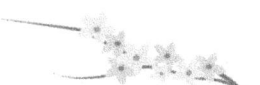

Princess Tamar's stunningly beautiful pottery is intentionally smashed into pieces by a malicious rapist, her brother, who should have cherished and protected her. Her pottery is further broken by her father's uncaring neglect and public humiliation. Where is the Great Potter when we hurt?

Princess Tamar is the beautiful daughter of King David, the sister of his favourite son Absalom. She is lovely, kind, precious, and has a servant's heart. Her morning begins with her happily preparing food for her sick brother, the crown-prince,—a plot planned by him and his cousin. Little does she know she soon will be brutally raped and her beautifully decorated and painted clay pottery will be intentionally smashed and thrown into the streets of Jerusalem like a piece of trash.

Tamar's father King David failed to observe his own characteristics in his eldest son. Instead, he sends his daughter into the wolf's den, as it was David who asked Tamar to take care of Amnon, who pretended to be sick—as if they did not have servants to do that. Why send a princess to take care of an ill prince?

Tamar's story is difficult to hear—excruciating.

No, my brother Amnon! Don't force me!

An incest and rape should not be done here in Israel!

---

[12] *Read also*: 2 Samuel 13–19.

Don't do this wicked thing.
Don't do this to me!

It is heartbreaking that Tamar's shouts for help go unheeded. Perhaps they are heard, but no one cares. Or they dare not interfere, not knowing whose side to choose: prince or princess?

Tamar tries everything to avoid her rape. She tries to reason, to explain how dreadful it would be for both him and her. In her final desperation, she even offers herself for marriage.

But Amnon is not good or decent, and nothing Tamar says means anything to him, for Ammon and his friend have been planning this for weeks. Nothing will stop him now! And since he is stronger, he overpowers and rapes her.

It is heartbreaking and gruesome!

For Amnon, nobody else matters. Narcissistic, he is not interested in considering how this will affect Tamar. To him, she is a toy to be brutally played with and then thrown away, destroyed and demolished. Like all rapists destroying so many innocent girls' lives. A big brother, Amnon should protect her, but he does the opposite. Tamar's screams heighten his lust for power and control. A perfect rape. Just as he planned!

The way Amnon treats Tamar after the rape is outrageous. It was not enough that he cruelly used and hurt her; he also intensively hated her and wanted to destroy her. An intentional blow breaking the clay pottery was not enough, so he grounds the clay crumbles until nothing is left, only to be thrown to the streets like garbage and kicked, ensuring no dignity remained to recover.

"Get up and get out!" Amnon shouts at Tamar after he has done his nasty business with her body.

How heartbreaking it is to see Tamar trying to hang on to a shred of dignity and hope. *No! Sending me away would be a greater wrong than what you have already done to me!*

But Amnon, the perpetrator enjoying his victim's total humiliation, throws her to the streets. "Get this woman out of my sight and bolt the door after her."

This woman! After raping Tamar, Amnon treats his sister, a princess, as if she were some disdainful drifter manipulating her way into his house.

She is tossed into the street for all to witness her humiliation.

Silenced Rape Victim

That day Tamar's clay pottery smashes into a thousand pieces. The attack breaks any trust she once had in her brothers, her relatives, and anyone who is supposed to protect her, including her father.

It touches me to imagine Tamar staggering on the streets of Jerusalem… The defiled, teenager tearing her beautifully embodied robe, the symbol of virgin daughters' of the King, pouring ash from the dirt of the streets on her face. She weeps in desperation as she knows her life is ruined, her dreams destroyed.

We do not know how long she wanders on the streets in shock and horror but we *do* know that she was silenced as many rape victims are. I find it horrific how the whole episode was hush-hushed by his father and even by Absalom: *"Be quiet for now, my sister; he is your brother. Don't take this thing to heart"* (v. 20).

How can he construe a ruthless rape as 'a thing'? How can he counsel Tamar who was just brutally violated, not to take it personally, not to take it wrong, not to be upset; asking her to simply swallow and suppress it; pretend it never happened and keep it a secret! Did anybody take Tamar's side? Were they only concerned with protecting the reputation of the royal institution?

Sadly, isn't this how rape victims are often treated? The abusers, and those who witness the abuse, project the responsibility of the crime onto the victims thus encumbering them with the shameful secret.

It is obvious the 'love' Amnon felt towards Tamar in the beginning was not love. There is no room for raping and forcing in realm of love. Amnon *hated* Tamar with *intense hatred*. But why did he? Why did he also kick her on the street? According to Deuteronomy 22:28-29, if a man rapes a virgin he must marry her and he can never divorce her. Although, the Levitical law forbids siblings to have intercourse (27:22), perhaps with the King's permission, it might have been possible for Amnon to marry Tamar, just like Tamar suggested in her desperation.

We could speculate that by treating Tamar as if it was *her* who shamed him, Amnon projected his shame onto her. Perhaps his guilt manifested as repulsion and belligerence. Perhaps Amnon hated Tamar because he hated everything she represented? Or because he hated Absalom, brother of Tamar, who was their father's favorite?

It's cruel revenge but typical for Abraham's lineage: favoritism, betrayal, revenge, failing to protect... The cycle of evil repeating generation to generation. Transgenerational trauma breaking new potteries.

Humiliation

Rape and humiliation always go hand in hand. Anybody who has experienced it knows this. Everything one believed in is destroyed, feeling that it is impossible to even imagine how to collect the broken pieces! Humiliation is the instrument of the perpetrator. It is an effective weapon not only to torture the victims but also to contribute to their rejection by their families and communities. It is the perfect destruction of the clay pottery. A Vietnamese proverb characterizes the sad, distorted self-image of many violently raped women: *"The bowl was clean and someone ate out of it, leaving it dirty."* [16] In the victims' minds they falsely believe their pottery is dirty, too dirty to be loved by anyone, even themselves. They see themselves as forever tarnished, damaged goods. Perhaps humiliation is closely linked to how one sees themselves, as well as how they think others see them, after the rape.

> *Humiliation takes away a person's power. Its goal is to turn you into a powerless person who cannot perform, who cannot work or take care of his family and friends.*[17]

> *It is a state of being, characterized by feelings of uncleanliness, worthlessness, embarrassment, and shame. It takes away the dignity or self-respect of an individual. There is a complete absence of love, affection, and empathy."* [18]

Sadly, Amnon enjoyed humiliating Tamar, typical of narcissistic rapists who count on their victim's bafflement and bewilderment, and who desire to humiliate them along with destroying trust, happiness, hope, security, and justice.

We know Absalom never verbally confronted Amnon, but did eventually kill him two years later. His relationship with his father David broke down, he threatened to kill him, and raped his ten concubines.

But none of this violence healed Tamar.

Despite finding refuge in Absalom's home, and her niece being named after her, Tamar never recovered. She died desolate and broken.

There is something deeply heart-wrenching to have no other identity than allowing the projected shame to veil your very existence for the rest of your life and dying as a desolate.

It takes a victim a lifetime to clean off the defilement of a single act of rape, and that the [...] community may never again fully accept her, causing irreparable damage to all persons involved.[19]

News stories and documentaries describing civil war scenes are often full of disturbing images of rape victims and horrendous group terror. In the Middle East, not far away from the episodes in Tamar's life, thousands of women and girls are abducted, raped, and humiliated by ISIS and other terrorist groups. Many refugees who manage to escape are utterly broken potteries. Joy and hope are gone, with worthlessness and shame taking their place. These victims have been stripped of dignity and self-respect. Many refugee women feel that everything normal and beautiful is destroyed, with their trust, values, and beliefs torn to pieces.

Intentionally Broken and Neglected

Tamar's clay pottery is intentionally broken by Amnon and his cousin who plan this plot. Sadly, not even their father, David, does anything to provide her justice.[13] He is furious but chooses not to intervene, just as his phlegmatic ancestors did so many times prior when they should have protected their wives and daughters.

---

[13] *Tamar*-name means palm tree. In the Jewish tradition it is a symbol of justice.

It could also be that David allowed his guilt surrounding Bathsheba to cloud his judgement of his son's behaviour thus neglecting Tamar's rights altogether. Perhaps Tamar didn't appeal to her father at all because she knew he was tolerant on his sons' evil behaviour.

The transgenerational trauma of favoritism and lack of protection spirals, and as a consequence, David loses all three children. Absalom kills Amnon, and later, Absalom is killed. Interestingly, it is only for Absalom that David shows deep grief. He does not grieve for Tamar or Amnon. "O my son Absalom! My son, my son Absalom! If only I had died instead of you—O Absalom, my son, my son!" (2 Samuel 18:33 NIV). David cries after Absalom as if he were his only child, but he is not moved by Tamar's tears. He did nothing after learning of Tamar's treatment. He did nothing to ease her devastation and humiliation. As the king, he could have called in all the powers to restore her daughter's dignity. Instead, he does nothing to help Tamar as she weeps aloud in her torn robe.

Interestingly, according to statistics, 93% of juvenile sexual abuse victims knew their perpetrator.[20] More than half of female rape victims were assaulted by an intimate partner, and almost half by an acquaintance; more than half of male rape victims were assaulted by an acquaintance.[21] Sadly, there have been too many sexual violence crimes taking place in Church communities as well.

No rape victims should ever be shamed and silenced!

This is critical for those investigating violations in Christian communities. The victims should always receive full support, not stigmatization, blaming, guilt-trips or pressure to 'forgive and forget,' because the perpetrator (who was caught) apologizes. There should be transparency and accountability. Any suggestion of suppressing a legal investigation to protect the institution only reinforces the notions of hypocrisy that exists from those outside the church. There should be zero tolerance on any sexual violence in church communities or inside marriages.

No Happy Ending till Heaven

Why didn't the Great Potter intervene?

Sometimes the Great Potter intervenes in ways we do not understand. He does not always answer our cries in the way that we think He should. His thoughts are not our thoughts. As the heavens are higher than the earth, so are His ways higher than our ways (Isaiah 55:8–9).

For some, there is no happy conclusion until in heaven. Then their broken potteries will be brand-new. Then there will be no more tears in their eyes as the Sovereign Great Potter "will wipe away the tears from all faces" (25:8 NIV).

Our Tears Recorded

Have you ever kept a diary or journal in which you recorded your heartbreaks and sorrows? Some people write these in the form of poetry. I used to write long poems describing my feelings as teenager. And so does the Great Potter for our tears. He keeps count of our crying and track of all our sorrows. None of our tears go wasted. He has collected all our tears in His bottle. He has recorded each one in His book (Psalm 56:8 NLT).

The Great Potter did this with Tamar's tears, just as He does with yours and mine. He cries with us while He bottles our tears; We need not bottle them up and store them within our pottery.

Isn't it a beautiful thought that the Great Potter, the Creator of the universe, cares and takes notice when we cry tears of sorrow, pain, anguish, repentance, confession, and joy? He is touched by our burdens, our broken hearts, and our feelings of grief.

Can you imagine it: a bottle of tears and a book of tears? It must be an enormous database and storage room full of those bottles.

The Great Potter will gather us into His arms and hold us close. He will comfort us and wipe the dirt and tears from our eyes. Perhaps, that day He will show us those bottles of tears that He has been collecting. He might just select one of mine and say, "Heidi, do you see *this* bottle here? These are the tears you cried when this or that took place in your life. You see, my child, *you were never forgotten*. I did care that your heart was broken. I was there comforting you."

The Great Potter did this with Tamar as well. Though she died as an outcast in her smashed clay crumbles, He restored her in eternity, where He wiped away all of her tears and created her a new pottery.

No broken piece is meaningless.

None are wasted, and all have a divine purpose, some which will not be clear until that day, when He wipes our tears.

And then, the stunning episode between the Great Potter and Tamar, who lived and died desolate, is revealed: "I will also give that person a white stone with *a new name written on it*, known only to the one who receives it" (Revelation 2:17 NIV).

Imagine that moment.

The Great Potter gives Tamar a white, brilliant pebble as a sign of her innocence, her victory, and her ultimate position in front of the Great Potter.[14] The new name written on it is known only by Tamar. Tamar's hands shake as she holds her stone. Looking at it, she sees letters written on it. Looking closer, she reads it. And then like a warm breeze filling her, bringing the new knowledge to flood every cell, her mind, her thoughts, her emotions, *it all makes sense*!

She immediately understands the new name; the *secret* between her and the Great Potter—the secret for her broken pottery.

Though we don't know what's written on the stone, we can guess that it entails something *opposite* of the painful names tattooed on Tamar like a stigma that defined her during her lifetime: abused, rape victim, desolate, outcast, unclean, tarnished, spoiled, damaged goods...[22]

---

[14] According to various commentaries there are many speculations on the meaning of the white stone. (1) In the ancient Greek court system, a white stone signified innocence. (2) In ancient Rome sports games, it indicated a victory. The winner's name was written in a white stone as a "ticket" to the awards celebration. (3) A white stone refers to diamonds as the original word *leukos* means "bright or brilliant." (4) And a white stone refers to the twelve stones of the high priest's breastplate that contained names of the twelve tribes of Israel. The priest wore this when he entered into the Holy of Holies, the presence of God, once a year. (5) For Christians, the new name could also refer the name of Jesus, the ultimate winner, who reconciled us, or (6) it could refer His standing in God's presence with our names written on Him. [22]

Perhaps this name on the stone was meant for her from the beginning of time, before her pottery was smashed and broken. The name reveals how the Great Potter has always seen her: beautiful and precious—*Beloved.*

Perhaps it contains the Great Potter's name or refers to the Great Potter's unfailing love, never-ending grace, and everlasting faithfulness. —This name is a new beginning for Tamar, where all of the old hurts are wiped away, even from her memory.

Now Tamar's pottery is new and whole, soft and shining. No scratches, no memory of the old injury. Perhaps something golden or diamonds have replaced earlier cracks.

Can you relate with the sense of projected shame? It may be something nobody else knows about, a shameful secret you've kept since childhood, yet it has killed you inside. Or you are publicly stigmatized in your community, marked and branded by something you didn't choose but it now defines your very being, and you feel that nobody sees anything else when they look at you. A refugee, divorcée, disabled, bankrupted, addicted, orphan, foster kid, raped…

Did someone intentionally crash your pottery into little pieces? Perhaps today you are searching for answers to your tears and broken pieces. Maybe your world has only recently crashed into pieces. Maybe your hopes and dreams have been cruelly shattered on the floor. Perhaps the great deceiver has whispered to your heart that nobody understands your pain, nobody cares, and that you don't deserve any good treatment.

What do you do when it feels like Job when he said: "… But if I go to the east, he is not there; if I go to the west, I do not find him? When he is at work in the north, I do not see him; when he turns to the south, I catch no glimpse of him" (Job 23: 8–9 NIV). There isn't any of us who hasn't sometimes felt all alone amongst our broken pieces.

Have you felt this way with your broken pottery? Remember, even if you don't *feel* that the Great Potter has heard your cries, He has already collected your tears into His bottle and recorded your sorrow and grief into His book.

It is comforting to know that the tears and broken pieces of this suffering world of broken potteries are not forgotten or forsaken.

Isn't it breath-taking that *you also* will receive a white stone with your new name written on it—a sign of your innocence, victory, and redeemed position with the Great Potter.

CHAPTER 17

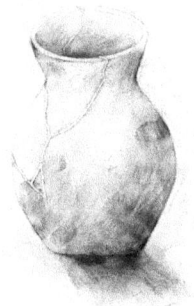

ELIJAH
THE PROPHET BROKEN UNDER A MOUNTAIN

Now Elijah said to the prophets of Baal,
"Choose one bull for yourselves and prepare it first,
for you are many; and call on the name of your god, but put no fire under it."

So they took the bull which was given them, and they prepared it, and called on the name
of Baal from morning even till noon, saying,
"O Baal, hear us!" But there was no voice; no one answered.
Then they leaped about the altar which they had made.
And so it was, at noon, that Elijah mocked them and said,
"Cry aloud, for he is a god; either he is meditating, or he is busy, or he is on a journey,
or perhaps he is sleeping and must be awakened."
So they cried aloud, and cut themselves, as was their custom, with knives and lances,
until the blood gushed out on them. And when midday was past, they prophesied until the
time of the offering of the evening sacrifice.
But there was no voice; no one answered, no one paid attention.

1 Kings 18: 25–29 NKJV

And it came to pass, at the time of the offering of the evening sacrifice,
that Elijah the prophet came near and said, "Lord God of Abraham, Isaac, and Israel,
let it be known this day that You are God in Israel and I am Your servant,
and that I have done all these things at Your word.
Hear me, O Lord, hear me, that this people may know that You are the Lord God,
and that You have turned their hearts back to You again."
Then the fire of the Lord fell and consumed the burnt sacrifice,
and the wood and the stones and the dust, and it licked up the water that was in the trench.
Now when all the people saw it, they fell on their faces; and they said,
"The Lord, He is God! The Lord, He is God!"
And Elijah said to them, "Seize the prophets of Baal! Do not let one of them escape!"
So they seized them; and Elijah brought them down to the Brook Kishon
and executed them there.

vv. 36–40

Now it happened in the meantime that the sky became black with clouds and wind,
and there was a heavy rain. So Ahab rode away and went to Jezreel.

Then the hand of the Lord came upon Elijah;
and he girded up his loins and ran ahead of Ahab to the entrance of Jezreel.

vv. 45–46

Elijah Escapes from Jezebel

And Ahab told Jezebel all that Elijah had done,
also how he had executed all the prophets with the sword.
Then Jezebel sent a messenger to Elijah, saying, "So let the gods do to me, and more also,
if I do not make your life as the life of one of them by tomorrow about this time."
And when he saw that, he arose and ran for his life, and went to Beersheba,
which belongs to Judah, and left his servant there.
But he himself went a day's journey into the wilderness,
and came and sat down under a broom tree. And he prayed that he might die, and said,
"It is enough! Now, Lord, take my life, for I am no better than my fathers!"
Then as he lay and slept under a broom tree, suddenly an angel touched him, and said to
him, "Arise and eat." Then he looked, and there by his head was a cake baked on coals,
and a jar of water. So he ate and drank, and lay down again.
And the angel of the Lord came back the second time, and touched him, and said,
"Arise and eat, because the journey is too great for you." So he arose, and ate and drank;
and he went in the strength of that food forty days and forty nights as far as Horeb,
the mountain of God.
And there he went into a cave, and spent the night in that place; and behold,
the word of the Lord came to him, and He said to him, "What are you doing here, Elijah?"
So he said, "I have been very zealous for the Lord God of hosts;
for the children of Israel have forsaken Your covenant, torn down Your altars,
and killed Your prophets with the sword. I alone am left; and they seek to take my life."

God's Revelation to Elijah

Then He said, "Go out, and stand on the mountain before the Lord."
And behold, the Lord passed by,
and a great and strong wind tore into the mountains and broke the rocks in pieces

before the Lord, but the Lord was not in the wind;
and after the wind an earthquake, but the Lord was not in the earthquake;
and after the earthquake a fire, but the Lord was not in the fire;
and after the fire a still small voice.
So it was, when Elijah heard it, that he wrapped his face in his mantle and went out and stood in the entrance of the cave.
Suddenly a voice came to him, and said,
"What are you doing here, Elijah?"
And he said, "I have been very zealous for the Lord God of hosts;
because the children of Israel have forsaken Your covenant, torn down Your altars, and killed Your prophets with the sword. I alone am left; and they seek to take my life."
Then the Lord said to him: "Go, return on your way to the Wilderness of Damascus; and when you arrive, anoint Hazael as king over Syria. Also, anoint Jehu son of Nimshi king over Israel, and anoint Elisha son of Shaphat from Abel Meholah to succeed you as prophet.
Jehu will put to death any who escape the sword of Hazael, and Elisha will put to death any who escape the sword of Jehu. Yet I reserve seven thousand in Israel —all whose knees have not bowed down to Baal and whose mouths have not kissed him."

19:1–18[15]

Elijah's clay pottery unexpectedly smashes into crumble. The first blow comes from Queen Jezebel. After the Great Potter's gentle restoration attempts, Elijah smashes it himself. Although Elijah's story is one of trauma, burnout, and depression—as well as a suicidal pottery hiding in a cave—his story doesn't end there. It is a beautiful example of the Great Potter who cares about His clay potteries so much that He meets them in unique and unexpected ways—even if they are buried under a mountain.

[15] *Read also*: 1 Kings 17–19, 21; 2 Kings 1–2; Deuteronomy 18:18; Malachi 4:5–6; Hebrew, 3:23–24; Matthew 11:14–15; 16:13–16; 17:1–3; 9–13; Mark 6:14–16; 9:2-13; Luke 1:16–17; 9: 28-36; John 1:19-27; Isaiah 40:3; Revelation 11:1-14.

Elijah's story can't be told without including mountains. The first scene takes place on Mount Carmel, the second one on the mountain of Horeb, and the third one on the mount of Jesus's transfiguration.

Is there something special about these mountains in Elijah's life? Or do they simply point to us humans finding ourselves sometimes on a mountaintop experience and other times smashed under a mountain? For some of us, our lives are like stressful climbing from one mountain to another.

Mount Carmel

The Mount Carmel rain dance episode was dramatic! It was an amazing, victorious, exhausting experience for the prophet Elijah. Had the press been there, the headlines would've read:

> The Great Potter vs. Baal Competition: Which Is Most Powerful?
> The Baal Prophets' Impressive Rain Dance: Yelling and Self-Mutilation!
> Fire and Brimstone Falls onto the Elijah's Altar!
> Rain Clouds Building on the Horizon!
> Who Is This Hairy Prophet? Oprah Interviews Elijah.

The Great Potter showed up in a mighty way. Not only did He consume the drenched sacrifice from the altar Elijah had built but He also consumed the water, wood, stones, and soil. His almighty power evidenced He is the one true God. It is all glorious and magnificent as all the prophets of Baal are defeated and destroyed.

After the days of stress, total devotion, and the horrendous racket from Baal's prophets, Elijah was exhausted, mentally and physically. Certainly, Elijah should have taken a well-deserved vacation on the seaside somewhere. Or a nap, at least. But he doesn't.

Instead, he launches on a marathon of thirty kilometers to the city to meet Queen Jezebel. And what a sprinter he is, running faster than King Ahab's horses. He must be filled with supernatural powers.

What inspired him to go to the evilest queen of all time? Perhaps he was excited and enthused by the outcome of the contest between the false god and the Great Potter—which really was no contest at all. What might his thoughts have been as his feet ate up the kilometers?

It's revival time!

Surely, Queen Jezebel will be the next to repent!

She will accept the Great Potter as the true God!

I, Elijah, the great prophet, will go down in history!

Elijah is reveling in his mountaintop experience. However, his clay pottery is about to be suddenly and unexpectedly smashed.

Bad News

Have you ever received an unexpected message? Reading the content, you are dumbfounded, hardly believing your eyes? This is what happens when Elijah reads the queen's message. Maybe when he received it, he figured that the queen was praising him. Or that the queen was so excited about his victory on Mount Carmel against Baal's prophets that she can't wait until he arrived at the palace to lead her in the worship of the Great Potter.

Stunned and shocked, Elijah stares at the written text. His head spins as he re-reads it from the beginning: *Tomorrow you die!*

Suddenly his situation turns upside down. Elijah's self-confidence turns into panic. He goes from ecstasy to horror. His shiny clay pottery is smashed into a thousand pieces.

And running he goes. But instead of heading to the palace, he turns to escape for his life, hunted by the dismay and dread of his imagination.

It's his fight-or-flight response.

Elijah flees and runs approximately 170 kilometers into the desert of Beersheba, where he departs from his servant and continues by himself. Isolating himself, a typical reaction to trauma.

Of course, Elijah must be utterly fatigued by now, unable to think clearly, and full of fear. He cannot take another step and collapses under a broom bush.

Under the Broom Bush

Elijah's pottery is smashed into a thousand pieces, and he realizes how broken he is. He feels utter despair. And all he can do is hope to end it all. Hoping to die, he begs the Great Potter to give him the final blow.

Elijah believes this is the end. He closes his eyes, expecting to never wake up, but the Great Potter has something better for Elijah.

Gently and tenderly, He collects the broken pieces, placing them on His table, launching an ICU specially planned for Elijah: *food, water, and rest.* That's what this broken pottery needs—no theological discussion, no sermons. Just basic needs this "hero" had neglected for days.

"Get up and eat," the angel sent by the Great Potter says. "Get up and eat, or the journey will be too much for you."

That the Great Potter Himself, the great Creator of the universe, sees to the basic needs of His broken pottery is comforting. Beautiful. The Great Potter does not forsake His own.

Under that broom bush in the middle of nowhere, Elijah is without hope. He was so far from anyone and any place, that he could never reach there alive. He needed the Great Potter. He needed to be placed on His table to receive the special care planned for him only.

The journey from the desert of depression is long. The Great Potter knows this.

Get up and eat, or the journey will be too much for you.

It may feel hopeless to even think about getting out of there. And He knows that as well. Even if the wish is for Him to deliver the final blow, His plans are still good.

No, He never wants us to do anything that is too much for us!

When He gently collects the broken pieces, He provides refreshment and strength for the journey.

The Great Potter never forsakes His own to die under any broom bush.

And so, Elijah continues his journey. Altogether, he travels around 500 kilometers from Mount Carmel to Mount Horeb, the mountain of the Great Potter, which takes forty days and forty nights—from the mountain of miracles to the cave of depression; from the mountaintop to under another mountain.

Have you felt like Elijah: burned out and depressed, feeling a deep emptiness that reaches to the core of your soul? Have you ever neglected your basic needs because of doing the Great Potter's work? —Pumped-up, running like a headless chicken, living irrational fears that *feel* real—like a nightmare, questioning the reality of what you know actually took place. For whatever reason, have you isolated yourself in some sort of wasteland, thinking it is all about *you?*—Thinking *you* do not need anybody because *you* must be a superman or superwoman with superpowers.

If you have been at the end of yourself then you know how Prophet Elijah felt.

Slouched, exhausted, and smashed to pieces, realizing that this must be the end—no strength to go on, too exhausted to think or feel and numbed by the horror of your life. You have no more tears to shed, and you have been silenced in shattered stagnancy.

Welcome to Mount Horeb!

Mount Horeb

By the time Elijah reaches Mount Horeb, he seems to have forgotten the many miracles and supernatural interventions, including the most recent 'under-the-bush'-episode, the Mount Carmel Miracle, and the 'ravens-feeding-him-on-the river'-episode. Although there have been plenty of them in Elijah's life, it is as if they never happened.

Depressed, he crawls to his cave, thinking it a perfect pit to die.

"What are you doing here, Elijah?" the Great Potter asks. "What are you doing on this mountain? What are you doing in this cave?"

Oh, do not even consider that the Great Potter did not know the answers. He asked because *Elijah did not know* why he had traveled these hundreds of kilometers. Why had he come to this mountain, or why was he hiding in this cave?

Elijah, what are you doing here?

As Elijah reflects on the answers to these questions, his fears rise to the surface—some real and others irrational. He ran away because of the dread, the revenge of Queen Jezebel. His life was in danger. He also imagined threats. His trauma triggered insecurity and mistrust. He mistakenly thought he was the Great Potter's last prophet alive.

Fear is an emotion that warns about a threat. It is our unique interpretation of the situation. It takes place in our brains when physiological changes in the body indicate a perceived threat. A sound, smell, color, or atmosphere can trigger a flashback of a trauma experience, making us feel that the original trauma is repeating although we are perfectly safe. The body reacts first, preparing to fight, flee, or faint, based on the reaction to the original trauma experience.

Discussing and clarifying our falsified thinking process is *the first step* out of the cave of fears. That is why The Great Potter calls to discuss with Elijah. But Elijah is not eager to leave his cave. The *status quo* feels safer than the outside reality. Outside is the source of his anxiety, so avoidance is his best defense. Misery has become his best friend, and anxiety is the new normal.

The Great Potter does not want Elijah to waste his life in the cave of his fears, living with lies and misconceptions.

Finally, Elijah speaks to the Great Potter from the depth of his cave. And the Great Potter listens. It is not a face-to-face dialogue as Elijah is still hiding in his cave. Nevertheless, it is the first step toward freedom.

The threatening images developed during Elijah's exhaustion and isolation have stolen his peace and replaced it with fear. As Elijah continues to share his fears, the Great Potter listens.

The second step is to move away from the cave, at least moving closer to the entrance of the mountain of depression and hopelessness.

Mercifully, the Great Potter does not give up on Elijah. He comes to Elijah because Elijah does not come to Him.

Would Elijah recognize the Great Potter passing by? How does it sound when the Creator of the universe moves? Is it like a mighty wind storming into the mountains and shattering rocks? Perhaps like a thundering earthquake shattering the ground and foundations? What about a terrifying fire burning everything to ashes?

Many attribute these to the Great Potter. Well-meaning friends tell us: "Hear! Hear! It must be the Great Potter speaking to you in this lightning! In this storm, in this fire, in this earthquake… It must be the Great Potter sending *you* a message in your sickness, your loss, your desperation."

But these are destructive forces to describe Him. Of course, He is mighty and great and powerful, but is this how He passes by His beloved potteries?

> Then a great and powerful wind tore the mountains apart and shattered the rocks before the Lord, *but the Lord was not in the wind.* After the wind there was an earthquake, *but the Lord was not in the earthquake.* After the earthquake came a fire, *but the Lord was not in the fire.* And after the fire came *a gentle whisper.* When Elijah heard it, he pulled his cloak over his face and went out and stood at the mouth of the cave. (1 Kings 19:11–13)

I can easily imagine Elijah crawling deeper into his cave. Shaking violently, he wants to die, but does it have to be a violent death? The loud noises flood the mountain. Explosions after another. The stony foundation of the entire cave shakes. And then the fire and smoke. —This must be the end! Who can bear the wrath of the Great Potter! However, whatever were those manifestations—they were *not* the Great Potter passing. It was not Him sending any messages.

> *And then— suddenly it is all quiet.*
> Can you imagine it? All quiet. Not a sound.
> *And then a small voice.* A gentle whisper…
> Now, *this* is the Great Potter.

No storm, earthquake, or fire forced Elijah from his cave. After all of that noise and supremacy came silence. Then *a gentle whisper,* almost too quiet to hear. So soft.

No force, yet it was the Great Potter's gentle whisper that drew Elijah out.

Though weak, Elijah comes to the entrance of his cave. He cannot resist. He knows it is the Great Potter. It is *His love* that gently pulls him out.

And that is enough of a step toward recovery: Away from the cave, self-inflicted fears, self-pity, and bitterness. Away from being trapped. It is a move toward the light and liberation.

That's all Elijah has to do. The Great Potter will do the rest.

Now is not a time of fire and brimstone. There was enough of that at Mount Carmel. Mount Horeb is about a gentle whisper of the Great Potter as He lifts Elijah's clay pieces from the ground and gently places them on His table and begins to restore his pottery. This gentleness ministers to Elijah's exhausted soul.

The Great Potter is not violent. He is not looking to punish, to give the clay pottery the final blow. This is a false image. Rather, He calls with a gentle whisper.

Elijah had an incorrect view of the Great Potter. But His gentle whisper encourages Elijah to move out of his cave of fears. And the therapeutic discussion with the Great Potter continues.

What are you doing here, Elijah?

He wants Elijah to learn the roots of his burnout, the reasons for his brokenness, and the source of his fears. The Great Potter's questions are never trivial. They are carefully crafted questions to pinpoint the issue and launch a healthy self-reflection process.

It is safe to have this discussion with the Great Potter. There is no need to try to hide any broken pieces because He already knows it all—past experiences that trigger current reactions, inner hidden pain.

Only the Great Potter knows what questions to ask.

Elijah tells the Great Potter his emotions, honestly sharing his fears, insecurities, anxiety, self-pity, and anger. He confesses his grandiose self-image of bearing the responsibility for the nation of Israel on his shoulders and irrationally thinking that he is the only living prophet of the Great Potter.

Elijah must allow the truth to liberate him.

After discussing with the Great Potter, Elijah learns the truth about himself, others, and the Great Potter. He is not the only survivor, for the Great Potter has reserved seven thousand people who have not worshipped Baal.

Trading irrational thinking with the truth, fears and anxiety fade.

Elijah's turning point is to decide between terror or trust, fear or faith, cave or future.

Even though Elijah's pottery is in a thousand pieces, smashed and strewn on the floor of the dark cave, it is not the end of his story. The pieces are not buried under the mountain. The Great Potter makes Elijah a new vessel prepared for a new task and new adventures. He also provides him a prophet friend so that he needs not do everything alone—a good idea for any of His vessels.

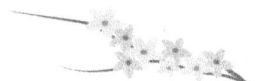

Have you also crawled into a cave? As a temporal safe zone for a while for your broken pottery but soon turned it into your 'home-sweet-home', a permanent dwelling, a new normal? Beth Moore in her book, *Get Out of That Pit,* introduces the idea of permanent pit-dwellers who refuse to leave their pits behind even though it would be possible.[23] I think it could be similar with cave-dwellers.

Perhaps you first built some rough wall installation to help with the moisture and hung a flashlight on the ceiling. Then you brought your favourite rugs and a comfy armchair. After a while you even painted some fancy artwork on the stony walls. You may have developed ways to keep the creepy creatures hiding under a mountain out of your mind. Perhaps power rituals or humming a comfort song.

> *I love my cave in the springtime.*
> *I love my cave in the fall.*
> *I love my cave in the winter when it drizzles,*
> *I love my cave in the summer when it sizzles.*

Who cares if it is a bit moldy, unavoidably dark. During the hot summer months, it's pretty cool, and in the winter months, well… it's pretty cool—you can't get everything, eh?

There isn't an honest person who hasn't occupied the cave of fears—yet all too many have been trapped and paralyzed for years. That cave of fears fogs our common sense; it limits our lives, stealing the joy. What kind of threats typically trigger your sense of insecurity; how do you determine whether they are real or imagined?

The realization of irrational thinking is necessary to leave the cave of fears. Understanding that the childhood experiences can unconsciously cause fears as adults may help with your reflection process. Whatever you believe about the world, yourself, and the others affect your anxiety levels and how much you allow yourself to trust.

Now, standing at the entrance of the cave, you can let your irrational fears go.

Mount Tabor

Later, alongside Moses, Elijah stands with the Great Potter at Mount Tabor, the place of the transfiguration, where the Great Potter fulfilled the law and the prophets. Elijah and Moses, both broken potteries, each had several encounters with the Great Potter, yet they never saw His face (Matthew 17:1–8).

Elijah is surrounded by His glory and magnificence. This proves that Elijah's past brokenness did not diminish his value as clay pottery.

Elijah's brokenness did not affect how the Great Potter saw him. He hand-picked Elijah to be with him at the transfiguration. Elijah was chosen to be taken to heaven in a fiery chariot. The angel Gabriel told Zacharias that his son, John the Baptist, would preach in the spirit and power like Elijah. And Elijah is believed to be one of the witnesses who appear in Jerusalem during the end times.

Though Elijah was broken, he was one of the most powerful vessels in the Great Potter's service. It was as if gold filled the fractures in Elijah's clay pottery—gold to glorify the Great Potter.

As we learned from Abraham's family tree, the past affects and even shapes the future. To refuse to deal with past mistakes is to create a greater negative impact in the future—passing on the misery to children, grandchildren, and beyond.

But it doesn't need to be this way.

Reflection on the past is like turning on the light while isolated in that dark cave. Nothing has changed except the light allows what is there and what is not to be seen, as well as the scattered pieces of broken pottery.

There is no magic eraser that wipes away a damaging experience and magically puts the broken pieces together. The only way is the process on the Great Potter's table. Facing your brokenness, allowing Him to collect your broken pieces, and working through your emotions is the first step.

By reflecting on your breaking experience, you steadily diminish its power over your life, choices, thoughts, and emotions.

Gradually, you begin to understand what triggers your emotions and reactions. And little by little, you may gain more empowerment over those reactions until it no longer has the power to limit your vision or longer falsify your image of the Great Potter. It can no longer limit your creativity and potential or the ways the Great Potter can use you as His vessel. Remember, your brokenness does *not* define your identity. You do not need to use the same defenses you did as a child. You no longer need to succumb to trauma-triggered reactions.

Your fears need not distance you from the Great Potter.

"What are you doing here? Why are you here? How did you get here?" the Great Potter asks you, not because He doesn't know the answers but because *you* don't, and you need to. Take time to reflect on these questions and honestly answer them. To be free to make good choices today and to understand your present, you must understand your past and the choices you made.

The Great Potter invites you with a *gentle* whisper. "Come to me, all you who are weary and burdened, and *I will give you rest"* (11:28 NIV).

Maybe, for some reason, you expect something other than rest from the Great Potter. A reprimand, perhaps? A list of duties, a performance-oriented to-do list?

Or an order to try to fix your past failures? It is incredible how the Great Potter describes Himself: "for I am gentle and humble in heart" (v. 29). How astonishing that instead of a new burden, the Great Potter offers rest—His yoke is easy and His burden is light.

Always remember that the Great Potter will even turn the mountains to find broken pieces hiding in caves.

Step out of your cave and let Him start His restoration process with you.

He will meet you at the entrance and make you a new vessel for His work.

CHAPTER 18

JEREMIAH
THE WEEPING PROPHET

The Call of Jeremiah
The word of the Lord came to me, saying, "Before I formed you in the womb I knew you,
before you were born I set you apart; I appointed you as a prophet to the nations."
"Alas, Sovereign Lord," I said, "I do not know how to speak; I am too young."
But the Lord said to me, "Do not say, 'I am too young.'

You must go to everyone I send you to and say whatever I command you. Do not be afraid of them, for I am with you and will rescue you," declares the Lord.

JEREMIAH 1:4-8 (NIV)

Jeremiah was put into a vaulted cell in a dungeon, where he remained a long time.

37:16

So they took Jeremiah and put him into the cistern of Malkijah, the king's son, which was in the courtyard of the guard. They lowered Jeremiah by ropes into the cistern; it had no water in it, only mud, and Jeremiah sank down into the mud.

38:6–13 [16]

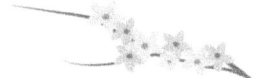

Jeremiah's clay pottery was utterly smashed. Not once, not twice, but throughout his lifetime it was repeatedly smashed. —Yet it was Jeremiah who wrote beloved words about the Great Potter's faithfulness and the prosperous plans He has for us. What did Jeremiah understand when his smashed pieces were pressed into the mud?

Jeremiah's story stands in stark contrast to the prosperity gospel that preachers paint as the picture of a victorious Christian. Jeremiah's clay pottery was horribly broken, and unlike Job, Hagar, Joseph, and Elijah, his story did not have a happy ending. He was supremely qualified to write the book of Lamentations, which is full of laments and passionate expressions of grief and sorrow. No wonder his nickname is the Weeping Prophet.

As a child, he was called by the Great Potter, who set aside Jeremiah's clay pottery as His particular vessel as a prophet who spoke His words. Jeremiah took His message to the nations and preached the destruction of Jerusalem. But it came with a mighty promise of the Great Potter: "Do not be afraid of them, for I am with you and will rescue you" (1:8).

---

[16] *Read also*: Jeremiah 1, 11, 20, and Lamentations 1–5.

Why did Jeremiah weep if he had the Great Potter's promise, and He would be with the prophet and rescue him?

He wept because of the unpleasant events the nation of Israel would experience, the destiny of his fellow potteries, and the helplessness he felt over it all. He wept because he was alone, a lonesome cowboy, no prophet colleagues to chat with, no wife or children. His only companion was Baaruk, his secretary, his one and only friend who wrote down his prophetic words.

I am sure that as a newbie prophet, Jeremiah had dreams and hopes. However, from the very beginning, he encountered nothing but opposition and hardship—over-the-top anxiety. Jeremiah's pottery was cruelly tortured and smashed... repeatedly.

And then he wept...

- when his family betrays him,
- when the guys of his village curse and want to kill him,
- when he is sitting in the stock outside the temple that day,
- when his writings are destroyed,
- when his prophecies are not received and respected,
- when he is hated, hunted, and imprisoned for the rest of his life, and
- when the first stone strikes him. The next stone blows his pottery into pieces.

Jeremiah's clay pottery remained miserably smashed most of the time—hunted by his enemies, deserted by his friends, and finally killed by his countrymen. *Not rescued* by the Great Potter, despite the promise.

Yes, it makes perfect sense that Jeremiah would weep. *"Why is my pain unending and my wound grievous and incurable? You are to me like a deceptive brook, like a spring that fails"* (15:18). Reading Lamentations 3 makes it sound as if he was greatly dismayed with the Great Potter:

> *I am the man who has seen affliction by the rod of the LORD's wrath.*
> *He has driven me away and made me walk in darkness rather than light;*
> *indeed, he has turned his hand against me again and again,*
> *all day long.* (1–3 NIV)

> *Like a bear lying in wait, like a lion in hiding,*
> *he dragged me from the path and mangled me and left me without help.*
> *He drew his bow and made me the target for his arrows.*
> *He pierced my heart with arrows from his quiver.*
> *I became the laughingstock of all my people;*
> *they mock me in song all day long.* (vv. 10–14)

Do you see Jeremiah sitting in a water cistern where his enemies smashed him a few days ago? He's been sitting in the cold mud for several days now, shivering and feverish. He is just a clay pottery, not a hero or a superman. He's broken into pieces on the cold, moldy floor. He has no blanket, no pillow. He is alone in the darkness and aching pain.

> *Where is the Great Potter? Where are you? Hey, you promised to rescue me!*

But nobody is rescuing Jeremiah.

And he continues weeping:

> *He has made my skin and my flesh grow old and has broken my bones. He has besieged me and surrounded me with bitterness and hardship. He has made me dwell in darkness like those long dead. He has walled me in so I cannot escape; he has weighed me down with chains.* (vv. 4–7)

Another time, Jeremiah's pottery is smashed into a deserted well, with no water but lots of smelly mud.

> Mud in his eyes.
> Mud in his ears.
> Mud in his mouth.
> Full of trash and rats.

Hey, Great Potter, why don't You keep your promises? Why don't you help me? Jeremiah cries in an agonising despair.

> *Even when I call out or cry for help, he shuts out my prayer. He has barred my way with blocks of stone; he has made my paths crooked"* (vv. 8–9). *"He has filled me with bitter herbs and given me gall to drink. He has broken my teeth with gravel;*

he has trampled me in the dust. I have been deprived of peace; I have forgotten what prosperity is. (vv. 15–17)

Jeremiah's clay pottery is repeatedly smashed and cruelly demolished by his enemies. They torture him, and he remains their prisoner until the city is conquered. You'd think he'd have a happy ending, but the end is just as nasty.

After the city is conquered, Jeremiah is taken against his will to Egypt, where according to the traditional sources, he is stoned to death by his infuriated fellow countrymen. No rescue by the Great Potter's forces. Just a tortured end.

So I say, 'My splendor is gone and all that I had hoped from the LORD.' I remember my affliction and my wandering, the bitterness and the gall. I well remember them, and my soul is downcast within me. (vv. 18–20)

Laments after Lamentations

Reading Jeremiah's laments, you can feel his pain, hear his anguish, and imagine his hopelessness.

Anxiety. Despair. Devastation.

Thus, what follows really puzzles me…

"Yet *this* I call to mind and therefore *I have hope*" (v. 21).

Hope?

Where does this hope come from?

Stuck in the muddy well, and deserted among the rats. *Not there!* Not in prison and not when smashed into crumbles. *How can he have hope in those circumstances?*

Visiting the Auschwitz concentration camp, a couple of years ago, I walked among the hundreds of barracks, electric fences, and guard towers. I heard the horrible history, saw the heartbreaking photos of the prisoners, and thought it impossible that anyone could have held on hope while imprisoned there. Yet, in such a brutally violent environment built to rip off the humanity from the prisoners, a few of them, such as Corrie ten Boom, held on to hope in the Great Potter.

So did Dietrich Bonhoeffer, thirty-nine-year-old on April 9, 1945, right before his brutal execution. However, in his last letter to his family, he writes about "The Loving Forces Silently Surrounded"— the Great Potter's supernatural goodness.

> *By loving forces silently surrounded,*
> *I feel quite soothed, secure, and filled with grace...*[24]

Undoubtedly, Dietrich Bonhoeffer, like Jeremiah, knew *the secret of hope* in the direst circumstances.

> *By loving forces wonderfully sheltered,*
> *we are awaiting fearlessly what comes.*
> *God is with us at dusk and in the morning*
> *and most assuredly on every day.*[25]

Most horrendous circumstances and terror, yet Jeremiah writes about hope. Despite circumstances, he is *wonderfully sheltered by His loving forces*. Jeremiah knew that the Great Potter was beaming in the night, that He was with him at dusk and in the morning, that whatever happened, he belonged to Him.

Great Is Thy Faithfulness

Do you know the hymn "Great Is Thy Faithfulness"? The song speaks of blessings and health, happiness and wealth. It is often sung around the Thanksgiving dinner table, and it is linked with abundant life. However, out of all the other prophets and great authors, it is Jeremiah who discovers *great is His faithfulness!* It was Jeremiah, the Weeping Prophet, who learned this characteristic of the Great Potter. *Great is His faithfulness in every situation.*

> Because of the LORD's *great love* we are not consumed, for *his compassions never fail*. They are new every morning; *great is your faithfulness.*
> (v. 22–23)

Now Jeremiah *knew* this secret of broken potteries. Great is Your faithfulness... *especially* when it does not feel so. It has nothing to do with circumstances or feelings, which come and go. But His faithfulness lasts forever and ever and is new every morning.

Jeremiah felt miserable, and he didn't hide the fact. However, *he does not base the facts on his feelings but on the One who renews every morning.*

The Great Potter's love, compassion, and faithfulness are new every morning. Because Jeremiah knows this, he has hope despite his misery. *This is supernatural.* Even in the middle of the evilest circumstances, *His faithfulness surrounded Jeremiah.*

> The LORD is my portion; therefore I will wait for him.
> The LORD is good to those whose *hope* is in him, to the one who seeks him;
> *it is good to wait quietly* for the salvation of the LORD. (vv. 24–26)

Though Jeremiah is half-sunken, smashed into pieces in a muddy well, and devastated, he quietly waits for the Great Potter. Because he knows He is faithful, Jeremiah has hope:

> For no one is cast off by the LORD forever.
> Though he brings grief, he will show compassion,
> *so great is his unfailing love.* (vv. 30–32)

It was Jeremiah, the Weeping Prophet—who did not prosper during his lifetime—who wrote about the good and prosperous plans of the Great Potter:

> For I know the plans I have for you,' declares the LORD,
> 'plans to prosper you and not to harm you, plans to give you hope and a future.'" (Jeremiah 29:11 NIV)

Jeremiah knew the heart of the Great Potter better than anyone.

And then one day, the Great Potter rescues His clay pottery as He promised. He gently collects the pieces broken by the sharp stones on the field where His prophet breathed his last. He gently cleans the pieces, adds some new clay, and creates new pottery. Perfect. No cracks. No faults.

> And I heard a loud voice from the throne saying,
> Look! God's dwelling place is now among the people,
> and he will dwell with them.

> They will be his people,
> and God himself will be with them and be their God.
> *He will wipe every tear from their eyes. There will be no more death*
> *or mourning or crying or pain,*
> for the old order of things has passed away. (Revelation: 21:3–4 NIV)

And finally, Jeremiah weeps no more. The Great Potter has wiped away all his tears. The broken pottery is restored for good. "I have good plans for you. Good plans, though I know it was not as you imagined," the Great Potter says.

Jeremiah had it all—every element of a nasty trauma. Broken by his malicious enemies and killed by a frustrated countryman, he was helpless. He felt pain and the lack of empathy, but he reminded himself of the One who has it all under control and *saw beyond* what we think should be a happy ending.

It was enough to receive the Great Potter's compassion. The Great *I Am* was with Jeremiah despite the circumstances.

This is what mattered.

Can your pottery relate in some way to Jeremiah's experience? Perhaps someone threw your pottery into a muddy well. When you were a child, even before you knew how to speak, did you suffer from abuse, abandonment, parents' mental health issues or addictions? How easy it is for broken clay pieces to sink into those dark cisterns.

Did you also feel that the Great Potter was not keeping His promises? Did you weep and cry in self-pity, feeling He was nowhere nearby?

Jeremiah did not choose to be smashed the way he was. None of us do. But it happens. And when it does, remember "Great Is Thy Faithfulness." *Remember the facts beyond your feelings.* His compassion never fails. His grace never ends. And nothing, absolutely *nothing* will separate you from the Great Potter's never-failing, unconditional love.

He who called you in your mother's womb *sees* you broken in the trash yard of broken potteries, buried under mud. He who wonderfully made you, can find all of your broken pieces and restore your clay pottery.

You may be broken into a thousand pieces, smashed and half buried in a smelly, muddy cistern; however, you have the Great Potter's promise. He has good plans for you, even when it may not feel so at that moment.

The Great Potter has a plan for you, but it may mean that He will not always rescue you from nasty circumstances. But it is a promise that whatever happens, you are safe because He holds your future—and you are never without hope.

CHAPTER 19

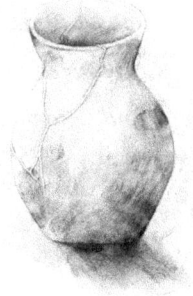

MARY
THE MOST BLESSED AMONG WOMEN

Now in the sixth month the angel Gabriel was sent by God
to a city of Galilee named Nazareth,
to a virgin betrothed to a man whose name was Joseph, of the house of David.
The virgin's name was Mary.

And having come in, the angel said to her,
"Rejoice, highly favored one, the Lord is with you; blessed are you among women!"
But when she saw him, she was troubled at his saying,
and considered what manner of greeting this was.
Then the angel said to her,
"Do not be afraid, Mary, for you have found favor with God.
And behold, you will conceive in your womb and bring forth a Son,
and shall call His name Jesus.
He will be great, and will be called the Son of the Highest;
and the Lord God will give Him the throne of His father David.
And He will reign over the house of Jacob forever, and of His kingdom there will be no end."
Then Mary said to the angel, "How can this be, since I do not know a man?"
And the angel answered and said to her,
"The Holy Spirit will come upon you, and the power of the Highest will overshadow you;
therefore, also, that Holy One who is to be born will be called the Son of God.
Now indeed, Elizabeth your relative has also conceived a son in her old age;
and this is now the sixth month for her who was called barren.
For with God nothing will be impossible."
Then Mary said, "Behold the maidservant of the Lord! Let it be to me according to your
word." And the angel departed from her.

Mary Visits Elizabeth

Now Mary arose in those days and went into the hill country with haste,
to a city of Judah, and entered the house of Zacharias and greeted Elizabeth.
And it happened, when Elizabeth heard the greeting of Mary,
that the babe leaped in her womb; and Elizabeth was filled with the Holy Spirit.
Then she spoke out with a loud voice and said,
"Blessed are you among women, and blessed is the fruit of your womb!
But why is this granted to me, that the mother of my Lord should come to me?
For indeed, as soon as the voice of your greeting sounded in my ears,

the babe leaped in my womb for joy.
Blessed is she who believed,
for there will be a fulfillment of those things which were told her from the Lord."

LUKE 1:26–45 (NKJV)[17]

Mary's clay pottery is broken by the Great Potter Himself. A sword pierced her heart as she helplessly watched her son brutally tortured. Crushed into pieces, how could she be blessed of all women? If this is a blessing, what must it feel to be cursed? Blessed—but not the way she expected. Blessed through brokenness. A blessing for the entire world of clay potteries.

I wonder what was going in young Mary's mind when Gabriel, the angelic army leader, announces that she is favored by the Lord. And what does she feel when her aunt prophesies that she is the most blessed of all women?

Of course, bearing the Son of God is magnificent and exhilarating. Being a mother of the Messiah was the dream of many teenage Jewish girls. However, I doubt Mary feels incredibly blessed when pondering how to disclose the unexpected pregnancy news to her fiancé, or when she considers her parents' reactions and the neighbors' malicious gossip. Who would believe a wild story like hers—a virgin pregnancy? Oh, for sure. Camels fly too.

We do not know how Joseph learned about the pregnancy. Possibly Mary told him after returning from Elizabeth's, or maybe Joseph confronted Mary after hearing rumors. Perhaps there was suggestive innuendo from his coworkers at the carpentry shop. Did Mary see shock and disbelief in Joseph's eyes when she tried to explain the angelic visit? Did she also see hurt in them?

Mary must have been thinking about what could happen in case Joseph did not believe her. If Joseph were to report her to the priests and make it public that she was pregnant, and he was not the father, she would be treated as an adulteress,

---

[17] *Read also*: Luke 2; Matthew 1:18-25; 2; John 18:28–40; 19; 20; Micah 5:2.

stoned or at least sent away and sold into slavery.[18] Does Mary feel blessed when she contemplates these possible consequences and question what kind of a blessing is this? Does her clay pottery begin to crack a bit?

We cannot blame Joseph for being skeptical and not believing this crazy, pathetic tale of a virgin pregnancy.

Joseph and Mary were betrothed, and he had paid the dowry according to the contract. Sleeping together would only be seen as a the final step in the consummation of their marriage. Her getting pregnant wouldn't have been such a big deal in that community, perhaps only a common violation of the custom to wait a year between the betrothal and wedding. However, we see kind-heartedness in Joseph. Since he had never slept with Mary, he rightfully assumes she had been unfaithful. If she had been raped, she probably would have trusted him enough to tell him about it instead of coming up with that wild story about Gabriel and becoming pregnant from the Holy Spirit.

Even though Joseph must feel hurt and cross about his fiancée having been with another man, he doesn't want to humiliate her so he plans to divorce her quietly without putting her in a bad situation. Joseph does not want Mary to be stoned to death for adultery. He is ready to let everyone assume that he is the biological father and that they had just rushed the wedding night. He is even willing to take the shame and heat for divorcing her. Either Joseph is exceedingly kind, or he loves her, or both.

Of course, after the angel Gabriel visits Joseph and confirms Mary's story, Joseph will no longer doubt her angelic visitation and commits to protecting her and the child (Matthew 18: 18–25). But did all the villagers *truly* believe Joseph was the biological father?

There were the rumours…[19]

---

[18] Deuteronomy 22: 23–24

[19] Even today, conjecture persists. Were Joseph and Mary aware of these malicious rumours? Gossip such as Mary having an affair with a Roman soldier? He was even named—Tiberius Julius Abdes Panthera. Or another rumour, Mary raped by a Roman soldier of Syrian origin, living in the military camp near the village of Nazareth? Another had Mary being raped on her way to see Elizabeth; It was ninety miles from Nazareth to Ein Karem, Judea and would have taken several days. Although Mary

Can you imagine how Mary feels as a target of daily gossip and malicious statements? Also, for Joseph, it must have been difficult to hear her wife's reputation being bashed, and himself being seen as a man who raises another man's child.

When we think about Mary's life, many of her experiences certainly do not sound like one being blessed among women. Lots of brokenness and tears, yes, but not precisely blessings.

Were there fears in Joseph's mind causing him not to leave his heavily pregnant wife in Nazareth with her family, but instead, dragging her on a rough road trip lasting several days to Bethlehem? Was there shame involved for Joseph not staying with his relatives in Bethlehem, rather, he has his wife delivering their baby in an animal shelter? Was there a threat that either Joseph's family, Mary's family, or some furious neighbours, or religious leaders could have hurt her or the baby? Did Joseph need to ensure she always remained under his protection?

Interestingly, after the baby is born in the humble stable in Bethlehem, where they had traveled to meet the demands of the census, the family feels no urgency to return to Nazareth. Instead, they stay in Bethlehem for another couple of years until the visitation by the eastern magi precipitated their flight to Egypt to avoid the child being caught up in the massacre of every child under the age of two.

Did Mary feel blessed and favored by the Lord as a refugee in Egypt while hearing the news of King Herod's order to murder the babies in Bethlehem? Mary was no doubt frightened.

When I visited the house in Cairo that Coptic tradition claims to be where the family stayed, I leaned out the window, imagining young Mary doing so over 2000 years prior. Looking from that window, I saw the ruins of a former Roman fortress. Perhaps Mary looked upon it, possibly fearing that the Roman soldiers would hunt

---

surely would have traveled with a caravan, it was not safe for a young girl. When she then returned home after few months and was not able to hide her belly from the prying eyes of newsmongers, is this when the whispers and gossips began? It even continued into Jesus's adulthood—Mark 6:3 reports Jesus being described as Mary's son, which in that culture is unheard of, as everyone was recognized according to their father's lineage. Moreover in John 8:41, the priests hint of Jesus's background being illegitimate. Busybodies and talebearers? Or the opening salvo in a spiritual war? Months later, looking to kill the child, soldiers sweep the countryside massacring every child under two.

down the particular Hebrew toddler in Cairo as well. Maybe she sat by that window, pondering the meaning of being blessed among women. I wonder if she felt blessed while being scared for Jesus's safety.

If this is what being blessed means, I wonder what else it is to come on us?

When did she embrace the blessing and the Lord's favor part? We wonder how Mary felt as she realized the mission Jesus was on. When He was only twelve, He blatantly declares that His place is in the synagogue doing His father's business. A few years later, she seemed to push Him to speed the process a bit by asking Him to turn the water into wine at the wedding at Cana. As a mother who is proud of her children, I can understand Mary's eagerness for Jesus to step into the limelight, for she knew her son was extraordinary and special.

When Mary heard stories about her son's miracles—healing the sick, casting demons, and raising people from the dead—and about the multitudes who followed Him, I wonder if she also followed and heard His sermons. Did His teachings make sense in her heart considering all that she knew about Him before he was even born?

I am sure Mary cherished the good news and felt blessed, but perhaps it was tinged with worry because of rumors about the priests and Pharisees going against Him and trying to stop His ministry. Did Mary's pottery crack as a result? No doubt more cracks formed when He told His disciples that He does not have a mother (Matthew 12:48). Surely that pierced her heart.

I'm sure Mary was bursting with joy on seeing her son ride into Jerusalem and all the folks greeting Him with joyous hosannas. Possibly she experienced a little healing in her worried heart.

This is what the angel Gabriel meant all those years ago.
My son is the Messiah, the Redeemer!

Mother Observing Her Son Tortured

Never in her wildest dreams did she imagine her son's circumstances going south the way they did. Early morning on what is now known as Good Friday, she hears from the horrified disciples about the previous night's chaotic events: Jesus's arrest and appearance before the Sanhedrin and high priest. Heart pounding, she hurries to Pontius Pilatus's crowded place and feels the hostility and hears the angry murmurs. Questions fill her mind:

What is happening?
Of what are they accusing my son?
Why are the Roman soldiers beating Him and whipping Him, ripping off His skin?
What is all this?

With every lash of the whip and punch of fist, Mary's clay pottery crushes to hundreds of pieces. She simply cannot believe her eyes.

This is not how the story was supposed to end?
This is not what I expected as a blessing I was promised!
No, this cannot be happening.
It must be a nightmare.

But it is not. Feeling foggy and bewildered and indifferent standing there in the crowd, Mary realizes she is indeed awake, but her life has suddenly turned into a nightmare.

And then a sword pierces her heart.

In every whipping sound, she hears her heart pierced deeper.

Can you imagine how it all feels for a mother? Just watching there in utter helplessness and not being able to help her dear son. She probably had to cover her ears against the agitated crowd grousing frantically and then begin to shout like manic that He should be crucified. Angry racket pounding like a primitive beat, "Crucify Him! Crucify Him! Crucify Him! Crucify Him!"

Aren't these the people who only a few days ago greeted Him in joy? The very same people He healed and helped so much? Why would they choose to release Barabbas, a murderer, in exchange for her son, who has done nothing but kindness to everyone? Mary is bewildered:

Did I understand it all wrong?
All those promises, were they all my imagination, some crazy hallucination?

She helplessly watches the soldiers beating her son, His skin shredded, and so much blood. She cannot recognize Him. They spit on Him and mock Him, placing a red robe on His shoulders while another soldier shoves a crown of thorns onto His head. Pushing so hard the thorns pierce deep into His battered flesh.

Blood trickles down His puffy, bruised face.

Blessed among the women? You must have been joking, Gabriel!
No, not joking, brutally mocking!

Mary can barely hold herself up as she stands in the middle of her shattered pieces, bewildered and devastated. But she must endure more horror.

How can they do this to my son?

She follows Jesus as He trudges the Via Dolorosa, a narrow street ascending toward His final misery, His rough cross digging into His wounded back. Folks line the road, mocking, insulting, and spitting on Him. They are bent on inflicting on Him all of their pain, hate, and cruelty. The soldiers continue their kicking and whipping until He collapses, His strength spent from the onslaught of violence.

Mary locks onto His eyes, which are pools of sadness and pain and unbearable agony. His beaten body is bruised and crushed beyond recognition. Her battered son bears little resemblance to a human being.

Perhaps mother and son exchange a special look. Mary wants to run to Him, hold Him, as she did when He was a little boy and He had hurt himself. But the Roman soldiers roughly shove her back. Thank God, a strong man, Simon, is helping Him by carrying the cross.

At the top of Golgotha, Mary finds her friends. The women are wailing in horror of what is to become of their Lord, while the crowd chants in excitement and hostility, "Crucify Him! Crucify Him!" Perhaps she is trying her best to go to her son despite the soldiers' sharp weapons, but they don't allow her. "Stay away, woman!

Stay where you are! Not a step closer!" And the other women held her so that she will not run to her son despite the soldiers.

Disbelief, sorrow, and grief mingle within Mary as she helplessly watches the soldiers holding her son down on the wooden cross. Pushing his feet together, they hammer an iron stake through them into the wood. Then they spike His hands to the cross. The strike of metal on metal tears through Mary's heart as if the nails are piercing it. Each blow smashes against her pottery. As long as she lives, she will never forget that sound. Even years after, whenever she heard it, the flashbacks of this morning would shake her entire being.

My son is being crucified.

The soldiers raise the cross on which her son is nailed. Mary gasps at the intolerable pain she sees in her son's eyes when the flesh and nerves of his hands and feet are ripped as the heavy cross is dropped into the waiting hole. The jarring sends a ripping pain through His body.

If this is to be favored by the Lord, what is it to be despised?

And Mary, broken and crushed, helplessly observing the tremendous suffering of her eldest son. Hanging on that horrible wooden cross in unimaginable pain, hanging so that it is hard to breathe. Oh, His eyes so full of pain. Yet even in his last moments, His caring attention is on her (John 19:25–27).

As a mother myself, I cannot even begin to imagine how horrible and helpless that must have felt for Mary? That sense of utter helplessness. Not being able to lessen her son's pain at all. Unable to comfort Him. Not being able to do what the mothers do best.

Blessed among women? Cursed, perhaps. But does not feel blessed for sure!

If only she could, she would do anything to stop that agonizing torture of her son. Looking at His anguished face. His chest visibly rising and falling with each throbbing, painful breath he takes.

Oh, how much longer must he suffer?

I can imagine Mary screaming to the Great Potter, "Please, please! Since You are not going to rescue my son, please end His agony! Finish it now!"

"My God! My God! Why have you forsaken me?" Jesus utters.

Oh, it hurts Mary like a spike plunging through her heart!

Yes, Great Potter, why? Why did You forsake my son?
Isn't He supposed to be Your Son? Why did You abandon Him?

And then finally, *it is finished.* Mary's son is dead.

When the soldier plunges his spear into His side, and water and blood flow down His dead body, Mary stares in shock and disbelief. Later, she listens as Joseph of Arimathea and Nicodemus ask permission to remove the body from the cross. After He is lifted down, she collapses onto His dead body, wailing in agony. She removes the thorny crown and throws it away in anger. She dabs at the dried blood on His face and rocks Him as she had when He was a child.

How does it feel for a mother to hold the body of her dead son?

Blessed? I doubt it.

A sorrow and agony so deep, words cannot express. *Why, oh, why did they do this to my son?* Taking His body covered with white linen, the men place Him gently on the bed in the garden tomb. She says her final good-bye, "Sleep peacefully, my son," and perhaps sings Him the last lullaby, the one she sang when He was a baby in her arms.

Sleep my child, sleep my darling.
All too soon, my song will cease.
When you have left my arms so loving,
May you then find a life of peace.[26]

As she sings, memories fill Mary's mind: the night He was born; how tired, weary, and frustrated she was after the long trip, finding no room available, the pains of labor in a stable. Perhaps she remembers holding her newborn son, looking into His bright eyes, and kissing her baby's cheek. Oh, the love she felt for this baby of hers!

The love she feels holding her son's brutally bruised, dead body.

Perhaps Mary wonders at how quickly the years had passed: His first smile. His first teeth. His first step. His helping his father at the carpentry shop. Going fishing with His friends. Doing so well at the school, and discussing so smartly at the synagogue. Oh, how proud she had been! And when He left home the first time, setting out on His calling, how her heart had swelled with love and pride. What a fine young man He was, so full of compassion and gentleness. Blessing Him as He walked away from home, she prayed for Him every day. Her son had helped hundreds of potteries as He poured out love wherever He went. Now He is dead. Life brutally ripped away in one torturous day.

Her son is dead, and she cannot fully make sense of it all.

Did Mary feel blessed at that moment? Or did she feel like a broken mother whose son had been tortured and slaughtered? This kind of brokenness can only be understood by a mother who has violently lost her child.

Her heart heavy and bewildered, her body stubbing in grief, Mary leaves the garden tomb after Joseph and Nicodemus place a heavy stone on the doorway.

> *My son is dead, and I don't understand.*
> *Didn't that angel say that Jesus would become the King and Saviour?*
> *Didn't those old folks at the synagogue tell me that He is the Messiah?*
> *Didn't Elizabeth call me the most blessed of all of the women?*
> *They were all mistaken, or they were lying.*

The End is the New Beginning

The next day, Saturday, Mary cannot eat or sleep. She cannot stop crying or remove the haunting image of the soldiers torturing her son. She shudders at the agonizing looks in His eyes. She moves in a fog of hopelessness and despair.

Early Sunday morning, Mary returns to the garden tomb with her friends. Her eyes are swollen and heavy from all the tears. They come with the herbs and ointments, hoping to properly prepare His body.

You know how the story ends. The tomb is empty, and He is not there. He had been resurrected by the power of the Great Potter. He *is* the Messiah, the King of Kings, the Savior of the world.

Mary's clay pottery was broken beyond seeming repair. It was smashed like no other pottery. However, there was a secret in her brokenness. There was indeed a blessing; however, it is not only for her but for all of us. "But he was pierced for our transgressions, He was crushed for our iniquities; the punishment that brought us peace was on him and by his wounds we are healed" (Isaiah 53:5 NIV).

There *is* a happy ending in Mary's story.

There can be a happy ending to any broken pottery's story.

The happy ending is possible because of what the Great Potter did. Because of Jesus, because of His brokenness, we have hope.

The end of Mary's story is the new beginning for all the broken clay potteries. "For God so loved the world that he gave his one and only Son, that whoever believes in him shall not perish but have eternal life" (John 3:16 NIV).

As He promised to the thief hanging on the one side of Jesus's cross—You shall be with Me in paradise—this promise is also for all who believe in Him as Lord and Savior. It does not matter how little we have to give Him. The thief was dragged right from the trash yard, being punished for his crimes. He had nothing to offer but the last moments of his miserably lost life.

However, it was enough. He *believed* the One suffering next to him is the Messiah. And it was enough for the Great Potter, who says "Whosoever believes."

The blessing is for all of kinds of pottery: rich and poor, healthy and sick, wise and simple, right and sinister, happy and sad, successful and losers, popular and loners, you and me, whosoever believes in Him. He will pour His everlasting love and never-ending grace on us.

Mary, blessed among women!

CHAPTER 20

NAMELESS WOMEN ON THE GREAT POTTER'S TABLE

The Lord is a refuge for the oppressed.

Psalm 9:9 (NIV)

Heidi McKendrick

The following four stories include seriously broken women meeting the Great Potter. These women are all nameless, which is telling about women's status of their times. In Jewish courts, women were not allowed to be witnesses because they were seen as over-emotional, hysterical, and unreliable. The Great Potter models a radically different treatment of women. He asks a woman (Luke 8:2; John 20:10–15) He had earlier freed from seven demons to be His first witness after His resurrection.

Isn't it interesting that the Great Potter chooses a woman with a questionable reputation to witness the most crucial moment in history?

Breaking the taboos is the way the Great Potter often mends broken potteries. By seeing the unseen, He changes their identity, the way they see themselves. He permits them to value themselves. By giving a voice to them, He restores the dignity of the most oppressed in society. The Great Potter not only heals their physical sicknesses or forgive their faults but also restores their self-esteem and returns their self-worth.

The Great Potter esteems women as much as He values men. Similarly, He treasures slaves as much as He respects the wealthy, He regards simple fishermen as much as scholarly teachers. The Great Potter speaks to unnoticed women on the street, at a dinner party, or an ancient well, a screaming example for the disciples, which is exceedingly difficult for them to comprehend. He refers to women as daughters of Abraham, equally to the reference of Jews as sons of Abraham, and He praises women as examples of faith, modeling to the disciples the equality of women and men.

There are no men, no women, no slaves in Christ (Galatians 3:28).

The next few chapters introduce four potteries, all broken for different reasons, all at the end of their rope, all thirsty for change. The Great Potter was their last resort.

Their names were not recorded, so they were likely unknown by the gospels' authors, but the Great Potter knew not only their names but their life histories. Perhaps by learning their stories, you will reflect on your life and allow yourself to receive the same new identity as the Great Potter offered these anonymous women.

Meet the Great Potter meeting women who were bleeding, about to be stoned, weeping, and oppressed.—All destined to be transformed.

CHAPTER 21

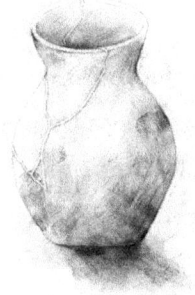

THE BLEEDING WOMAN HEALED WITH NEW IDENTITY

Now a certain woman had a flow of blood for twelve years, and had suffered many things from many physicians. She had spent all that she had and was no better, but rather grew worse.
When she heard about Jesus, she came behind Him in the crowd and touched His garment. For she said, "If only I may touch His clothes, I shall be made well."

Immediately the fountain of her blood was dried up, and she felt in her body that she was healed of the affliction. And Jesus, immediately knowing in Himself that power had gone out of Him, turned around in the crowd and said, "Who touched My clothes?" But His disciples said to Him, "You see the multitude thronging You, and You say, 'Who touched Me?'" And He looked around to see her who had done this thing. But the woman, fearing and trembling, knowing what had happened to her, came and fell down before Him and told Him the whole truth. And He said to her, "Daughter, your faith has made you well. Go in peace, and be healed of your affliction."

MARK 5:25–34 (NKJV)[20]

This nameless woman's clay pottery first breaks because of an unmerciful disease. Painful operations by the doctors of that time failed. She is cast down and smashed by others who despised and rejected her. After twelve years of suffering, a meeting with the Great Potter not only restores her broken pottery but also gives her a new identity.

Nobody knows her name. But for sure, they know that she is unclean—dirty and filthy according to Jewish law. Anything she touches she contaminates.

After twelve long years, she can barely remember life before the onset of the disease. It was an odd disease, vaginal bleeding, chronic hemorrhaging, which first smashed her clay pottery. It was as if her monthly menstrual periods were permanent, continuing day after day, making her permanently unclean according to her culture's laws (Leviticus 15:19–33).

Year after year her pottery kept breaking when each doctor conducted horrendously painful treatments that provided no relief, only worsening symptoms. She tried everything: traditional healing with herbs, weird rituals, odd treatments prescribed in the Talmud, primitive medicines, painful procedures, and most humiliating techniques. I once observed some of those while in the Museum of the History of Medicine in Paris, France, and immediately thought about this woman's tre-

---

[20] *Read also*: Mark 5:25–34; Luke 8:43–48.

mendous suffering at the hands of those gruesome apparatuses. She spent all of her money on trying to find a cure.

Nothing worked.

The final blow for her pottery was that the illness caused her to be ostracized from society. And this had gone on for twelve long years. The food she cooked was unclean. The table at which she ate was unclean. The coffee mug she drank from was unclean. If anyone touched her, they would become unclean as well. If she had children, she could never hug and hold them, for they would become unclean. If she still had a husband, he could never touch her, or he would become ritually unclean for seven days. No intimacy, no cuddles, not even a brief hug. No dinner parties, breakfast with loved ones, no tea and fancy cakes with her girlfriends—if she even had any.

A horrible situation! She was isolated and reviled. Her permanent social distancing was worse than what people experienced during the COVID-19 pandemic.

Of course, in this condition, this woman was barred from attending synagogue. If she dared approach the tabernacle she would be put to death.[27] When she walked along the streets, she was bound to ring a little bell so that everyone would know an unclean creature was about to pass them. Even her shadow was considered contaminated. Her touching any Pharisee or religious leader, even accidentally, would have been an outrageous and punishable act.

Indeed, this woman's future is dark. Destitute and broken, she was possibly facing having to live in caves outside of town with the lepers, demon possessed, and other outcasts. We can barely imagine her agony. She was not only chronically ill but also an outcast of her society—an untouchable castaway.

If Only I Just Touch His Clothes...

Oddly, this woman is in the middle of the crowd the day the Great Potter was to arrive. She knows she should not be there and the consequences if discovered not following social distancing rules. She purposefully doesn't ring that nasty little bell because she needs to go to the center of the crowd to get close to the Great Potter.

She thinks it is worth taking the risk. The Great Potter is her only hope. She already had faith and believed in the Great Potter.

If I just touch His clothes, I will be healed.

Hiding behind her veil when He passes in the crowd, she reaches for just one quick touch. And she touches Him, just the edge of His garment. She knows in an instant that she is healed. She feels no more bleeding. Before she can lift her face from the covers of her veil, she knows the miracle just took place.

But the joy dies quickly when the Great Potter abruptly stops. While looking right at her, He demands to know, "Who touched my clothes?"

She swallows hard. Why did she think He would be anything different?

Trembling and fearing her punishment, she lifts her head, looks at Him, and admits that it was she. But something more incredible than being physically healed happens. Peering into the Great Potter's eyes, all fear vanishes. Rather than hate and recrimination, His eyes convey love and tenderness. There is utmost healing in His look. It feels like being accepted and sincerely seen—who she is, her suffering, pain, shame, and despair. For the first time in forever, this despised woman is seen. The Great Potter acknowledges her with all of her broken pieces, the clay rubble, and the ways she has been trying to put herself back together. He sees it all. And at that moment, He restores her from inside out. He gives her a new identity. "Daughter," He says to her. "Daughter."

A new identity.

It is beautiful that the Great Potter did not let this rejected no-name woman leave without recognition. He did not merely leave her healed and unnoticed. To the Great Potter, a no-name woman was as important as the rich and mighty Jairus to whose house He and His disciples are traveling. It was not enough that He healed the poor woman's physical condition, quenching the flow or restoring only the cover of the broken pottery. He wants to do more!

Daughter.

He wants to heal her emotional wounds, her bleeding heart, and restore her deeply inflicted scars from living twelve years as an outcast; He wants to heal her aching soul. The Great Potter did not see this woman as unclean. "Daughter, your faith has healed you."

Yes, The Great Potter wants to make this clay pottery beautiful. "Go in peace and be freed from your suffering."

Make it glorious, so He adds gold to the fractures. He removes the veil of shame and silence and frees her from any suffering and oppression.

My daughter.

Princess.

Daughter of the King.

This is who we are to the Great Potter. This no-name woman, you, and me. He is the foundation of her identity, my identity, and your identity. "See what great love the Father has lavished on us, that we should be called children of God! And that is what we are!" (1 John: 3:1 NIV). We are His children. His unfailing, unconditional love and His presence heals our potteries' bleeding hearts just as they healed this woman with bleeding issue.

If you feel like a castaway today, remember that the Great Potter wants to restore your dignity. He wants to give you a new name, a new identity. On the cross, the Great Potter did not only pardon you and delete your name from the book of penalties, but He also gave you His name. From an outcast, full of shame and fear, you were transformed into a fully adopted child of the Great Potter. You belong to Him. You are royalty. Not only did you receive a new name but also a new home, a new family, and a new legal standing as heir, equal with previous children, and a relationship with the new father.[28]

What a transformation it is!

"See, *I have engraved you on the palms of my hands*; your walls are ever before me" (Isaiah 49:16 NIV). Isn't that wonderful that our names are carved on the palms of the hands of the Great Potter? In Bible times, a slave had their masters' names written on their hands, just as clay potteries have the Potter's thumbprint on them.

But the Great Potter has his clay potteries' names written on the palms of *His* hands.

I thought about this as I sat in an important meeting a few years ago. A colleague wrote a student's name on his hand so he'd remember to call him. When he noticed I was watching him, he laughed, saying, "If I write the name on a piece of paper and put it in my pocket, I will forget. But if I write it on my hand, it's there for me to see and remember." Understandable for an absent-minded professor, but why would the Great Potter, the sovereign Creator, bother to write our names on His hand?

Oh, that we are always on the Great Potter's mind!

Our names are there to continually remind Him about us. Furthermore, His commitment and the new covenant are written on our hearts (Jeremiah 31:33). His thumbprint is on our clay potteries, just as it is on the saints' foreheads (Revelation 3:12; 14:1).

The names of His children were on His palm when the Roman soldiers ferociously pierced it.[29] Their names are on His palms by the scars from the nails. It is because of His scars, that His children cannot wipe away their names from His palms. Nobody and nothing can wipe them off. My name is there permanently, and His thumb print is on me permanently. It is the new covenant between the Great Potter and His potteries so that we will never forget His unfailing love, never-ending grace, and everlasting faithfulness.

CHAPTER 22

THE WOMAN CAUGHT IN ADULTERY AND ALMOST SMASHED BY STONES

*At dawn he appeared again in the temple courts,
where all the people gathered around him, and he sat down to teach them.
The teachers of the law and the Pharisees brought in a woman caught in adultery.
They made her stand before the group and said to Jesus,
"Teacher, this woman was caught in the act of adultery.*

In the Law Moses commanded us to stone such women. Now what do you say?"
They were using this question as a trap, in order to have a basis for accusing him.
But Jesus bent down and started to write on the ground with his finger.
When they kept on questioning him, he straightened up and said to them,
"Let any one of you who is without sin be the first to throw a stone at her."
Again he stooped down and wrote on the ground.
At this, those who heard began to go away one at a time, the older ones first, until only Jesus was left, with the woman still standing there. Jesus straightened up and asked her, "Woman, where are they? Has no one condemned you?" "No one, sir," she said. "Then neither do I condemn you," Jesus declared. "Go now and leave your life of sin."

JOHN 8:2–11 (NIV)

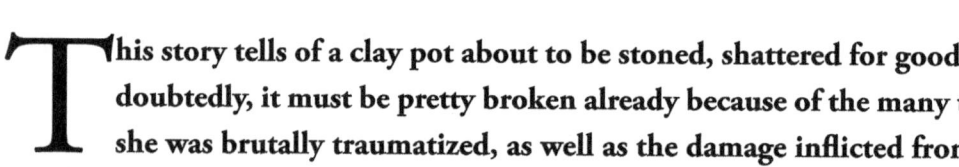

This story tells of a clay pot about to be stoned, shattered for good. Undoubtedly, it must be pretty broken already because of the many times she was brutally traumatized, as well as the damage inflicted from her wrongdoings. However, the aim here is to give the pottery one deadly last blow. Mercifully, the Great Potter has another plan. He beautifully restores the pottery and writes a new story.

Oh, how this woman must have been trembling with fear, half collapsed on the ground in the temple court. She desperately tries to cover her face and half-naked body with what little veil was not ripped from her as she was violently dragged through the narrow city streets.

But it's impossible to hide her shame.

She is aware that she is about to be stoned. The angry religious leaders' accusations and onlookers' murmurings fill her burning ears. Some followed as she was hauled here, collecting sharp stones along the way.

Nothing will save her from the painful death.

We don't know much about this woman. The religious leaders called her an adulteress, which, according to the law, meant she was married but had committed a marital infidelity, illicit intercourse with a man other than her husband. Whether this was a one-night stand, a continuous affair or set up in this sting to entrap Jesus, we are not told, so we just don't know. Her past is mere speculation, but as often is the case, wrong choices lead to more wrong decisions. Regardless, it really doesn't matter what this woman had done or why. *The Great Potter had already decided to forgive her and stop her stoning that morning.*

However, the woman has no idea who she is dealing with.

Could this woman blame anybody else but herself for her predicament? Many try to justify their bad decisions, but I believe she hasn't for the longest time. Perhaps in the beginning, with her first bad choice she did, but not anymore. She quickly learned that nobody cared about her. For a long time, no one had asked about her well-being. She's so full of cracks from previous trauma that she does not say anything in her defense.

How easy it is and has always been to stone a sinful woman. Burn the Jezebels on the stake. Dismiss them from the congregation of perfect potteries. All through the bloody church history, holier than holy men projected unwelcome thoughts and feelings onto sinful women, who then became scapegoats for those gents' own weaknesses. How many women through the ages were judged, ostracized, or killed because a "religious man" participated in forbidden sexual sin? Many women know how it feels to be shunned, their beautiful pottery smashed because of someone else's issues projected onto them.

This woman, about to be stoned, has no reason to believe that this is not her end. Horror fills her. She covers her face, not wanting to look at these men witnessing her shame, her executioners.

Her body prepares to receive the first painful blow.

Now, What Do You Say?

And there He is—that new Teacher, the One who is the judge they said. Indeed, He will agree with these shouts of righteous indignation. "Teacher, this woman was caught in the act of adultery. She got caught red-handed! In the Law, Moses commanded us to stone such women. Now, what do you say?"

What does He say?

What does He think about *such* a woman?

Interestingly, nobody asks the woman what *she* thinks of it all. She has no say, no voice, in the matters of her life or death. What could she say as a defense? She knows the rules, and she was caught in that man's bed—not her husband's. She might ask for mercy, but why bother? Her life is inconsequential. She is merely an expendable pawn. When they came, the man was not there anymore. Had he put something in her drink so that she would fall asleep? Was this prearranged for some other end? Little did she know that she was bait to trap this new Teacher.

"Now, what do you say?" they ask again.

But He says not a word. He stoops down and writes something on the dusty black stones of the Temple courtyard with His finger. She cannot read but she recognizes that they are words. Perhaps He is writing something about the book of Law; something to justify her stoning. Her name, charges, and punishment. A cold shiver runs up her spine, and she trembles so hard it is difficult to stand.

He straightens. "Let anyone of you who is without sin be the first to throw a stone at her."

She holds her breath and shelters her face with her hands, quivering in anticipation of the first blow, in horror and silent sobs. It will be a slow, excruciating stoning. Even without witnesses, which is against the law, the stones will fly. One stone after another. Dozens of moral men surrounded her, most hefting stones, waiting for someone to start.

But nobody throws any stones.

The new Teacher again stoops and resumes writing in the dirt. In stagnant silence, everyone watches as he writes.

She can hardly believe her eyes. One by one, the men back away and leave. The older men first. The stones thud as they drop them when they depart. Others go abruptly, almost storming away. Some slip away discreetly, as if they were not there at all.

Hesitantly, she lifts her eyes to see the courtyard strewn with stones.

"Woman, where are they?"

But this time the Teacher's voice is *not* authoritative and stern, as it was when He had spoken to the men. Instead, it's gentle, tender, almost soothing—as if He is smiling.

She quickly glances at Him.

Yes—He *is* smirking, almost sneering, as he watches the men slink away. It's as if He's asking, "Where are they?"

She looks around. She cannot help a forbidden grin. They are all gone. Only she and the Teacher remain. She hastily drops her eyes.

"Has no one condemned you?" Now she can hear the smile in His voice.

She lifts her face to Him. "No one, sir."

She dares to look into His eyes. She's unsure what she sees. Compassion? Love? It is as if He sees deep inside her heart—everything she has experienced, wrong decisions, pain. Looking at her tear-stained eyes and trembling heart and pouring His everlasting love and never-ending grace. She cannot look away.

"Then neither do I condemn you."

Pardoned without penalty.

The Great Potter gently collects the broken pieces of this fragmented pottery. He sees her inner being, her past, her self-destructive behavior. He sees the source of each crack: her brokenness and defenses, her clumsy attempts to self-mend, those who transgressed and hurt her.

She'd given up on herself, accepting that she was hopelessly trapped in this vicious cycle, hurting herself more. What she is today is what she will be for the rest of her life. She deserved nothing good, and nobody could ever love her. But she couldn't fully comprehend the Great Potter and why He would give her pottery another chance. After all, she brought this on herself. She was guilty of smashing her pottery herself.

She didn't know the Great Potter, but He knows her.

He has known her since before her birth. He would not condemn her. Not for a moment did He intend to allow her to be stoned. In the Great Potter's presence, this woman's broken pottery is not only safe but it immediately begins to heal.

"Go now and leave your life of sin."

But He says it softly.

It reminds me of the child who falls while climbing on a high rock. She goes running and crying to her father. He gently tends her wounds, then tells her, "Go now, back to your playing, but don't climb on that rock anymore so that you won't hurt yourself."

No condemnation.
No judgment.
No fire and brimstone.
No listing of broken rules or rebuke.
No lecture.

The Great Potter does not even ask the woman to confess and repent. He simply forgives her because He has the power to do so.

He forgives because He can.
Instead of condemnation, He pours His grace.
Instead of judgment, He gives His love.
Instead of demands, He offers His compassion.
Instead of punishment, He forgives.

Saved

Can you imagine how this must have felt for this woman? Just moments before she was awaiting a brutal killing; now she is saved. Moments ago all hope was gone; now stepping into her new beginning.

This woman is indeed guilty. But she is no more blameworthy than any of us. Where her sin increased, the Great Potter's grace increased all the more (Romans 5:20). She does not deserve His mercy, but neither do we.

The Great Potter's compassion is always a gift, not a reward. She did nothing to earn His love, and neither have we. The Great Potter's love is unconditional.

What message did the Great Potter write in the sand?

It was significant as these pious zealots were one moment weighing their stones, and the next wishing they could be anywhere but there. Some scholars have suggested He wrote the Ten Commandments, focusing mainly on "you shall not murder." Stoning someone without following the law would be murder and those present were very aware that the law was not being appropriately followed. Let's not forget that she never committed adultery by herself.[21] Where was the partner in crime? Why was he not charged? The Great Potter followed the law to the letter. He did not even break the Sabbath law as He did not write on papyrus or parchment. In other passages where the Great Potter confounded His critics, the religious leaders always huddled, debating how best to respond to His criticisms. They did not this time. Now they simply left the scene one by one.

That's why I think the Great Potter wrote the Pharisees' names and some sort of list of their sins, starting with the eldest man. Perhaps He wrote details of adulterous thoughts, or a dark, shameful secret. Maybe the Great Potter judged them the way they judged this woman. Whatever metric they used was now being meted to them (Matthew 7:2). We can only speculate as to what He wrote.

Often the emphasis of this event is "leave your life of sin", or "go and sin no more," delivered as a stern, punitive decree. It is as if many preachers continue what the Pharisees were doing before dropping their stones and leaving the scene. These preachers seem opposed to *such* a woman getting off the hook. *They continue con- demning her* despite the Great Potter notably stating that *He* would not condemn her.

Some feel safer focusing their main message on law and order rather than amazing grace. Is it because the Great Potter's grace is so overwhelming? Or is it merely

---

[21] During the time of Christ, divorce was the most common punishment for adultery (Matthew 5:32). The Roman government did not approve of Jews administrating capital punishments (consider the cruxifiction). However, according to Leviticus 20:10 both the adulterer and the adulteress were ordered to be put to death and adulterous betrothed virgins (and their partners) to be stoned (Deuteronomy 22: 23-24). There had to be two witnesses (who did not have any biases or conflicts of interests); those two witnesses had to throw the first stones (13:9; 17:6-7). In this case, the law was not followed, and the 'witnesses' left the scene. Their main interest was to trap Jesus but it is not possible for clay potteries to trap the Great Potter!

because it is easier to judge someone who sins differently than I do. How often are we guilty of collecting the stones? Yet our Potter only collects our broken pieces!

How amazing to be dramatically forgiven!

How beautiful that the Great Potter restores His broken potteries with His everlasting love, never-ending grace, and nonstop faithfulness—even if the pottery's brokenness is our own doing or a combination of our wrong choices and others' malicious behavior. The Great Potter wants to restore and reinstate. He wants to clean all the mess and dirt away and give our pottery a fresh new start.

> "How blessed is the one whose transgression is forgiven; whose sin is covered" (PSALM 32:1 NIV).

CHAPTER 23

THE WEEPING WOMAN THROUGH THE EYES OF THE GREAT POTTER

A Sinful Woman Forgiven
Then one of the Pharisees asked Him to eat with him.
And He went to the Pharisee's house, and sat down to eat.
And behold, a woman in the city who was a sinner,

when she knew that Jesus sat at the table in the Pharisee's house,
brought an alabaster flask of fragrant oil,
and stood at His feet behind Him weeping;
and she began to wash His feet with her tears,
and wiped them with the hair of her head;
and she kissed His feet and anointed them with the fragrant oil.
Now when the Pharisee who had invited Him saw this,
he spoke to himself, saying,
"This Man, if He were a prophet, would know who and
what manner of woman this is who is touching Him, for she is a sinner."
And Jesus answered and said to him,
"Simon, I have something to say to you."
So he said, "Teacher, say it."
"There was a certain creditor who had two debtors.
One owed five hundred denarii, and the other fifty.
And when they had nothing with which to repay, he freely forgave them both.
Tell Me, therefore, which of them will love him more?"
Simon answered and said,
"I suppose the one whom he forgave more."
And He said to him, "You have rightly judged."
Then He turned to the woman and said to Simon,
"Do you see this woman?
I entered your house; you gave Me no water for My feet,
but she has washed My feet with her tears and wiped them with the hair of her head.
You gave Me no kiss, but this woman has not ceased to kiss My feet since the time I came in.
You did not anoint My head with oil,
but this woman has anointed My feet with fragrant oil.
Therefore I say to you, her sins, which are many, are forgiven, for she loved much.
But to whom little is forgiven, the same loves little."
Then He said to her,
"Your sins are forgiven."

Secrets Of Broken Pottery

And those who sat at the table with Him began to say to themselves,
"Who is this who even forgives sins?"
Then He said to the woman,
"Your faith has saved you. Go in peace."

LUKE 7: 36–50 (NKJV)

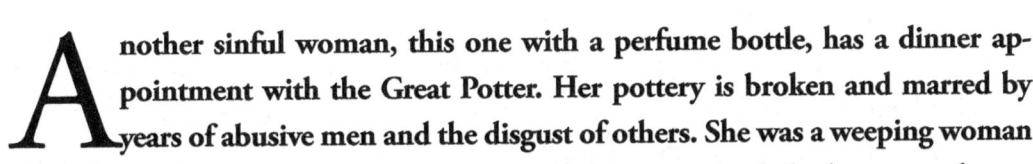

Another sinful woman, this one with a perfume bottle, has a dinner appointment with the Great Potter. Her pottery is broken and marred by years of abusive men and the disgust of others. She was a weeping woman yearning for love but seen by the Great Potter the way nobody had ever seen her.

A dinner party is in full swing with high-powered guests in a high-end mansion to which Reverend Simon invited only a select few—selected potteries. The best food and wine are served alongside the latest entertainment.

It was an ancient Roman tradition to recline while eating. I cannot imagine it being a very comfortable way to eat or suitable for the digestive system. The Great Potter was one of the dinner guests. But He is not there to eat. He is there to restore one seriously broken pottery.

Imagine a 'sinful' woman daring to enter this scene—a woman with a not-so-good-reputation, another nameless woman in the Bible. Even Luke, who writes detailed reports, does not mention her name. Instead, he reveals that she has a particular reputation. Sadly, nothing else mattered in her case. She was "that" woman, well-known and stigmatized, a woman who lived an immoral life—a loose woman, a working girl, a hooker, a prostitute.

A Lady of the Night

A woman who sold her body was emotionally wounded, and most likely abused and battered, entered the house. Her broken pottery was evidence that life had not treated her gently. It had cracks and blows and self-efforts to restore it—heavy makeup masking the fractures.

She had been dropped to the floor a few times, intentionally smashed against the wall as well, kicked, crushed, and blown into pieces. Her spirit, heart, and emotions hardened with each crack and blow. Life taught her to build a wall around herself as protection. She was fixed like cement, deeply frozen, totally numb, and feeling nothing.

Perhaps she masked any hint of vulnerability. Maybe she was a bit pushy, a little too loud, or vulgar and aggressive. Her armor served to scare away the intruders. Her frozen emotions protected her against overwhelming pain.

Out of place among these religious holier-than-thou type folks who could never imagine being caught dead near the shadowy streets and hideouts of her kind.

What is she doing here? Doesn't she know that this party is by invitation only? Hopefully, she is not thinking to seduce any of these respectable vessels.

But she is not there for customers or money. She is there because she heard about the Great Potter and the living water and bread of life He offered. She overheard where she could find Him that evening. It was urgent that she encounters Him. She would die of hunger and thirst if she waited any longer. Her soul would not survive another night.

It was the custom that the poor and less fortunate were allowed to receive the leftovers of any great dinner party. But it was unheard of for uninvited folks to wait around the dining area. Nevertheless, the dinner's guests and hosts did not exactly like it when *this* particular woman entered the property.

But she risks being thrown out and enters the house. Perhaps she stands off to the side, in a corner of the room, or behind the pillar. She searches the room, seeking the Great Potter, the man with the gentle and compassionate eyes. The man so unlike any man this woman ever encountered—and she had experienced many men.

She may have already met the Great Potter in passing, or maybe He had spoken to her. Perhaps she is the adulterous woman the Great Potter earlier saved from stoning.

She had likely heard some of the Great Potter's radical thoughts, possibly hearing them for herself on a nearby mountain when He preached. Of course, she had to remain on the fringes, ignoring the whispers of the respectable townsfolk. What did

He mean when He declared that He came to proclaim the good news to the poor, to heal the broken-hearted, and to proclaim liberty to the captives and oppressed?

This woman certainly knew about being poor, was an expert of broken-hearted—her heart had been torn in the 1001 nights under the Middle Eastern moon—she had extensive experience in being oppressed, bound with inner chains of shame, humiliation, and sorrow. No wonder the Great Potter's message hit home. It sounded like a real deal for her and sparked something within her—the slightest thawing of her stone-hard heart. This glimmer of hope perhaps ignited a seed of faith, enough to yearn more from the Great Potter.

It's an enormous risk, but something in her heart has opened, urging her forward. She has nothing to lose as she has already lost everything. Already broken as broken can be.

There's nothing else to lose and everything to gain.

Liberation

She approaches Him, coming near to where the Great Potter eats. Then she collapses at His feet. In the presence of the Great Potter, something bursts inside of her. She begins to weep. Unstoppable. She is unable to move, to speak through her tears. It is as if a dam, constructed years before, has broken. Her tears have been held inside for a long time, swallowed back too many times. Tears long frozen are melting. And now the waters from deep inside are running free, *liberated*, watering the Great Potter's feet. She is breaking on the Great Potter's table.

There is something deeply touching at this moment.

With only one look from the Great Potter's gentle eyes is enough to melt her frozenness, remove the protective numbness. In the Great Potter presence, her tears are permitted to flow, the defenses torn down. All these long held, petrified tears—sorrow, deep pain, disappointment, regret, shame, humiliation. All these feelings in the Great Potter's gentle presence.

It is simple, but it is life changing.

Her heart of stone is changed to a heart of flesh. The suppressed pain that was hidden, pretending not to hurt, and masked behind a fake smile is exposed to the light for the first time.

Perhaps for the first time in her life, it is safe to be open, vulnerable, uncovered. It is safe to lower her barriers. Exposed and raw, she has no fear of the Great Potter. Now, the first time this pain sees the daylight. And her tears flow down like a Niagara Falls, down from her eyes, down her cheeks, down her neck.

At last she meets someone who understands her essential self.

Though a man, He looks at her eyes not her body and sees into her heart and past; her emotional woundedness and needs; her dreams, fears, and hopes. He looks at her differently from the others, who stared at her with disposing and rejecting looks with eyes full of anger and lust, of course. However, *this man's* eyes are clear with love, gentleness, compassion, and grace.

Yes, that look could melt a stone heart! It could melt a stone fortress!

It is beautiful that the Great Potter does not wipe away her tears or pat her hand. He does not send her away. Neither is He concerned that His dinner gets cold. He does not patronize her. Rather, He allows her tears, lets her pour her love over Him, and happily *accepts* it. As she gives Him everything she has, He does not belittle it or take offense.

He appreciates her loving heart and admires her love.

Usually, the Great Potter poured love onto the potteries, but this time love flowed to Him. Perhaps, for the first time in this woman's life, it is *safe for her to love.*

The Great Potter accepts and cherishes this woman's love.

He does not flinch when she kisses His feet watered by her tears. He does not wince when she dries them with her long hair.

Onlookers must have gasped in horror and choked on their food.

Outrageous! Scandalous!

Unveiling and opening her hair in public is a shameful display, seductive according to the Pharisees. Using it as a towel and *touching* a man in public is even more appalling, strictly forbidden. A hooker touching a religious teacher is beyond taboo.

Simply contemptible in their eyes, but it is *a beautiful encounter* between the woman and the Great Potter.

No words are needed when she gently kisses the Great Potter's feet before pouring expensive perfume on His feet, emptying the alabaster bottle. There is something dainty about this woman bringing her perfume with her that night. Most likely, this jar was all the perfume she had. One drop was potent enough to mingle in the air for the whole night's business.

But the Great Potter is worthy of all she has.

Finally, this woman has met someone who loves her without conditions, without any demands, without any hidden agenda. Her heart is full of faith, hope, and love. Anointing his feet is her way of pouring her love into Him. Despite the guests' hisses of disdain, the only thing she cares about is that *she has finally met the Great Love*. And she wants to demonstrate her love to Him.

So, she gives Him the best she knows.

Do You See What I See?

The Great Potter looks at Simon, the host of the evening, *knowing* his thoughts. *"Do you see this woman? Do you see what I see"*

The Great Potter sees her differently than does Simon or any of the dinner guests. Simon sees a law-breaking woman, someone who is sinful, unclean, and utterly outrageous. One who should be arrested and stoned. The Great Potter sees a weeping woman in terrible pain. Simon loathes this woman because of what she represents. The Great Potter loves her with His unconditional love, despite what she does, does not do, has done, or has not done. Simon condemns her. The Great Potter offers her His never-ending grace. Simons sees the external, dirty pottery. The Great Potter sees her heart, her core, her needs.

We do not know whether Simon ever understood what the Great Potter was trying to explain to him. However, we know what happened to this woman: her entire life and future changed at that moment with the Great Potter.

"Your sins are forgiven. Your faith has saved you. Go in peace!"

She came to the Great Potter with her shame and pain, her thoroughly smashed pottery. But she departs relieved of her burdens. She leaves with His supernatural peace, forgiven and not condemned, not even a critical thought.

It is crucial to know what the Great Potter sees when He sees you, when He looks at you with His special look.

How can you know what He sees?

Imagine a mother cradling her newborn baby. What does the baby see in the mother's face and eyes? That special look the mother has only for her baby. And the baby recognizes it and knows that it is the mother communicating, "You, my baby, you are the most beautiful, most precious baby in this entire universe." The baby then begins to see herself in this same way.

This look is the foundation of the baby's unique value and self-worth.

Sadly, many children never experience this look for any number of reasons. Whatever the cause, many children struggle throughout their lives and into adulthood to find that look and acceptance. They look in all kinds of places or substitute sources. To be seen and loved is a basic need of every human being. When the Great Potter meets His clay potteries, He looks at us with the look that says, "*You are the most beautiful, most precious child of the entire universe.*"

His love is *not* conditional. He sees all of our cracks and brokenness, but He looks beyond them and to our core. He sees what we hide from others, even the stuff we hide from ourselves—pain, shame, self-defences, and our most primitive needs buried deep under the trash and broken shards of life. The naked truth.

It is not hard to put yourself in the room and imagine the feelings of discomfort and confusion of those watching this scene unfold. But Simon's reaction went beyond misunderstanding to condemnation. "If only you knew what kind of woman she is!"

Even today, many religious leaders endeavor to whitewash or even change this narrative. They gloss over this woman's character and water down the rare love exchanged between her and her Potter. The concept of a Christ who died for us does not make them cringe. Yet this same Savior looking into the eyes of His child in this manner does. *"You are my most beautiful, most precious child."*

Some preachers seem to worry about the Great Potter's reputation. Or perhaps they feel they should not let the sinner (especially a sinful *woman*) get off the hook so effortlessly and so do not show the Great Potter as compassionate as He is. Therefore, some simply claim that the prostitute in Luke 7:36–50 is *not* a prostitute but Mary of Bethany, Lazarus and Martha's sister and the Great Potter's highly respected disciple. They claim Luke's episode is the same one described in Mathew 26:6–13; Mark 14:3–19; and John 12:1–8.

It is not.

To alter the encounter between this weeping woman and the Great Potter and present her in any different light than what she was, we must ask how we can fall to our knees and worship at His feet yet be like Simon regarding this woman. It is sad if the pure love that poured between her and the Great Potter is so overwhelming that we must change the narrative to satisfy our puny image of the Great Potter.

This rare, real, exposed love should be irresistible, enticing, and tantalizing. A meeting between a sinner and her Redeemer is the greatest love story. The unfailing love poured from the Great Potter into this broken pottery while she pours her authentic, raw love onto Great Potter's feet should move us like no other love story.

This woman loved greatly and deeply because she was forgiven much. She came to the scene full of agony but left forgiven and at peace.

How beautiful is this? [22]

---

[22] After reading numerous contradictory opinions of Mathew 26:6–13; Mark 14:3–19; and John 12:1–8 episodes from many Bible Commentaries, I ended up concluding that although these accounts share similarities, they are in fact two different instances, with two different women, Jesus, and perfume.

(1) The dinner in Luke 7:36–50 takes place in Capernaum, Galilee, years before the Passover episodes. The dinner at which Mary of Bethany anoints Jesus before His burial takes place in Bethany, near Jerusalem, only three to six days before Passover.

(2) The host of Luke's dinner is Simon the Pharisee, while the other dinner host is Simon the Leper, most likely someone Jesus had healed and His disciple. Luke would not have confused him with a Pharisee.

(3) Luke's woman is introduced as the "woman who lives sinful life," which is discussed several times in the story. She is a prostitute. Matthew, Mark, and John introduce her as Mary of Bethany, Martha and Lazarus's sister, or simply a woman. — No mention of her living a sinful life or being a "sinful woman."

(4) Luke knew Mary of Bethany because he discusses her in Luke 10. If this woman were her, Luke would have mentioned her name.
(5) Luke's weeping woman cries like a waterfall, washing the Great Potter's feet with her tears and using her hair as a towel. Mary of Bethany does not cry but simply pours the perfume on Jesus's feet.
(6) In Luke, Simon the Pharisee is outraged because the Great Potter has the nerve to speak to and touch a prostitute. In contrast, Matthew, Mark, and John's dinner guests (disciples) are offended at the waste of money that could have been used to help the poor.
(7) In Luke, Jesus has a lengthy discussion about forgiveness of sins with the Pharisee, while in Matthew, Mark, and John, He declares His burial and reminds the disciples that they will always have the poor but He will no longer be with them.
(8) In Luke, Jesus chastises the host because the weeping woman washed his feet, something the host should have done but didn't. In Mark, Matthew, and John, He states that Mary poured the perfume in preparation for His burial.
(9) Jesus tells the weeping woman that her sins have been forgiven and that she can go in peace. He does not say anything like this to Mary of Bethany but declares that her anointing Him should be preached as a memory for her.
—Different scenes, different actors, different narrative, different message. Two different episodes.

CHAPTER 24

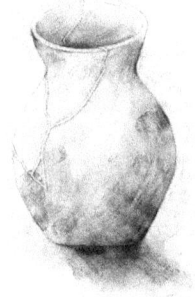

THE SAMARITAN WOMAN PREDESTINED TO MEET THE GREAT POTTER

But He needed to go through Samaria. So He came to a city of Samaria which is called Sychar, near the plot of ground that Jacob gave to his son Joseph. Now Jacob's well was there. Jesus therefore, being wearied from His journey, sat thus by the well. It was about the sixth hour. A woman of Samaria came to draw water.

Jesus said to her, "Give Me a drink."

For His disciples had gone away into the city to buy food.

Then the woman of Samaria said to Him,

"How is it that You, being a Jew, ask a drink from me, a Samaritan woman?"

For Jews have no dealings with Samaritans.

Jesus answered and said to her,

"If you knew the gift of God, and who it is who says to you, 'Give Me a drink,'

you would have asked Him, and He would have given you living water."

The woman said to Him, "Sir, You have nothing to draw with, and the well is deep.

Where then do You get that living water? Are You greater than our father Jacob,

who gave us the well, and drank from it himself, as well as his sons and his livestock?"

Jesus answered and said to her,

"Whoever drinks of this water will thirst again,

but whoever drinks of the water that I shall give him will never thirst.

But the water that I shall give him will become in him a fountain of waterspringing up into everlasting life."

The woman said to Him, "Sir, give me this water, that I may not thirst, nor come here to draw."

Jesus said to her, "Go, call your husband, and come here."

The woman answered and said, "I have no husband."

Jesus said to her, "You have well said, 'I have no husband,' for you have had five husbands, and the one whom you now have is not your husband; in that you spoke truly."

The woman said to Him, "Sir, I perceive that You are a prophet.

Our fathers worshiped on this mountain,

and you Jews say that in Jerusalem is the place where one ought to worship."

Jesus said to her, "Woman, believe Me, the hour is coming when you will neither on this mountain, nor in Jerusalem, worship the Father. You worship what you do not know; we know what we worship, for salvation is of the Jews. But the hour is coming, and now is, when the true worshipers will worship the Father in spirit and truth;

for the Father is seeking such to worship Him.

God is Spirit, and those who worship Him must worship in spirit and truth."

The woman said to Him, "I know that Messiah is coming" (who is called Christ).
"When He comes, He will tell us all things."
Jesus said to her, "I who speak to you am He."

The Whitened Harvest

And at this point His disciples came, and they marveled that He talked with a woman;
yet no one said, "What do You seek?" or, "Why are You talking with her?"
The woman then left her waterpot, went her way into the city, and said to the men,
"Come, see a Man who told me all things that I ever did. Could this be the Christ?"
Then they went out of the city and came to Him.
In the meantime His disciples urged Him, saying, "Rabbi, eat."
But He said to them, "I have food to eat of which you do not know."
Therefore the disciples said to one another, "Has anyone brought Him anything to eat?"

JOHN 4:4–33 (NKJV)[23]

The Samaritan woman was broken because of many hurts over the years. She'd been married five times and all had ended. Now she meets her Maker who acknowledges and restores her. She becomes a beautiful vessel for His service.

It is almost noon at the well-known Jacob's well in Samaria, surrounded by the city of Sychar. This was the well that Jacob had dug when he lived in the Shechem area long ago (Genesis 33:19). The well provided physical water, but today the Great Potter will explain that He has come to provide His children with living water that will quench their spiritual thirst. The Great Potter wisely sent His disciples into town for supplies. He does not need their disapproving looks and insensitive comments to hurt the woman He will soon meet at a divine therapeutic appointment planned ahead of time.

---

[23] *Read also*: John 4: 39-42.

The Great Potter sits and waits.

Here she is already coming carrying her water jar.

Many sermons suggest that this woman does not come to the well to draw water in the morning as all the other women are there, for even though the heat is brutal at noon, it is emotionally simpler not to deal with their looks, whispers, and hurtful statements. However, nothing in the text validates this notion. On the contrary, the passage refutes it.

I believe she often goes to the well in the morning with the other women. However, today she comes at noon because she has a divine appointment by the well with the Great Potter. He needs to meet her alone, without the other women, without His disciples. He has a personal message for her.

He has already chosen her to be His messenger.

For some reason, many religious teachers eagerly misalign this lady's character, willingly stamping her into some convenient class. It makes one wonder what it is with these preachers. It is easier to categorize this Samaritan woman with loose immoral character than as an overtly strong woman abused by the system, oppressed by men, yet *still* trying to preserve her sense of dignity—broken but carrying her hurt with poise.[24]

Perhaps she is a woman who irritated some folks for not knowing her place. Maybe she was a tad too bold, a little too smart, a bit too outspoken. She was too much something and not enough something else: not timid, not ashamed, not apologizing for her shadow. Instead, she dared to enter into dialogue with this Jewish teacher. No wonder this woman still irritates some preacher folk and is thus stamped as a "loose woman."

Admittedly, I quite like this Samaritan woman. She has spunk!

---

[24] Presenting certain Bible women in a certain light is an interesting phenomenon as it is an inconsistent application. Most of the time the light is determined based on *what looks better for men dealing with these women*. The same religious teachers who represent Rahab as the innkeeper, not as a prostitute, and ignore Ruth seducing drunk Moab, seem to have no problem lust-shaming Bathsheba for seducing poor David, although, in reality, David sexually exploited her.

That being said, I am sure this woman is aware that her life is not as it should be. She is not your average Sunday school poster child. Nothing went as she dreamed as a little girl. Nothing any mother would hope for their daughter, either. And she has been trying to cope as well as she can. She's cemented her broken pieces together, adding grout and glue to ensure they will not break, no matter how hard the next blow.

It's not appealing but resilient for sure.

No doubt she has adapted to the shocks and disappointments of life, being smashed again and again, and each time trying desperately to put it all together. Could anybody understand when one's hopes and dreams are crushed repeatedly? She fixed her pottery as well as she could. She made it strong.

I believe she doesn't mind coming to the well with the other women, but she does not heed their gossip about her. She is self-sufficient, taking care of herself as well as she can—self-reliant rather than trusting in those who fail. Too many blows too many times taught her that. And then her five husbands, all gone.

We don't know what happened to her husbands, whether they all died, they all divorced her, or a combination.[25][30] We can only speculate. But we know that all five marriages ended for one reason or another, and the implication was a nasty stigma of a woman who cannot keep her man.

---

[25] In the Bible times, barrenness was one common ground for divorce. It was seen as a curse as bearing children was a central role of married women. Moreover, a man without a son was also viewed as cursed. A childless Jewish scholar was not eligible to sit on the Sanhedrin and was limited in his business relations. However, it is unlikely that someone was divorced more than once because of not being able to bear children or because she could only deliver daughters rather than sons. Women were not allowed to initiate a divorce in that society. For men, on the other hand, it was pretty straightforward. If she finds no favor in his eyes and he has found some unsuitability in her, then he only needed to write her a certificate of divorce and put it in her hand while simply sending her out from his house (Deuteronomy 24:1-4). However, the Jewish rabbinical teaching condemned divorcing more than three times, and of course, the more often it happened, the greater the stamp of being 'damaged goods' became. [30]

It could also be that this woman at the well was widowed several times. Perhaps, she was a widow who married four brothers-in-law after her first husband died. It could be that after this, the family ran out of sons or the next in line simply refused to marry the woman with the black widow's reputation. She could also be a widow who had married her kinsmen (Deuteronomy 25:5-10; Ruth 4:1-17).

She would have been easily considered a castaway of society because the culture placed little value on women. They were considered property. But the Great Potter valued them as His beloved children.

We also know that her living arrangement is with a man who is not her husband, stigmatizing her further. As if there were any doubts, few sermons preached about this poor woman don't allude to our perception of her low moral character. But we can't forget that being a concubine was not immoral at this time. Ponder also that only the freeborn, not former slaves, could legally marry each other according to Roman marriage laws. There are numerous possibilities as to why this woman was not married to the man. Solely based on her vulnerable situation, it may have been the lesser of two evils. Divorced or widowed, women without male relatives could quickly end up as prostitutes to support themselves.

Although the popular slandering of this Samaritan woman is inappropriate, there's little doubt in the eyes of many folks that this woman is damaged goods, an outcast of some sort, oppressed for sure. Broken pottery for whom rejection and loss are "normal" may have sent her into depression. It's not unrealistic to believe that she did not see herself worthy of receiving love. Therefore, she did not trust people and did not need anything from anyone. She would not allow others to come too close, for she had to protect herself from being hurt further. Her grout-covered pottery appeared strong while hiding her tears and vulnerability. It was safer that way.

Breaking Taboos

Somehow, this woman carries her shame with dignity and a bit of royalty. It's evident in the way she speaks with the Great Potter: her head up, she asks thought-provoking questions and discusses with Him theological doctrines as if she is equal to Him. Something in her brokenness is almost venerating. She has an authentic honesty about her—beauty in the middle of the clay crumbles smashed over the years.

Her answers to the Great Potter's questions, without any embarrassment, indicates she is not a prostitute. She does not fall weeping at the Great Potter's feet like some other women did the moment He approached them. Furthermore, the Great

Potter neither tells her "your sins are forgiven" nor instructs her to "go and sin no more."

He acknowledges her hardships but never accuses her or blames her for them. When He mentions her past husbands and present living arrangement, He is not judging but only confirming that He knows her. There is no hint of sarcasm or ridicule about speaking half-truths or that she is a loose woman needing to repent. To the Great Potter, she is broken pottery, having been smashed many times.

The way the Great Potter treats this woman at the well is beautiful. He acknowledges her beauty despite her broken pieces resulting from difficult circumstances and gives her empathy and validation.

For this woman's sake, the Great Potter does many things that shatter cultural prohibitions. He purposefully stops in this Samaritan town; a place Jews would traditionally avoid because of prejudice. A single Jewish man discussing theology with a multi-married Samaritan woman in public breaks several taboos. It's not only the topic being discussed that is forbidden but also His speaking with a woman in public. Some Pharisees closed their eyes when passing by a woman on the street. Some started their day expressing thanks that he was neither a gentile, a slave, or a woman.

Indeed, this conversation is the most prolonged private exchange recorded in the New Testament. When the disciples returned, they question the Great Potter's behavior. For them, if conversing with women was socially inappropriate, debating with a Samaritan woman was insane. Didn't He know that this Samaritan woman was unclean? "A menstruant from the cradle," as the Babylonian Talmud put it. And anything she touched would become unclean for any Jew. But the Great Potter asked her to draw water from the well in her jar and give Him a drink. Shocking. The disciples know it. The woman knows it. The Great Potter knows they know it. But He does not care! I'm sure He chuckles a bit at the look on Peter's face when he tries to hide what he is thinking.

To the Great Potter, this woman is not unclean. She is not an outcast, not tarnished. To Him, she is beautiful, smashed but precious.

Unlike any other man, the Great Potter treats this woman as an equal. He discusses with her as if she has intellect, which validates her dignity and restores her value and more.

The Great Potter's discourse with this woman is on a similar metaphorical level as what He earlier discussed with Nicodemus, a prominent scholar, and the way He deliberates matters with his disciples (although they usually do not understand much of anything).

Remarkably, it is with this woman that He first openly reveals himself as the Messiah.

This simple woman, not Nicodemus or the disciples, understands what the Great Potter is saying. Just like the angels at Christmas night revealed the good news to the outcasts, so does the Great Potter.

Living Water

The conversation at the well between this oppressed clay pottery and the Great Potter is stunningly beautiful. He does what no other scholar of that time would have done, believing that teaching the Torah to women was so out of the question that one rabbi even said that the Torah should be burned rather than given to a woman.

"Will you give me a drink?"

"Sir, You are a Jew and I am a Samaritan woman . . . how can you ask *me* for a drink?"

"If you knew who I am, you would ask *me*, and I would give *you* living water."

"Sir, but you do not have a jar. The well is deep, so how will you draw this living water?"

"Whoever drinks the water I give them will never thirst. Indeed, the water I give them will become in them a spring of water welling up to eternal life."

And then she knows!

It is *this* water He speaks of that she desperately needs. Her self-fixed dry pottery thirsts for this living water. Oh, how weary she is of her fruitless efforts! Tired of being so strong and hiding her vulnerability.

"Sir, give me this water so that I won't get thirsty. I'm tired of coming here and drawing it myself. I'm tired of trying and failing to fix my broken pottery…, of pretending that I don't need anyone…, of pushing everybody away…, of being scared. I'm dying of thirst. Sir, give me this water!"

"*I am* the Messiah—*I Am He.*"

No wonder this woman drops her water jar, lifts her skirts, and hurries back to the town, inviting everyone she encounters to come to meet this Great Potter, the Messiah. And they come, and that day many believe because of this woman's testimony.

The Great Potter not only restores this oppressed woman's broken pottery but also makes her His beautiful vessel. She became the second evangelist of the gospel. The first were the shepherds running to Bethlehem on Christmas night. After her, countless others became followers of and evangelists for the Great Potter, many of whom were outcasts in the eyes of society.

None of this woman's broken pieces were wasted. The Great Potter restored them as new pottery. He made it glorious, and all the shame projected onto her broken pieces are wiped away. Everything changes for the woman at the well. With her pottery restored, she has a new identity in the One who rescued her and made her a beautiful vessel of evangelism.

How can you relate to this Samaritan woman? Do you also need a new identity from the Great Potter?

Go to Him and let Him restore you today.

CHAPTER 25

PETER PITIFULLY SMASHED AND REINSTATED

Peter declared, "Even if all fall away, I will not."
"Truly I tell you," Jesus answered,"
today—yes, tonight—before the rooster crows twice you yourself will disown me three times."
But Peter insisted emphatically, "Even if I have to die with you, I will never disown you."

MARK 14:29–31 (NIV)

They took Jesus to the high priest, and all the chief priests, the elders and the teachers of the law came together. Peter followed him at a distance, right into the courtyard of the high priest. There he sat with the guards and warmed himself at the fire. The chief priests and the whole Sanhedrin were looking for evidence against Jesus so that they could put him to death, but they did not find any. Many testified falsely against him, but their statements did not agree.

vv. 53–55

While Peter was below in the courtyard, one of the servant girls of the high priest came by. When she saw Peter warming himself, she looked closely at him. "You also were with that Nazarene, Jesus," she said. But he denied it. "I don't know or understand what you're talking about," he said, and went out into the entryway. When the servant girl saw him there, she said again to those standing around, "This fellow is one of them."
Again he denied it. After a little while, those standing near said to Peter, "Surely you are one of them, for you are a Galilean." He began to call down curses, and he swore to them, "I don't know this man you're talking about." Immediately the rooster crowed the second time. Then Peter remembered the word Jesus had spoken to him: "Before the rooster crows twice you will disown me three times." And he broke down and wept.

vv. 66–72

As they entered the tomb, they saw a young man dressed in a white robe sitting on the right side, and they were alarmed. "Don't be alarmed," he said. "You are looking for Jesus the Nazarene, who was crucified. He has risen! He is not here. See the place where they laid him. But go, tell his disciples and Peter, 'He is going ahead of you into Galilee.

16:5–7

"I'm going out to fish," Simon Peter told them, and they said, "We'll go with you."
So they went out and got into the boat, but that night they caught nothing.
Early in the morning, Jesus stood on the shore, but the disciples did not realize that it was Jesus.
He called out to them, "Friends, haven't you any fish?" "No," they answered.
He said, "Throw your net on the right side of the boat and you will find some."

When they did, they were unable to haul the net in because of the large number of fish.
Then the disciple whom Jesus loved said to Peter, "It is the Lord!"
As soon as Simon Peter heard him say, "It is the Lord," he wrapped his outer garment around him (for he had taken it off) and jumped into the water. The other disciples followed in the boat, towing the net full of fish, for they were not far from shore, about a hundred yards.
When they landed, they saw a fire of burning coals there with fish on it, and some bread. Jesus said to them, "Bring some of the fish you have just caught."
So Simon Peter climbed back into the boat and dragged the net ashore. It was full of large fish, 153, but even with so many the net was not torn. Jesus said to them, "Come and have breakfast." None of the disciples dared ask him, "Who are you?" They knew it was the Lord. Jesus came, took the bread and gave it to them, and did the same with the fish.
This was now the third time Jesus appeared to his disciples after he was raised from the dead. When they had finished eating, Jesus said to Simon Peter, "Simon son of John, do you love me more than these?"
"Yes, Lord," he said, "you know that I love you." Jesus said, "Feed my lambs."
Again Jesus said, "Simon son of John, do you love me?"
He answered, "Yes, Lord, you know that I love you." Jesus said, "Take care of my sheep."
The third time he said to him, "Simon son of John, do you love me?"
Peter was hurt because Jesus asked him the third time, "Do you love me?"
He said, "Lord, you know all things; you know that I love you." Jesus said, "Feed my sheep."

JOHN 21:3–17 (NIV)[26]

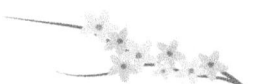

Peter bragged about his bravery and strength mere hours before shattering his pottery by his own hand. But the Great Potter beautifully restored his pottery. Later, the church was launched on the ruins of his rubble.

---

[26] *Read also*: Matthew 26:69-79; Luke 22:54-62; and John 18:15-18, 25-28.

Peter's clay pot shattered into a thousand pieces as the sad events of that first Good Friday unfolded. This rough and strong fisherman, refined by wind and storms, becomes timid and scared at the prodding of a young servant girl. Three times he denies his Master. Losing his composure, he curses and swears that he does not know the Great Potter. This from the disciple who only hours earlier had sworn his allegiance that *he* would never betray his Master even if everyone else did. Peter who, in defense of Jesus, unsheathed his sword and cut off a soldier's ear. Who only a short time before had walked on water in his flash of faith. Who had asked the Great Potter not only to wash his feet but all of him. Peter who was the first disciple who realized that Jesus is indeed the Messiah. (John 18:15–27; Matthew 36:69–75; John 21:15–18.)

Impulsive Peter. Brave Peter. Courageous Peter. Peter, the leader of the disciples.

As soon as Peter's third denial is out of his mouth, "the Lord turned and *looked right at Peter*. Then Peter remembered the word the Lord had spoken to him: "Before the rooster crows today, you will disown me three times" (Luke 22:61 NIV).

Oh, that look! His eyes full of pain looking right at him…

To realize he had denied his Master in His most desperate time of need was incomprehensible but to have the Great Potter *witness* his cursing and swearing while denying he ever knew Him must have been the crushing moment of Peter's pottery's composure. …The rooster crowed!

It is The End.

I'm Going Out to Fish!

Peter weeps bitterly, sobbing like a man who has just lost his kingdom and destiny, his calling and self-respect. Realizing what he has done, the last fragments of his clay pottery collapse. He has smashed his pottery and has no clue how the tiny crumbles could fit together. He moans like a man who has just betrayed his best friend and lost face with his brothers.

No doubt Peter would have been even more horrified had he been aware at the time that his denial would be recounted in all four gospels, word by word, and that billions of readers would learn about it even two thousand years later.

Do you know this feeling of standing in the middle of your smashed pot? Shards in your hand are evidence that it was you who threw it to the floor. A marriage in ruins. A family destroyed. A failed business. A career crashing in flames. Addictions. The shame, the looks, the hushed whispers are aimed at you alone.

Standing there, Peter figures that he is too tarnished to be a good enough vessel for the Master. His pieces are too crumbled ever to be fixed. Peter sees the reality of the situation. It's not worth the bother to try gluing his broken pieces together. Instead, he lets it be and gives up. He hangs up his sandals. "I may not be worthy as a fisher of men anymore, but the real fish don't care if some coward of a fisherman is trying to hook them."

So maybe he should go back to fishing. Back to the life he was familiar with before meeting the Great Potter and following Him. The Great Potter called him to follow Him about three years prior, but now he knows better. He doesn't measure up; he will never meet the bar; destined for greatness, he's a colossal flop.

But the angel at the tomb instructs Mary Magdala to tell the disciples *and* Peter to meet their Master in Galilee. *Why mentioning Peter separately?* Possibly Peter and the other disciples no longer considered him as one of the twelve.

Maybe—when receiving the angelic meeting-message, Peter believes it will be his day of reckoning to which he has been subpoenaed. The Judge will berate and disown him in front of the brethren, telling everyone what a cowardly creature he is, before shunning and banning him forever. Perhaps that's why Peter jumps from the boat and swims to the land when he sees the Great Potter standing there. Hoping the worst of the reprimand would be over before the others get there.

But he is so wrong!

Whatever Peter expected and feared was not what happened. It starts with hearty breakfast, which the Great Potter prepares for His disciples. They sit around the fire, just like in the old days. The disciples are full of questions, but Peter sits quietly, chewing the savory fish and avoiding the Master's gaze.

Heidi McKendrick

Take Care of My Sheep

The Great Potter takes Peter away, and they walk a bit farther up the shore. I've visited that lake and imagined Peter and the Great Potter sitting on the boulders by the water. Peter's heart pumping, his blood pressure rising, expecting the inevitable scolding and rebuke.

"Peter, do you love Me more than these?"

Oh, here we go. "Yes, Lord, You know that I love You." Peter hardly dares to raise his eyes to meet the Great Potter's.

"Feed My lambs."

Feed My… what? What does the Great Potter mean? Why would He trust me to feed his lambs? I publicly disowned him.

"Peter, do you love Me?"

The rebuke is coming for sure. "Yes, Lord, You know that I love You." *But does He know? Why would He think I love Him after what I did? After swearing that I never knew Him.*

"Take care of my sheep."

Puzzled, Peter lifts his eyes to meet the Great Potter's gaze. *Oh, that look!* Peter sobs quietly.

"Peter, do you love me?"

Oh, the pain because the Great Potter asks for the third time. What can he say to defend himself?

"Lord, *You know all things*; You *know* that I love You."

"Feed my sheep."

And that's it… No condemnation. No rebuke. No lecture. No shunning. No bans. No ordering any penalty bench. No conditions. No reprimand.

Instead, the Great Potter gives Peter a mission, a new assignment, and a new job. The first one, years ago, was to become a fisher of people. Now he is to take care of and feed His sheep. From a fisherman to a rancher, eh?

A fresh start! The broken pottery made new—a vessel for His service. Although Peter had given up on the Great Potter, the Great Potter had not given up on Peter.

Peter, feed My sheep. Take care of My lambs.
You know how they feel when they think they are lost for good...
When they weep in the darkness alone, assuming there is no going back,
when they are shivering in the cold in the night.
You know how it feels, Peter, don't you?

Isn't Peter's treatment different from what many failed potteries have experienced in several Christian churches? Is it different from what you have experienced?

How Do You Love Me?

John overheard this conversation. According to his report,[27] the Great Potter uses *agapao*-love in His first and second do-you-love-me-questions, but Peter uses *phileo*-love in *all* his You-know-I-love-you-answers. The Great Potter also uses *phileo*-love in His third question.[28] [31]

Agapao-love refers to the highest form of unselfish, unconditional, and self-sacrificial love, such as God's love towards people. *Phileo*-love refers to deep, tender, intimate affection between friends. The Bible scholars and commentaries debate what this means but it seems that the Great Potter (twice) asks Peter, if he loves Him with unconditional, unselfish, and self-sacrificial love. However, Peter both times responds that he loves Him as a dear friend. In His third query the Great Potter no longer probes after self-sacrificial love but simply confirms that Peter loves Him as a dear friend.

The level that Peter is able to love is *enough* for the Great Potter.

Interestingly, when Peter answers 'you *know* that I love you', he uses a term that refers a general knowing. However, in his third answer he also uses a term that means an *experiential* knowing: '*You know all things*; You *know* that I love You.' There he refers to the fact that the Great Potter personally saw and heard Peter

---

[27] Jesus and Peter discussed in Aramaic but John's gospel is written in Greek.
[28] *Agapao* [#25] refers to the highest form of unselfish, unconditional, and sacrificial love, such as God's love towards people. *Phileo* [#5368] refers to deep, tender, intimate affection between friends. *Oida* [#1492a] refers to general 'knowing,' perceiving. *Ginoskeis* [#1097] is experiential knowing, a knowledge that has been seen and experienced. [31]

denying Him on that horrible night before Good Friday—Peter knows He knows because He experienced what happened.

But Peter denying his Master never meant he didn't love Him. It merely meant he was scared.

Peter's *phileo*-love answers to the Great Potter's *agapao*-love questions imply he loves Him deeply, tenderly, and affectionally—The Great Potter *is* his dearest friend but Peter is no longer able to promise any self-sacrificial actions. Being a realistic square shooter, he no longer sees himself as a knight in shining armour, ready to be tortured, dying as a disciple or the last man standing. Lots of things have changed since that Thursday-night dinner when Peter was still swaggering in self-confidence.

I find it beautiful that Peter dares to be brutally honest in front of the Great Potter, and that He accepts his honesty as-matter-of-fact. The Great Potter does not demean Peter's *phileo*-love towards Him but receives it as precious. Peter seeing himself in a realistic light, not promising anything he is not ready to fulfil, does not diminish or change His calling. We need not to be hero-material in order to love the Great Potter, and have Him anointing our vessels for His service.

Interestingly, in John 21:18–19, the Great Potter indicates that in the end Peter will also love Him with *agapao*-love as he will die a martyr. All through the painful dialogue He saw the core of Peter, the very depths of his heart which even Peter was not willing to see at that point. While Peter saw himself scared and cowardly yet loving his Potter as his dearest friend, the Great Potter already recognized the seeds of *agapao*-love developing in his core.

The Great Potter always sees the depths of our heart—He sees the truth that even we may not be ready to see (1 Samuel 16:7). Most importantly, He accepts us '*as-is*'. None of us are too damaged, scared, or cowardly vessels for His Service.

He is not looking for polished super-hero-potteries but broken pieces!

Peter—Rock

And the Great Potter collects Peter's broken pieces and makes him a new pottery. A beautiful vessel for His service.

Only months after that, on the day of Pentecost, the day the church is founded, Peter rocks![29] Standing in front of thousands, testifying about his faith and preaching about the Great Potter and His plan for every broken pottery, Peter, the leader of the disciples, sounds fearless and clear with his message (Acts 2: 14–41). "Fellow Jews and all of you who live in Jerusalem, let me explain this to you; listen carefully to what I say…" (v. 14 NIV) "Therefore let all Israel be assured of this: God has made this Jesus, whom you crucified, both Lord and Messiah" (v. 36).

Peter understands the core of the gospel. "'He himself bore our sins' *in his body on the Cross, so that we might die to sins and live for righteousness;* 'by his wounds you have been healed'" (1 Peter 2:24 NIV).

Think about that. Despite Peter's miserable brokenness, the Great Potter continues to use his pottery. On the Day of Pentecost, its smashed clay crumbles become building blocks for His church's foundation when over three thousand are baptized. The Great Potter did not change His plans for Peter. He remained faithful despite Peter's unfaithfulness. "And I tell you that you are Peter, and on this rock, I will build my church" (Matthew 16:18 NIV). His name, Peter, still meant rock—even after his pottery was pitifully broken.

Do you have a false image of the Great Potter? Do you fear that He will reject or punish you for not measuring up, for not keeping your promises, for acting cowardly and denying or betraying Him? Do you mistakenly imagine Him banning and shunning your pottery? Do you see your broken pottery as not good enough or too cowardly for the Great Potter's service? Have you given up and gone back to whatever you were before He called you?

Perhaps because of the way other clay potteries in the church have treated you so poorly, you fear the Great Potter will treat you in the same manner, and you feel that you no longer have anything to offer other than your broken pieces and that you are not worthy of service to the Great Potter.

---

[29] The Greek word for *Peter* means "rock."

Even if you've given up on yourself, *He has not given up on you.* The Great Potter, whose character is love, grace, and mercy, will gather you to Himself, make you beautiful, and give you a purpose for service in His kingdom.

As He did for Peter's broken pottery, the Great Potter wants to do for you.

"Do you love Me?" He asks, calling your name with extraordinary tenderness. "_____ *[add your name]*, do you love Me as your dearest friend?"

"I have many vessels, but I am choosing *you* for *this* mission." His eyes sparkle as He continues. "I'm sending you to seek those who are hiding because they are scared… Those broken clay pieces scattered all around the trash yard of broken potteries, thinking they have no way back home. You *know* this because you have been there. I'm sending you to tell them that none of their broken pieces go wasted."

CHAPTER 26

JUDAS ISCARIOT SMASHED POTTERY AND SCAPEGOATED

Then the chief priests and the elders of the people assembled in the palace of the high priest, whose name was Caiaphas, and they schemed to arrest Jesus secretly and kill him. "But not during the festival," they said, "or there may be a riot among the people."

Matthew 26:3–5 (NIV)

Then one of the Twelve—the one called Judas Iscariot—went to the chief priests and asked, "What are you willing to give me if I deliver him over to you?"
So they counted out for him thirty pieces of silver.
From then on Judas watched for an opportunity to hand him over.

vv. 14–16

And while they were eating, he said, "Truly I tell you, one of you will betray me."
They were very sad and began to say to him one after the other,
"Surely you don't mean me, Lord?"
Jesus replied, ""The one who has dipped his hand into the bowl with me will betray me.
The Son of Man will go just as it is written about him.
But woe to that man who betrays the Son of Man!
It would be better for him if he had not been born."
Then Judas, the one who would betray him, said, "Surely you don't mean me, Rabbi?"
Jesus answered, "You have said so."

vv. 21–25

While he was still speaking, Judas, one of the Twelve, arrived.
With him was a large crowd armed with swords and clubs, sent from the chief priests and the elders of the people. Now the betrayer had arranged a signal with them:
"The one I kiss is the man; arrest him." Going at once to Jesus, Judas said,
"Greetings, Rabbi!" and kissed him.
Jesus replied, "Do what you came for, friend."
Then the men stepped forward, seized Jesus and arrested him. . . . But this has all taken place that the writings of the prophets might be fulfilled." Then all the disciples deserted him and fled.

vv. 47–50, 56

Early in the morning, all the chief priests and the elders of the people made their plans how to have Jesus executed. So they bound him,
led him away and handed him over to Pilate the governor.

*When Judas, who had betrayed him, saw that Jesus was condemned,
he was seized with remorse and returned the thirty pieces of silver to the chief priests and
the elders. "I have sinned," he said, "for I have betrayed innocent blood."
"What is that to us?" they replied. "That's your responsibility."
So Judas threw the money into the temple and left. Then he went away and hanged himself.
The chief priests picked up the coins and said,
"It is against the law to put this into the treasury, since it is blood money."
So they decided to use the money to buy the potter's field as a burial place for foreigners.
That is why it has been called the Field of Blood to this day.
Then what was spoken by Jeremiah the prophet was fulfilled:
"They took the thirty pieces of silver, the price set on him by the people of Israel,
and they used them to buy the potter's field, as the Lord commanded me."*

27:1–10[30]

Judas Iscariot thoroughly smashed his clay pottery. Then he tried to undo the damage but without success. Perhaps he was scapegoated by the other clay potteries who also failed the Great Potter and fled. Not finding any other solutions, he gave his pottery the final blow.

Four deaths are recorded on the first Good Friday. Three are killed on wood crosses by Roman soldiers' hands: two are criminals; the third is perfectly sinless and innocent; the fourth hangs himself.

His name is Judas Iscariot.

I wonder if anyone misses Judas Iscariot—mother, wife, siblings, children. Do any of his friends miss him? What about the remaining eleven disciples? After all, they had spent three years together following the Great Potter.

Was Judas Iscariot so much worse than the others?

Judas Iscariot betrayed his Master, but didn't Peter deny Him three times? Indeed, didn't all of the disciples flee that night, hiding after He was arrested? The Bible does

---

[30] *Read also*: Mark 14: 10–52; Luke 22: 1–53; John 13:18–30; 18:1–12.

not mention any of them being near when He carried His cross to Calvary. John and the women were at His crucifixion site, but the Bible does not mention the others' whereabouts during these events. They seemed to be drained of courage and scared to be recognized as His friends.

The women were not as scared. Nor were two of His secret disciples, Joseph of Arimathea and Nicodemus[31] who jeopardize their reputations and ask Pontius Pilate's permission to remove Jesus's body for burial. But the disciples were nowhere to be found (John 19:39–42).

Betrayal

According to the Merriam-Webster definition, "betrayal" is: *to deliver to an enemy by treachery* or *to fail or desert especially in time of need.*[32] Judas Iscariot was not the only disciple of the twelve who betrayed their Master; according to Matthew, "all the disciples deserted Him and fled" (26:56 NIV). They all failed Him that night. One of His followers even fled naked, leaving his clothes behind (Mark 14:51–52)!

None are present to support Him during His most grueling hours of suffering. They are not there because they are hiding, locked behind their doors, fearing that they, too, will be arrested. Even after hearing the news about His resurrection, they continue to hide so that the Great Potter has to come to them, passing through the closed door because they are too scared to open it even to Him.

It is sometimes convenient to focus on a scapegoat. Highlighting what this particular pottery did may make the others' responses look less significant, not as bad. But the sad fact is that all of His disciples deserted Him. Although Peter tried to protect Him with his sword, and John stood by the cross alongside His mother, none of them stood as a witness for Him before the Sanhedrin, although they *could* have. None of them defended Him when Pontius Pilatus questioned Him. None opened their mouths to shout to the crowd, "No! He is innocent!" If it were left

---

[31] Both men were Pharisees, and members of the Sanhedrin. Joseph of Arimathea was also Minister of Mines to the Roman government. Although, in many sermons wrongly characterized as coward approaching Jesus at night, this was not the first time Nicodemus stood up showing his courage. For example, John 7:32–51 describes him defending Jesus against the other Pharisees.

to them no one would have removed His body from the cross and buried it in the tomb.

It is comforting that the Great Potter's disciples, of whom eleven became the great apostles, are pretty much like most of us. No hero material. Not exactly brave either. They were broken into pieces by fear.

The earliest canonical Gospel writers Mark (Mark 14:10–11) and Matthew (Matthew 26:14–16) portray Judas's actions in a neutral tone, without interpreting his behavior. In contrast, both Luke (22:3) and John (13:27) seem to introduce him as demonic or possibly Satan himself. Sadly, only a few months later, Peter also bashes Judas badly (Acts 1:15–20). Had he forgotten that he failed the Great Potter by denying him? Lacking empathy for another vessel, broken strikingly similar to how his pottery had been, was he unaware of his bias, thus projecting onto Judas? Did he forget first to dig the tree trunk from his own eye?

Of course, possibly the four authors of the Gospels had a different perspective or different focus. As human beings, isn't it often easier to write about one who was evil personified, ruined, demonic, or the devil himself than to divulge that we *all* are capable of doing tremendous wrong? Perhaps Judas Iscariot, who was unable to defend himself, was a scapegoat, thus allowing others to feel better about themselves.[33] [32]

Judas' name, in many languages, is used as a synonym for *betrayer*. In art, he is stereotypically portrayed as red haired villain, and in literature his character as the archetype of the traitor. Interestingly, *"the names of children everywhere commemorated all the disciples, except Judas,' his name was always reserved for the antihero of the story. [...] It seems that since Luke and John's times, Judas' destiny became a cautionary tale of what happens to those who don't remain faithful to their group."* [34]

---

[32] The idea of Judas Iscariot being scapegoated is a topic discussed in many research articles and books, and even illustrated in various novels, poetry, screenplays, and Broadway musicals, such as Dante's Inferno, Shakespeare's Othello, Andrew Lloyd Webber's Jesus Christ Superstar (Lyrics Tim Rice), Bach's St. Matthew Passion, Philip Seymor Hoffman's The Last Days of Judas Iscariot. Judas (as well as Apostle Peter) is also portrayed in Dostojevski's Crime and Punishment. Interestingly, as Judas (Hebrew name Judah) was the only disciple originated from Judea, he also later became the stereotyped representation of all Jews, as a traitor and greedy thief; a similar scapegoating idea being visible during antisemitic persecution, i.e. the religious prejudice against Jews as 'Christ killers.'

I feel sorry for Judas Iscariot. I can imagine how devastated he must have felt. His betrayal led to his Master's arrest, torture, and death.

Friend, Why Have You Come?

It is interesting to note the Great Potter's reaction to Judas when he walks to Him from the garden's shadows. *"Friend, why have you come?"*

> What? What did He say to him?
> Did the Great Potter call Judas Iscariot his *friend*?
> How could He call him His friend when He *knew* why he had come to Him in the garden?
> Oh, Matthew must have misheard or misunderstood…

It was not a misunderstanding. The Great Potter indeed called Judas His friend. I can imagine the Great Potter's expression when He says this to Judas. It's "that" look, as if Judas was His most precious and beautiful child. Without judgment. *"I know why you've come. I've known it all along. And I want you to know that it does not change anything. You are my friend, Judas Iscariot."*

He *was* a friend of Judas.

He *is* a friend of Judases.

Did Judas see that look of love? Did He read the message from His eyes? "Greater love has no one than this: to lay down one's life for one's friends" (John 15:13 NIV). There is no greater love than the Great Potter's. How He gave his life for His friends. *Me, you, and Judas Iscariot.*

And later, didn't He also pray in a tremendous agony when they were nailing His feet and hands on the cross? *"Father, forgive them,* for *they don't know* what *they* are *doing"* (Luke 23:34 NIV).

Did He pray for Judas's forgiveness as well?

We know that Judas's clay pottery was smashed, broken into unrecognizable fragments, and crushed into the ground when he realized what he had done. Whatever reason for his betrayal—greed, money, irritation, or the disappointment of the kingdom not coming as they had all imagined—we do not know. However, based on his remorse afterwards, we do know he did not intend to get His Master condemned—questioned and straightened out perhaps, but not tortured and brutally crucified. After all, he was His friend.

It can be agony to comprehend the magnitude of the consequences of your actions. The cost is too high, the price too vast. Sitting in the middle of the pieces of your broken pottery and somehow trying to fix what you have just done, hoping to turn back the clock before time runs out. You have just released the tragedy, the avatar, the perfect storm, and you know that if you cannot fix it right now, it will be too late and disastrous.

Perhaps there's a bit of Judas in all of us. Haven't we all done something we wish we hadn't? Something we were not able to undo, thus we broke our own pottery and ruined innocent potteries around us.

Judas Iscariot was *trying* his hardest to undo what he had done. Seized with remorse, he hurries to the chief priests and elders, and returns the blood money he received. He tries to make them change their minds about His verdict, to make them release Him. *"I have sinned, for I have betrayed innocent blood."*

I have sinned. I have betrayed. He is innocent.

However, it was too late.

"What is that to us?" The priests replied, shrugging their shoulders. "That's *your* responsibility."

It seems a simple matter to transfer our responsibility to someone else's shoulders, to wash our hands of it. Wouldn't it be easier if we all could simply blame Judas Iscariot?

And yet, wasn't Judas the only one on that Good Friday who openly disclaimed both, Jesus' innocence and his personal responsibility for the episodes? Herod Antipas did not take any responsibility; Pontius Pilatus washed his hands. Nobody else stepped in to declare Jesus innocent in front of the Sanhedrin and the High Priest, but Judas. Nobody else regretted their guilt.

I wish Judas Iscariot had understood that the Great Potter is never tired of giving new starts, always willing to forgive anything. He is ready to collect our broken remains—even if our blow breaks other potteries too, even if our explosion destroys the entire oven of potteries.

Father, Forgive Him, for He Doesn't Know What He Is Doing

And Judas Iscariot does what he can—throws the money, the thirty silver coins, to the ground and runs away in throbbing agony, trying to escape his horror and despair. Regret and remorse fill his body and mind. Fleeing blindly in shock as if it is a nightmare that does not stop.

One thought pounds in his mind like the hammer that nails his Master to the cross at the same time.

> *My responsibility.*
> Mine only.
> I've sinned.
> I've betrayed.
> *My responsibility.*
> He is innocent.
> I'm a murderer.
> *My responsibility.*
> I've betrayed my friend.

A burden of guilt and responsibility crushes him. He knows it was he who caused his loved one to suffer. This knowledge is too heavy for Judas Iscariot to carry. He can never forgive himself. "How could I live with this load another day? How could I carry this burden even another hour?"

Around the same time as his Master collapses under the weight of the wooden cross, Judas Iscariot buckles under the weight of his sin and responsibility and gives up living.

Oh, if only he knew that in that very moment, His Master was praying. "*Father, forgive him, for he doesn't know what he is doing.*" Just as He prayed for all of us at that moment, for all those times we failed Him.

We do not know what happened for sure as Matthew and Luke write about the episode differently. He either hanged himself (Matthew 27:5) or fell headlong from the cliff (Acts 1:18). If only had he still been alive on Resurrection Sunday! If Judas Iscariot had still been alive, the angel at the garden tomb would have asked Mary Magdala to tell the disciples, Peter, *and Judas.*

Judas Iscariot would have had a similar meeting with the Great Potter at the lake of Gennesaret after breakfast. There would have been a beautiful restoration of Judas Iscariot's broken pottery, just as there was a restoration of Peter's.

How do I know? Because even if we are faithless, He remains faithful. And He remains faithful because He cannot deny himself (2 Timothy 2:13).

Why Did He Die?

Judas Iscariot was the first to acknowledge *his part* in the Great Potter's death. He was the first to understand and confess his guilt. Of course, after him, millions of people have understood their guilt, too. *Do you understand your guilt?*

It was *not* Judas Iscariot who killed Christ, nor the crowd demanding He be crucified, not even the Roman soldiers nailing Him on the cross. It wasn't even those nasty nails either… It was *all of us*. And it was *His choice*. It was all according to the Great Potter's divine plan, His sacrifice. It was all because of His unfailing love.

> You see, at just the right time, when we were still powerless, *Christ died for the ungodly.* Very rarely will anyone die for a righteous person, though for a good person someone might dare to die. "But God demonstrates His own love toward us, in that while we were *still* sinners, Christ died for us. (Romans 5:8 NIV)

Do you fully comprehend why He died on that cross? "But He was wounded for our transgressions, He was bruised for our iniquities; The chastisement for our peace was upon Him, And by His stripes we are healed" (Isaiah 53:5 NKJV).

Because He died and was resurrected, we have hope, and our broken pottery can be restored. *Because He lives, we can face tomorrow,*[35] and even our past mistakes.

"For God did not send his Son into the world to condemn the world, but that the world through him might be *saved*" (John 3:17 NKJV).

The Great Potter knew Judas Iscariot when he was in his mother's womb, just as He knew us. The Great Potter knew what Judas would do. Old Testament prophets wrote of it also. However, Jesus made no mistake in choosing Judas as a disciple. And no, I don't think he was selected so that he could become the perfect scapegoat![33] *There are no scapegoats needed in the Great Potter's kingdom.* The perfect Lamb has already been sacrificed to cover the sins of the world. "All have turned away, they have together become worthless; there is *no one* who does good, *not even one*" (Romans 3:12 NIV). We all have failed and deserted Him one way or another. But we can all be forgiven because of His never-ending grace; "for *all* have sinned and fall short of the glory of God, being justified freely by His grace through the redemption that is in Christ Jesus" (Romans 3:23–24 NKJV).

What does Judas Iscariot's story speak to you? Have you sometimes felt that there is no hope left? Have you become exhausted under the weight of your guilt and remorse? Here's some good news: "But where sin increased, *grace increased all the more*" (Romans 5:20). It does not matter what you have done. *The Great Potter's grace is never-ending.* You simply need to receive it as a gift.

Perhaps, Judas Iscariot's story speaks to you about a loved one's suicide and triggers emotions and unanswered questions. Maybe you've been left to hold an unnecessary stigma, guilt, or shame although, in reality, your loved one simply died after a long, painful illness that she or he may have suffered and battled for years. Remember, as the Great Potter sees every one's heart, He also knows the agony, stress, depression,

---

[33] "Aaron shall lay both his hands on the head of the live goat, confess over it all the iniquities of the children of Israel, and all their transgressions, concerning all their sins, putting them on the head of the goat, and shall send it away into the wilderness by the hand of a suitable man. The goat shall bear on itself all their iniquities to an uninhabited land; and he shall release the goat in the wilderness" (Leviticus 16:21–22 NKJV).

and despair often present before committing suicide. He sees, and we can rest on *the assurance* that His grace is *always* sufficient, *for all situations,* and for all of us. Remember that nothing can separate us from the love of the Great Potter.

The priests took the money Judas threw at their feet and purchased the potter's field, Hinnom Valley, south of Jerusalem. The potter's field became the graveyard for foreigners who died while in Jerusalem—a resting place for outsiders. This is comforting to know that the former potter's field became the resting place of broken potteries, a place for them to wait for the final call to the new beginning and the new time: the final restoration.

CHAPTER 27

PAUL THE PHARISEE BROKEN BUT POLISHED

The Damascus Road: Saul Converted
Then Saul, still breathing threats and murder against the disciples of the Lord, went to the high priest and asked letters from him to the synagogues of Damascus, so that if he found any who were of the Way, whether men or women, he might bring them bound to Jerusalem.

*As he journeyed he came near Damascus,
and suddenly a light shone around him from heaven.
Then he fell to the ground, and heard a voice saying to him,
"Saul, Saul, why are you persecuting Me?"
And he said, "Who are You, Lord?"
Then the Lord said, "I am Jesus, whom you are persecuting.
It is hard for you to kick against the goads."
So he, trembling and astonished, said, "Lord, what do You want me to do?"
Then the Lord said to him, "Arise and go into the city, and you will be told what you must do."
And the men who journeyed with him stood speechless, hearing a voice but seeing no one.
Then Saul arose from the ground, and when his eyes were opened he saw no one.
But they led him by the hand and brought him into Damascus.
And he was three days without sight, and neither ate nor drank.*

Ananias Baptizes Saul
*Now there was a certain disciple at Damascus named Ananias;
and to him the Lord said in a vision, "Ananias." And he said, "Here I am, Lord."
So the Lord said to him,
"Arise and go to the street called Straight, and inquire at the house of Judas for one called Saul of Tarsus, for behold, he is praying. And in a vision he has seen a man named Ananias coming in and putting his hand on him, so that he might receive his sight."
Then Ananias answered,
"Lord, I have heard from many about this man, how much harm he has done to Your saints in Jerusalem. And here he has authority from the chief priests to bind all who call on Your name."
But the Lord said to him,
"Go, for he is a chosen vessel of Mine to bear My name before Gentiles,
kings, and the children of Israel.
For I will show him how many things he must suffer for My name's sake."
And Ananias went his way and entered the house; and laying his hands on him he said,
"Brother Saul, the Lord Jesus, who appeared to you on the road as you came,*

has sent me that you may receive your sight and be filled with the Holy Spirit."
Immediately there fell from his eyes something like scales, and he received his sight at once;
and he arose and was baptized.
So when he had received food, he was strengthened.
Then Saul spent some days with the disciples at Damascus.

Saul Preaches Christ
Immediately he preached the Christ in the synagogues, that He is the Son of God.

Acts 9:1–20 (NKJV)

Paul the Pharisee's pottery[34] is shiny outside, polished, and perfect, with no visible cracks. Admirable, self-sufficient, self-righteous but completely broken inside. Meeting the Great Potter is life-altering. It changes Paul's destiny.

Everyone who saw Paul the Pharisee's pottery admired its refined, scholarly looks, sharp mind, and deep devotion. It was polished clay, glazed with classic decorations, nothing too much, simply perfect. A highly educated Pharisee, he is elegant and distinguished by strict observance of the law. What fine pottery it is!

And why not? Since childhood, he has mastered the art of concealing cracks, repairing, polishing, and perfecting his appearance. Once giving his pledge to his brotherhood, Paul was consumed every waking moment with observing the minutest aspect of the law. He was a Hebrew of Hebrews; a Pharisee born from Pharisees.

Devout Paul tried to follow all of the legal traditions ascribed in the Talmud and Torah, as well as rules of the codified scribal law: 613 commandments of the Mosaic law (365 negative commands and 248 positive laws). The Mishnah, the oral tradition of Jewish law and the first part of the Talmud, that contained thousands of new ordinances created to clarify the original commandments.[36] Rigorously

---

[34] Paul is his Latin and Greek name, whereas Saul of Tarsus is his Hebrew (Jewish) name. Paul was born in Tarsus, and he was Roman citizen. In this chapter, I call him Paul.

following the many layers of complicated regulations, performing prayers a certain way, fasting frequently, carefully observing ritual purity, while becoming fanatical about his and others' cleanliness was Paul the Pharisee's life. He "was advancing in Judaism beyond many of [his] own age among [his] people and was extremely zealous for the traditions of [his] fathers" (Galatians 1:13 NIV).

No doubt, Paul is the impeccable Pharisee. Overtly legalistic and ritualistically obsessed with his pottery's strict outward manifestation, he wears his phylacteries with his tassels conspicuous. Paul may close his eyes when women pass on the street. He may start every morning thanking he was not born a slave, a woman, or like those miserably broken and unwashed potteries unfit for use. Paul could have been sitting in the synagogue's best seat, sitting in honor at banquets, and wearing pretentious clothing. He likely blew his own trumpet when giving for the poor. He is so observant of the law that he even tithes the herbs and spices from his garden. I wonder if Paul is also the hypocrite, straining at a gnat but swallowing a camel (Matthew 23:15–22). Or perhaps he judges himself as he judges others, demanding an equally perfect performance from everyone.

Healthy Don't Need a Doctor...

If Paul is such an accomplished and impeccable pottery, you may wonder why I have included him in a book of broken potteries. It seems he would be a better fit for the edition titled *Prototypes of the Perfect Pottery*. Incongruous as it may sound, my impression of Paul the Pharisee is that he is the most miserably broken pottery presented so far. Prodigious façade with a dreary and wretched core. A whitewashed tomb.

> Woe to you, teachers of the law and Pharisees, *you hypocrites*! You are like *whitewashed tombs*, which look beautiful on the outside but on the *inside are full of the bones of the dead and everything unclean.* In the same way, on the outside you appear to people as righteous but on the inside you are full of *hypocrisy and wickedness.* (vv. 27–28 NIV)

This pottery is more miserable than any other presented so far because it completely denies it is broken and therefore rejects any help. These are the potteries the Great Potter refers to when He declares that healthy potteries do not need a doctor but only sick potteries do (Luke 5:31). He did not mean that the potteries are so healthy they do not need inner healing; rather, He meant that some potteries, in their self-sufficient piety, *falsely* think they do not need it. In their self-righteousness, they believe that by their works, following the law, they have salvation. Therefore, they do not need grace, mercy, or reconciliation.

No doubt, some Pharisee potteries would be deeply offended if somebody were to claim that *they* need the Great Potter's gift of grace. With their squeaky-clean credit, perfect performance, a lengthy list of good works, and evidence of a lifelong sin-avoiding behavior, why would they need a Savior? Unmerited grace is for vagabonds and beggars who have no merits of their own and cannot hope to earn their wages. Hardworking Pharisees will have no problem collecting their well-deserved salary. Suggesting a free grace handout is simply a shameful and insulting proposition!

Of course, this is a sad position. As these delusional broken potteries believe they are perfectly healthy without the "need" of a doctor, they have missed the basics of the gospel. Just as Paul the Pharisee hated the gospel of grace, reconciliation without works, and righteousness without law when he persecuted the early Christians, the modern legalistic teachers intensely dislike the Great Potter's unmerited grace and unconditional love. They do not focus their messages on those topics as doing so would liberate their congregations' potteries, and the preachers might lose their control over them. The Great Potter had some harsh words for them: "Woe to you, teachers of the law and Pharisees, *you hypocrites! You shut the door of the kingdom of heaven in people's faces. You yourselves do not enter, nor will you let those enter who are trying to*" (Matthew 23:13 NIV). He did not sugar-coat the situation: "Truly I tell you, the tax collectors and the prostitutes are entering the kingdom of God ahead of you" (21:31).

Paul the Pharisee, like many legalists, held a false idea of the Great Potter. Getting so gritty with the law, they missed the big picture. They did not understand the Great Potter's everlasting love and never-ending grace because they never experienced it. So adamant were they in following their works-based salvation, they neglected the Great Potter's grace thus leading other potteries astray as well, burdening them instead of liberating them. However, after meeting the Great Potter, Paul no longer despised His grace: "I do not set aside the grace of God, for *if righteousness could be gained through the law, Christ died for nothing!*" (Galatians 2:21 NIV). The Great Potter's grace is not for us to earn; it is there for us to accept.

The Older Brother-Syndrome

Sadly, many churches are full of broken potteries who suffer the same syndrome as one of the characters in a parable Jesus spoke to the scribes and the Pharisees. In the story of the prodigal son, the older brother is infuriated with his father because, unlike his brother, he has served his father and obeyed all the rules. He feels deep bitterness because his brother, who had squandered his inheritance on riotous living, is now not only savoring his father's unmerited grace as a gift but is the centre of celebration and recognition (Luke 15:11–13). Without speculating how the older brother knew about his brother's ungodly living while away, I sadly point out that it was the elder brother's *choice* to see himself as an unfairly treated servant and slave instead of claiming his rightful place as his father's son and fully authorized heir.

> *Look!* All these years *I've been slaving for you and never disobeyed your orders.* Yet you never gave me even a young goat so I could celebrate with my friends. But when *this son of yours* who has squandered your property with prostitutes comes home, you kill the fattened calf for him! (vv. 29–30 NIV)

It was also the older brother's choice *not to enjoy* the estate that was available to him. "'My son,' the father said, 'you are always with me, and *everything I have is yours*'" (v. 31). Although everything his father had was also his, yet the older brother behaved as if he had no right to it. The distorted image of his father led him to believe that he had to earn his keep. He mistakenly believed that he had to work to please him whom he thought was unpleasable and made no allowance for fun. This distortion was so complete that the older brother failed to understand that his father saw both him and his brother as *precious sons*. Ironically, both brothers misused their inheritance. The younger one threw it away while the older brother ignored it. *Refusing to enjoy it, touch it, use it, not even taste it, he falsely believed he did not even have it.* This is how some people growing up in a legalistic church community feel. Their legalistic prison cell is locked, but, in reality, they are free to leave. Instead, they choose to just sulk in their cells.

Many Christian potteries do not admit to being broken, such as Paul the Pharisee or the prodigal son's older brother. They keep working to perfect their whitewashed potteries while ignoring what is inside: broken pots held together with white chalk, polished and shiny outside (the cracks and fractures are carefully hidden) as they work to keep up appearances. Their worship of the Great Potter "is based on merely *human rules* they have been taught" (Isaiah 29:13 NIV). They ignore red flags in their lives: tension, stress, burnout, and worrying at night if they are doing enough, being enough.

What if this incredibly religious pottery with the right pedigree, this absolute model Jew, is not enough? "Circumcised on the eighth day, of the people of Israel, of the tribe of Benjamin, a Hebrew of Hebrews; in regard to the law, a Pharisee; as for zeal, persecuting the church; as for righteousness based on the law, faultless" (Philippians 3:5–6 NIV). Paul, a sincere Pharisee, was sincerely misguided.

A Model Member?

No doubt Paul the Pharisee would be a model member in many congregations. He never questions authority, even when the leaders are hiding blatant wrongdoings, even crimes. He would think that he had no right to criticize the self-righteous leaders who call themselves "God's anointed". He might also feel that it would be his Christian duty to keep up appearances, even sweeping dirt (sin) under the carpet to ensure the worldly outsiders see only the polished image of his pious righteous community. No doubt, he would be the member who obeys the rules, written and unwritten, without hesitation. Accepting without reserve the leadership controlling his time, money, hairstyle, even pronouncing what the Great Potter's will for his life, education, job, or marriage is. Of course, as a model member, he never misses any church gatherings, is the first to arrive at the early morning prayer meeting and the last to leave the evening assembly. He willingly serves on every board and committee, does kitchen duty, does not calculate his hours, and tithes generously. He is enthusiastic about declaring the "truth" as his group is *the only one* getting it right. Other groups, even those with similar doctrines, have it wrong as they are not holy enough, not devoted enough—just not enough.

Paul the Pharisee may see it as his Christian duty to spy on the other potteries' walks and report those who do not follow the rules or are about to go astray. He shuns and bans and smashes those who do not live up to the criteria and projects onto others his own secret or unconscious flaws. Did he also look for a reason to accuse just like the modern day pharisees do whenever something or somebody does not agree with *their* particular perspectives?

Say 'NO' to legalism—Let the Truth Liberate You!

In my grace-focused ministry, I long ago realized the reality of the old saying: the dogs bark but the caravan goes on. Sounds a bit harsh but sadly, in many Christian communities the legalistic spirit of the pharisees is alive and well. Their advocates are loud and outrageous, and have no fear breaking potteries under their jurisdiction; hiding the fact that the truth is supposed to liberate them. The only way to avoid getting verbally lynched as 'free-grace-heretical', 'false apostle' or 'jezebel' would be to pipe down and quit preaching the gospel. At the beginning of a church service, (in the middle of a series of my grace-filled seminars in a foreign country), I was told: "you've already infected too many churches with this message therefore we will not allow you to speak today." I must admit, it felt almost surreal when my husband had to go and collect my PowerPoint projector and laptop from the pulpit in front of the congregation of hundreds, before being escorted out. However, afterwards I've been comforted by the idea that at least

I got the chance to 'infect' several groups before being silenced.—We all know how fast infections spread! Similarly, if this book contaminates someone with the Great Potter's *completely* unconditional love and never-ending grace, then the mission of the book was clearly accomplished!

Perhaps your childhood church was legalistic and taught a works-based salvation such as what I have described. The Bible-banging, narcissistic "spiritual" leaders used fearmongering to control the congregants; they discredited and gagged anybody who taught anything opposite. Possibly some of them did not *mean* to be abusive but were simply misled themselves, repeating what they had been taught. Nevertheless, your pottery took the toll and suffered the consequences of insecurity, fears, anxiety, and completely distorted idea of the Great Potter. Maybe this describes the church you are attending now, which is filled with whitewashed, self-perfected, tight-haloed potteries— snooping, shaming, and silencing.

If your pottery never cracked, suffocated, starved, and demolished because of legalistic teaching, be blessed and joyful that you were spared! But remember do feel empathy for those who were not so fortunate.

What if a little Pharisee is sitting inside all of our clay potteries? Our broken potteries then become stuck in legalistic mind-sets in which everything is based on fulfilling human-designed regulations or traditions. We believe in the Great Potter's reconciliation on the Cross but deep inside we think we need to *earn* our position with Him through our achievements. Or maybe we were saved by grace but believe it is our conduct that will *keep* us saved.

Like the Pharisees, we often miss the main point.

If we misunderstand the Great Potter's love and grace, *we misunderstand everything* He taught. Remember, the Great Potter never aims to load shame or humiliation on His clay potteries. *He desires to liberate them.* Contrary to the Pharisees, it is *never* the Great Potter's intention for any of His potteries to be stoned because of their failures.

Yet too many broken potteries have been smashed by the churches that follow these legalistic policies; fatally wounded in the name of religion, spiritual abuse, and then left to die, believing they no longer have access to the Great Potter. No wonder many potteries have left the church, walking away from the gospel because of those who have twisted it into something else.

If this is you, know this: *The Great Potter has not thrown your broken pieces away*, nor will He ever! Even if you believe *you* cast the Potter away along with your broken pieces, He indeed *has not gone anywhere*; rather, He is ready to restore your pottery as soon as you give Him your consent.

I hope you understand that the image of the Great Potter portrayed by legalistic and spiritually abusive church communities is distorted and false. *It is not who the Great Potter is*. In a Christian church, there should be no legalism, no works-based salvation, no spirit of Pharisees, and no abuse in the name of God as *it is right from hell* (Matthew 23:15). Interestingly, although the Israeli society two thousand years ago had many social problems and injustice, the Great Potter never stood against anything but the damaging impact of the legalistic Pharisees and their turning the church into a marketplace. The Great Potter loudly voiced His disgust of their abusing His potteries, controlling their lives on every level, and forcing them to obey their rigid rules. The Pharisees claimed that *they* represented God on earth and were God's anointed to prevent any criticism of their actions, but their lives and attitudes were contrary to the Great Potter and His mission. The Great Potter has nothing to do with legalism nor 'industrialized religious complexes' that only seek to exert control, monetary gain and profit. The works-based salvation is *not* His doctrine but theirs who indeed, in their piousness, do not even need Him.

However, the Great Potter *desires* to liberate legalists too, just like He liberated Paul the Pharisee! *He loves them also.*

Spiritual Blindness

Paul the Pharisee was on a crusade to do the Lord's work. Paradoxically, he had devoted his whole life for the Great Potter before he had even met Him! Isn't this typical in many legalistic settings even today?

The spirit of religion that goes through the motions of doing right and follows a checklist of activities and duties or pottery-made traditions has nothing to do with worshipping the Great Potter. He does not want His vessels to serve Him out of guilt or fear but purely out of love. Being trapped in a legalistic religion creates a delusion for the potteries. Though they are broken and spiritually blind, they have been so duped that they deny they are broken; in fact, they don't realize they are broken. Although it may look the opposite—perfect and polished—it is still miserably broken at the core. They do not understand their self-polishing is nothing but filthy rags in the eyes of the Great Potter (Isaiah 64:6). The legalistic broken pottery is a sad phase, denying their desperate need for the Great Potter.

> Jesus said, 'For judgment I have come into this world, *so that the blind will see and those who see will become blind.*' Some Pharisees who were with him heard him say this and asked, 'What? Are we blind too?' Jesus said, 'If you were blind, you would not be guilty of sin; but *now that you claim you can see, your guilt remains.*' (John 9:39–41 NIV)

Some could argue that Paul the Pharisee had more spiritual insight than most. But according to the Great Potter, Paul was as spiritually blind as a dead man; he mistakenly thought he had perfect vision—a dangerous combination, especially for someone who does not admit they are blind and appoints himself to serve as others' guide.

If you are currently in a legalistic church community, the Great Potter's advice is very clear: "*Leave them*; they are blind guides. If the blind lead the blind, *both will fall into a pit*" (Matthew 15:14 NIV).

We know what happened to Paul the Pharisee when he dramatically meets the Great Potter while traveling on Damascus's dusty road. As spiritually blind, not understanding he needed healing, he had to lose his distorted vision to see the Great Potter and his broken pottery in the true light. Paul's self-constructed, whitewashed walls had to crumble for him to realize how broken his pottery was and how much he needed the Great Potter's grace and divine restoration. His pottery's shell had to be exposed in the Great Potter's divinely bright light so that the clay crumbles could be genuinely washed. However, during this process at the Great Potter's table, Paul's pottery is fully restored as a beautiful vessel for His service.

The Great Potter opens Paul's eyes to finally see how blinded his pretended vision had been, how smashed his pottery is, and how desperately He needs *true* vision and healing. As Paul receives the Great Potter's grace on His table and learns the truth about Him, he receives his new purpose: to be the preacher of grace to gentiles. He became the most potent purveyor of the Great Potter's grace. Two thousand years later, we still read his blatant writings against legalism and self-righteousness in which he calls the legalistic potteries nothing less than foolish and bewitched (Galatians 3:1).

He Will Give You Rest

If your pottery is trapped in legalism's white-chalked shell, the Great Potter wants to liberate you. He invites all who are burdened because of any performance-oriented religion to come to Him. "Come to Me, all *you* who labor and are *heavy laden*, and I will give you rest" (Matthew 11:28 NKJV). *He wants to give us rest!*

Can you imagine no more burdensome tasks, no more to-do lists, but merely rest in Him? He did the work that bought our salvation; *there's nothing left for us to do but to believe and accept His free gift.* This rest is essential for the restoration and reinstatement of any clay potteries. For ex-legalistic clay potteries, the rest is life-altering. How the Great Potter introduces Himself here is beautiful: ". . . for I am gentle and lowly in heart, and you will find rest for your souls" (v. 29).

How different from the Pharisees and other self-righteous religious potteries—gentle and humble in heart. No harsh words, no rebuking those who are already burdened. This is nothing like Pharisees' crushing and unbearable religious demands; they never lift a finger to help ease the burden (23:4).

And what is it that the Great Potter says about His yoke? "For My yoke *is* easy and My burden is light" (v. 30). We do not need to try to earn His love or grace by chuffing, wheezing, drudging, and hard labor. It is not only that He restores our broken pottery but also that we exchange our false image of Him for the correct image.

An easy yoke and a light burden: because He carried all of the burdens to the cross and in the cross, we now learn from Him by taking His yoke, *with Him*. The picture is of two oxen yoked together: a stronger, experienced ox and a younger, weaker ox. The stronger ox carries the burden! This is what the Great Potter does for us. He gives His never-ending grace; He carries the yoke for us. There is no need to burden ourselves with any religious demands. "It is for freedom that Christ has set us free" (Galatians 5:1 NIV).

With gentleness and no violence, the Great Potter invites us. Light yoke. No more performance-based burdens under which we will collapse sooner or later. Instead, grace is a gift; we can do nothing to earn it. It's already paid; we don't have to pay it afterward! Grace is even for those of us broken by legalism.

In the parable of the prodigal son, two potteries were equally lost. However, the father does not rebuke either of them. He humbly leaves his house for both of their sakes: for the younger son, when he sees him approaching from a long way off, and for the elder son when he goes out and pleads with him to come inside the house. The father does not judge either of his sons but offers his love for the pottery who broke himself in the foreign land and for the son trapped in legalism while living in his estate.

The Great Potter desires to reconcile His potteries to Himself: those openly smashed by their own hands, like the prodigal son, and those pretending to be perfect and polished, like the elder brother or Paul the Pharisee. He loves them equally! He feels empathy for both of them! Both of them have a place at the Potter's House, on His table. He wants to collect our broken pieces and make our pottery new. He wants to clean away all the filth, dirt, and wax polish; welcome us back home, and make us a unique and beautiful vessel for His service. Over the years, I've heard many testimonies of 'returning' prodigal sons' but not so many of returning older brothers. Our Father is waiting for all of us!

Heidi McKendrick

PART 3

SECRETS OF BROKEN POTTERY

Heidi McKendrick

INTRODUCTION

If only I knew where to find him; if only I could go to his dwelling!"
I would state my case before him and fill my mouth with arguments.
I would find out what he would answer me, and consider what he would say to me.

JOB 23:3–5 (NIV)

Bad stuff does happen to decent clay potteries, and we all break one way or another. There isn't any who hasn't questioned why the good and Sovereign Great Potter allows all this pitiful agony and not simply stop the torment for His clay pots.

It's not that your pottery *isn't* going to break; it's the aftermath that matters—what you *choose* to do with your broken pottery. Do you let that brokenness define the rest of your life or do you trust the Great Potter to launch the restoration process?

Some potteries are smashed beyond comprehension yet inducing the insight of the ages: *What else* is there *but* to trust the Great Potter, even in the trash yard of the broken potteries? To rest during the distinct phases at the Potter's House, whether waiting on His shelf, being marred on His wheel, or fired in the oven.

Trusting that…

- He has come to seek those who are lost.
- He will find my broken pieces and collect them.
- He will never forsake my pottery.
- None of my pieces go wasted.
- His hands are skillful when molding the pottery the way He wants to.
- His divine plan is perfect, although sometimes impossible to understand with my clay brain.
- In eternity, there will be no more brokenness or cracks, no spots or wrinkles or blemishes. That day is when my clay pottery will be complete and whole.

In the next few chapters, I have collected a few secrets for broken potteries. Many of them were already visible in the stories of broken Bible heroes. All of them are something I have discovered at various times of my brokenness or during my recovery at the Great Potter's table. Several of them I learned after realizing that, although unexpectedly, my broken pieces had fallen right into His loving hands. Perhaps you have discovered even more secrets. After all, the Great Potter is never short with His love and grace.

I encourage you to claim these secrets for your pottery, allowing them to sink deeply into your core, bringing you hope during your broken pottery episodes.

I desire that you will receive the Great Potter's unfailing love and never-ending grace as His perfect will for you. His grace is enough. His faithfulness never ceases. These beautiful secrets of His perfect gifts are for not-so-perfect clay pots struggling on an earth full of brokenness.

Please join me as we explore twenty secrets of broken potteries.

CHAPTER 28

SECRET #1
A TREASURE INSIDE YOUR CLAY POTTERY

For it is the God who commanded light to shine out of darkness, who has shone in our hearts to give the light of the knowledge of the glory of God in the face of Jesus Christ. But we have this treasure in earthen vessels, that the excellence of the power may be of God and not of us.

We are hard-pressed on every side, yet not crushed;
we are perplexed, but not in despair;
persecuted, but not forsaken;
struck down, but not destroyed
— always carrying about in the body the dying of the Lord Jesus,
that the life of Jesus also may be manifested in our body.

2 Corinthian 4:6–10 (NIV)

The first secret is *treasure inside our clay potteries*. Like the priceless Dead Sea scrolls stored inside cheap clay pots, the treasure within our clay pots has nothing to do with us. The treasure is the Great Potter, His light, as He *is* the light (John 1:5; 9:5; 18:12; Isaiah 9:2). "His brightness was like the light; He had rays flashing from His hand" (Habakkuk 3:4 NKJV).

Without the Great Potter, there would be no light on the earth. Neither would there be light inside our clay potteries. He makes His light shine inside of our potteries, in our hearts. As clay potteries, we are called to reflect His light that shines into our clay potteries.

We are not only called to do this but also *equipped* for the job, both *justified* and *glorified*. "Those he called, he also justified; those he justified, he also glorified" (Romans 8:30 NIV).

In Bible times, the most common lamps were clay pots that held olive oil for fuel on which a wick floated. Similarly, we are the clay pot that holds the Great Potter's light. Often, it shines through our cracks, breaks, and fractures.

That the Great Potter chooses us to store His treasure is a mystery beyond mystery, explainable only by His grace. Like the broken potteries' stories revealed, there is no pottery in His service that is not chipped or fractured. King David was guilty of adultery and murder, but the Great Potter proclaimed him a man after His heart. Abraham, whom is called a hero of faith and friend of the Great Potter, was miserably broken many times. Moses, another broken pottery, with his quick temper was chosen by the Great Potter to receive the Ten Commandments and guide His nation from slavery into the Promised Land. Recall a few others: Elijah, running in fear for his life; Jonah, another prophet, first absconding his calling then pouting because the Great Potter showed mercy; Peter disowning the Great Potter. In all of these cases, the treasure was placed within less-than-perfect clay potteries *to show that the all-surpassing power is from the Great Potter and not from them.*

Therefore, it is crucial not to confuse the contents with the container.

Isn't it remarkable that something so valuable is placed inside our fragile clay potteries, chosen by the Great Potter for His glory to shine through us? The priceless treasure of eternal life is a gift. The Great Potter stepped down into our worldly trash yards of broken potteries and reconciled the world to himself (2 Corinthians 5:19). This treasure contained the good news, the truth that can fully liberate anyone who simply believes.

Reading 2 Corinthians 4:6–10 as a therapist, I find it interesting that the apostle Paul mentions all imaginable, traumatizing experiences that any clay pottery could ever have. He not only lists them but also reveals the paradoxical and supernatural opposite way to approach these trials.

We are sometimes hard-pressed on every side but not crushed. At least not so much that the Great Potter can't collect our pieces. We may feel perplexed or ashamed, but we are not in despair, again because of the Great Potter's presence. We may be persecuted and hunted, but we are never abandoned by the Great Potter. We may be struck down and our pottery may be dropped but not destroyed because whatever happens to us is under the Great Potter's control.

EARTHLY EMOTION & EXPERIENCE	SUPERNATURAL SOLUTION
We are hard pressed on every side	→ but not crushed
We are perplexed	→ but not in despair
We are persecuted	→ but not abandoned or forsaken
We are struck down	→ but not destroyed

The Great Potter's light shining through us is His supernatural intervention. *A treasure beyond treasure.* Any possible trauma clay potteries could ever experience in their most horrible brokenness is one reality, yet the Great Potter's supernatural deliverance is another reality.

All the experiential elements of traumatization—horrendous psychological pain, helplessness, and lack of empathy from other potteries—are under the control on the Great Potter's table. He turns all events into something useful, a blessing, according to His good plans for us. We have hope and a future that go beyond our ability to conceive. We have supernatural peace that only the Great Potter can give us, a new meaning for our most traumatizing experiences, and post-traumatic growth because none of our broken pieces go wasted.

What a treasure the Great Potter stores inside our clay potteries! *A treasure that glorifies His name.*

The apostle John told a story about a man who had been blind since his birth (John 9:1–12). The disciples, whose sense of logic never stops astonishing me, contemplate why this man was born blind. "Rabbi, who sinned, *this man* or *his parents*, that he was born blind?" (v. 2 NKJV). The Great Potter does not expound on the typical self-righteous folk blaming the downtrodden. His answer is blunt: "*Neither this man nor his parents sinned, but that the works of God should be revealed in him*" (v. 3).

Another similar encounter is with Lazarus, the Great Potter's good friend who is seriously sick. However, the Great Potter proclaims, "This sickness is not unto death, but for the glory of God, that the Son of God may be glorified through it" (11:4). Sometimes the Great Potter allows brokenness so that His works might be displayed in us and that His glory may shine through our pottery.

The light of His treasure within our broken clay pottery shines through our cracks.

I sometimes wonder which is the bigger miracle: a miraculous healing in a blink of an eye, or the Great Potter's continuous, supernatural peace, joy, and hope during life's most traumatizing events. During the death of loved ones, loss of health, heartbreak over children, divorces, poverty, bankruptcies: does the sudden miracle *or* the continuous, supernatural peace, joy, and hope that lasts for decades despite the unchanging difficult circumstances glorify the Great Potter more?

In which are His works displayed louder: in an instantaneous recovery or His continuous supernatural peace when struggling with chronic illness or depression?

His light…

- continuously shines in the middle of the darkest times,
- is peace amid a horrendous agony and pain,
- is joy during a continuous sickness or poverty,
- is hope in the most difficult circumstances, and
- is safety when everything around us is failing.

Leonard Cohen had it right when he sang: *"There is a crack, a crack in everything—that's how the light gets in."*[37] Perhaps the Great Potter repairs our broken pottery *with seams of His Light*—restoring our brokenness in a way that makes the vessel even more gorgeous.

CHAPTER 29

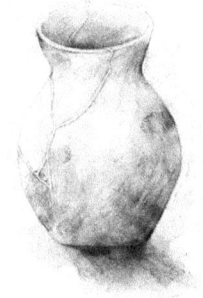

SECRET #2
YOU'RE LOVED WITH THE GREAT POTTER'S UNFAILING AND UNCONDITIONAL LOVE

Your love, LORD, reaches to the heavens, your faithfulness to the sky.

Psalm 36:5 (NIV)

> *Give thanks to the LORD, for he is good; his love endures forever.*
>
> 106:1
>
> But I am like an olive tree flourishing in the house of God;
> *I trust in God's unfailing love for ever and ever.*
>
> 52:8

Every story of every broken pottery reveals this secret as it reclaims the Great Potter's attributes of love, grace, and faithfulness. These are but a few characteristics of the great "I Am."

The second secret essential for us broken potteries is to embrace the Great' Potter's unfailing and unconditional love toward us. Because the Great Potter *is*, love *is*. Love is His existence. It is something so enormous that we cannot even begin to comprehend with our clay brains. The Great Potter does not just love us, He *is* love. Love is the essence of who He is.

"And so we *know* and *rely* on the love God has for us. *God is love*" (1 John 4:16 NIV). —The Great Potter's unshakable love!

Love so enormous.

Love that exceeds every boundary in every direction.

Love without limits.

Love without restrictions.

Love so long and high and deep and wide, we cannot reach the end of it—Endless Love. Love that endures forever (Psalm 136).

It is a life-altering experience to be wholly immersed in the love of the Great Potter.

Love that exists as His character and cannot increase or decrease with anything we do or not do. Even if we wanted to, we could not add anything to that love. *It is perfect as-is.* No wonder the Apostle Paul was praying that you, being *rooted* and *established in love*, may have power, together with all the Lord's holy people, to *grasp* how *wide and long and high and deep is the love of Christ*, and to know this love that surpasses knowledge. (Ephesians 3:17–19 NIV)

Moreover, even if we tried, *nothing can separate us from that love*. The Great Potter keeps loving even when our potteries are smashed or lost, even when we have rejected Him. No matter how shattered or rebellious we are, He still loves as much as He has from the beginning of time. Nothing— *I mean nothing*— will be able to separate us from His love (Romans 8:38–39).

Though the mountains be shaken and the hills be removed, yet *my unfailing love for you will not be shaken* nor my covenant of peace be removed," says the Lord, who has compassion on you." (Isaiah 54:10 NIV)

I wholeheartedly agree with King Solomon: "What a man desires is *unfailing love*" (Proverbs 19:22 NIV). We desire it all our lives and often look in entirely wrong places.

The Great Potter's love is not only unfailing but it is also *unconditional*, which means it has *no conditions* or restrictions, no strings attached. There are no ifs or buts. He does not say I love you *if* . . . or I love you *but* . . . It is not possible for His love to fail, and it does not diminish even if we fail in some way. The Great Potter's love never ceases; it enfolds us without measuring us first. It is striking that His love for us is not comparable even with the best ways we love one another.

It is not possible for the Great Potter to love us conditionally.

It is difficult to comprehend the Great Potter's love as we are only familiar with the limited ways we love and are loved by our parents, spouses, and friends. For many of us, most of our experiences with love involve conditions—love that must be earned and deserved. However, the Great Potter's love has no prerequisites. His love *is* because *He is*.

Allow this to sink in: As clay pottery, "there is *nothing* I can do or not do to make Him love me *more*. There is *nothing* I can do or not do to make Him love me *less*." [38]

There is nothing I could do (or not do) to change the very characteristics of the Great Potter. Whatever I do, His love towards me remains unchangeable!

The core of the gospel is straightforward. "For the Great Potter so *loved* the world, that he gave his one and only Son, that whoever believes in him shall not perish but have eternal life" (John 3:16 NIV). Whoever believes; not 'whoever achieves'!

The Great *I Am* came to my trash yard to save me from myself, to collect my crushed pieces, take them home, and put them on the Potter's table. *It is all finished* because of His death and resurrection. I only need to believe Him and accept the free gift He offers. I only need to believe and *receive*.

This is all you need to do.

I trust the Great Potter's unfailing love. I know it *is* even if I am not always able to feel it in my brokenness. I know He loves me even when I don't feel lovable or lovely, even when I cannot love myself.

I rely on it in every situation because I know it is true. His love is *who He is*, and He never changes. His love is His gift.

I'll take it!

CHAPTER 30

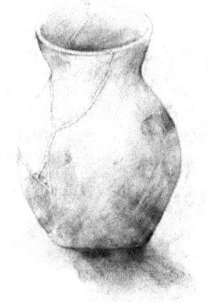

SECRET #3
YOU ARE THE RECIPIENT OF THE GREAT POTTER'S NEVER-ENDING GRACE AND MERCY

But God, who is *rich in mercy*, because of His *great love* with which He loved us, even when we were dead in trespasses, made us alive together with Christ (*by grace you have been saved*), and raised us up together, and made us sit together in the heavenly places in Christ Jesus, that in the ages to come He might show the exceeding riches of *His grace in His kindness* toward us in Christ Jesus. For *by grace you have been saved through faith*, and that not of yourselves; it is *the gift of God, not of works*, lest anyone should boast.

Ephesians 2:4–9 (NKJV)

As the Great Potter's love is who He is, so is His grace and mercy. Because He *is*, grace *is*. Because He *is*, mercy *is*. The Great Potter "is gracious and full of compassion, Slow to anger and great in mercy" (Psalm 145:8 NKJV). The third secret to internalize is that *the Great Potter's grace and mercy are absolute, unmerited, and never-ending.*

- *Absolute*, as there is nothing to add to His grace.³⁹ ³⁵ No clay pottery can do anything to diminish it. Likewise, it is impossible to receive only "a little bit" of grace or "some" grace. Neither is it possible to receive "more" or "less" grace.
- The nature of grace is that it is *unmerited*, undeserved. The Great Potter does not take back His grace, and it never runs out no matter what we do or do not do.
- The Great Potter's grace is *never-ending*. It is "exceedingly abundant" (1 Timothy 1:14 NKJV).

The Great Potter's grace and mercy are His unmerited favor to His clay potteries, to be received as a gift. Both are free in the sense that we are getting something we do not deserve, something we have not, and cannot, earn. Mercy also means that

---

³⁵ *Xáris* #5485 means "*favor, disposed to, inclined, favorable towards, leaning towards* to share benefit" - properly, *grace*. The Lord's *favor* – freely *extended to give Himself* away to people (because He is "always leaning toward them"). *Xáris* is similar with the Hebrew (OT) term 2580: *Kaná* ("grace, extension-toward"). Both refer to God *freely extending* Himself (*His favor*, grace), *reaching* (*inclining*) to people because He is *disposed* to bless (be near) them. [39]

we are *not* getting something we *do* deserve. We deserve punishment for our sin, but because of mercy, we are not punished; rather, He took our punishment upon Himself, which satisfied the requirements of justice. He pardoned us. "For the wages of sin *is* death, but the *gift* of God *is* eternal life in Christ Jesus our Lord" (Romans 6:23 NKJV).

Isn't it comforting that it is not possible for mere pottery to change the Great Potter's grace, that it does not matter what they do or how badly they break themselves? The Great Potter's grace is the essence of His character. From the beginning of time, He planned a way to reconcile His clay potteries to Himself. He "was in Christ *reconciling the world to Himself,* not imputing their trespasses to them, and has committed to us the word of *reconciliation*" (2 Corinthians 5:19 NKJV). It is crucial to internalize the nature of the Great Potter's gift, which exists merely because of what He did and who He is, and it has nothing to do with anything we did or did not do.

We cannot do anything but accept and receive it.

It is not easy to comprehend grace because it does not meet our clay potteries' criteria of fairness and equality. Just as in the parable in Matthew 20:1–6 the vineyard workers who were hired early morning and worked the full day did not think it was fair that those who worked only one hour received the *same* salary as they did. We mistakenly think that it would be easier to accept grace if we worked for it or earned it or received it as a competition prize. But if this were so, it is no longer grace. In the Great Potter's justice system, it is perfectly equitable for one pottery to receive more grace, more often, than another.

Grasping the concept of unmerited favor that is not fair can be difficult because we are not familiar with it in our everyday lives.

The Great Potter's gift of amazing grace has nothing to do with our works or justice but everything to do with Him and what He did at Calvary about two thousand years ago. He took our guilt and punishment onto Himself and paid the price. What He did was perfect and complete.

A story of a clay pottery who arrives late to a revival tent meeting—only to find workers taking down the tent. Desperate at missing the altar call, he inquires one of the workers what he should do to be saved. The worker says, "You cannot do anything. It's too late." "What do you mean? How can it be too late?" the clay pottery says. "The work has already been accomplished. There is nothing you need to do but believe it."

This is grace: The work has already been accomplished.

There is nothing you need to do but believe it.

Legalistic Mixture of Grace and Law—Not the Living Bread!

Unfortunately, many Christian churches do not focus on the Great Potter's grace. Or they somehow mix His grace with the law as if it would make it somehow "safer." They may teach about grace a little bit, but it is almost as if they dare not teach about it too much for fear they will lose control over their members, or their members will somehow lose control over themselves. The bread they offer in their church services is *not* the living bread the Great Potter offers but some artificial or no-name brand mixture of little bit of grace with many rules—no wonder it tastes like a shoe sole and folks do not want to taste it another time.

It is sad when any church excludes the Great Potter's marvelous treasure that includes His never-ending grace and replaces it with their works-based doctrine. I experienced this type of church in my childhood, and it took me over three decades to rid myself of the fearmongering and legalistic views deeply carved into my core. Of course, I now understand how dangerous this type of false doctrine can be as it, indeed, drove me away from the Great Potter into a guilt-ridden perfectionism trying to gain His acceptance and approval.

This teaching of my childhood church community was the same issue the Galatian church fell prey to and the apostle Paul had to address. False teachers had come in and convinced some of the people that the Great Potter's grace was no longer sufficient, but they had to go back to the law to be holy. They also had fallen away from the true Christ-centered, grace-focused teaching—and Paul had some harsh words to shake them from the false teaching: "You have become *estranged from Christ*, you who *attempt to* be justified by law; you have *fallen from grace*" (Galatians 5:4 NKJV).

Interestingly, in my childhood church, I often heard preachers warning us not to take grace lightly. "Not to hold it cheap" meant that we had to try to measure to it . . . as if receiving it as a gift would be holding it cheap. As I came to understand, it is quite the opposite. Every drop of the grace is exceptionally precious, particularly because of what the Gift-giver had to sacrifice for it. To treat grace cheaply occurs when we think we can earn even a drop of it with our achievements instead of admitting that we could never deserve it no matter how long or how hard we worked.

Growing up in a legalistic church community, I tried desperately to avoid those items on the sin lists. I tried my best to fulfill all kinds of odd requirements of righteous living without understanding that the Great Potter had already fulfilled every iota of the letter of the law for me.

Yet I didn't know there was *nothing else* for me to do but to *receive His gift.*

I held a distorted image of the Great Potter, imagining Him as a thrifty pharmacist measuring His grace with the tiniest pipet, drop by drop, and firmly stating that I had better watch myself if I had already received my daily share—or my weekly, monthly, or annual...

"My, don't *you* have lots of nerve ever asking more after how you've screwed up."

I imagined the Great Pharmacist declaring with a stern, disapproving look.

"No more grace left for *you*!"

I accepted that I must have wasted my share of grace for my lifetime.

To fall away from grace, even into that religious-looking and holy-sounding legalistic trash yard of broken potteries, is a severe diagnosis to broken pottery. Brokenness that is often not even figured out, as it is something that extends behind all kinds of polished facades.

Falling away from grace is the same as falling away from Christ, the very foundation that saves (1 Corinthians 10:4). *Falling away from grace means we are falling into a swamp of our works.* No matter how good they may be, we have fallen away from the foundation of salvation, the rock, thus disparaging the Great Potter's grace and His redeeming work on the cross.

Even though there is nothing wrong with good works, they are not the basis of our salvation or the preservation of our salvation, not even a foundation of our sanctification or blessings. If we work hard to justify receiving the grace, we have *already* fallen away from it, just like the Galatians did—grace is not grace if we work for it. If we feel the Great Potter's grace is not quite sufficient without adding a mixture of law, we are as foolish as the Galatians.

> O foolish Galatians! Who has bewitched you that you should not obey the truth, before whose eyes Jesus Christ was clearly portrayed among you as crucified? This only I want to learn from you: Did you receive the Spirit by the works of the law, or by the hearing of faith? Are you so foolish? Having begun in the Spirit, are you now being made perfect by the flesh? (Galatians 3:1–3 NKJV)

Furthermore, if we do not understand the concept of free, unmerited grace, we quickly begin to see the Great Potter as impatient and frustrated with our brokenness. We begin to see Him as punishing and judgmental. We may soon find it difficult to trust Him as we will feel unsafe to draw closer to Him.

Sadly, some clay potteries try to diminish the Great Potter's grace and mercy, even try to remove it altogether from themselves and others. They believe they always need to feel at least some guilt. They have difficulty letting it go simply because they *were* guilty before accepting Christ! They may think that His grace is too much or too good to be true. They may even reason that some sins are too vast or too vile for His grace. Or they may feel that because they have taken His grace so lightly, they deserve no more.

Of course, all of this reasoning is based on their distorted idea of the Great Potter. He wants you to correct that image and simply receive His amazing grace! *Sola Gratia.*

CHAPTER 31

SECRET #4
THE GREAT POTTER'S GRACE—
EVEN IF YOU CANNOT FEEL IT

But when the kindness and the love of God our Savior toward man appeared, *not by works* of righteousness which we have done, but according to *His mercy He saved us*, through the washing of regeneration and renewing of the Holy Spirit, whom He poured out on us abundantly *through Jesus Christ our Savior,*

that having been *justified by His grace*
we should become *heirs* according to the hope of eternal life.

TITUS 3:4–7 NKJV

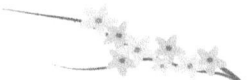

Misaligned teaching about the Great Potter can leave deep wounds in our clay potteries and damage our emotions, making it difficult to immerse ourselves into the secrets of broken potteries, including the Great Potter's grace. We may understand the concept of grace at a theoretical and cognitive level but cannot *feel* anything on any emotional level. In this state, it is difficult, if not impossible, to handle grace.

There are many reasons for this. It may be that our capacity to feel our feelings was damaged during our trauma experiences when others brutally broke our clay pottery. Our trauma-defined, distorted self-image may make it difficult for us to feel the grace. Our unconscious tendency to repeat our trauma may make it impossible for us to experience anything different from what our past has determined to be normal. For example, for clay potteries abused as children by one or both parents, it may not be easy to think of the Great Potter as the loving Father. They may also have problems feeling any assurance of being His fully redeemed child.

If you have difficulty emotionally experiencing the Great Potter's grace, it is essential to accept this secret: *The Great Potter's grace is poured onto your pottery even if you cannot feel it.*

The *objective truth* about the Great Potter's grace is *not* dependant on your subjective emotion about it.

The truth is that the Great Potter's grace

- exists despite your emotions,
- is not an experience but an ontological and existential *fact*,
- is poured into you whether or not you can feel it, and
- is not based on your feelings.

I hope you understand that 'believing' or 'not believing' is not a feeling—it is a *choice*. We can simply *choose* to believe that the Great Potter's grace is bigger than our brokenness and doubts. And, if we have difficulties to believe, we can always pray: "Lord, I believe; help my unbelief!" (Mark 9:24 NKJV). When we ask, The Great Potter will be happy to supply His faith as He *is* both: the author *and* perfector of our faith (Hebrew 12:1–2).

The Great Potter's grace does *not* increase or decrease based on our emotions as it has nothing to do with our feelings. It has nothing to do with our faith, either. If it did, none of us have hope, not even for the amount of a mustard seed. Furthermore, the Great Potter's grace for us will not end if we question it or doubt it, not even if we think that we cannot believe it. It is entirely by grace that we have been saved, through faith, which is *also* the gift of the Great Potter (Ephesians 2:8). Nothing to do with *our* works. All because of the Great Potter's fully completed work during the Good Friday and Resurrection Sunday episodes over two thousand years ago.

Be assured that the Great Potter understands us better than we understand ourselves. As He sees our hearts and our unconscious cores, He always finds a good reason to feel authentic compassion for us. *His grace will never run off*, leaving us alone, for it is never-ending. Martin Luther said it well: *"Faith is a living, daring confidence in God's grace, so sure and certain that a man could stake his life on it a thousand times."*[40]

Because our emotions can be trauma inflicted and send us distorted messages about ourselves and others, we cannot always rely on them; however, we can always trust the Great Potter. Our emotions come and go, but the Great Potter remains the same yesterday, today, and forever. Even if I cannot feel His grace, I am still immersed in it. I cannot escape it.

The Great Potter's grace and mercy *are* because He *is*.

Even if I smashed my clay pottery into a thousand pieces, its every shard and each crumble still belongs to the Great Potter. Wherever "sin abounded, grace abounded much more" (Romans 5:20 NKJV).

Amazing grace, isn't it? Absolute and complete. Nothing to add, existing despite anything I feel about it. — "Let us therefore come *boldly* to the throne of grace, that we may *obtain mercy* and *find grace* to help in time of need" (Hebrews 4:16 NKJV).

Come boldly! You will be treated with enormous kindness!

And finally, "Do *not* be carried away by all kinds of strange teachings. It is good for our hearts to be *strengthened by grace*" (13:9 NIV).

If you haven't already, it is time to immerse yourself in the secret of Great Potter's grace for your broken pottery. "But grow in the grace and knowledge of our Lord and Savior Jesus Christ. To him be glory both now and forever! Amen" (2 Peter 3:18 NIV).

It is good to be strengthened by His grace.

It is good to grow in His grace.

CHAPTER 32

SECRET #5
THE GREAT POTTER ACCEPTS YOU AS-IS

For when we were still without strength, in due time Christ died for the ungodly. For scarcely for a righteous man will one die; yet perhaps for a good man someone would even dare to die. But God demonstrates His own love toward us, in that while we were still sinners, Christ died for us.

ROMANS 5:6–8 (NKJV)

One of the most rejuvenating secrets for my broken pottery was realizing that *the Great Potter accepts me as-is*, even when I am smashed into a thousand pieces in the trash yard of broken potteries.

Hear the secret: The Great Potter accepts you *as-is*. Even if you did the smashing. Even if you have done nothing trying to make it easier for Him to find you. Even if you think you no longer need His interventions.

As the Great Potter accepts us as-is, we must accept ourselves. This is not always easy because we may have been conditioned to believe that nothing good is in us or that we should always try our best to become something *else* that we are not.

An interesting concept relating to distorted self-images is fulfilling the Great Potter's call to love other potteries as ourselves (Matthew 22:39). This means that we must love our clay potteries before we can love others. If I have issues accepting myself, I may also have problems accepting others. If I do not like myself, I may have difficulties enjoying others. If I cannot stand myself, I might have problems tolerating others. A vicious cycle!

Furthermore, it is challenging for any relationship if we feel we must prove our self-worth or have difficulties trusting other potteries. Jealousy, clinging, using another pottery to fulfill our needs, or expecting others to make us feel competent while we are convinced that we are not: these are typical relationship problems that derive from not being fully content with our clay potteries.

Distorted or Healthy Idea of Self?

Do we even know where we received our current idea of self?

Because of past brokenness, trauma experiences, and odd, legalistic teachings, we may have internalized the nagging false guilt as our driving force. Perhaps our past hurts still define us. Or that piercing shame projected onto us a long time ago distorted our self-image. Perhaps, even after several years, it does not allow us to see ourselves likable and lovable, as if we feel we do not even have the right to exist.

Perhaps, our idea of self comes from the distortions of our childhoods, such as toxic emotions that never belonged to us but to those who projected them on us.

Or they may be remnants of our pottery's past brokenness, from false ideas that some- one programmed into us while breaking our potteries. Remember, it is not your responsibility to carry someone else's projections as your burdens.

A healthy self-image includes several aspects: a sense of belonging and knowledge of being accepted, wanted, cared for, enjoyed, valued, loved, and competent, for example. When the Great Potter accepts us as-is, He welcomes us with all of our failures. All of them. He is not disillusioned with us as He knows everything about us inside out, not only our current misery or our past screw-ups but also all the messes we are capable of orchestrating in the future.

As an entrance gift, accepting us as-is into His family, the Great Potter immediately offers us full belonging with all the benefits. He offers His love and care, fully knowing our extraordinary capacity to make mistakes.

Because the Great Potter accepts us as-is, we have no reason not to accept ourselves as well. We need never doubt that the Great Potter would not want or value our broken pieces. After all, He has already paid a hefty price for us. He declared it so clearly that He gave His life for us. And, not only that, the Great Potter, who created our innermost being, who knit us together in our mothers' wombs, who made each of us fearfully and wonderfully, who knows us completely from the beginning of time, planned us to be His children.

Sadly, many Christian clay potteries are not comprehending this secret of being accepted as-is by the Great Potter. Many continue entertaining self-whipping or self-belittling mind-sets, even while at the Potter's House. I used to be one of them, never feeling good enough, wondering whether my faith was not big enough or my achievements not sufficient. Instead of resting in the Great Potter's grace and mercy, and enjoying His peace, my mind was filled with apprehension and feelings of inadequacy. I ended up exhausted in my efforts to find favor with the Great Potter as I misguidedly thought He was displeased with me.

Maybe this sounds familiar to you. Have you projected onto the Great Potter your struggles accepting yourself? Have you transferred onto Him the characteristics of your meaningful relationships, their limited grace, and conditionalized love toward you? Do you think that the Great Potter treats you the same way you treat others or as they treat you? Have you tried to squeeze the Great Potter into a clay pottery of your creation? Have you, in your mind, created an image of the Great Potter who possesses your limitations?

If so, you are holding the wrong idea of the Great Potter. "Please, consider the incredible love that the Father has shown us in allowing us to be called *children of God*. And, *that is what we are*" (1 John 3:1 NIV). We *are* His children (Romans 5:7–8, 11), accepted as-is and deeply loved. Just as the prodigal son approaching his father's estate had no reason for apprehension, neither do we. We are His children, heirs, and this is our *permanent* position.

Our brokenness will not change this position.

CHAPTER 33

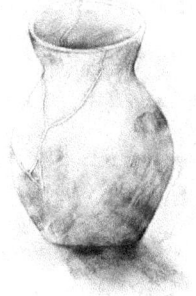

SECRET #6
THE GREAT POTTER'S CHILD—
BEING AN HEIR IS PERMANENT

But as many as received Him, to them He gave the right to become *children of God*,
to those who believe in His name: who were born, not of blood,
nor of the will of the flesh, nor of the will of man, but *of God*.

JOHN 1: 12-13 (NKJV)

Heidi McKendrick

In order to fully comprehend the secret of *our permanent status as the Great Potter's child and heir*—even if our pottery breaks— it is helpful to understand the origin of the Apostle Paul's writing and the concept of sonship in the AD first century. Jewish family law differed from the Greek and Roman family law. Writing to Jews, Peter and James used the concept of sonship as "new birth." However, when Paul wrote to Greek and Romans (gentiles), he used the idea of "adoption" instead of "new birth."

- "In his great mercy he has given us *new birth* into a living hope through the resurrection of Jesus Christ from the dead" (1 Peter 1:3 NIV).
- "He chose to give us *birth* through the word of truth, that we might be a kind of first fruits of all he created" (James 1:18 NIV).
- "He predestined us *for adoption to sonship* through Jesus Christ, in accordance with his *pleasure and will*" (Ephesians 1:5 NIV).
- "But when the fullness of the time had come, God sent forth His Son, born of a woman, born under the law, to redeem those who were under the law, that we might receive *the adoption as sons*. And because you are sons, God has sent forth the Spirit of His Son into your hearts, crying out, "Abba, Father!" Therefore you are no longer a slave but a son, and if a son, then *an heir* of God through Christ." (Galatians 4:4–7 NKJV).
- "For you did not receive the spirit of bondage again to fear, but you received *the Spirit of adoption* by whom we cry out, "Abba, Father." The Spirit Himself bears witness with our spirit that we *are* children of God, and if children, then heirs—heirs of God and joint *heirs* with Christ..." (Romans 8:15–17 NKJV).

The concept of adoption comes from the Greek word: *huiothesia*,[41] meaning "*the place and condition of a son given to one to whom it does not naturally belong,*" or "*to formally and legally declare that someone who is not one's own child is henceforth to be treated and cared for as one's own child, including complete rights of inheritance.*"[42] [36] Although in Jewish family law being a naturally born child is the most secure position

---

[36] *Huiothesia* is also used in Romans 8:23; 9:4; Ephesians 1:5.

in the family, according to Greek and Roman law, it was the opposite, and that's why Paul, when teaching the gentiles, applied the term *adoption* instead of *birth*.

The Roman historian William M. Ramsay clarifies the Greek inheritance law as follows:

> The Roman-Syrian Law-Book . . . lays down the principle that *a man can never put away an adopted son,* and that he cannot put away a real son without good ground. It is remarkable that the adopted son should have *a stronger position* than the son by birth, yet it was so. [43]

> The Romans recognized that when a baby was born, "you got what you got," whether you liked it or not. ... Thus, according to Roman law, a naturally born baby could be disowned from the family. However, people *adopting* a child knew exactly what they were getting, and no one adopted a child unless that specific child was wanted as a family member, so according to law an adopted child could not be disowned. He or she was *permanently* added to the family. Many early believers were Roman citizens, and using the word "adoption" was one of God's ways to let the Church know that *He chose the children brought into His family, and they could not be taken from it.* [44]

Comparing their spiritual childhood with a naturally born child makes sense in Jewish culture in which both genealogy and birthright were paramount and permanent. However, when writing to Romans or Greeks, natural birthrights were not 100 percent secure in these cultures. Therefore, Paul used the concept of adoption to illustrate the permanent nature of spiritual sonship.

Of course, one reason for Paul's usage of the term 'adoption' was to assure the gentiles, who had been excluded by Jews, that adoption makes them family. However, another reason—stunningly touching—was that Paul understood that *if* his readers thought there could be *a slightest possibility* a naturally born child *could* be disowned, this would easily give them a misleading idea of their position as God's children.

Although—sadly— this does not stop many works-based salvation and legalism-driven preachers, I find it beautiful that Paul did *everything possible* to impede *any of his readers* to develop a wrong image about their status with the Great Potter. Paul did not want his readers to think their position in the Great Potter's family could *ever* be insecure, or that there could be *any* reason for them to become disavowed by the Great Potter. He wanted to avoid anybody living in fear that their potteries *could* be repudiated or put away if they did not perform well enough. Paul wanted to avoid any works-based salvation doctrines thus he emphasized that our permanent position as children and heirs have *nothing to do with our works*, but it is the Great Potter's divine gift.

When the Great Potter planned our salvation, He planned it to be permanent, secure, with no grounds to disown us or refuse us. *Whosoever believes...* He said—and it indeed *is* that simple! Yes, we *are* His potteries, His children and heirs, and *nothing* can remove us from this position. (Romans 8:31-39). We are *permanently* placed on His family; we bear *His* name, His thumbprint, and His home is our new address.

Being fully aware of our potteries' flaws and cracks, the Great Potter *chose* us—He adopted us as-is, so that "having been *justified by his grace*, we might become heirs having the hope of eternal life" (Titus 3:7 NIV).

The Great Potter will never put away our pottery no matter how many mistakes we make or how miserably we break ourselves. Even if we fail and intentionally smash our pottery, we are *still* His child and His heir. David's broken pottery is an ample example of this!

Yes, we can lose everything, our health, sense of dignity, security, or reputation. However, nobody can steal our place at the Great Potter's table.

It is permanent.

Just like it was for the prodigal son and his brother, although the brother chose to sulk outside the house instead of joining the celebration table!

And in the future, let's not let any legalism-driven fears or false guilt dwell in our clay potteries. Let's not internalize any toxic, self-belittling attitudes or allow anybody to project their shame onto us. Let's eliminate intergenerational trauma and unhealthy assumptions perhaps carried in our families for generations. Let's tune our warning bells to alert us for any false doctrines accusing us without basis.

Because of the Great Potter's never-ending grace, we are forgiven and redeemed—permanently.

Please, at this moment, allow yourself to receive the Great Potter's acceptance of you as-is. You don't have to try to change yourself to be somehow more acceptable or likable. *He already welcomes you.* Just let this truth sink into your clay pottery as a fantastic treasure.

Just say thank you. It's already yours!

CHAPTER 34

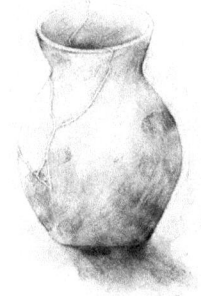

SECRET #7
THE GREAT POTTER IS FAITHFULL EVEN WHEN YOU ARE NOT

Your faithfulness continues through all generations;
you established the earth, and it endures.

PSALM 119:90 (NIV)

Who is like you, LORD God Almighty? You, LORD, are mighty,
and *your faithfulness* surrounds you.

89:8

As it is with the Great Potter's love and grace, so is His faithfulness. He is faithful because He *is*. He cannot deny His own because of His name. Therefore, an important secret for the broken pottery to internalize is that *the Great Potter remains forever faithful even if we are faithless.*

Yes—it is in the Bible: "If we are faithless, he remains faithful, for he cannot disown himself" (2 Timothy 2:13 NIV).

The Great Potter remains faithful because He *is* who He *is*, eternally the same, the same yesterday, today, and forever (Hebrews 13:8), as, according to His promise, "I the LORD do not change" (Malachi 3:6 NIV). He is the first and last, the Alpha and the Omega, "who is, and who was, and who is to come, the Almighty" (Revelation 1:8 NIV).[37]

With our clay brains, it is impossible to comprehend the existence of the Great Potter. As potteries, we keep changing, breaking, and reshaping. We also keep breaching our promises, whereas the Great Potter never does. His promises are true and sure. We can believe them and count on them. "Every good and perfect gift is from above, coming down from the Father of the heavenly lights, *who does not change like shifting shadows*" (James 1:17 NIV). *Even if we are faithless, He remains faithful* is a fantastic secret that defines the security of our relationship with the Great Potter.

Remember this secret the next time you fail and feel miserable; when you doubt His love, fearing that He may never want you back; when you mistakenly conclude that He will never want to use you in His service again; or when you think that He will not be able to trust you anymore because you incorrectly start believing that you do not deserve second, third, six, tenth, or more chances.

The next time you question why anyone would remain faithful for faithless, remember that the Great Potter does because faithfulness is His who He *is*. The Great Potter's faithfulness is far above the way we clay potteries think. His commitment is *absolute*. It does not change, no matter what. It is much stronger than our unfaithfulness could ever be. The Bible stories of broken potteries are good examples. Although some of the heroes were called giants of faith, they were still faithless and

---

[37] See also Lamentations 3:22–23, Psalm 102:25–27; Isaiah 41:4; Hebrews 1:10–11.

broken. The defining factor was not what *they* did or didn't do but that *the Great Potter claimed ownership of them*, which meant *they could claim the Great Potter's faithfulness.*

The Great Potter's faithfulness is *not* grounded in my faithfulness. It is grounded in *His* faithfulness. "If we confess our sins, *he is faithful* and just and will forgive us our sins and purify us from all unrighteousness" (1 John 1:9 NIV).

It is good to know that the Great Potter never regrets making any of His clay potteries. He does not repent His calling nor His gifts (Romans 11:29), not even when we intentionally break His beautiful creation. His faithfulness has been the framework of His dealings with us clay potteries since the beginning of time, and it will remain so. Absolutely nothing can separate us from Him, even if we may sometimes feel that *we* might because of something we have done. Charles Spurgeon said it well: *"The glory of God's faithfulness is that no sin of ours has ever made Him unfaithful."* [45]

Eternal Security

Moreover, we have eternal security because of the Great Potter's faithfulness. Can you believe this? If not, then remember that even our faith is a gift from the Great Potter, and He never gives us bad gifts. It is because of the powers of His *grace* that we can grasp the faith, that teenier than a mustard seed part of it. And when we do, the Great Potter already holds our hands—before we had a thought to reach for His.

"Now faith is confidence in what we *hope* for and assurance about what we *do not see*" (Hebrews 11:1 NIV). Having faith simply means that we *trust* and have *hope*. If having hope means that we see something that is not yet visible, then faith must mean to have hope. Does this sound complicated? It's not, because "now these three remain faith, hope and love. But the greatest of these is love" (1 Corinthians 13:13 NIV). The Great Potter is love (1 John 4:8).

It is *the Great Potter's faith* that counts as well as His faithfulness, not *our* faith or faithfulness! Both faith and grace are *His presence in us* and *His presents to us*, something too enormous for our clay brains to measure. As it is all of the Great Potter's work, faith, hope, and love are not dependent on anything we could possibly do (or not do).

It's all because who the Great Potter is. Our part of the equation is to *choose* to believe in Him; *trust* that He *is* who He *says* He is and that He *does* what He *promised*. "anyone who comes to him must *believe* that *he exists* and that *he rewards those who earnestly seek him*" (Hebrews 11:6 NIV).

Imagine faith only the size of a mustard seed is *all* that is required! Faith so small yet powerful enough to even cast off the Mighty Mountain of Religion that falsely taught us about the works-based-salvation. This mountain will be removed from our heart and moved into the depths of the sea (Matthew 17:20). [46]

Even if *we* forsake the Great Potter, He does not leave us. Even if we cast Him off, He will not cast us off (Romans 11:1). Just like the Good Shepherd does, the Great Potter goes looking for His lost potteries. He searches until He finds every broken piece and then carries them home. After that, He faithfully restores our potteries on His table. And one day, when we reach our final home heaven, He perfects the process He launched here on the earth (Philippians 1:6).

Interestingly, it is when sitting among our broken pottery pieces that we often question the Great Potter's faithfulness. Yet it is during these times that we learn about this attribute of His essence; when we experience that He will *never* let us go.

Yes, it's true—this is also in the Bible: "Never will I leave you; never will I forsake you" (Hebrews 13:5 NIV).

What a promise for any of us broken potteries!

"Let us hold *unswervingly* to the *hope* we profess, for he who promised is *faithful*" (10:23) —His faithfulness is forever. Just like His love is everlasting and His grace is never-ending.

The Great Potter's everlasting faithfulness will last to the last minute of your life. And after that, as you are entering heaven, the gates will open for you *because* His faithfulness never ceases.

Blessed assurance, indeed!

CHAPTER 35

SECRET #8
THE TREASURE, CHRIST IN YOU, WILL NOT DISAPPEAR WHEN YOUR POTTERY BREAKS

But you are not in the flesh but in the Spirit, if indeed the *Spirit of God dwells in you.*

ROMANS 8:9 (NKJV)

A little while longer and the world will see Me no more, but you will see Me. Because I live, you will live also. At that day you will know that I am in My Father, and you in Me, and I in you.

JOHN 14:19–20 (NKJV)

WOW! Are you thinking that there is a typo in this title? When I grasped this reality for my broken pottery, I felt like a heretic. It sounded too good to be true: *The treasure, Christ in me, will not disappear in my brokenness!*

When He created us clay potteries in His image, the Great Potter made us dimensional as well. *Spirit*, His breath of life, was placed in our *bodies* that He formed from the earthly dust. As the union of these two, the man became "a living soul" (Genesis 2:7 KJV) or "living being" (NIV). *The soul* is our core being, including our emotions, feelings, thoughts, motivations, wills, intelligence, cognitive processing, memories, and unique personalities, not to be confused with our spirits. We are *living souls*, including both spirit and body. The soul inhabits our bodies. As clay potteries, we stand between these two worlds: body and spirit. With my body, including my senses, I live on the visible and material earth. And with my spirit, I simultaneously live in the invisible spiritual world. My spirit allows me to *be in a relationship* with the Great Potter and worship Him.[47]

When I make a statement such as "Christ dwelling in me," I refer to Christ, *His Spirit*, dwelling *in my spirit*, while my senses dwell in my *body* and my *self* dwells in my *soul* (John 16:7). In a way, this means that if my *body* contains my world-consciousness, my *soul*, my self-consciousness, then my *spirit* must contain my Great Potter–consciousness.[48] To clarify these concepts, *"Man is not a body, he has a body, he dwells within a body—man is a 'living soul.'"*[49]

Just as my life begins when spirit and body are united, it will end when they are separated. When I die, my spirit, the breath of life, returns to the Great Potter, who gave it to me.⁵⁰ "Then shall the dust return to the earth as it was: and the spirit shall return unto God who gave it" (Ecclesiastes 12:7 KJV). While they were stoning Stephen, he prayed, 'Lord Jesus, *receive my spirit*" (Acts 7:59 NIV). Furthermore, Christ, "was put to death in the body but *made alive in the Spirit*" (1 Peter 3:18 NIV).

It is important to understand these concepts of our existence because therein is a vital secret to grasp. Though our bodies may be broken because of illness, our souls, minds, and emotions may end up crushed in thousands of pieces because of trauma; therefore, both body and soul may be devastatingly broken at the same time, each impacting the other. An emotional pain affects my body, and physical pain influences my emotions. However, even amid most horrendous brokenness, we can have enormous faith that has nothing to do with wishful thinking or even hope: *Christ indwelling the spirit.* The spirit is His castle as He is our King and Saviour. Nothing, I mean nothing, no power whatsoever, can ever separate us from Him (Romans 8:38–39). "*The Spirit himself* testifies with *our spirit* that we are God's children" (v. 16 NIV).

Do you believe it? Do you believe this secret is true? Christ still dwells in you even if your clay pottery is broken into a thousand pieces, totally shattered into minute pieces that are lost and buried under the trash.

It is true. Christ dwells in His precious potteries (1 Corinthians 3:16; 6:19). However, it's *not* because of any honorable deeds we may do or our actions in trying to stay clean and unblemished but only because of the Great Potter's grace. "But you know him, for *he dwells with you* and will be in you" (John 14:17 NKJV).

This is a revolutionary secret to embrace. No matter what, your every broken piece and your tiniest smashed crumble belongs to the Great Potter, and He continues to dwell in you.

If you are smashed into a thousand pieces, He then dwells in those thousand pieces!

CHAPTER 36

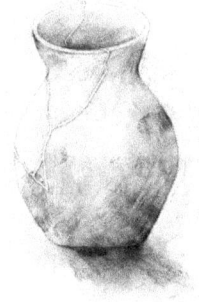

SECRET #9
YOU ARE A NEW CREATION, RECONCILED AND RIGHTEOUS EVEN WHEN BROKEN

Therefore, if anyone is in Christ, he is *a new creation;* old things have passed away; behold, all things have become new.
Now all things are of God, who has *reconciled us* to Himself through Jesus Christ,

> and has given us the ministry of *reconciliation,* that is,
> that God was in Christ *reconciling* the world to Himself,
> not imputing their trespasses to them,
> and has committed to us the word of *reconciliation.*
>
> 2 Corinthians 5: 17–19 (NKJV)

> And if Christ is in you, the body is dead because of sin,
> but the *Spirit is life* because of righteousness.
>
> Romans 8:10 (NKJV)

Christ dwelling in your pottery contains another secret remarkable amid brokenness: *You are a new creation, and you remain reconciled and righteous, even when broken.*

You may be in a thousand pieces, dwelling in a trash yard, but it is temporarily. You are *still* inwardly a new creation, created by the Great Potter. Not because of anything you did or deserved but all because of what He did when He redeemed all the potteries to Himself on the cross. "*Whatever you once were, God views you not as you were in yourself, but as what you are in Christ Jesus.*"[51]

As a new creation, it means that your *spirit* (not your body or emotions) has been born again (1 Peter 1:3). Your spirit has been created by the Great Potter (John 3:6) as something new and fresh; you are in Christ and Christ is in you (Galatians 2:20). In your spirit you are a new entity, like a newborn baby. According to the Great Potter's plan, the connection Adam and Eve broke, the second Adam, Christ, has now restored, making it possible for Him to dwell in us.

As born-again clay potteries, we are the Great Potter's creation as we did not create ourselves (Ephesians 2:8). We are entirely His handiwork and not our own, "…created in Christ Jesus to do good works, which God prepared in advance for us to do" (v. 10 NIV).

The old pottery has gone, and the new one has replaced it.

Because of the Great Potter's grace, *we are reconciled with Him*, 100 percent reconciled and 100 percent righteous. None of our trespasses will count anymore, and they will not be held against us.[52] We are admissible before the Great Potter, *pardoned for good*. Not just 50 percent, not even 99 percent, but 100 percent pardoned. Not because we could ever earn that position with our deeds but simply because we have received His righteousness as a gift during the reconciliation. Apostle Paul preached: "We implore you on Christ's behalf, be *reconciled* to God. For *He made Him* who knew no sin to be sin for us, that *we might become the righteousness of God in Him*" (2 Corinthians 5:20–21 NKJV). And: "for all of you who were baptized into Christ have *clothed* yourselves with Christ" (Galatians 3:27 NIV), *His* righteousness.

Edward Mote's old hymnal says it well: [53]

1. My *hope* is built on nothing less
Than *Jesus' blood and righteousness*;
I dare not trust the sweetest frame,
But wholly lean on Jesus' name.

On Christ, the solid Rock, I stand;
All other ground is sinking sand.

2. When darkness veils His lovely face,
I rest on His unchanging grace;
In every high and stormy gale
My anchor holds within the veil…

4. When He shall come with trumpet sound,
Oh, may I then in Him be found,
Clothed in His righteousness alone,
Faultless to stand before the throne! …

So, when the Great Potter looks at us, He no longer sees our flaws and cracks, no matter who or what caused them. Instead, He sees Christ and we rest in His grace! *He sees His righteousness* because Christ reconciled us to Himself. It is according to

His righteousness that the Great Potter both measures and treats us. You will always be His perfect child, no matter how broken your pottery may be, even if you intentionally break it.

Because of His perfect sacrifice, the Great Potter no longer defines us as sinners nor sees your dirty clothes; instead, He clothes us in Christ's righteousness, which is perfect. *Forever.* "For by one offering He has perfected *forever* those who are being sanctified" (Hebrew 10:14 NKJV). This has absolutely *nothing* to do with anything we have or have not done. *It is the perfect gift.* It's ours forever and forever, and nothing can steal it away from us! "I give them eternal life, and they shall *never* perish; *no one will snatch them out of my hand*" (John 10:28 NIV).

No one will snatch us out of the Great Potter's hand!

This gift is for you. If you have not accepted it, I ask you to do this: Thank the Great Potter for sending Jesus for dying on your behalf, for the forgiveness of your sins, and that He reconciled you to Himself. Then simply tell Him anything that is on your heart. He will listen to you as your new identity is now His daughter or son, and He will forever stand by your side. No need to live in fear, and never again doubt the Great Potter's love or question whether His grace is sufficient.

Isn't it special and comforting to remain utterly righteous without deserving it? Completely justified without any merit, as was the prodigal son in Luke 15: 11–31. To anyone brought up in a legalistic church community, this may sound heretical, but I've provided numerous Bible verses to show that it is true.

> This righteousness is given through faith in Jesus Christ to all who believe. There is no difference between Jew and Gentile, for all have sinned and fall short of the glory of God, and *all are justified freely by his grace* through the redemption that came by Christ Jesus. (Romans 3:21–24 NIV)

You may not always live a Christ-like life, and your actions and thoughts might not always glorify Him, yet *He lives in you* (Galatians 2:20). Even if your pottery is broken, He *still* lives in you because He has redeemed you, once and for all (Ephesians 3:17). You remain righteous because *He* is righteous.

"Christ in you, the hope of glory" (Colossians 1:27 NKJV).

CHAPTER 37

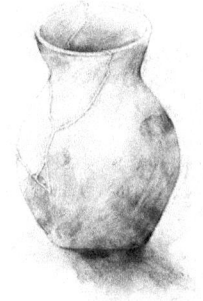

SECRET #10
THE GREAT POTTER IS YOUR CONTINUOUS SAVIOR

Who then is the one who condemns? *No one*. Christ Jesus who died—more than that, who was raised to life—is at the right hand of God and is also *interceding for us*.

ROMANS 8:34 (NIV)

> My dear children, I write this to you so that you will not sin. But *if* anybody *does* sin,
> we have *an advocate* with the Father—Jesus Christ, the Righteous One.
> He is the atoning sacrifice for our sins, and not only for ours
> but also for the sins of the whole world.
>
> 1 John 2:1–2 (NIV)

Even if you are buried in the most miserable trash yard of broken potteries, the Great Potter is still your Redeemer. Even if you continue breaking your pottery, *He remains your advocate and continuous Savior.* "Because we trust in the living God, who is *the Savior* of all men, *especially of those who believe*" (1 Timothy 4:10 NKJV).

He is our Savior—*especially us who believe*! The Great Potter is our *continuous* Savior.

I grew up in a legalistic church that taught that although the Great Potter reconciled me to Himself when I first came to Him, the onus fell on me to *stay* reconciled. So *the Great Potter remaining as my continuous advocate and Saviour for as long as I live* was a revolutionary secret. He redeemed me once and for all, which is still in effect today, and He *continues* as my Savior forever. "The Lamb of God, who takes away the sin of the world!" (John 1:29 NIV) does not mean that it was *only* one chance, one short moment of forgiveness, rather that *"His mercies never come to an end*; they are *new every morning*" (Lamentations 3:22–23 ESV).

In my youth, although I fully understood that I was saved only because of His grace, I completely misunderstood that He continues being my Savior after salvation. For some reason, I thought that while the Great Potter's grace was sufficient to squeeze me through the narrow gate once, for me to *remain* on that narrow road leading to heaven, and indeed *staying saved*, was entirely dependent on me. I didn't just think this up; rather, it was instilled in me. The old ladies at the church who kept asking me after every Sunday service whether I was *still* saved fed this misconception. Those preachers who encouraged the continuous self-scrutinizing statements I can still hear after fifty years ring in my ears reinforced it:

"Are you *sure* you are *still* ready to meet the Groom?"

"Is your dress *still* cleansed with the Lamb's blood?"

"Are you *certain* all your sins are *still* washed away?"

Similarly, I remember the first night's bonfire at the church summer camps. We were asked to reflect on our position with the Great Potter and whether we were *still* saved.

"Are you ready if the rapture of the believers was to take place tonight?"

"Anyone with the salvation assurance, please, lift your hands!"

I recall only a few kids cautiously lifting hands. Cautiously because how could we ever be *certain*?

"And now, those of you without the salvation assurance, please lift your hands!"

This time only a couple of the bravest and rebellious ones dared to lift their hands. This was a bold statement to make in front of the pastors who knew our parents and were sure to inform them.

The third question was the one most of us camp oldies expected.

"If you feel uncertain about your salvation, please lift your hand."

Most of us lifted our hands. Yes, I was certainly uncertain.

And, of course, after a week of Bible studies, bonfire revival meetings, and nightly prayer vigils, most of us felt the sweet assurance of our salvation *again*. After leaving camp, the feeling lasted a couple of days, sometimes even a week. However, after a couple of weeks, I was usually back into my familiar anxiety, fearing my parents' sudden rapture and being left behind to the apocalyptic horrors. If nobody was at home when arriving from school, I called a particular church granny. If she answered the phone, I breathed in relief that the rapture had not taken place—not yet.

The specific topics and Bible verses indeed increased my anxiety level, such as:

- How can I be *sure* I am one of those predestined? (Ephesians 1:4–5)
- What about if I've done an unforgivable sin *accidentally*? (Mark 3:28–29; Matthew 12:31–32)

- Because of failing, did I crucify Christ again and now there was no hope for me? (Hebrews 6:4–9; 10:26–31). What about if I am an apostasy?

Of course, I did not understand that "blaspheming the Holy Spirit," "falling away," "trampling the Son of God underfoot", or "insulting the Spirit of grace" referred to *rejecting the grace of Christ*, His perfect sacrifice (Hebrews 9:28) just as the legalistic Pharisees had done in their self-righteousness. I did not understand that His grace never ends, and it was a free gift for me to receive. To make matters worse, as a child, I accentuated Bible passages that emphasized the Great Potter's punishment, judgment, and eternal hell.

I also had the tendency to take the most loving statement and twist it to fit with my distorted image of the Great Potter. For example, Romans 8:16, The-Spirit-Himself-testifying-with-our-spirit-that-we-are-God's-children Bible-verse *certainly* increased my apprehension levels. I could never be sure if I *felt* any inner witness or if I only imagined it. The more I assessed my feelings, the less assurance I felt. 1 John 4:18, There-is-no-fear-in-love-but-*perfect-love-casts-out-fear* Bible-verse only *proved my fears right. Having fears was an evidence for not having the Great Potter's love. A vicious circle!* Oh, how I wish I had understood that the witness of the Spirit in my spirit is *not* dependent on my spirit, emotions, or feelings but based on His Spirit; the Great Potter redeeming me 100 percent. Nothing I do can make Him forsake me or love me less!

He is the Gate and the Road

Another misunderstanding I had because of my legalistic upbringing was the idea of a squat, tight gate at the beginning of a narrow road leading to heaven. In my mind, I had to somehow squeeze through the narrow gate, obeying the rules and leaving behind anything I enjoyed, all the worldly stuff, and the sin, of course.

Similarly, I believed that to *remain* on the narrow road that dangerously wound upward and to *stay* saved was entirely dependent on me. The road not only was filled with "forbidden" signs but also was slippery and crammed with roadblocks, potholes, and traps. The fiery lake was waiting for those who fell. Trying to stay saved required cautious steps. And only few succeeded.

Certainly, there would have been less anxiety and insecurity if only I had understood the idea of Christ as my continuous Savior. Instead of believing the works-based gate and road to heaven, understanding that *He* is the gate *and* the road would have relieved me of untold anxiety. I now understand that the road is narrow because there is *no other way* but His grace; none of our works qualify.

"Jesus said again, 'Very truly I tell you, *I am the gate* for the sheep... *I am the gate*; whoever enters through me will be saved" (John 10:7, 9 NIV). "Jesus answered, 'I am *the way* and the truth and the life. No one comes to the Father except through me'" (14:6).

How opposite the *truth* is from the legalistic teaching that focused on achievements and efforts! Since Christ is both the gate and the road, He indeed leads me to a pasture and fulfilled life. I can rest on His already finished accomplishments!

The Great Potter does not save, then abandon us to make it on our own, struggling in agonizing uncertainty for the rest of our lives. Instead, *He keeps saving us every day* (Lamentations 3:22–23). Every morning, His grace is brand-new and fresh like living water and living bread meant to be received and enjoyed every single day.

CHAPTER 38

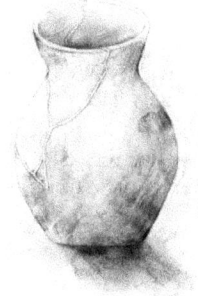

SECRET #11
YOU ARE THE GREAT POTTER'S MOST PRECIOUS AND BEAUTIFUL CLAY POTTERY

For you created my inmost being; you knit me together in my mother's womb.
I praise you because *I am fearfully and wonderfully made*;
your works are *wonderful*, I know that full well.

PSALM 139:13–14 (NIV)

That look in the Great Potter's eyes. It's full of love, gentleness, and compassion when He sees you—even those secret areas that are deeply hidden where you don't even want to see yourself.

Seeing your dreams and fears.

Your joy and grief.

Your pride and shame.

Your deepest desires and most profound disappointments.

Seeing also all your failures. Every crack and bruise of your broken pottery. Even if you have tried your best to fix it with those superglues or cover it with the heaviest makeup—even if you have polished your pottery so that it looks like stainless steel.

The Great Potter sees your inmost hurt—that most excruciating wound that ever pierced your heart and broke your clay pottery. Even the most shameful episode of your very being—that most humiliating event that withered your pottery for the rest of your life. And not only that, He launches the healing process. He collects your broken pieces and takes them home. He mixes them with the new clay of His unfailing love and never-ending grace.

I hope you allow yourself to see what He sees when He looks at your eyes?

If you have never dared to lift your eyes and look at His eyes while He is looking at you, just allow this process to enfold right now. Even if you are *still* scared and fear that He looks at you with a glimpse of disappointment, disapproval, dismay, disbelief…

He doesn't.

He *is* looking at you right now. Lift your eyes to see what He thinks about you when looking into the core of your clay pottery. You can read it in His eyes. This is the message of love and tenderness for your heart to treasure: *You are the most precious and the most beautiful child of mine!*

You.

Most precious.

Most beautiful.

Mine.

My child.

Even if you never experienced this love from your parents. Even if you were never held gently, cradled in their arms, even if you never heard your name softly whispered, and even if you never read this message in your parents' eyes, the Great Potter claims you as His most precious child.

Perhaps you've searched for that look all of your lives. You've yearned to hear soft words of comfort. Maybe it's difficult for you to feel fulfillment, to accept yourselves as you are. In the Great Potter's presence, this primitive need can be satisfied.

Take this into your core and let it fill not only your cognitive brain cells but also your feelings and emotions, allowing this truth to liberate your pottery.

You are the most precious and the most beautiful child of mine!

Transformation

Sadly, many Christians are conflicted between what they read about the Great Potter's love and grace in the Bible and what they *feel* about Him. They also have distorted ideas about what they believe *He* feels toward them. Even though their theology is biblical, their assumptions and expectations about Him are defined by trauma and are therefore distorted. Just as I had imagined in my childhood and youth the Great Potter as a vindictive judge who measured my mistakes and saw my pottery as a tragic waste of clay and His efforts! This kept me from hearing, "You are the most precious and the most beautiful daughter of mine!"

Exhausted, after trying to meet the bar all my youth, in my mid-twenties I had quit trying to measure up anymore. I had let go of legalistic rules I had mistakenly believed were prerequisites to stay on good terms with the Great Potter. Frustrated, I accepted the bittersweet reality that never again would I squeeze myself back into that constricted square in which I had to spend my childhood. However, although seemingly calm and taking it as my new normal, I couldn't help feeling a pang of guilt and fear, although I tried to silence it. While I acknowledged that I had been a victim of legalistic and spiritually abusive teaching, I did not yet realize how that had also distorted my idea of the Great Potter.

It wasn't until my mid-thirties when I finally immersed myself in the truth of what the Great Potter thinks when He looks at me.

You are the most precious and the most beautiful daughter of mine!

Grasping this truth *transformed* my life. Accepting and believing this changed my distorted image of Him and then transformed my fearful and anxiety-driven relationship with Him. At the same time, this truth also renovated my damaged self-image, as I had always thought that I was not good enough, so it didn't matter how much I tried. Learning what the Great Potter thinks of me was life-altering. The revolutionary before-and-after experience I will remember for the rest of my life.

Interestingly, no Christian book or sermon launched this liberating process in my soul. It started as I was writing my research paper for my Advanced Psychotherapy studies and came across Donald Winnicott's, a British psychoanalyst, ideas about the mother-baby relationship.[54] He wrote about the message the mother conveys with her eyes as she looks into her baby's eyes: "You are the most beautiful baby of this entire universe."

What does the baby see when he or she looks into Mother's face? How she looks at her baby is somehow related to what the baby sees in her. If the mother *"looks with love and with tenderness, the baby experiences him or herself as joyfully alive."*[55]

Reading Winnicott's ideas of the mother-baby relationship launched my process to understand the Great Potter's thoughts and feelings toward me. I suddenly recognized that the Great Potter had *always* looked at me with love and tenderness—*and He always will*. And it is because of this look that I can experience myself as joyfully alive (instead of full of fears).

Suddenly, it all made all sense to me because I was a mother of my four-year-old curious little boy and a gorgeous baby girl, only a couple of months old. My heart bursts every time I looked at them or even thought about them. Realizing what I felt toward my son and daughter helped me comprehend how the Great Potter must feel about me, His daughter. Just as my children are most precious and beautiful to me in the whole universe, so was I in the Great Potter's eyes.

I am the most beloved and most beautiful clay pottery of His.
You are the most beloved and most beautiful clay pottery of His.

Just as I loved my children so much that I would die to protect them; the Great Potter did, and not just to protect me from physical harm, but His bursting love that sacrificed His life for me keeps me eternally safe. And He did it for you, too.

This is a life-changing secret for any broken pottery to adopt.

In this secret is the foundation of all Great Potter's dealings with us. Everything He did and will do and any work He is going to do with our clay potteries is because we are His most precious and beautiful potteries. And all along, He has good plans for you and me.

As broken pottery, you are not only perfectly safe and loved in the Great Potter's hands but also cherished.

> In His eyes, you are…
> "a rose of Sharon, lily of the valleys, " (Solomon 2:1 NIV);
> "… your voice is *sweet*, and your face is *lovely*" (v.14).
> "How *beautiful* you are, my darling! Oh, how b*eautiful*!" (4:1);
> "… my dove, my *perfect* one, is *unique*." (6:9).

Allow this truth to engross your core and *immerse yourself in the way the Great Potter sees you.* You are loved with His unfailing love, a divine love that surrounds your clay pottery, inside out. Immerse yourself in this divine truth, letting it into the core of your clay pottery at this moment.

> *You, yes, you, are My most beautiful and precious child!*
> *You are treasured.*
> *Beloved, Adored, Cherished*—is your new name.

CHAPTER 39

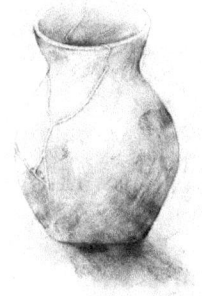

SECRET #12
YOU LEARN ABOUT THE GREAT POTTER WHEN YOU SURRENDER

> And after my skin has been destroyed,
> yet in my flesh *I will see God;*
> *I myself will see him with my own eyes*
> —*I, and not another.*
> How my heart yarns within me.
>
> JOB 19: 26–27 (NIV)

As Job experienced the Great Potter in his brokenness, so you can experience Him in yours. When all is good in your life, it is as if you rely on stories of others who share what the Great Potter has done in their lives yet not understanding who the Great Potter *is*. But when He intervenes for your brokenness, rescuing and restoring your broken pieces, you perhaps for the first time "see Him" with your own eyes. When He becomes the Redeemer for your disasters, you grasp how much He cares about *you*. You learn something unique about His divine love, something different about Him, as Job, Hagar, Paul, Elijah, and Peter did.

The secret is that *you learn about the Great Potter when you surrender to Him.*

Over a decade ago, I had the opportunity to see the Great Potter with my inner eyes and saw Him differently than ever before in my life. This encounter deeply enriched my relationship with Him. I learned that even though He oversees the galaxies, He is *also* interested in my heartbreak.

It was the end of July, one of those scorching and humid days. Although the sun was shining with its hottest force, I was shivering in the darkest valley of my life. I felt foggy and was in the shock phase of all that had happened within a week. I did nothing but cry. Waking up in the morning, I experienced a moment of relief, thinking that what I was going through was a nightmare, then I realized it was all too real. *My life had become a nightmare.*

Crying in my car on this sweltering day as I didn't want to cry at home in front of my children. My pottery was smashed, crushed into shards, suddenly and unexpectedly. I felt helpless, with no idea how to begin to clean the horrendous mess. I felt desperate facing the loss and unknown taking place.

Suddenly, amid my bawling, I clearly heard a voice. It sounded like a choir singing, first quietly and then as if the singers were in the car with me. It seemed a multitude of beautiful, harmonic voices had surrounded me.

I surrender all . . . That is what I heard first. *I surrender all...*

And the idea of surrendering to the Great Potter filled me in an instant, like a refreshing breeze.

I surrender all. I surrender all.

> *All to Thee my blessed Savior.*
> *I surrender all.*[56]

And—so I surrendered. In that heated car on that late-July sunshine surrounded by this divine choir singing in my soul, I surrendered.

> *I surrender because I cannot do it by myself any longer.*
> *I surrender because I cannot pretend to hold it together anymore.*
> *I surrender because I do not know where to start to make it right again.*
> *I surrender because I am so tired and exhausted.*
> *I surrender because there is nothing left of my beautiful clay pottery.*

And I asked the Great Potter to collect my broken pieces, to clean the mess, to take all of the crumbled bits. Take it all because *I surrender*. I surrendered to His table, to His wheel, to His shelf, to His firing oven . . . whatever it takes. I gave it all to Him.

> *Here it is, take my pottery and take my misery! I surrender my heart.*

And then I heard another voice speaking deep in my heart: *Nothing. NOTHING can separate you from the love of Christ!*

My pottery was miserably broken; however, the Great Potter would *not* allow *anything* to separate me from Him and His love.

> *Neither* death nor life, *neither* angels nor demons, *neither* the present *nor* the future, *nor* any powers, *neither* height *nor* depth, *nor* anything else in all creation, will be able to separate us from the love of God that is in Christ Jesus my Lord. (Romans 8:38–39 NIV)

We do not always understand why our pottery is broken so badly. And we don't need to. It is enough that we know that we are perfectly safe. Whatever happens to us, nothing can separate us from the love of the Great Potter.

Job also surrendered to the Great Potter's will in the end. He realized that all that happened in his life was too big for him to understand. Therefore, he surrendered, and he gave his situation to the Great Potter. Similarly, once *we* surrender, the Great Potter *will* say the last word for our situation. How different from our trying to desperately glue our broken pieces together or trying to hide our cracks from others and even from Him. When we surrender to Him, we are relieved of the stress that comes with trying to clean our messes.

This is quite a remarkable secret for us broken potteries: *We learn about the Great Potter when we surrender.* When we surrender, we no longer only hear about His wondrous works for the others but see Him with our *own* eyes. We experience Him working with our clay crumbles and making something new out of them.

We also learn to trust the Great Potter instead of being horrified by our circumstances. Not even the tiniest detail of our broken pottery pieces is outside of His control and His purpose. He can change even evil to serve His good plans. He can use the worst situation to bring good into our lives. His solutions are so creative, they are beyond our clay brain imaginations.

We learn that the Great Potter is never far away but very close. Even when we don't feel His presence, He is there. *Immanuel, God with us.* He is with us in our darkest valleys.

I saw the Great Potter while in the messiest trash yard of my broken pottery. And He saw me. Before this, I had only heard about Him. But after I saw Him, in my soul, with my own eyes, I *learned* that He cares about me, my pottery, and its tiniest cracks. After that episode on that heated day in July—what followed the next months—was nothing less but the Great Potter taking care of the smallest details while walking with me through my valley of death. His loving attention, and daily miracles—as I call them—embraced me to see the stars lightning the sky of my darkest valley. I learned I can survive all things through Him who strengthens me (Philippians 4:13).

As broken pottery, when we surrender is when the Great Potter takes over. That is when we see our Redeemer in His glory and compassion standing on our ashes. When Stephen was being stoned, he surrendered his life to the Great Potter, and—at that moment, Christ stands up (Acts 7:54–60). He could not just continue sitting calmly and observing. He stands up for Stephen because He wants to *demonstrate*

His empathy in that horrible moment. I imagine Jesus saying to him, "I am with you at this moment. I'm *standing* right here, with you, waiting for you." Yes, Stephen surrendered, but Christ stood up in all His glory. There was a moment in my life too that I actually imagined Christ standing up!

Can you relate with this? With your mind's eye, can you see Him *standing* on the ruins of your broken pieces and demonstrating His empathy for your pottery that was smashed in pieces? —He is indeed able to empathize with you (Hebrew 4:15). He will never abandon a broken pot.

In the middle of your uttermost brokenness, when you saw the Great Potter with your own inner eyes, what did you learn about Him? If you've never surrendered to the Great Potter, what would you want to learn about Him?

CHAPTER 40

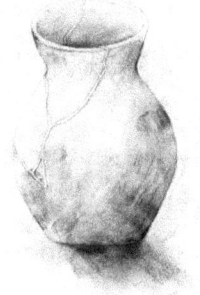

SECRET #13
NO MATTER WHAT, THE GREAT POTTER IS ALWAYS IN CONTROL

I know that you can do all things;
no plan of yours can be thwarted.

JOB 42:2 (NIV)

As potteries blown violently onto a stone floor and breaking into millions of pieces, we often wonder in anguish, where is the Great Potter? Or when recalling our times in the trash yard of the broken potteries, we wonder where He was when we most needed Him. However, we can look back and see that He was always there. All the time, in our darkest valleys, driest deserts, deepest caves, muddiest pits, and the most stinky trash yards of broken potteries, *He was there.* We have indeed fallen into His loving arms without even knowing it until after the fact.

When you surrender your broken pieces to the Great Potter, you surrender control over your life. Then you can relax and give yourself to the process. *No matter what, the Great Potter is always in control as He oversees your restoration.* Trust that the Great Potter knows what He is doing with your pottery and that He will make all things work for your good.

This is the secret the Great Potter's potteries can learn only during brokenness. Job realized that the Great Potter's ways are too marvelous for us to grasp; His creativity goes beyond our wildest imaginations. Dealing with the Sovereign Creator who deeply loves us, it makes sense to trust Him as He holds and renews our pottery. Our brokenness, as well as our recovery, are under His control. As Joseph's and Hagar's stories demonstrated, the Great Potter works in and through the most threatening situations, causing everything to work out for our good. He can even change the meaning of something miserably broken into something beautiful. Jacob, Judah, Tamar, David, Bathsheba, Rahab, Ruth, and many other broken potteries mentioned in the Messiah's lineage prove that the Great Potter can redeem anything to serve His purpose, even those traumatizing episodes.

Yes, it may look a total mess in the moment, but I may not see the whole picture. *"Although the threads of my life have often seemed knotted, I know, by faith, that on the other side of the embroidery there is a crown."*[57]

The Great Potter can bring blessing from our brokenness, meaning from misery, and secrets from suffering. He works all things for the good according to His purposes (Romans 8:28).

In the Great Potter's hands, even the darkest moment of our broken potteries may turn into our most valuable resource. As a therapist, I have experienced this many times. My broken pottery has best taught me to understand other broken potteries. Although it is impossible to see any meaning for most of our traumatizing events when we are in the middle of them, looking back, it often makes sense. We are broken and wounded potteries but vessels for His Service, wounded healers to empathize with the suffering world.

Trust that the Great Potter, who formed you in your mothers' wombs and began this good work in you will take responsibility for it. "Being *confident* of this, that he who began a good work in you *will carry it on to completion* until the day of Christ Jesus" (Philippians 1:6 NIV).

The Great Potter does not tire of working with us, even if we don't cooperate. He will never tire of us even if we resist. He will not make mistakes in our process or mix our pieces with the wrong ingredients. He knows what we need as He has known us from the beginning. It does not matter how many times He must start the process over or how many times He must collect our pieces when we've been smashed.

His love remains.

His grace remains.

His faithfulness remains.

When we shout, "Help!" from the middle of our broken mess, He is already there. He is in control no matter what. He is in control even when you feel out of control and miserable.

Corrie Ten Boom chose to trust Him while at the Nazi concentration camp: "*Never be afraid to trust an unknown future to a known God.*" [58]

CHAPTER 41

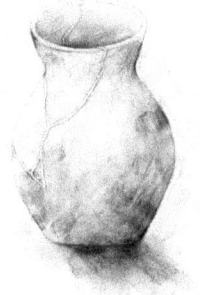

SECRET #14
THE GREAT POTTER'S
SUPERNATURAL PEACE GUARDS YOU

Peace I leave with you;
my peace I give you.
I do not give to you as the world gives.
Do not let your hearts be troubled and *do not be afraid*

JOHN 14:27 (NIV)

Although the Great Potter never promised His clay potteries a life without struggles and brokenness, He promised *to be with us* "to the very end of the age" (Matthew 28:20 NIV). He also left us something supernatural, *His peace,* as "he himself is our peace" (Ephesians 2:14 NIV). The Prince of Peace is with us every day (Isaiah 9:6).

Peace I leave with you, my peace I give you...

Because of His supernatural, royal peace, our potteries can tolerate brokenness. Because of this peace, we have the assurance that the Great Potter is always in control, even if we don't feel so at the moment. Instead of relying on feelings that come and go and can be damaged by traumatizing experiences, our *trust* is in the Great Potter.

Interestingly, the Great Potter's peace, "which transcends all understanding, will *guard* our hearts and our minds" (Philippians 4:7 NIV). Like a powerful military safeguard, His supernatural peace protects and surrounds our hearts and minds, which keep us from stress, worry, and fears.

This secret is vital for your broken potteries to embrace: No matter what, *the Great Potter's supernatural peace guards you.* Even if your external circumstances do not change, His peace never leaves. Moreover, no circumstances can steal it from you. The Great Potter's peace continuously guards your clay pottery even if it's thrown onto the floor and smashed into pieces. There is His peace for each of your pieces, no matter how broken they are.

As clay potteries, we have His peace when at the Potter's house and He is working with our clay. Even though it is not always comfortable to be shaped and formed on His wheel, we trust Him to know what He is doing. We will not lose His peace even when placed in His firing oven, an uncomfortable experience, especially on the lower shelves where potteries are fired at the highest temperatures and prepared to become the sturdiest vessels. However, the Great Potter always has a plan when he works with our clay. Anything that happens to us in the Potter's house is for a purpose, and it is always under His full responsibility.

I'm sure both the prophet Jeremiah and Dietrich Bonhoeffer knew this secret of supernatural peace. I imagine it was because the Prince of Peace was nearby guarding their hearts and minds in their cruel circumstances. They were able to hold on with hope and experience. *"The loving forces silently surrounded"* thus I *"feel quite soothed, secure, and filled with grace."* [59]

Although we do not know why something happened to break our pottery, we learn to trust that the Great Potter has all the answers. His presence in our lives is the existential reality that does not shatter even though the world around us is falling apart. His peace will not leave us even when our potteries are crushed into a million pieces.

Remarkably, we do not have to *feel* His presence, it is enough that we *know* He is always there. He may not calm the storm around us, but His *presence* calms our heart. "Fear not" is declared in the Bible 365 times, once for every day of the year!

The Apostle Paul often started or ended his letters by wishing grace and peace. This makes sense because grace always comes with peace, and peace always comes with grace.

Grace and Peace!

CHAPTER 42

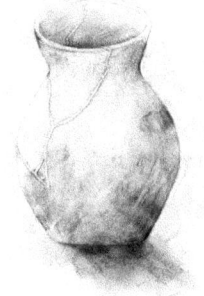

SECRET #15
YOUR EMPTY POTTERY WILL BE FILLED

I can do all things through Christ
who strengthens me

Philippians 4:13 (NKJV)

The prophet Elisha wanted to do something miraculous for a penniless widow (2 Kings 4:1–7). Elisha tells the widow to collect as many empty potteries as she can find and then start to fill them with oil from her meager supply—enough for one loaf of bread. The widow pours into one pottery then another and still another. She keeps pouring, filling all of the jars. She gathers more potteries from her friends and still keeps pouring. In the end, all of the empty potteries are filled to the brim with oil.

There is a secret in emptiness we often experience as clay potteries. *Our empty potteries will be filled!*

The one filled with our self-sufficiency does not need any filling; it needs to be emptied first so it can be filled with the Great Potter's oil, gifts, and power. It is only when we have nothing to pour from ourselves that the Great Potter begins His divine miracle of pouring from us into other potteries, blessing them.

> And He said to me, '*My grace is sufficient for you,*
> for *My strength is made perfect in weakness."*
> Therefore, most gladly I will rather boast in my infirmities,
> that the power of Christ may rest upon me. . . .
> For *when I am weak, then I am strong."* (2 Corinthians 12: 9–10 NKJV)

The apostle Paul learned this secret. No longer a legalistic, works-based-salvation Pharisee boasting in his deeds, he knows that he has nothing to offer. He had in his life what he described as a "thorn in his flesh," which sounds painful and irritating, something that was constantly cracking his pottery. Paul says that he had three times pleaded with the Great Potter to take it away from his pottery (vv. 7–8). However, instead of removing it, the Great Potter assured Paul that His grace is *sufficient* for him.

With His grace—all is good!

The Great Potter's grace is all we need, a vital secret for any broken pottery apprehensive about apparent emptiness and the palpable reality that when broken we are empty. Whatever was stored in that pottery before the breakage, is no longer inside but mixed with the broken pieces and dirt.

The Great Potter's grace goes hand in hand with His power, just as our weaknesses go hand in hand with His strength and our emptiness with His refilling service. There is no need to pretend that we are stronger or sturdier than we are, or emphasize that we are only half empty or half full. We need not fantasize that we are a Braveheart type, power-girls, or unbreakable pottery made of cast iron. The Great Potter does not want us to try to be anything but what we are. All He needs from us is to rely on Him, to acknowledge our emptiness and weakness so that He can freely fill us with His treasure.

His power is made perfect in our weaknesses.

Furthermore, we never need to focus on our cracks or emptiness. That would fill us with anxiety, despair, and inadequacy. But when we focus on the Great Potter's treasure stored inside us, we are filled with peace, hope, love, and grace.

The broken potteries' stories in this book clearly show that the Great Potter does not use supermen or superwomen as His vessels. When we stop staring at our flaws and cracks, and start seeing the Great Potter instead, that is when we are equipped vessels for His Service.

No need to feel embarrassed or ashamed if we are empty and utterly wretched. It is undoubtedly a better position than being filled with any DIY fixes or narcissistic tendencies, driving us to shine *our* light. When empty without anything to offer on our own, it is easier to receive everything the Great Potter has for us—and then share for others.

The Great Potter's power that becomes perfect in our weaknesses means that we can receive His renewing grace every morning, just as we can trust the renewal of His strength every day. His strength equals our days (Deuteronomy 33:25). Furthermore, we need not worry about tomorrow either, "for tomorrow will worry about itself. Each day has enough trouble of its own" (Matthew 6:34 NIV).

For the Great Potter's power within our potteries, we do not have to concentrate on ourselves and be disheartened because of our issues. Instead, we are encouraged to consciously empty our potteries from anything that does not belong there.

We should let go of self-pity and bitterness as well as any shame that was projected onto our potteries as a result of traumatic experiences. False guilt should be evacuated. Self-dismay and self-belittling thoughts should not be given space in our potteries. Any vicarious trauma-related symptoms transferred onto us while helping others should also leave our potteries as they do not belong to us. We can ask the Great Potter to empty our potteries of everything that does not belong there, and fill it with His secrets.

So, let's start *receiving* what the Great Potter designed for us to hold. Once He has filled us with all that He intended, we can pour into other potteries. Allow His mighty light to shine through your many cracks and holes.

Let your brokenness and emptiness become your ministry in His service.

When we stop staring at our nothingness but instead focus on the Great Potter's almighty power, our strength is renewed. He replaces our weaknesses with His power and our worry with His peace.

And every morning, our pottery will receive a new filling of grace—*abundant* grace.

CHAPTER 43

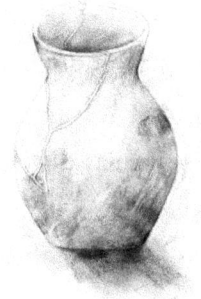

SECRET #16
YOU ARE NEVER DAMAGED GOODS FOR THE GREAT POTTER'S SERVICE

*And the vessel he was making of clay
was spoiled in the potter's hand,
and he reworked it into another vessel,
as it seemed good to the potter to do.*

Jeremiah 18:4 (ESV)

Our self-image, which is developed early in life, most likely differs from the way the Great Potter thinks about us. When the Great Potter accepts us *as-is* and sees us as precious and beautiful, our self-image may be so damaged and trauma-inflicted that we do not see ourselves in a good or accurate light at all. Sadly, a typical self-image for many broken potteries includes guilt-driven, self-belittling, and ascetic 'wretched worm' attitudes that in some Christian circles may even be confused with good old Christian humility. Some may even think that mentally whipping oneself is the holy way to treat ourselves. It is not.

One of the great demolisher's best weapons to *sabotage* our service with the Great Potter is to load us down with the trauma-driven inferiority complex and a profound sense of incompetence. He accuses us with a list of failures and cracks, and then berates us as to why we are not enough or fit for the Great Potter's service. His words convince us to resign ourselves to avoid any hassles and further embarrassments. We may agree with his false assessment and meekly step down from our posts. Considering ourselves damaged goods, we slink away in dejected silence. We rip off our pottery rights, and allow projected shame and humiliation to determine that we do not deserve anything else. Just as Peter ran away after the rooster-event, so do we. Perhaps first digging the worms behind a woodshed, and then go back fishing… or whatever it was we were doing *before* the Great Potter first called us for His Ministry.

Maybe your Christian community has told you that you better step onto the sidelines and position your pottery on a shelf for the rest of your life. Because of your problems—bankruptcy, divorce, addiction, mental health issues, children's troubles…, you are no longer welcome to *serve* in your community amongst the more polished potteries. Your ministry has been cancelled or suspended for ambiguous period of time.

In my childhood church community, I witnessed the humiliating episodes of many young women being caught pregnant out of wedlock, and then asking forgiveness sobbing in front of the congregation. Although forgiveness was always granted, in many cases, the 'sin' was never forgotten so much that they were permanently displaced to the sidelines, not good enough to serve in any ministry, despite their God-given gifts and talents. *What a waste!*

There isn't anyone qualified to put themselves into the position of authority to suspend someone's ministry. The Great Potter does *not* regret His calling, He never wastes clay—every talent He gave He *meant* to be utilized in His Service.

Have you fallen for the destroyer's lies after a devastating broken pottery experience?

Being positioned on the Great Potter's table and comparing yourself with other potteries can be embarrassing. Shamefully exposed, full of cracks, smashed into pieces, it's easy to think that you have no right to contribute to the Great Potter's kingdom because of your less than perfect witness and your often-broken pottery. Have you assumed that the Great Potter could no longer trust you and have no use for your vessel?

Please, do *not* allow the devil to sabotage your Christian service! Do not allow him to use your bad report-card or poor track record as evidence against your pottery. Do not let him plant a distorted image of the Great Potter in your mind and replace the Great Potter's truth with his insipid lies. The Great Potter is *already* doing something new out of your broken pieces. "Forget the former things, do not dwell on the past. *See,* I am doing a new thing! *Now* it springs up; *do you not perceive it?*" (Isaiah 43: 18-19 NIV).

Whenever you find yourself with disturbing thoughts filling your mind, ask yourself: Which one am I to believe—the devil's lies about my pottery being damaged goods and thus not qualified for the Great Potter's service? Or the Great Potter's assurance that He accepts me as-is, and that He loves me with His unfailing love, never-ending grace, and everlasting faithfulness?

Which one do you believe? The devil or the Great Potter?

Do you really think the devil has any say in whom the Great Potter uses? For sure, *he does not hold the HR position in the Great Potter's house!*

Why not listen to the Great Potter?

He desires to use all of His clay potteries as vessels for His service. No matter what trash yard of broken potteries we dwell in, we are never too tarnished for the

Great Potter. You are never too broken! He desires His light to shine through your cracks! Therefore, it is time to bathe yourself in this significant secret of broken potteries: *I am never damaged goods for the Great Potter's service.* You may be damaged all right, but you are not *so* damaged as *not* to qualify for His service.

Dream Big!

Even amid the most horrendous brokenness in the trash yard of broken potteries, the Great Potter still wants us to dream big! He wants us to see His *good* plans, embrace His promises, and trust that everything is possible for Him. Just as the exhausted Israelites kept moving in the wilderness because of the beautiful image of the Promised Land the Great Potter had planted into their clay hearts, we should accept the image of what He sees when He looks at us.

The Israelites reacted tragicomically (or simply potter-ishly) when they finally entered the Promised Land. When it was time to move in and fill their potteries with the milk and honey, their irrational fears were instead filled with visions of giants and grasshoppers! "We seemed like grasshoppers in our *own eyes*, and we looked the same to *them*" (Numbers 13:33 NIV).

I always thought that we Canadians have low self-esteem as our national symbol is a beaver. Undoubtedly, a grasshopper would be even a more humiliating national image. If the Israelites saw themselves as grasshoppers, they had a distorted picture of the Great Potter as well. Luckily, Caleb and Joshua did not stare at their empty potteries nor entertain the devil's impotent-complex boosting whispers. Instead, they poured the content of their potteries from the Great Potter onto the people: "The LORD is *with us*. Do not be afraid of them" (14:9).

Yes, a distorted vision can certainly be misleading—the devil wants to blind us!

Claim Your Talents!

The parable of the talents (Matthew 25:14-30 NKJV) tells the story of a generous and trusting master who shares talents for his servants to oversee while he is away. One receives five, another two, and the third fellow receives one talent. However, something that puts this story into a different context from what I was taught at Sunday school, is the fact that there is no reason to call the fellow who received one talent, a *poor* fellow with *only* one talent! The fellow is not poor—even this one talent is *a large amount of wealth*, equal to 16 years worth of labor![38] [60] The point of the story is that while the others happily invest and multiply their talents, the one talent recipient acts in a pretty peculiar way: As if he had received hardly anything and therefore needed to play so safe that he was not playing at all! Instead of mobilizing the enormous wealth and opportunity that had landed in his hands, he immobilizes and totally undermines the opportunity.

Is it because of envy? Is he so scared to fail that he does not bother even trying? Is he so blinded by his distorted notions of his master, seeing him as harsh, stingy, greedy, and malicious, fearing his anger and rejection? Or is he infuriated because he sees the situation as unfair? Because someone else received five talents he does not allow himself to enjoy what he has. As if, it was his concern what someone else had received. It had nothing to do with him, nor was it taken away from him.

Ruled by his irrational fears this guy is a sad example of someone *who dares not to live*—just like the prodigal son's older brother. Rather than appreciating the value of his highly prized talent, the angry fellow buries it in the ground. In his self-pity and cynical sullenness he shoots his own foot—then blurts out to his master: "Look, *there* you have *what is* yours!" (v. 25)

Likewise, it is tragic if we bury our own unique talent in the ground. If we hold a distorted image of the Great Potter we may miss the good plans He has for us.

I have a question for you: Do you, for some reason, doubt your qualifications for your current calling and ministry? Do you think that you are not 'good enough' to continue? Do you compare your pottery with others and feel that it would be better for everyone if you quit?

If so, I seriously want you to consider the following: It's *not* about *you*! Your calling is not about you but it's all about the Great Potter and *His* Great Mission. Your

---

[38] A *talent* was a unit of weight of approximately 80 pounds. As a unit of money it was valued for that weight of silver. A talent was worth about 6,000 denarii. One denarius was the normal pay for a day's work. One talent was worth of 16 years of labour. [60]

talent is not *yours*, it's His; it was given to you by Him and it *still* belongs to Him. It's not about you not being qualified enough or not as qualified as someone else but the fact that *it is the Great Potter's project.* Your calling was *His choice* and, bluntly put: you have no right to bury *His* talent in the ground!

""Can the pot say to the potter, "You know nothing"?" (Isaiah 29:16 NIV). "Does not the potter have *the right* to make out of the same lump of clay some pottery for special purposes and some for common use?" (Romans 9:21 NIV). If you feel inadequate for the ministry the Great Potter is calling you, so did Moses, Isaiah, Peter, David, and many other Bible-heroes—yet *sent they were!* (Exodus 4:13; Isaiah 6:5; Luke 5:8). Just like it was not a good reason for them to refuse it is not for you. The Great Potter reinstatating your pottery is not regulated nor limited by your brokennes, no matter how tarnished you may be in your *own* (or somebody else's) mind.

If the Great Potter decided to make your pottery for a certain purpose, why would you doubt His wisdom for doing so? Why would you think that He does not know what He is doing or that you are not the best choice for the job?

It is not a 'wretched worm' mentality to emphasize that the Bible never says, 'whosoever believes in *themselves*'… but rather: whosoever believes *in Him*! Us answering to our calling is not about us 'believing in ourselves' but us believing in the Great Potter, the author and finisher of our faith. Instead of staring at our pottery's obvious cracks and flaws, and allowing this to paralyze us, we should be "looking to Jesus, the founder and perfecter of our faith (Hebrew 12:2 NIV). Instead of trusting our infirmities we should trust the Great Potter.

Today when you hear the Great Potter calling you: "Whom shall I send? And who will go for us?" simply, reply like Isaiah did: "Here am I. Send me!" (Isaiah, 6:8 NIV)

If your Christian community demands you *only* utilize *half of your talents*, suppressing the rest simply because you are a woman or some member of a discriminated minority, it is time to go and dig your Great Potter-given talents from the ground! "There is neither Jew nor Gentile, neither slave nor free, nor is there male and female, for you are all *one* in Christ Jesus" (Galatians 3:28 NIV). The Great

Potter does not discriminate or oppress any of His clay potteries. He does not victimize or exclude.

Let's utilize our full potential as the Great Potter's vessels. It's time to claim back the *full* ownership for our pottery's talents, calling, and ministry!

Let's shoo away any grasshoppers in our clay potteries!

CHAPTER 44

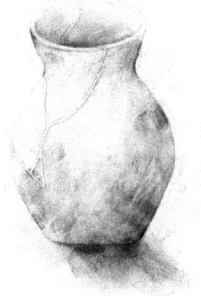

SECRET #17
YOUR BROKEN PIECES AREN'T WASTED

Lord my God, *I called to you for help, and you healed me.*

PSALM 30:2 (NIV)

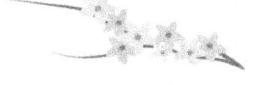

Heidi McKendrick

In Canada, the Prairie Indians tell a touching story about making clay potteries. If clay pottery breaks in the kitchen, the broken pieces are thrown into the trash yard with the other trash right outside the kitchen.

We could assume that this is the end of that pottery's life, *but it is not so*. Although broken, the pottery is not useless. Better days are coming. When the potter of that village is ready to make new clay potteries, he visits each trash yard behind every home and collects the broken clay pieces, including the smashed clay crumbles. He gathers them carefully and carries them to the potter's house. There he mixes the pieces with new clay. The broken pieces, already fired several times, are needed for the new pottery to become stronger.

The Great Potter desires our broken pieces, even the crushed clay and the most smashed crumbles. He visits every trash yard of this world to find and collect the pieces. He carries them to His house, the place where we belong. It does not matter how broken we are; He will never forsake us or throw away any of our pieces because we are His precious potteries and even our broken pieces belong to Him.

I often wonder why the Great Potter bothers using our broken pieces. Why doesn't He just use new clay or sturdier and less disappointing material? However, perhaps in this broken world, these are the only materials He could find to make new potteries. After all, didn't He make His image out of the earthly dust? He could have used gold or diamonds if He wanted spectacular vessels. He could have used cast iron or stainless steel if He wished His vessels to be durable and not easily damaged. However, He chose clay, and, as the Creator of the universe, He was fully informed of the qualities of clay. He chose clay because it is through clay that He can work and shine *His* glory. The Great Potter "chose the lowly things of this world and the despised things—and the things that are not—to nullify the things that are" (1 Corinthians 1:28 NIV).

None of our broken pieces are wasted. Our trauma, our suffering is never worthless. The Great Potter will never abandon a broken pot as He never wastes His clay. The Great Potter always has your back. When He mixes our broken pieces with His new clay, He not only restores the old pottery but also creates something new. The stories of the broken potteries illustrated in the Bible are full of these examples, and we've learned about a few of them. On His table, the broken potteries were not only restored but also reinstated. Some potteries received new names and identities, new callings and missions, new destinies.

Despite their origin or current state, the Great Potter makes the broken potteries His vessels. In His mighty hands, the evil will turn to serve good, and the chaotic mess will turn into order. On His table, the hopeless receive hope and the desperate receive divine peace. This is an empowering secret for any broken pottery to memorize: *None of your broken pieces are wasted.* This is because the Great Potter "works for the good of those who love him, who have been called according to his purpose" (Romans 8:28 NIV). He works all things, good and bad, for good—but often behind the scenes.

The beautiful fact is that our pain is not vain. The strongest potteries are made of powdered clay ground from the broken, already fired potteries. It does not matter how many times our pottery breaks, the Great Potter will always give us a fresh start, making us new. Even if we break hundreds of times, His grace never runs out. He collects our pieces and mixes them with His new clay of love, grace, and faithfulness. He takes us through the washing, kneading, drying, resting, and firing phases as many times as needed.

Our pottery needs a tender touch of our Maker.

Our broken pieces are the material of the new pottery.

CHAPTER 45

SECRET #18
YOUR BROKENNESS MAY BECOME YOUR MINISTRY

*For we are God's handiwork,
created in Christ Jesus to do good works,
which God prepared in advance for us to do.*

Ephesians 2:10 (NIV)

But what is that ultimate secret of brokenness? Why do we always have to break first?

As a DIY gardener enjoying the flowers that blossom in early April, even through the snow, I am amazed at the new life emerging from a tiny broken seed. Just as our broken pottery does, they also first fall to the ground and sink into the black dark ground, where they break—they must break if they hope to sprout and blossom.

"Unless a kernel of wheat falls to the ground and *dies*, it remains only a single seed. But if it dies, it produces *many* seeds" (John 12:24 NIV).

Something falls, something breaks, something dies—and then multiplies.

And then the seed is broken again, and a bread is baked out of those broken seeds. And then that bread is broken again—then shared.

And it becomes a blessing.

There is a secret in our brokenness: *Our brokenness may become our ministry to help other broken potteries.*

Wasn't the Great Potter the only one who saw the potential of the laughably humble beginning in the story of the small boy's lunch feeding five thousand folks? After *blessing* and *breaking* the bread, it shared so miraculously that there were plenty of leftovers reserved for future blessings (Matthew 14:19). Similarly, our pottery—first broken— then shared as a blessing for another broken pottery.

I've had this experienced many times.

When I take the risk and choose to share my brokenness, other broken potteries may feel empowered to share too. And then they begin to grasp onto that Hope I did.

When I no longer hide on the self-administered penalty bench trying to cover my cracks, but instead begin to share my broken pottery experiences, my vulnerability validates others' experiences too—*I am not the only one experiencing this.*

It's like having a kinship with other 'soldiers' who shared the same long, deep trenches.

Sharing something we thought is not shareable diminishes the sense of shame—the shared experience turns into an empowering experience and recovery. If the core of trauma is disempowerment and disconnection, *"recovery, therefore, is based upon the empowerment of the survivor and the creation of new connections."* [61]

The trash yard of broken potteries breaks our *connections*.

Traumatic events, someone smashing our pottery onto the stone floor, not only break us into thousands of smashed pieces but *also* call into question our basic relationships, destroying the attachments of family, friendship, love, even church community. The breakage shatters the construction of sense of self that was formed and sustained in relation to others; it undermines the belief systems that assisted us to give *meaning* to our experiences. When someone breaks our pottery, they not only violate our faith in a natural or divine order but also cast us into a state of existential crisis.[62]

Trauma always isolates, but a therapeutic encounter—sharing with another broken pottery—can re-create a new sense of belonging. While trauma stigmatizes, humiliates, and shames, the therapeutic encounter validates and affirms, even providing witnessing for our most difficult experiences—even those we thought cannot be shared. Trauma degrades the victims but the empathy exalts them.[63]

Whenever our clay potteries break into a thousand broken pieces, and when those thousand pieces bury in the darkness it never feels like a blessing at that moment. Usually, it is impossible to imagine that this tragedy could bring anything good. However, in the Great Potter's divine plan, our brokenness may become a great blessing for *someone else*.

A link exists between first breaking and then producing something stunningly beautiful. It is similar to a butterfly breaking out from its ugly cocoon, or a broken alabaster bottle releasing its aroma.

It may be the very reason why, as broken potteries ourselves, our own woundedness may become the source of the empathy needed for our helping hand, listening ear, and compassionate heart. Because of our own brokenness we do not put ourselves on any pedestals, we do not judge another broken pottery; neither are we too eager to advise.

As wounded healers, our own pain and suffering—our tacit knowledge— has trained us to gain deeper understanding of others' suffering.[64] Our own trash yard experience has taught us how important it is to break the isolation, and how therapeutic it is to receive empathy and validation for our traumatizing experiences—we know how lonely it is to mourn alone.

Sharing makes the load lighter!

Medice, Cura Te Ipsum

Physician, heal thyself (Luke 4:23) refers to the helpers' self-care—we all need to launch our own healing process before we qualify helping others. Yet, this does *not* mean we have to be perfect—none of us are.

It is our brokenness that equips us with compassion—it is our cracks and fractures that help us to attune the pain without words.

Before helping other potteries, each of us need to reflect on our own brokenness, understand its reasons, and our own trauma reactions—we need to launch our *own* healing process first. It would not be therapeutic if we end up using those we help to fulfill and compensate our *own* unmet needs.

It's like trying to help someone out of a swamp—I must come close enough in order to reach my hand. Yet, I must remain *on a secure ground myself*, or I will *also* fall into the same swamp—and that would not help anyone. Some of these swamps are familiar for many of us: swamp of bitterness, unforgiveness, grudge, or self-pity, for example.

Helpers *"who deny their own conflicts and vulnerabilities are at risk of projecting onto [others] the persona of 'the wounded one' and seeing themselves as 'the one who is healed'."*[65]

This kind of a 'helpers-syndrome' can be prevented when we first admit *we also* need healing.

The Great Potter—Broken for You

What about that most incredible blessing of the most significant brokenness ever taken place on the trash yard of broken potteries?

For I received from the Lord that which I also delivered to you: that the Lord Jesus on the same night in which He was betrayed took bread; and when He had given thanks, He broke it and said, "Take, eat; this is *My body which is broken for you*; do this in remembrance of Me." (1 Corinthians 11:23–24 NKJV)

The Great Potter Himself is our Wounded Healer. He turned pure evil into the most amazing blessing. The evil that crucified the perfect sacrifice—wanting to destroy Him for good, miserably failed. Although the darkness celebrated His death, resurrection power and the Great Potter's divine plan was victorious! Christ, the Wounded Healer is the most outstanding role model in His broken body for the blessing of the world.

His body was broken for *your* pottery.
His body was broken for *my* pottery.

His definitive brokenness produced blessings for everyone who believes. Broken, so that our clay potteries can live.

Please, *first* receive the Great Potter's blessing for your clay pottery. Receive His compassion—His unfailing love, never-ending grace, and supernatural peace. Receive the whole package. His treasure shining inside of you.

And then—be ready to spread it around you, at the trash yard of broken potteries.

Become His Ministry—His hands and feet—His light shining through your broken cracks—His compassion pouring from your pottery to the other potteries.

CHAPTER 46

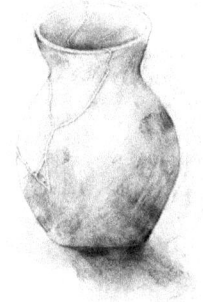

SECRET #19
ONE DAY YOUR TEARS WILL BE WIPED AWAY, AND YOUR POTTERY WILL BE WHOLE

The Sovereign Lord will wipe away the tears from all faces;
he will remove his people's disgrace from all the earth.
The Lord has spoken.

ISAIAH 25:8 (NIV)

Some broken potteries do not have happy endings. For some reason, there seems not to be an indication of a release from agony.

For those broken potteries who do not find relief for their brokenness, this secret is life-altering: *One day, your tears will be all wiped away forever, and your broken pottery will be whole.*

It is that day when this dark valley of life on earth will be turned into everlasting joy. "He will wipe every tear from their eyes. There will be no more death or mourning or crying or pain, for the old order of things has passed away" (Revelation 21:4 NIV).

That day, all broken potteries will also understand the reason for their suffering. Suddenly, we will have the answers to our currently unanswered questions.

"For you, LORD, have delivered me from death, my eyes from tears" (Psalm 116:8 NIV). And, better later than never, our tears will turn into shouts of joy (John 16:20) that will last forever.

Just imagine the Great Potter's bottles full of your tears (Psalm 56:8). Every pain and sorrow are written down; your sufferings are recorded. No matter if no one else noticed your tears, He did and has not forgotten them. The Great Potter saw your tears, every one of them (2 Kings 20:5). Not only did He *see* but also, He *heard* your weeping. Just as no sparrow falls to the ground without His knowing (Matthew 10:29), neither is He unaware of your pottery's knocks and blows. It was for you that He promises: "Blessed are you who weep now, for you will laugh" (Luke 6:21 NIV).

The Great Potter also promises that our current troubles are achieving for us an eternal glory that far outweighs them all (2 Corinthians 4:17). I'm confident, that's how it is for Princess Tamar or Prophet Jeremiah.

Always remember that just as the seasons change, there is a "time to weep and a time to laugh, a time to mourn and a time to dance" (Ecclesiastes 3:4 NIV). "Those who sow with tears will reap with songs of joy. Those who go out weeping, carrying seed to sow, will return with songs of joy, carrying sheaves with them" (Psalm 126:5–6 NIV).

You may wonder how your heartaches or anguish could ever be turned into anything positive. They will because the Great Potter promised. If not right now, at least in heaven. In the meantime, trust Him and cleave to Him through your suffering and pain.

> *Here are my shattered pieces—here are my ruined dreams.*
> *Here is my pierced heart—here is my crushed spirit.*
> *Here I am—Your pottery, still carrying Your thumbprint.*

And remember—if it is your lot in life to break often, you will *always* fall straight into the Great Potter's loving arms.

He holds your broken pieces.

If you have thousands of them, let it comforts you to know that you belong to Him thousands of times.

CHAPTER 47

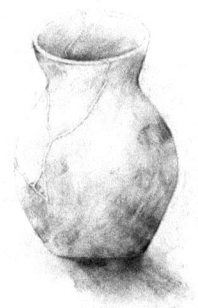

SECRET #20
THERE IS BLESSING IN YOUR BROKENNESS

And the God of all grace,
who called you to his eternal glory in Christ,
after you have suffered a little while,
will himself *restore you* and make you strong, firm and steadfast.

1 PETER 5:10 (NIV)

Heidi McKendrick

Whenever we think about blessings, we associate them with a list of good things for our clay potteries, including health, wealth, success, wellness, good relationships, and more. But what about brokenness, struggles, and sickness? Can we be grateful for these? Why would we even think broken pottery could contain any blessings?

But the secret is that *there is a blessing in our brokenness.*

The visible blessing and restoration *right after* a broken-pottery experience we can accept as good results. Job is our go-to example because the Great Potter blessed the rest of his life and replaced everything he had lost during his horrendous trial. Hagar is another example of a blessing that came after being abandoned by Abraham. Joseph's life ended up with a visible blessing for not only himself but his family and adopted nation.

However, many of our broken potteries' blessings are *not visible* while we remain in the broken state. Sometimes the blessing shows up generations later, as we see in the broken lives of Leah, Tamar, and the lineage of Christ. Out of Bathsheba's misery from King David's adultery and murder episodes, the Great Potter brought His blessing, the Messiah, to all of us.

Mary, whom the angel proclaimed to be blessed among all women, likely did not feel blessed when her pottery smashed to pieces as she helplessly observed her son's slow and torturous death. I can imagine Mary thinking that her blessing felt more like a curse. Yet her son, the Son of God, became cursed so that the generations that followed could be redeemed from the curse and receive the greatest blessing ever poured over us clay potteries.

> Christ has redeemed us from the curse of the law, having become a curse for us (for it is written, "Cursed is everyone who hangs on a tree"), that *the blessing* of Abraham might come upon the Gentiles in Christ Jesus, that we might receive *the promise of the Spirit* through faith. (Galatians 3:13–14 NKJV)

Although we may never see it during our lifetimes, *it does not mean it is not there.* That the Great Potter makes all things, even evil, work together "for good" is interesting as it refers not just to our lifetimes. When scattered in broken pieces in the trash yard of broken potteries, we may be clueless as to what the Great Potter is doing beyond what we see. Also, it may be that we will not see how everything worked for good according to the Great Potter's plan until we enter heaven.

Thus, instead of disputing why this or that broke our clay potteries, perhaps we could start envisioning its purpose according to the Great Potter's perspective. Is there *a divine reason* for your pottery being broken into a thousand pieces? If there are no visible blessings for you, then is the Great Potter planning a blessing for someone else because of your brokenness? Or, is He preparing your pottery for His plans in eternity?

Eternal Blessings

We know that our broken pieces make the new clay pottery stronger, and our brokenness produces both endurance and steadfastness (Romans 5:3; James 1:3). Therefore, we could argue that clay potteries whose lives remained devastated until their deaths (Prophet Jeremiah, Princess Tamar and Dinah, for example) are being prepared for a particular task here in this broken world or for a task in eternity. They are ground into a fine powder and fired on the lowest and hottest shelves of the Great Potter's oven for a particular task in heaven.

> Blessed are you when people insult you, persecute you and falsely say all kinds of evil against you because of me. Rejoice and be glad, because great is your *reward* in heaven, for in the same way they persecuted the prophets who were before you. (Matthew 5:11–12 NIV)

If our broken pottery's pain prepares us for the glory in heaven, it means that the Great Potter working everything "for good" also refers to eternal goodness, which is so good that we cannot even imagine.

Therefore, none of our broken pieces are wasted, and none of our pain is meaningless. "For this light momentary affliction is preparing for us an eternal weight of glory beyond all comparison" (2 Corinthians 4:17 ESV).

A heavenly blessing has blessed thousands of broken potteries over the last thousands of years, giving them hope and reason to continue during the most horrendous circumstances. "I consider that our present sufferings are not worth comparing with the glory that will be revealed in us" (Romans 8:18 NIV).

PART IV
HEALING BROKEN POTTERY

INTRODUCTION

I am the Lord, who heals you.[66][39]

EXODUS 15:26 (NIV)

This final part of *Secrets of Broken Pottery* introduces thoughts on the healing process of broken pottery. The idea is that *none of us will be finished during our lifetimes; the healing process continues as long as we live*. Another is that we can trust the Great Potter during the ongoing process and be confident that "He who began a good work in will carry it on to completion until the day of Christ Jesus" (Philippians 1:6 NIV).

---

[39] "*Raphah*" #7495, means a primitive root; properly, to mend (by stitching), i.e. (figuratively) to cure:--cure, (cause to) heal, physician, repair, X thoroughly, make whole. [66]

As for us clay potteries, "We are in His hands just like clay in the potter's hands" (Jeremiah 18:6 NIV). Our spiritual recovery process is in His hands and under His responsibility. When we surrender to Him on His table, He takes over, and everything that happens to our potteries is under His control. Because the Great Potter oversees our healing process, we are safe as we rest while He molds us according to His plan. None of our broken pieces will be wasted; they are needed to make our new pottery stronger, a unique vessel, either for everyday use or a particular purpose, in His service. "In a large house there are articles not only of gold and silver, but also of wood and clay; some are *for special purposes* and some *for common use*" (2 Timothy 2:20 NIV).

The foundation of our broken potteries' healing process is announced in Isaiah 61:1–4 and Luke 4:18, the Great Potter's first sermon in the synagogue, His mission statement that proclaims His plans for us broken potteries. Let it sink into your core then claim ownership of this proclamation the Great Potter speaks into our hearts...

> *The Spirit of the Lord is upon Me,*
> *Because He has anointed Me*
> *To preach the gospel to the poor;*
> *He has sent Me to heal the broken-hearted,*
> *To proclaim liberty to the captives*
> *And recovery of sight to the blind,*
> *To set at liberty those who are oppressed.* (Luke 4:18 NKJV)

> *The Spirit of the LORD God is upon Me,*
> *Because the LORD has anointed Me*
> *To preach good tidings to the poor;*
> *He has sent Me to heal the broken-hearted,*
> *To proclaim liberty to the captives,*
> *And the opening of the prison to those who are bound;*
> *To proclaim the acceptable year of the LORD,*

And the day of vengeance of our God;
To comfort all who mourn,
To console those who mourn in Zion,
To give them beauty for ashes,
The oil of joy for mourning,
The garment of praise for the spirit of heaviness;
That they may be called trees of righteousness,
The planting of the LORD, that He may be glorified.
(Isaiah 61:1–3 NKJV)

The Great Potter's proclamation introduces a variety of cracks and fractures found in broken potteries. He announced His good news for each of them: those of us poor in spirit, brokenhearted, captives, oppressed, spiritually blind, mourning. It is quite a proclamation, a long list of typical painful experiences familiar to many of us broken potteries and often resulting in our clay potteries being thrown to the floor by others or ourselves, either accidentally or intentionally.

The proclamation announces the continuous Year of Jubilee, the year of the Great Potter's special favor, which, during the Old Testament times, was celebrated once every fifty years (Leviticus 25:10). In that year, anyone who had been sold as a slave was now liberated. Anyone who had lost their land because of unpaid debt could claim it back and return to it. After the Great Potter redeemed and reconciled with us on the day of Calvary, the Year of Jubilee was released for every day and everyone.

The next chapters of this book proclaim this year of the Great Potter's favor, the Year of Jubilee right now, right here, for every reader.

If you feel you have somehow lost your original "land" and your calling at the Great Potter's house, you will get it back because you are invited to come back home. If you are bound or oppressed, the Great Potter desires to liberate you. If you are grieving because of your heartbroken pottery, and if you are weary and burdened, the Great Potter Himself will comfort you with His Word. He will give you rest (Matthew 11:28). If you feel spiritually poor, there is good news for you from the Great Potter Himself.

The Great Potter invites all of His broken potteries to rest in His house while He works with our broken pieces on His table. He knows that the breaking hurts, and sometimes recovery does too. It may be painful to recall the traumatizing event or even reflect on and discuss it. It might be so painful that we think it would be easiest to burrow into the broken potteries' trash yard and bury our broken pieces, pretending the breakage never happened.

If you deal with painful memories of your clay pottery's past blows, it is essential to understand that trauma and brokenness always tends to *isolate* us. It is the nature of trauma to *silence* and boost *secrecy* because dealing with false guilt and shame is often projected onto us by those who broke us. Another characteristic of trauma is entertaining lies, such as *"Nobody would understand my experience or be interested in helping me."* Therefore, I highly recommend any broken pottery to discuss their experiences with a professional therapist or counselor. Sharing burdens with others usually lightens the load. Discussing will also help us to see our situation from a new, and perhaps healthier, perspective. It allows us to gain insight into what happened and why.

Isaiah 61:4 contains a therapeutic balm for all broken potteries: "And they shall *rebuild the old ruins*, They shall *raise up the former desolations*, And they shall *repair the ruined citie*s, The desolations of many generations" (Isaiah 61:4 NKJV). The Great Potter desires to totally rebuild your broken pottery from the foundations of your past experiences, and restore His design and purpose for your pottery, no matter how long devastated it has been. After identifying, reflecting, and understanding your broken pottery's ruins and old foundations, you no longer need to hide in them; even those ruins that are result of a transgenerational trauma. You can break free from the destructive tendencies, self-images, and worldviews inherited from your family tree or inflicted on your pottery by an acute brokenness. You can allow the renewing process to launch on the Great Potter's table.

The Great Potter, who is also the Wonderful Counselor (9:6), desires to arrange His Divine personal appointment with you as soon as possible. He wants to launch your healing process although He does not promise complete healing or perfection for anyone until eternity.

He desires to pour His unfailing love, never-ending grace, and everlasting faithfulness into your pottery. He wants you to know that His grace *is* sufficient, and that He genuinely accepts you as you are. He fully reconciles you to Himself and redeems you. He wants to assure you that none of your broken pieces are wasted and that He is in control over your brokenness and recovery.

CHAPTER 48

GOOD NEWS TO THE BUMS

The Spirit of the LORD God is upon Me,
Because the LORD has anointed Me
To preach good tidings to the poor.

Isaiah 61:1 (NKJV)

The Great Potter came to our broken potteries' earthly trash yard to proclaim the good news. He shuts down performance-oriented thinking and works-based salvation with the first sentence of His famous Sermon of the Mount to the *poor* in spirit: "Blessed are the poor in spirit, for theirs is the kingdom of heaven" (Matthew 5:3 NIV).

Imagine a surprised, perhaps perplexed, murmur running through the crowd around that mountain. "What does he mean by blessed are the *poor*? How can a poor person be blessed? Shouldn't he rather say that blessed are the rich? Or those who do it all right or at least try?"

Certainly, proclaiming the poor to be blessed was something unheard of in that society full of poor people, some of whom did not even own a pair of sandals. It was a revolutionary message. Indeed, it was the opposite of what the Pharisees and religious leaders taught. None of them appreciated anything poor, neither those who were poor in body nor spirit. They never invited the idea that a poor spirit could be anything honorable. Have you ever heard somebody wishing to be poor when they grow up?

An Unmerited Mercy for Losers Only

Typical of the Great Potter, He confuses our earnings-based thinking by proclaiming that the spiritually poor are blessed. This flew in the face of those who thought (or think today) they had it all together in their self-sufficient self-righteousness. The next story illustrates what the Great Potter was trying to capture with His message:

> Also He spoke this parable to some who trusted in themselves that they were righteous, and despised others: "Two men went up to the temple to pray, one a Pharisee and the other a tax collector. The Pharisee stood and prayed thus with himself, 'God, I thank You that I am not like other men—extortioners, unjust, adulterers, or even as this tax collector. I fast twice a week; I give tithes of all that I possess.' And the tax collector, standing afar off, would not so much as raise his eyes to heaven, but *beat his breast, saying, 'God, be merciful to me a sinner!'* I tell you, this

man went down to his house justified *rather* than the other; for everyone who exalts himself will be humbled, and he who humbles himself will be exalted." (Luke 18:9–14 NKJV)

The tax collector, broken pottery in a thousand smashed pieces, was painfully aware of his misery and how despised he was in everyone's eyes. He stood at a distance as he did not have the nerve to come to the front of the synagogue where the good, righteous folks were sitting. In the back corner behind a pillar, he stood with his head bent low, staring at his dirty sandals. Full of shame, he dared not to look up to heaven or lift his eyes. Quite the opposite from the Pharisee who puffed his chest like a peacock showing off his colors. The tax collector beat his breast in agony, begging for mercy while the Pharisee hollered, hoping everyone nearby would learn how amazing he was. But the tax collector left the synagogue justified and righteous, whereas the Pharisee is left with his self-sufficient smugness.

In the Pharisee's estimation, his pottery was polished and perfect. As he was not inclined to acknowledge his need for even a morsel of mercy, he would see no advantage in accepting it as a gift either. Undoubtedly, he would have been offended if someone were to offer him one.

In the Pharisee's mind, the free, unmerited grace is for *losers only*, not for someone like himself with a long list of merits. He would never humble himself to receive anything *that* humiliating. He was not a charity case, accepting the alms or crumbs dropped under a table.

Sadly, the gift of mercy was under that Pharisee's nose, fully paid, *meant for him also*. Yet in his self-satisfaction he rejected it; in his self-righteousness, he saw no need for the righteousness of Christ. It is a sorrowful position when someone in their pious delusion refuses to acknowledge his pottery's brokenness and need for a doctor, thus refusing recovery. To acknowledge that we are broken, poor and sick, and in need of the divine Doctor means that we are *not* claiming self-righteousness. We need His generous charity and His gracious pardoning. *We cannot survive without it!*

Heidi McKendrick

Unmerited or Earned?

It is tough to understand the Great Potter's unconditional love and unmerited grace with our clay brains. The concept of collecting something we do not deserve is deemed humiliating and not acceptable in our society. To earn anything through hard work is considered noble.

This is why the world is full of churches that teach works-based salvation. It is something much more understandable, fair, honorable, and acceptable than the concept of unmerited grace.

But this is the key to what the Great Potter is trying to capture in His opening sentence of the Sermon on the Mount. Interestingly, the term He uses to describe the poor in spirit[40][67] refers to *humiliating poorness*, potteries entirely at others' mercy, penniless bums; an idle scrounger who has no possessions but dirty clothes, not even a pair of shoes, and who haven't showered for weeks.

This level of beggar has no accomplishments, no CV, no resumé, no faith, no hope, no love. Nothing. These poor in spirit (who are blessed and the heirs of the kingdom) are wholly reliant on the Great Potter's mercy and grace. They are painfully aware that they don't deserve even a drop of it, yet this is precisely the attitude the Great Potter is looking for.

Like the robber crucified next to the Great Potter—the completely smashed pottery about to die in minutes. Nothing to offer but his last minute seed of faith "…remember me when You come into Your kingdom" (Luke 23:42 NKJV)— *but it is enough for the Great Potter.* "Today you will be with Me in Paradise " (v. 43). Nothing less is offered for this wretched lowlife. *Today. With Me. In Paradise.* And in few minutes, right after it is all finished, the King of the Kings and the freshly pardoned outlaw will walk to the Kingdom, together.

Now that is grace!

---

[40] Poor / *ptōchois* # 4434 means: beggarly, poor, "of one who crouches and cowers," "one who can only obtain his living by begging," "one who has nothing at all." A beggar (as cringing), i.e. pauper. [67]

The thief on the cross achieves no bucket-list of doctrinal rituals or religious traditions. He enters in without displaying any evidence of a Christian walk, character development, holiness pedigree, fruits of the Spirit, good fight, or victorious race. For him it was only a moment, a deathbed confession, but a job well done. He did not need to do anything but *believe* in the Great Potter and *receive* His grace.

As with every lost pottery that is found, that night there was a celebration in heaven!

Just as with the prodigal son (Luke 15:11–32) who returned home wearing filthy rags, his father dresses him in the best clothes and sandals. He knew that he had shamefully disgraced his father yet his father places his signed-ring on his finger. The son would've been happy if his father had taken him as a slave, yet suddenly he finds himself celebrated as a son and heir, without any reprimand or judgment.

> *Amazing grace, indeed.*
> *How sweet the sound*
> *That saved a wretch like me.* (John Newton)[68]

The Great Potter does not want our tight-haloed performances. He is not impressed by our so-called holiness lists or catalog of sins we didn't do. On the contrary, He is offended by plans of works-based salvation—a mixture of grievous laws sprinkled with grace. The Great Potter wants an authentic relationship with His potteries. He wants clay pots willing to surrender because they are so poor in spirit that they would die of thirst and hunger without His living water and bread.

The empty pottery is filled with the Great Potter's unmerited grace, glory, and treasure. However many potteries proudly display their good-conduct portfolios, rule-following routines, exhaustive sin-avoiding demeanors, and self-sacrificing exercises are so full of themselves that there's no room left for the Great Potter.

> *Blessed are the poor in spirit.*

Isn't it beautiful that it is for us broken potteries that the Great Potter proclaims the Year of Jubilee, the year of His favor, the gospel, the good news? His kingdom belongs to us who are troubled, tormented, oppressed, depressed, mourning, and emotionally wounded. Because we *need* good news is why He blesses us. Those perfect (rich) in their minds don't need Him (or so they think); it's easier for a camel to go through the eye of a needle than for a 'rich' to enter God's Kingdom.

The gospel the angels sang on that first Christmas night was the Great Potter reconciling Himself with us because none of His potteries could make the right choices and rise to the bar. Good news for all clay potteries living on this earth! Interestingly, even then the low-class, poor, dirty shepherds were the first to receive this heavenly announcement.

How do you understand the Great Potter's grace today? In your mind, who fulfills it, the Great Potter or you? Are you saved because you earned salvation through good works? Or is your salvation because of what the Great Potter did on your behalf on the cross? Are you justified as a reward for good behavior or because of His grace? Are you a wage earner or a charity case? Or do you think a bit of both is needed to make it fair and reasonable?

Receive the gospel as one of the poor in spirit.

CHAPTER 49

HEALING THE BROKEN HEARTED

He has sent Me to heal the brokenhearted. [69] [41]

ISAIAH 61:1 (NKJV)

---

[41] 'Brokenhearted' / *Chabar* means "to burst, break (down, off, in pieces, up), broken(-hearted), bring to the birth, crush, destroy, hurt, quench, quite, tear." 'The heart' / *leb (labe)* also means feelings, will, and intellect. 'To bind up' / *Chabash* means "to wrap firmly"; bind (up), gird about, govern, healer, put, saddle, wrap about." [69]

A broken heart, a painful soul, and a crushed spirit: does this describe your clay pottery's brokenness? How was your heart broken? Did somebody thrash it with a demolition hammer? Was it stabbed in the back with a knife? Did a sophisticated yet cruel arrow pierce your heart?

Betrayal, rejection, dishonesty, fake promises, abandonment, and abuse are just some of the many reasons that can break the heart of clay pottery, thrashing its core and leaving it bleeding. "A broken spirit who can bear it?" (Proverbs 18:14 NASB). A painful, bleeding, aching mess results from a heart violently crushed and ripped apart, a soul tore apart, leaving us unable to know how to collect the broken pieces.

Yes, our enemy, the devil, is a brutally skilled butcher, specialized in tearing our potteries' flesh heart in pieces, damaging our self-image and world-view for the rest of our lives!

The good news is that Great Potter particularly came to comfort the broken-hearted. He heals "the broken-hearted and binds up their wounds" (Psalm 147:3 NIV). He "is close to the brokenhearted and saves those who are crushed in spirit" (34:18). He "will search for the lost and bring back the strays" (Ezekiel 34:16 NIV). He "will bind up the injured and strengthen the weak" (Ibid.). Yes, the Great Potter lives "in a high and holy place, but *also* with the one who is *contrite and lowly in spirit*, to revive the spirit of the lowly and to revive the heart of the contrite" (Isaiah 57:15 NIV).

A profound spiritual truth is tucked within these verses. Even though everyone else may reject or abandon us, the Great Potter never does. He remains close to us even if we think He is far away. It does not matter how badly we are crushed; He is right there, ready to collect our pieces. Because He has wonderfully made us, He remains interested in our destinies. Because of His love, He will not allow us to be destroyed. No matter how deadly our hearts are pierced, the Great Potter is still in control of our potteries. We do not stop belonging to Him even if we are thrown into a trash yard, blood gushing.

Certainly, in heaven we will have no heartache.

The Great Potter was pierced and crushed for our sake—His heart was broken. Yet by His wounds our broken potteries can commence their healing process (53:5). What a gracious message this is! The Great Potter, the High and Holy One, will collect our broken pieces. Although our healing process will continue for as long as we live, it is safe to be on the Great Potter's table.

The Great Heart Surgeon

Charles Spurgeon preached Christ's Hospital, *"There are many sorts of broken hearts, and Christ is good at healing them all."* [70]

> *Hearts are broken through disappointment. Hearts are broken by bereavement. Hearts are broken in ten thousand ways, for this is a heart-breaking world; and Christ is good at healing all manner of heart-breaks. I would encourage every person here, even though his heart-break may not be of a spiritual kind, to make an application to him who healeth the broken in heart.* [71]

The Great Heart Surgeon wants to replace our hearts of stone with a heart of flesh, that wall of stone we once built for our defense—a medieval citadel we formed to avoid feeling pain and to hide our vulnerability.

He wants to melt the freezing numbness of our stony hearts and then restore them to hearts of flesh, the kind we had before our potteries broke, the kind capable of feeling throbbing pain, aching agony, quiet content, and bursting joy. The Great Potter "will give you a new heart and put a new spirit in you" (Ezekiel 36:26). He "will remove from you your heart of stone and give you a heart of flesh" (Ibid.).

Being vulnerable and capable of feeling pain and repeated hurts, we must trust the Great Potter to conduct divine heart surgery. In His hands, we are safe, even if we feel vulnerable. We are safe, even if we feel unsafe.

Just as the Great Potter once wrote the rule of law on the tablets of stone that he revealed to Moses on Mount Sinai, He now desires to write His love letter on our clay potteries' hearts of flesh. Of course, He is writing on it with His blood, the new covenant between our clay potteries and the Great Potter. It is the letter He composed while on Calvary's cross.

He writes that we are fully reconciled to Him and recipients of His unfailing love, never-ending grace, and everlasting faithfulness. He mentions that we are His children, whom He loves as-is and sees as most beautiful and precious.

His letter is the contract detailing the treasure of His dwelling within our clay potteries and being in charge no matter what happens to us.

CHAPTER 50

LIBERATING THE CAPTIVES

*The Spirit of the LORD God is upon Me,
Because the LORD has anointed Me . . .
To proclaim liberty to the captives,
And the opening of the prison to those who are bound.*

Isaiah 61:1 (NKJV)

Heidi McKendrick

Captives are the third group the Great Potter mentions in His proclamation. Of course, we know that He came to proclaim liberty for all who are prisoners to any sin, paying our debt so that we can be pardoned, free, and forgiven. However, in this proclamation of Isaiah 61:1, the Great Potter also refers to clay potteries who are captives to emotional wounds caused by our brokenness and past injuries.

A captive refers to anyone who is bound or locked up in some manner, unable to escape their present reality. A clay pottery can be bound or trapped in the aftermath of brokenness and trauma experiences. We may bury ourselves under the junk of the trash yard we are thrown into, and then convince ourselves that there is no way we can liberate ourselves. Sometimes, even without realizing it, we may be stuck under heavy stuff that we have no strength to move and thus free ourselves. We can also be prisoners of our anxieties and fears, rational or irrational.

We can be prisoners of bitterness and self-pity, chained ourselves on the stone walls of a mighty, polished fortress of our own reconstruction; sulking, pouting, and feeling envy. Or holding on with our sense of victimhood, not wanting to let it go, re-telling the stories of injustice we experienced. Like the prodigal son's older brother, we keep listing our deeds, how *we* worked harder, suffered more, sinned less, had less fun, *yet* we are *not* treated as we should, we are not recognized, appreciated, celebrated...

We can also be captives of our own unrealistic expectations. We may be hostages of past traumatic experiences that still paralyze us, or prisoners of trauma triggers, not able to free ourselves and thus narrowing our lives and not reaching our full potential. Low self-esteem or low self-worth resulting from our painful past. Rejection or abusive treatment that still defines how we see ourselves can hold us captive. Of course, we may also be shackled with addictions, even good works that fill our time and prevent us from proper rest and reflection. Legalistic demands and expectations may detain us, even brainwash us in a spiritually abusive community.

Hear this! The Great Potter came to release all who are held captive or shackled for any reason. He came to liberate us jailbirds. He wants all of His potteries to fly free!

As broken potteries, we sometimes become our own worst enemies. Instead of resting, we try harder until we are exhausted. Instead of sharing our burdens with others to lighten our load, we bear them alone until we collapse and then isolate ourselves in deserts, mountains, or caves. Instead of seeking healing, we pretend we are not hurting. Instead of taking care of our bleeding wounds, we hide them, which allows infection to stall healing. Instead of reaching for help, we build thick walls around us so that nothing can come close and hurt us.

Does this type of self-built penitentiary sound familiar to you? I've certainly resided some of them a few times.

Some broken potteries have devised slogans that serve to further bind them:

- I will never be stupid enough to fall in love again.
- I will never again be weak or vulnerable.
- I will never be foolish to let anybody see my vulnerability.
- I will never trust anybody, no matter who they are.
- I will never allow anybody to steal anything from me or force anything on me.
- I will never let anybody use me, abuse me, betray me, cheat me, reject me, belittle me, laugh at me, or humiliate me.
- I will never let anybody see me cry in pain.
- I will never let anyone see even a glimpse of hurt in my eyes.
- I will never let anyone see how much they hurt me.
- I will never give anyone the satisfaction of seeing me helpless again.

If you are sitting in this type of a self-constructed prison, the Great Potter desires to liberate you. If you peek from your window, you will see Him by the prison door. He is knocking very gently, waiting for you.

If you knew Him, you would know that you no longer need to pretend anything with Him. The Great Potter has already seen your throbbing pain. He wants to launch your healing process. But first, He wants to liberate you from your citadel. Do you already feel some melting starting because of the warmth of His presence by your walls?

Heidi McKendrick

Jail of Legalism

One prison that holds many Christians captive is the jail of legalism. Works-based salvation is a clay pottery's attempt to earn the Great Potter's acceptance or approval by keeping His laws or the rules that some churches have established. As I mentioned earlier, I was born into a legalistic church, a third-generation member, my grandmother being one of the pioneers. I did not choose this for myself; rather, I was put into this tiny chamber that allowed no room to do anything but what I was told and not do anything strictly prohibited.

In my childhood church, it was expected that our inward changes would be deciphered by our outward changes. Not participating in worldly entertainment, and mastering the plain look of no make-up. I still remember how I seriously thought I would be hit by lightning because of that mascara hidden in my purse during a thunderstorm. Many church members were expelled because of drinking, dancing, dating (a non-member), divorcing, smoking... Even certain Christian music with electric guitars and drums was considered worldly.

Do you recall this childhood song?

> *Oh, be careful little eyes, what you see . . .*
> *Be careful little ears what you hear . . .*
> *Be careful little mouth what you say . . .*
> *Be careful little hands, what you touch . . .*
> *Be careful little feet, where you go . . .*

I sang it often. I even added a new verse: Be careful little brain not to think . . . The prison rules were nailed on the wall in my cell:

DO NOT TASTE!
DO NOT DRINK!
DO NOT TOUCH!
DO NOT LOOK!
DO NOT LISTEN!

DO NOT WANT!
DO NOT FEEL!
DO NOT PLAN!
DO NOT ENJOY!

Of course, I was taught that these rules were signed by the Great Potter. My prison door was locked, and in my distorted image of the Great Potter, I thought Him the warden, the One who closed the door to my cell. However, neither of these is true. He *never* wrote these rules or guarded my cell. Those were manmade rules that have no basis in Scripture. If only I had known that I could have pushed open the door and walked into freedom.

No doubt some inmates appreciate the dos and don'ts. These potteries prefer no shades of gray or ethical dilemmas to confuse their black-and-white reasoning. To know what to avoid every day and what to do is a relief. It requires no thinking and no relationship with the Great Potter. I was *not* one of these potteries. For as long as I can remember, *I questioned everything*. In my early twenties, I broke out from that prison; however, it was over a decade before I was inwardly liberated by the Great Potter. I experienced in my soul that He looks at me with the same love and gentleness I was looking at my little children. Such an opposite image of the Great Potter than what I was accustomed to in that prison of legalism.

Legalistic prisons exist today, and thousands of clay potteries are squeezed into narrow lodgings.[72] These cells allow no room to utilize the talents given by the Great Potter. From their tiny windows, the inmates are horrified as they observe clay potteries outside the prison living in outrageously blatant freedom and privileges. Sometimes they yell at them and judge them, preaching hell and brimstone.

Oh, how the Great Potter longs to remove the legalistic bonds that hold back His clay potteries from living in freedom as He designed.

Jail of Religious Perfectionism

Religious perfectionism is another captivity from which the Great Potter would like to free His potteries. Johan Wolfgang von Goethe grasped it well: *"A perfectionist is a man whom it is impossible to please because he is never pleased with himself.*" [73] Sadly, some Christians do not grow into freedom, but develop a performance-focused doctrine and move into the jail of religious perfectionism—they feel it is impossible to please the Great Potter.

The central atmosphere in this prison is the nagging feeling of never quite measuring up. Never being or doing enough to please themselves, others, or the Great Potter. Of course, in that prison, everyone is super sensitive to others' approval/disapproval. Everything they do is about performing and trying harder, usually spiced with a fierce self-belittling, self-contempt, false humbling, 'a wretched, poor, and helpless worm'- mentality, and, of course, heavy cloud of guilt—a well-known concept that if I'm not feeling guilty for anything, then I must feel guilty for not feeling guilty.

The rules, as well as values and priorities, are clear. Deeds, conduct, achievements, and work is all that matter. Indeed, performance goes beyond relationship. Like Martha's irritation—she feels unappreciated, unrecognized, poorly complimented, and unfairly treated when she complains of her sister Mary enjoying the Great Potter's fellowship.

The atmosphere in that prison is arrogance, self-righteousness with an undertone of hidden uncertainties, fears, and shame because you never know if you measure up to highly unrealistic goals. There is also the constant, paralyzing fear of failing, which promotes procrastination. The prisoners have all agreed to live their lives under continual self-evaluation, thus honestly feeling they always should do better and try harder. They exhaust themselves always smiling and looking cheery because that's how prosperous and *real* Christians should look—any brokenness is a lack of faith or proof of secret sin.

The prisoners develop complicated patterns of wishful thinking and action plans such as *if only* I have less fun, sin less, try harder, pray more, read the Bible more, tithe more, volunteer more, . . . I will *not* be disapproved, punished, or banned. Moreover, *if* I try even harder, I *might* be accepted, blessed, approved, and maybe even loved. There are two driving forces in this particular prison: *need to be accepted* and *fear to be rejected*. Every living moment is filled with a strenuous measuring activities and critical self-scrutiny. "What others think about us" has become so important that we may have totally forgotten what *we* think about anything.

In my childhood church community, we were constantly encouraged to guard our hearts against *anything* that *could* be rubbish. Sometimes it felt as if everything I liked was considered rubbish, if not sin. For example, post-secondary education was considered a waste of time because in those end-times the rapture was imminent. I also remember how exhausting it was to continually reflect on whether I was *true to the Lord* in my actions, spoken words, plans, decisions, and thoughts. Always feeling inadequate and needing to raise the bar.

Although these clay potteries' lives consist of climbing one mountain after another, they are never content. They like to think that they might be a bit closer to perfection after every new effort. They are a bit better than other clay potteries, or at least they try harder. That in itself should count as merit much like the Pharisees trying to find peace and contentment in their perfect deeds. Sadly, it is often only during a total burnout that these clay potteries realize how exhausted and lonely they are. Truthfully, this is the great demolisher's genius trap.

After freeing you, the Great Potter desires you surrender to Him, which is what perfection in Christ means. He wants to collect your polished yet broken pieces and place them on His table where you can rest. There, He desires to meet your deepest needs that went unmet because you had to deny all of them while in prison, where you had no choice but to do and be what others expected of you.

False Self vs. True Self

Of course, the Great Potter wants to free those trapped in the "I always have to please everyone" department of our religious prisons. If serving there too long, we lost ourselves entirely and even learned to smile behind our bruises. We were bound by our need to please others to earn their approval.

However, when the Great Potter liberates us, He shows us our true selves. While giving us a new identity as His beloved children, accepted as-is, and the most beautiful and precious, He liberates us from false self-identities.

Donald Winnicott,[74] a well-known English psychiatrist, founded the concept of the true self and false self. The false self usually develops in early childhood as we receive numerous negative and false messages about ourselves; thus, we believe that we can never be accepted or loved as-is. To be accepted and loved requires us to become somebody different from who we are: more robust, braver, happier, more serious . . . whatever it is that others expect and we are not.

This profoundly integrated lack of security and self-value is what the Great Potter wants to heal. He is aware of the sad fact that because of our distorted self-images developed during our prison years, we may not think that the Great Potter can love us once He learns about my real self.

Yet, He loves us *unconditionally.*

The Great Potter is not disillusioned; He is fully informed of who we are. He knows the good, the bad, and the ugly, and yet He loves us. The secret is that the Great Potter is charmed with our *real* selves, the potteries He created long ago. He is not interested in any fake or polished versions. He does not compare us with other clay potteries. Therefore, we need not compare ourselves either, not even with the clay pottery we used to be. Finally, we will know the truth, and *the truth will set us free* (John. 8:32). The Great Potter is the way, the truth, the life (John 14:6). Remember: "where the Spirit of the Lord is, *there is freedom*" (2 Corinthians 3:17 NIV).

When we get to know the Great Potter, His real character, not the false images formed in our prisons, the truth sets us free. *The divine truth.* The Spirit of truth (John 16:13). His light sees through everything, like a powerful, divine X-ray that shows our clay layers and all of our secrets. Yet *there is no fear* in this process as there is never any fear around His love (1 John 4:16). Therefore, it is perfectly safe to ask the Great Potter to "Search me, God, and know my heart; test me and know my anxious thoughts" (Psalm 139:23 NIV).

We do not need to fake anything any longer.

The Great Potter sees it all, gracefully peeling back one layer at a time. Indeed, we need a thorough cleansing of all of our broken pieces. We want Him to renew our potteries. Of course, during this process, the Great Potter also restores authentic feelings that were numbed during our prison life, when it was not safe to feel any- thing. Whatever He wants to do with our clay pieces on His table means that *the truth will set us completely free.*

Since the garden of Eden, the Great Potter is accustomed to seeing broken potteries trying to hide. He understands our tendency to cover up and look more polished and less fractured than we really are. Nothing surprises Him as He has already seen every possible DIY fix, grout, cement, superglue, makeup, cast iron masks, stainless-steel coating and more, including oversized leaves like Adam and Eve used after eating the forbidden fruit and hiding the Great Potter among the trees of the garden. But the Great Potter called to them, "Where are you?" He [Adam] answered, "I heard you in the garden, and I was afraid because I was naked; so I hid" (Genesis 3:8–10 NIV).

Since then, we clay potteries have feared being authentic, open, unprotected, and uncovered, vulnerable with naked emotions not only with the Great Potter but also with one another and ourselves. Rather than face and express our repressed memories and feelings because they cause pain, we cover and deny them.

But it is no longer necessary to pretend that we are brave when we are scared. We don't have to pretend strength when we are weak. We don't have to pretend we are happy when miserable. We no longer need to keep ourselves together with tricks and lies. We can safely collapse into His hands. *All we need to do is to surrender.*

The next time you hear the Great Potter's steps in your secret garden, please remember that there is no reason why you should hide from Him.

He did not come to arrest you; He came to free you.

CHAPTER 51

RECOVERING MACARONI VISION

*The Spirit of the Lord is upon Me,
Because He has anointed Me . . .
To proclaim liberty to the captives
And recovery of sight to the blind.*

Luke 4:18 (NKJV)

Heidi McKendrick

Alone in the dark. We've all been there at some point. When it is dark and we do not see well—even a familiar place can feel chaotic, startling, and confusing. When darkness grows around us, it may feed our imagination and fears. We could be paralyzed in one spot, too scared to move and explore. Or it may keep us in a constant fight-or-flight mode, fully alert, our senses heightened.

'Putting the lights on in a room'—a simple metaphor, but one I often use to describe my therapy work with broken potteries. Putting the lights on, at least, allows us to see what *is* there. It allows us to make an assessment and investigation of our whereabouts—real threats, or just imagined—it allows us to locate our broken pieces. There may not be any magical way to erase the brokenness—as nice as it would be—but at least now we will *see* it as it is.

Seeing, at once gives us a sense of control.

Once we learn more about our surroundings and our situation, we gain more control over it. While not being able to change it, we may learn how to be in the same room with it, without allowing it to freeze us, without allowing it to steal our full potential any longer. Even if we cannot remove the existence of brokenness from our lives, at least, we can claim or take back the control over our emotions.

The trauma no longer needs to rule our pottery's every living moment.

Was Blind, But Now I See

The Great Potter came to proclaim recovery of sight to the blind—both *spiritual* and *emotional* blindness. In both situations, blindness is *darkness*, difficulty to see clearly or unable to see at all. Distorted vision can sometimes lead to blindness. Naturally, blindness can create fear of the future, even horror, sometimes an irrational fear. It can develop into uncertainty, insecurity, mistrust, and blatant misunderstandings. We can also be blinded by bitterness and self-pity, and we can feel blind ambition or blind rage.

I find this topic thought-provoking, likely because I myself suffer an eye disease that could lead to blindness if not taken care. Luckily, I was diagnosed in its earliest phase and am hopeful the medication keeps it controlled.

The American Academy of Ophthalmology's definition of 'distorted vision' is quite fitting if used metaphorically as a 'spiritual disorder:' *"A condition in which familiar objects look wavy or bent incorrectly. [...] Lines that should be straight may appear bent or crooked, and it is difficult to see objects clearly."* [75]

When you embrace false images of the Great Potter, you perceive your position as His pottery in a precarious manner and you see Him erroneously. If you have difficulty claiming the secrets of the broken potteries, such as the Great Potter accepting you as-is, you may have a slanted vision of Him. If something that should be *straight and clear* appears crooked, it could be distorted spiritual vision.

There are so many reasons why we may need the Great Potter's healing to recover true sight. Paul the Pharisee was an example of one who *thought* he had more spiritual sight than most potteries. However, according to the Great Potter, spiritually, he was completely blind and could not see the truth but only *his* legalistic doctrine's narrow and distorted vision that directed his wrong actions.

David needed healing for his blindness after breaking his pottery: "For troubles without number surround me; my sins have overtaken me, *and I cannot see.*" (Psalm 40:12 NIV).

> John Newton felt the same:
> I once was lost
> But now I'm found
> Was *blind*, but now I see.[76]

Macaroni Vision

Macaroni vision is what I call extreme narrowness of viewpoint. It is seeing the Great Potter, reading the Bible, and understanding the Christian walk with one perspective only. Never questioning whether it is correct or distorted. Many legalistic preachers teach from a macaroni vision perspective. They fail to realize they are causing their flock to stumble or, like the Israelites wander aimlessly in the wilderness. A plank in my own eye may also produce macaroni vision, projecting my characteristics, feelings, and faults onto others and then accusing them—textbook example of scapegoating (Matthew 7:3–5).

Trauma experiences and the various blows to our potteries affect our vision, sometimes fatally distorting it but certainly making it difficult to perceive the Great Potter as healing and gracious. Our distorted vision may facilitate sabotaging our Christian ministry and assuming the Devil's lies that we are too broken for the Great Potter's Service.

A secretive childhood atmosphere could foster distorted visions impacting the rest of our lives—parents' addiction, psychiatric issues, abusive relationships…—an enormous elephant sitting in the family room.[77] Although the elephant is stealing away the living space, filling the room with its rumbling, trumpeting, and stench, everybody around the child is pretending *there is no elephant*. If the child even tries to discuss that elephant the others make him feel he is embellishing or imagining things. There may also be a serious prohibition for *never sharing* anything that happens inside the home. Like one of my therapy client's drawings of her childhood family—parents and children, all sitting on a living-room sofa with a huge band-aid around their mouths. She titled the picture: "The Holy Family."

A dysfunctional family backgrounds or legalistic church experiences not only wound and distort our image of the Great Potter but also how we view ourselves, others, and the world. I remember my childhood view of others and the world being damaged through the fearmongering and segregation, either 'one of us' or 'them'—we were not encouraged to interact unless, of course, we were witnessing to 'them'. The membership had to protect the community's image against the 'world'. Sometimes this meant silencing the victim and sweeping the dirt under the carpets.

Seeing You, Seeing Me

Clay potteries desperately need recovery of sight because without it we cannot come to an in-depth knowledge of the Great Potter. Nor will we learn who we really are. Without the recovery of sight, we will not know the secrets meant for us, and if we don't know them, we cannot see or claim them and let them liberate us spiritually and emotionally. Without the recovery of sight, we may not even notice that our prison doors are not locked at all, thus we fail to walk out into freedom.

Both Job's and Hagar's stories illustrate what it means *to see and be seen* by the Great Potter. "My ears had heard of you, but *now my eyes have seen you*" (Job 42:5 NIV). This eye-opening experience revolutionarily changed Job's perspective of the Great Potter and led him to understand that He is in charge in every situation. "You are the God *who sees me. I have now seen* the One *who sees me*" (Genesis 16:13 NIV), Hagar concluded in her therapeutic encounter with the Great Potter. Just as Hagar needed the Great Potter's divine intervention to see the well that she had not seen in the middle of her misery, so we need Him to take us to the living water.

Have you ever sat amid your smashed pieces feeling foggy and so exhausted that you lost your vision and sense of direction? Maybe—you thought the Great Potter's gathering your pieces were only an illusion, your imagination, and not real. Remember, even if you *think* your broken pieces are lost in the trash yard of broken potteries, the Great Potter has *already* seen them. Not one piece of your pottery has dropped to the ground without Him registering it (Luke 21:18).

It does not matter what your trash yard of broken potteries is—humiliation, betrayal, rejection, abandonment, injustice—the Great Potter has already seen you. And He wants to open your eyes also. He wants to give you a new vision for yourself, just as He did for Hagar, Peter, Elijah, and Paul. He wants to restore your lost identity. You *are* a son or daughter of the King of Kings, princess or prince of the Most High.

It is always desirable to see the Great Potter *correctly* while also being seen by Him. All the stories of the nameless women explore this. When the Great Potter looked at these women, He saw their innermost beings, what nobody else, even themselves, had never seen. These women left their encounter with the Great Potter in possession of a new identity and a new destiny.

When the Great Potter sees Peter after he had publicly disowned Him, He not only heals his emotional wounds and shame but also reinstates His relationship with him. The Great Potter sees Elijah sitting in His cave, blinded by his fears. He restores his vision and gives him new tasks as His beautiful vessel. Before restoring

Paul the Pharisee's vision, the Great Potter first blinds his distorted vision. Paul's healing is beautiful allowing him to see the Great Potter accurately. With the recovery of his sight, he becomes a beautiful vessel for the Great Potter's service. His letters continue to spread the good news of His love and grace.

When the Great Potter sees us, He notes the trauma symptoms and sees their sources and roots, even the original fractures that made us vulnerable. The Great Potter sees when, how, and why our potteries were broken. He acknowledges our pain and other feelings and is compassionate toward our suffering. He even sees our previous efforts of trying to fix our broken pottery. He sees our failings, defenses, and ways we try to cover up or hide. He sees our core needs, the naked truth.

I sometimes ponder what would happen if we were to see others the way the Great Potter sees them. As potteries we only see the outside of another pottery, the polished wall or the duct-taped cracks. "People look at the outward appearance, but the Lord looks at the heart" (2 Samuel: 16:7 NIV). *The Great Potter sees the inside.* When He saw the weeping woman pouring her tears on His feet, He really *saw* her. She was intimately seen and healed in His presence. When He saw the bleeding woman, He *saw* her deepest needs and thus reinstated her both spiritually, emotionally, and socially. When He saw the man who had been blind from his birth, Bartimaeus, the crippled and paralyzed, the lepers,[42] and many others, He *truly* saw them, their deepest needs—and felt compassion.

When we encounter other broken potteries, perhaps broken differently than ourselves, are we able to look beyond the obvious and show grace? Are we able to rid ourselves of biases, envy, stereotypes…, and see with the Great Potter's eyes?

Be Thou My Vision

"Thy word is a lamp unto my feet, and a light unto my path" (Psalm 119: 105 KJV). We can't see into the distance, only one or two steps ahead. But there is enough light to see the step I'm taking, preventing me from stumbling. Furthermore, when I walk with my Good Shepard, I trust He knows the way. Having *a vision of Him* guiding

---

[42] See: John 9: 1–12; Mark 2:1–12; 10:46–52; Luke 5: 17–26; 13:10–17; 17:11–19; Matthew 8:1–3, 5–13.

my every step provides me a clear sense of purpose and peace. He knows my past and my present. *He knows my future.* He holds a panoramic picture of everything, a Divine perspective; everything my pottery goes through is part of something bigger that makes sense to the Great Potter.

> …because of the tender mercy of our God, by which the rising sun will come to us from heaven to shine on those *living in darkness* and in *the shadow of death, to guide our feet into the path of peace."* (Luke 1: 78–79 NIV)

There is a secret fixing our eyes on the Great Potter rather than our circumstances. When we fix our eyes on Him, the storms of life may not quiet, but they do not overtake us. The Great Potter is the supernatural peace *with us.* Furthermore, when we fix our eyes on the Great Potter, we do not stare at our flaws and blemishes, and we let Him decide how He wants to use our vessels so that His light can shine through our broken fractures.

Blessed Are Your Eyes Because They See…

The clay potteries were never meant to live in the chaotic destruction of trash yards of broken potteries with no vision of their destiny or their Maker. The Great Potter came so that He could *be seen* by us; so that we could be transformed by believing in Him (1 Corinthians 3:18). He is no longer an unknown and invisible God whose name we cannot even pronounce.

"But blessed are your eyes *because they see*" (Matthew 13:16 NIV).

Seeing the Great Potter and *being seen by Him* is about being in relationship with Him. In that relationship we *see*, experience Him personally, and learn that He cares about our broken pottery. To be seen by the Great Potter is a profoundly intimate and touching moment, capable of changing the direction of our lives, our assumptions of ourselves, and our destinies. Being in the Great Potter's presence is healing because He sees our core, needs, fears, dreams, failures, and all those times our potteries were broken. He sees all of our pain, and

He has good plans for us. He wants to equip us as His vessels to spread the good news of His love and grace.

When we are healed from spiritual blindness, we see everything differently. Not only ourselves but the world around us: beautiful flowers and colors, nature's stunning beauty, the magnificence of creation—the tiny details that make our lives enjoyable and worth living. We also begin to value relationships as well as the precious clay potteries we encounter. We will see the beauty of the fellowship and share one another's burdens as we laugh and cry together. We see how the Great Potter is always present during our existential turmoil. In His presence, our hunger to be seen and accepted as-is is met as it fulfills our inner yearnings, bringing us purpose that only the Creator can bring.

I pray that you will see yourself as the Great Potter sees you and that this is a healing experience for your pottery. Let Him show you how deeply He values you, His most beautiful and precious clay pottery, for whom He has good plans. I hope you will see Him in the right light as well—as He is—and that you will be healed from any distorted images of Him, any blindness that prohibits you from internalizing His character.

I hope, when you think about the Great Potter, you see His unfailing love, never-ending grace, and everlasting faithfulness poured into you.

CHAPTER 52

LIBERATING THE OPPRESSED

The Spirit of the Lord is upon Me,
Because He has anointed Me . . .
To set at liberty those who are oppressed.[78][43]

LUKE 4:18 (NKJV)

---

[43] Those who are oppressed / *tethrausmenous* (Strong's Dictionary 2352): "to break in pieces, to crush, to bruise." [78]

The Great Potter came to liberate those who are oppressed. Any of us clay potteries trapped with paralyzing feelings because of our brokenness need a Liberator. We are oppressed when we experience being put down by others, tormented, trampled, tyrannized, beat up, mistreated, berated, bashed, and disheartened.

Difficult emotions are familiar to many of us, traumatizing experiences that smash our clay potteries: parents who abused and abandoned us, alcoholic fathers' vicious outbursts, spouses who belittled and betrayed, children who pierced our heart, friends who misused our trust, drug-addicted relatives who hurt us, as well as racist attacks, sexual abuse, physical abuse, emotional abuse, spiritual abuse... The world is a scary place for us clay potteries.

No wonder many of us are broken and oppressed.

The Great Potter, full of compassion toward us, *knows* how horrendous it is to be oppressed. Remember, He was oppressed Himself, "...and afflicted, yet he did not open his mouth" (Isaiah 53:7 NIV). He knows the helplessness of having no voice and no defense.

The complicated aspect of oppression is that it often stays with us, even after the action is long gone. Those belittling and berating remarks paralyze us. Emotional, physical, and sexual abuse damages our core and traps us, sometimes for decades, leaving an ugly scar.

Sometimes it looks as if the wound is healed, but only the surface has closed up, leaving the infection deep inside. Any small fracture for our clay pottery can split open the original injury, break the pottery, and throw us into agony.

It's not unusual that we wonder how such a small crack throws us into such turmoil. What we may not understand is that a deeper wound has opened.

Understanding the Impact of Projected Shame

Being broken causes emotional damage and distorts how we perceive others, ourselves, and the Great Potter. Our clay potteries' damage can harm our spiritual perceptions and impact how we understand our relationship with the Great Potter.

For example, it is typical for a child who has been mistreated by adults to justify it with the following unhealthy assumptions. It is also customary for victims of any violence:

- I must be bad because I am mistreated.
- I am not treated well because I am not good.
- Because I am bad, I don't deserve any better treatment.
- I deserve nothing good.
- If I feel good, it will not last because I do not deserve to feel good.

It is typical for abusers not to feel guilt or shame during an abusive encounter but instead project them onto the victims. The victims, not only abused, identify with this false guilt and unconsciously blame themselves for the abuse. Similarly, victims may identify with the irrelevant sense of shame projected onto their identities.

Sometimes this projected shame becomes such a heavy burden, the clay pottery isolates herself, which creates secrecy. If she visits a therapist, she is likely to inhibit sharing her burden. Mistreated potteries may also categorize themselves as dirty and tarnished, deserving nothing good from anybody, and having no self-worth. They diminish themselves, becoming invisible and voiceless to avoid conflicts. Yet they easily devote their lives to pleasing others while neglecting their own needs. All of this is a form of oppression.

The Great Potter longs to liberate the oppressed, restore their valuable vessels to His service. This is His mission statement He proclaims in His first sermon. It is also what the prophet Isaiah prophesied years earlier that He would do.

Sadly, many clay potteries suffering from projected shame and false guilt mistakenly think that their feelings and the demanding inner voices nagging are the Great Potter's. They do not realize it is their abusers' voices as well as unpleasable people, and those who offered their highly conditional love, who demanded unreasonable standards and best performances, top grades, and first prizes while never being satisfied.

Understanding the Impact of False Guilt

Sadly, our broken, false-guilt-ridden potteries keep us from understanding and feeling the Great Potter's unconditional love. We may fervently sing, "What wondrous love is this, O my soul, O my soul!" believing every word as our theoretical doctrine, honestly thinking the Great Potter is loving and forgiving. However, when this highly cognitive knowledge reaches the limbic system in our brains, the area that activates our emotions and controls our fears, something odd happens—we feel nothing. Or worse, the projected shame and guilt take over our emotions and we begin to fear the opposite! At the brain level, we know He loves, but on the emotional level, we fear He doesn't. Instead, we believe that it is ridiculous to think that the Great Potter could love someone like me! It is as if we simply do not allow ourselves to experience anything positive or that our emotions freeze before they reach our hearts.

Of course, this creates stress and anxiety. Whereas real guilt can be rooted in a particular action and thus dealt accordingly by forgiveness, it is more challenging to rid ourselves of false guilt entrenched in obscure notions of truth.

If we cannot experience the Great Potter on any emotional level, we may think that we must ask forgiveness at every altar call. However, even after doing that, we cannot hold on to peace and joy. Our inner consciousness is like an open wound that continually bleeds. We try our absolute best to believe our sins are forgiven, and we certainly do (on that smart cognitive level), and because we're good Christians, we believe what is written in the Great Potter's Word. However, by the time this knowledge should reach our emotions and liberate us, the same old guilt jumps up and takes over with the old nagging. In the end, we feel even more guilt because of our lack of faith and our problem of believing we are forgiven.

Silencing the False Guilt

The false guilt projected onto us as an aftermath of our oppressive experiences is entirely *false yet feels real*. Similarly, the Great Potter's forgiveness and grace are *entirely true but feel false* for those who are trapped with false guilt.

Whenever false guilt tries to sneak back, we can remind ourselves of the secrets of the Great Potter we learned:

- It was not only that He once looked at me with His look that says I am His most precious and beautiful child, but that He *continuously* looks at me with it.
- *I am accepted as-is*, appreciated as beautiful and precious, as long as I live, every single day, forever—*no matter what I do or do not do.*
- My relationship with the Great Potter is *a fact* that is not based on my feelings or anybody else feelings.
- I cannot do anything to make Him love me less. Nor can I do anything to make Him love me more.[79] His love for me is because of who He is and what He did. It is absolute, unchangeable, unmovable. He will never change, and there is nothing I could do to change Him!
- So, GO AWAY, false guilt. There is no room for your annoying voice in my system anymore!

I use these to drive away my false guilt. Sometimes I use them as a prevention, but for sure, as my first-aid reaction whenever I start to hear its first screech and niggling statements. Remember, the Great Potter did not plant false guilt or shame in any of us.

The Great Potter's unconditional love is difficult to embrace and share in for someone who has experienced only conditional love, abuse, or rejection. However, no matter how complicated a psychological phenomenon in your particular case, it is not impossible to be beautifully restored at the Great Potter's table. His unfailing love and His never-ending grace are most effective in healing emotional and spiritual wounds that have interfered with your relationship with Him.

It's worth reiterating the good news for any broken pottery with damaged emotions that we need not rely on or trust our emotions about the Great Potter. We only need to trust the Great Potter's *Word*. Even if our wounded souls will never heal during our lifetimes, and we could never *experience* forgiveness and grace on any *emotional* level, or even if we could never *feel* anything of the Great Potter's liberation, *the truth itself stands.*

The truth stays unchanged.

We are forgiven.

We are saved.

Christ dwells in us.

We are 100 percent righteous.

The Great Potter accepts us as-is.

Period.

The truth is what matters. *Not our feelings or lack of feelings.*

This was the spiritual truth I claimed for myself in my mid-thirties. More than two decades have passed since that moment I discovered the truth, and I still claim it for myself every day. I am not sure what would have happened to my clay pottery had I never understood the secrets of broken pottery. For certain I would not be where I am today writing this book.

As our beliefs about the Great Potter are affected by our feelings and brokenness, our cracks and wounds can disrupt even the most loving Bible verses and fill us with suspicion and mistrust. Like any burdens, the Great Potter also invites us to leave the false guilt and shame for Him as He wants us to have rest. He wants us to soar free like an eagle.

> Do you not know? Have you not heard?
> The LORD is the everlasting God,
> the Creator of the ends of the earth.
> He will not grow tired or weary,
> and his understanding no one can fathom.
> *He gives strength to the weary* and *increases the power of the weak.*
> Even youths grow tired and weary,
> and young men stumble and fall;
> but those who hope in the LORD *will renew their strength.*
> They will *soar on wings like eagles*;
> they will run and not grow weary,
> they will walk and not be faint. (Isaiah 40: 28–31 NIV)

CHAPTER 53

COMFORTING THOSE WHO MOURN

Because the LORD has anointed Me . . .
To comfort all who mourn,
To console those who mourn in Zion,
To give them beauty for ashes,
The oil of joy for mourning,
The garment of praise for the spirit of heaviness;

> *That they may be called trees of righteousness,*
> *The planting of the LORD, that He may be glorified.*
>
> Isaiah 61:1–3 (NKJV)

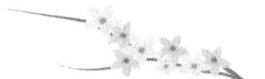

The Great Potter proclaimed that He came to comfort and console those who mourn. Every broken pottery can claim this beautiful promise. We can declare ourselves the beauty for ashes, even if we are now sitting buried in an ash pile of broken potteries. We can claim for our mourning the Great Potter's oil of joy. Perhaps it is the oil that is needed to ignite His light inside of us. For our spirit of heaviness, we can claim the garment of praise, amazingly soft and light, the opposite of the heaviness of oppression, shame, and guilt. We can claim our new permanent position as trees of righteousness, which the Great Potter planted. We did not earn or deserve this position by our works, but we received it freely because of His love and grace so that He may be glorified.

If You Were a Tree…

If you were a tree, what would you look like?
How big is it; how tall?
What does the trunk feel like?
What about its roots, its source of nutrition and water?
How is your tree continuously connected with the living water?
What kind of branches and leaves does your tree have?
What kind of fruit or flowers does it bear? How is it used, and by whom?
Do birds live in your branches; is it a shelter for animals?
How does your tree react to storms, sunshine, rain, and snow?
Did it grow in hard surroundings without water or nutrition?
Where in your tree do you see what it has experienced?

Does it have visible scars in its trunk or branches?

How does your tree demonstrate its resilience, its ability to bounce back?

Is there post-traumatic growth visible in your tree—growth after the traumatizing episode?

How does your tree celebrate the Great Potter's grace?

How does your tree reach towards the Light?

During my workshops with trauma survivors, I show them pictures of various trees and ask them to choose one that best describes their trauma-survivor story. I will always remember one workshop I conducted for refugees in the Middle East. A woman in her mid-fifties had recently arrived with a few of her family members. They had escaped an ISIS attack on her hometown of Mosul, Iraq. She chose a photo of a forest full of trees, all having a visible bend in the middle of their trunks but growing straight up above it. She explained that this is her remaining family and their future. They now have to bend, some of them have died, some are still lost, and there is lots of hardship; however, she hopes and trusts they will survive somehow, to overcome and grow strong and straight.

I met an elderly man in a workshop I conducted in the early '90s in Estonia, just before its independence. He was a former university professor who had survived almost two decades in Siberia. He drew a forest of miserable stumps. He said that all of the beautiful old oak trees had been violently cut down. He thought his tree would die also. Then he pointed to a stump in the foreground and said, "Recently, there has been a miracle. My stump has returned to life. Look! Do you see the new growth there?" Indeed, tiny green branches had sprouted with green leaves growing from the bruised stump. A few years later, I met this fellow again at a conference. He asked me if I still remembered him. I certainly did. He wanted to share with me that his tree had been growing, and it is was a sturdy bush full of life and green leaves.

Looking back on your life, how does your resiliency, your ability to bounce back, show in your life? Is post-traumatic growth visible in your life? How do you see the Great Potter's grace and His comforting presence in your life?

Blessed Are Those Who Mourn

According to the Great Potter, "Blessed are those who mourn, for they will be comforted" (Matthew 5:4 NIV). The Great Potter, the Comforter, comforts His mourning clay potteries. Whatever reason for their brokenness, even if they mourn because they intentionally broke their own pottery, He comforts them.

Blessed are those who mourn. Blessed are those who do not pretend all is fine when it is not. Who do not cover themselves with defenses of their own construction but confess their needs and ask forgiveness when they've done wrong, knowing the Great Potter will always grant it.

King David knew all about this in His mourning after sitting in the middle of the thousand pieces of his broken pottery. He was the opposite of his forefather, Adam, blaming nobody else but himself. "My sacrifice, O God, is a broken spirit; a broken and contrite heart you, God, will not despise" (Psalm 51:17 NIV). Good for David! He knew the Great Potter's heart. Therefore, He had no fear approaching Him to ask forgiveness. He did not harden his heart but cried for the Great Potter's help and comfort for his broken pieces (6:6–7). Yes, the Great Potter comforts the broken potteries who mourn because of breaking themselves.

The Great Potter also comforts the broken potteries who mourn because they were damaged by others or difficult circumstances. He feels compassion as He also "was despised and rejected by men, a Man of Sorrows and acquainted with grief" (Isaiah 53:3 NKJV). The Great Potter knows the devastation of being crushed by others' maliciousness. He knows the pain of a friend's betrayal as well as the sorrow of losing a loved one.

Whenever you go through your personal Gethsemane, be assured that, although it may feel like the loneliest corner on the earth, you are not alone. The Man of Sorrows cries with you. He is beside you, comforting you. He knows all about Gethsemane. The Lamb of God, so full of horror that He sweats blood, could have refused His mission, but He makes His decision to fully empty the bitter cup of suffering, thus fulfilling every demand of a perfect sacrifice.

Depression is Not a Spiritual Failure

If you're feeling depressed because of your traumatizing experiences and broken pottery, understand that depression is *not* a sign of a spiritual failure but rather *a symptom of a chemical imbalance* that can be helped with *proper medication.* Therefore, there is no need to deny your depression but gracefully receive help, including medication, available from medical doctors. Also, it is helpful to reflect on your life with a professional therapist. Indeed, *there is never a reason to feel guilty about feeling depressed.* We are all different, and we react in unique ways. Many of the Bible heroes experienced depression—Jonah, Nehemiah, Jeremiah, Job, Moses, Elijah, and David—so we certainly are in good company.

The writers of psalms express their sense of depression, turmoil, and anguish in their songs. See Psalms: 13, 34–35, 40, 42–43, 52, 54–57, 59, 63, 69, and 88. If you feel depressed these psalms may sound as your feelings feel.

Even Though I Walk Through the Darkest Valley…

I remember horse-back riding through the narrow valley leading to Petra, in Jordan. The trail snaked around making it impossible to see what was coming. Sometimes the rocky walls on both sides of the trail are so high one couldn't see the sky. I will never forget the sensation when the valley surprisingly opened—the lost city of stone was spectacular and breath-taking. Sometimes when I listen to other broken potteries' difficult experiences, I have to remind myself: Even the darkest valley always has a beginning and an end. *A valley is not a cave, it is not a ditch.* And— sometimes, just when we feel it is too dark, we begin to see the stars guiding our way.

> The LORD is my shepherd, I lack nothing . . .
> *Even though I walk through the darkest valley,*
> *I will fear no evil, for you are with me…* (Psalm 23:1, 4 NIV).

Sometimes life is so hard and the depression so heavy that we find ourselves in the shadows and valleys of darkness. But valleys are like tunnels with beginnings and ends. Because our Maker is the beginning and the end Himself, He knows the way (Revelation 22:13).

If we keep walking, merely taking one step at a time, one day we will reach the end of it. And at this point, we emerge with valuable lessons that we could learn only by going through the valley of shadows. Later, our experiences allow us to help others who need support during their valley experiences. Also, remember the stars shine brightest in the dark sky.

In your exhaustion, whenever you collapse under your broom brush as Elijah did, it is comforting to know that the Great Potter is with you, comforting you. If you fall in a desert in total despair, as Hagar did, the Great Potter not only sees and hears you but also comforts you.

And if you are too exhausted to spread your wings like an eagle (Isaiah 40:31), then you can simply "take refuge in the shadow of [His] wings until the disaster has passed" (Psalms 57:1 NKJV). You can ask the Great Potter to…"keep me as the apple of Your eye; Hide me in the shadow of Your wings" (17:8).

CHAPTER 54

HEALING THROUGH FORGIVENESS

*Bear with each other and forgive one another
if any of you has a grievance against someone.
Forgive as the Lord forgave you.*

COLOSSIANS 3:13 (NIV)

*Get rid of all bitterness,
rage and anger, brawling and slander, along with every form of malice.*

*Be kind and compassionate to one another,
forgiving each other, just as in Christ God forgave you.*

Ephesians 4:31–32 (NIV)

Be merciful, just as your Father is merciful.

Luke 6:36 (NIV)

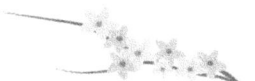

In the world of clay potteries, we break one another, accidentally and intentionally. We all need forgiveness from the Great Potter and one another. Of course, it may feel unfair to forgive someone who has done us wrong. However, life in this broken world is not always fair, but we want to live according to the Great Potter's heart. His grace toward us is also undeserved and unmerited. It is always a good idea to treat others the way we want to be treated.

As broken pottery, I certainly have much to forgive, but I also have much for which I need to be forgiven. And I must not only forgive others but also myself.

How Does the Great Potter Forgive?

"'Come now, let us settle the matter,' says the LORD. 'Though your sins are like scarlet, they shall be as white as snow; though they are red as crimson, they shall be like wool'" (Isaiah 1:18 NIV).

A story[80] tells of a priest who was burdened by a serious sin of his youth. He was unable to quell his sense of guilt. In his congregation was a lady who claimed to discuss with Jesus in her visions. The priest, although dubious, told the lady:" Next time you discuss with Jesus, ask Him if He knows what serious indiscretion I partook of in my youth." The lady agreed.

The following Sunday the priest asked her:" Did you meet with the Christ again in your dreams?" "Why, yes, we had a lovely discussion," the old lady responded.

"So, did you ask Him about my sin?"

"Yes, I did."

"So, what did Jesus say?"

"Jesus said that He does not recall."

The Great Potter thoroughly washes away our flaws. *He does not recall! He does not remember!* Unlike computer drives that retain data after deletion, He deleted them from His memory and never holds them against us. He does not preserve secret files in His heavenly hard drive but *chooses* to erase all evidence. When I need forgiveness, the Great Potter does not push the data recovery button to pull out my 'lost' files, duly stating, that according to His records He has already forgiven me one thousand and one times for one reason and two thousand and sixty four times for another. *He refuses to remember! He chooses to forget them forever.*

He has separated us from our wrongdoings "as far as the east is from the west, so far has he removed our transgressions from us" (Psalm 103:12 NIV). How far is the east from the west? Incredibly far away, meaning the transgressions can never be found again. Nor can they ever be held against us or embarrass us!

The Great Potter will also "tread our sins underfoot and hurl all our iniquities into the depths of the sea" (Micah 7:19 NIV). I imagine Him posting a Fishing Forbidden-sign on the coastline.[81] Of course, the great deceiver often organizes submarine sightseeing excursions, dredging up old mistakes and trying to convince us that not *all* of them are forgiven or forgotten. "Did the Great Potter *really* say . . .? Sounds familiar, eh? Yes, I've participated in those submarine tours few times...

Self-Forgiveness

So the Great Potter chooses to forget, but of course *we* still remember. We cannot simply reset our pottery's memory system back to the factory defaults. We still remember every single embarrassing detail. All the damage we caused... And so does the devil.

The great accuser desires that we *won't* forgive ourselves after breaking our pottery. His department is specialized in rubbing our noses in yesterday's mistakes.

Pointing out our lack of common sense, convincing us that it's not *realistic* to believe something *that bad* could ever be forgiven and forgotten—trying to steal away our joy and peace.

Wouldn't continuous self-blame be a compelling reason to bury our talents and not use our pottery for the Great Potter's service? It can effectively sabotage Christian ministries by making us believe that the Great Potter cannot or does not want to use us anymore. However, this is not what the Great Potter desires for us. He always has plans to use us as His vessels, but it starts with forgiving ourselves.

Self-forgiveness is crucial to allow us to emotionally immerse ourselves in the Great Potter's grace and not feel the guilt or shame for what He has already forgiven. Self-forgiveness targets compassion, kindness, and gentleness toward ourselves. Just as accepting ourselves is important as a foundation of accepting others, accepting our shortcomings makes us more compassionate for others' shortcomings. Additionally, self-forgiveness is shown to have many health benefits impacting cardiovascular diseases, cancer, addictions, and many issues related to high-stress levels.[82] This is understandable, as guilt and shame are heavy burdens to carry.

If we cannot forgive ourselves, we will have real difficulties forgiving others. Likewise, if we cannot forgive ourselves, unforgiveness will negatively affect our self-image and self-worth, which may affect all of our relationships, and so on.

Self-forgiveness is often a difficult and long process. However, the Great Potter can restore even our wasted years. He can "repay us for the years the locusts have eaten" (Joel 2:25 NIV). Sometimes we even get back more than what the enemy stole. This is one of those fantastic secrets of broken potteries to hold close.

Decisional and Emotional Forgiveness

We are called to forgive not only seventy times but seventy times seventy (Matthew 18:21–22), meaning we must forgive without keeping count. However, forgiveness is a *conscious decision* and needs not to have any connection to our emotions. If we only forgive those we *feel like forgiving,* many cracks of our broken pottery would remain unforgiven for the rest of our lives and we certainly would not be able to forgive ourselves! Although it is perfectly all right to feel anger, it is important not to let it turn into bitter unforgiveness and paralyzing self-pity. "In your anger do not sin": Do not let the sun go down while you are still angry, and do not give the devil a foothold" (Ephesians 4:26–27 NIV).

Forgiveness has many benefits. As a gift to ourselves it liberates *us* to move forward with our lives. Instead of carrying a loaded weapon (metaphorically speaking) and planning the perfect revenge, we can channel our energy toward growth, life, and creativity. As unforgiveness burdens, *forgiveness liberates*. If unforgiveness is a chain around *our* ankles, forgiveness is the key to unlock it (Matthew 18:34). Much secular research[83] proves that forgiveness has many health benefits linked with mental health and reduced anxiety and depression. According to Dr. Swartz, director of the Mood Disorders Adult Consultation Clinic at The Johns Hopkins Hospital:

> *There is an enormous physical burden to being hurt and disappointed. Chronic anger puts you into a fight-or-flight mode, which results in numerous changes in heart rate, blood pressure and immune response. Those changes, then, increase the risk of depression, heart disease and diabetes, among other conditions. Forgiveness, however, calms stress levels, leading to improved health.*[84]

There are two types of forgiveness, *decisional* and *emotional*.[85] Decisional forgiveness is a choice and requires letting go, releasing the resentment, and kissing revenge good-bye. It is deliberately deciding *not* to seek retribution against the perpetrator even if he or she does not deserve or seek forgiveness. Forgiveness is *a choice* to continue living without bitterness targeted toward the person who broke our pottery (Ephesians 4:30; Hebrews 12:15). It means choosing to move forward and not to expend energy on the toxic drudge. When deciding to forgive, we waive the right to pursue retribution. However, even if we let someone off the "hook," they may remain in the Great Potter's hook, but it is no longer our concern. "While they curse, you bless" (Psalm 109:28 NIV).[44]

---

[44] See also Romans 12:14.

Emotional forgiveness is something none of us can force because we are just clay potteries. The reality is that it is not always possible to regulate our emotions and feelings. If you cannot reach emotional forgiveness for someone who broke your pottery, rest easy; decisional forgiveness is enough. And if you feel you cannot do even that, you can ask the Great Potter to give you both the willingness and strength to forgive. It is often quite impressive what begins to emerge in our hearts when we ask for help.

It is empowering to choose to forgive. Our clay potteries are liberated from long-lasting toxic anger, rage, bitterness, vengeance, and hostility. When we let it go, we can concentrate on other things.

Forgiveness is not always easy. Often, a good start is to just leave the judgment in the Great Potter's hands. "Vengeance *is* Mine, I will repay" (Romans 12:19 NKJV).[45] You may be surprised to start feeling you no longer need revenge after taking this first step. *Gradually*, you might even feel like asking the Great Potter to bless your offender. Or pray as the Great Potter did: "Father, forgive them, for they do not know what they are doing" (Luke 23:34 NIV); or as Stephen did as his accusers were stoning his pottery: "Lord, do not hold this sin against them" (Acts 7:60 NIV). Sometimes, as we begin the conscious process of forgiveness, we may feel compassion for the person who wronged us.

Moreover, as the process of forgiveness launches from within us, we may begin to understand the offender's actions *without accepting or condoning them*. For example, we may understand the offender's perspective based on his childhood trauma experiences or something that may have affected his behavior. When that happens, it's the Great Potter's miraculous gifts for us, all happening because of His grace.

What Forgiveness is Not?

In Christian circles, it is typical to misunderstand what forgiveness is and what it is not. I have heard many stories about how Christian counselors demand their clients

---

[45] See also Deuteronomy 32:35; Hebrews 10:30.

forgive and forget without allowing them to work through legitimate feelings related to the broken pottery. The victims are blamed if they are unable to forgive immediately or unable to forget the episode. It is essential to understand what forgiveness is *not*, and not push anybody to do what they are not yet able to do.[86] There should be zero fearmongering, manipulation, or guilt-trips when reflecting with victims the topic of forgiveness.

Forgiveness is Not About the Offender

It is essential to realise that forgiveness is about *you*, the victim, *not* the offender. To forgive, you do *not* have to discuss the matter with the offender. You do *not* have to face him or her or reveal your plan to forgive. Your forgiveness does *not* need to be accepted.

In many cases, offenders would not acknowledge hurting you. In their minds, they don't need forgiveness. Because forgiveness is about *you*, it is even possible to forgive people who have passed away.

Forgiveness Is Not a Feeling

As forgiveness is a conscious decision, *not a feeling*, I sometimes must make it a daily ritual. Every morning, I choose *not* to give the perpetrator any power over my life. I must decide not to let them destroy *this* day as they destroyed my past. I decide I will not give them any emotional power to break my pottery again. Of course, this means that *I no longer provide them with the power to affect my emotions.*

We cannot change others' feelings or their behavior. We are responsible only for *our* choices and actions. We are empowered to *choose* to forgive.

Forgiveness Is Not Forgetting

Forgiveness does not mean that we *forget* our hurts. After a big blow, the wound can hurt for years. For us clay potteries, it is impossible to simply forget because of the number of scars remaining or the long-reaching consequences. The incident may have become a critical 'before-after' episode defining our lives and history.

We certainly will remember the event, the blow, for we cannot erase memories from our hippocampus. However, that episode needs not be the first thing on our minds when we wake up or the last thing before going to sleep. Although we cannot forget, *we can decide not to entertain those memories.* We can *choose* not to hold wrongdoings against others and not to keep records of wrongs (1 Corinthians 13:5), not to store and fuel them within our clay potteries (Hebrews 8:12).

We can also decide not to let the past hurt define who we are. Even though the next step in the recovery process is usually to see ourselves as *survivors* rather than victims, the goal is to no longer let the trauma episode define us, nor let the brokenness impact our self-image. Ultimately the goal is to define ourselves according to who the Great Potter says we are.

Forgiveness Is Not Approving

Forgiveness does not mean that we approve of others breaking our clay potteries. We do *not* accept or justify wrongdoings when we forgive. Forgiveness is not a sign of weakness but strength. It is brave to choose the higher road of forgiveness.

Forgiveness Is Not Denial

Forgiveness does not mean closing our eyes to what happened and thus pretending nothing happened. It does not mean *denying* the event or the hurt or rationalizing our emotions away. We don't need to *cover up* our brokenness nor *excuse* the offender's actions.

Forgiveness Is Not Belittling

Though we forgive, we do not belittle our experiences, pretending that they were not *that* bad. Even if we empathize with the offenders, we still take our experiences seriously. *If we belittle the impact of our hurt, the entire forgiveness process will be belittled as well.*

Broken pottery is always a serious business. Therefore, forgiveness moves through phases, more or less linear, just like any grief process does.[87] Although it seems more comfortable to ignore our pain and even belittle them, this does not do justice to ourselves.

Forgiveness Is Not Blind

It is impossible to forgive if we do not know what we are forgiving. That is why acknowledging and even expressing the emotions of our brokenness is a critical phase of our recovery process.

Any forgiveness may be a painful process as we will need to face anger, sorrow, bewilderment, humiliation, and more, including shame and guilt. However, these feelings are legitimate responses to our brokenness, and there is no reason to hide them from ourselves or the Great Potter. We must not hide or belittle our feelings. Before being able to forgive, we should understand the impact of the episode on our lives.

Only after we answer these questions is it possible to make an informed decision to forgive. Having a good counselor or therapist assisting through this process is always wise.

- How did this brokenness affect me and my relationships?
- How did it alter my life, behaviors, emotions, worldview, thoughts, finances, health, etc.?
- How did I feel when my pottery was blown to that wall or dropped to the floor?
- How did I feel when it was forgotten and not taken care of?

Forgiveness Does Not Stop Legal Investigations

Forgiveness does not pardon the offender from any legal consequences. Forgiving is liberating *ourselves* from holding any grudges and using our energy for revenge. It does *not* release the offender from penalties for a crime.

A demand to forgive should never be used to silence the victim, their feelings, and trauma processing. The victim does not relinquish their right to pursue a formal, legal investigation because a sexual predator says *sorry*. Saying sorry does not mean that the case is closed and the episode must be forgotten. *Apology should not be weaponized to silence the victim.* All too often this happens in religious communities. The roles are reversed, accusing the victim of unforgiveness, bitterness, and the depths-of-the-sea-digging. Similarly, the abuse victims have been blatantly accused of *provoking* the abusers; abusers whose only regret is that they got caught.

Forgiveness Is Not Reconciliation of Trust

An often-misunderstood concept is that *to forgive is the same as to reconcile, repair the relationship,* or *return to the relationship.* This is not so. Moreover, it is imperative to understand that forgiveness does not mean that trust has been restored. Neither does it mean that we pretend nothing happened. This is a form of dishonesty because not only did something happen but also something was miserably broken, and it may never be the same again.

Restoring the relationship as it was before the episode is not necessary for forgiveness. Though the Great Potter forgives us, fully reinstating His trust as He did with Peter and David, for example, we clay potteries do not possess supernatural powers or the eternal characteristics the Great *I Am* has. It is not always possible to reinstate the relationship the way it was after the breakage. Some relationships *shouldn't* continue because they are neither safe nor healthy.

Forgiveness and reconciliation are two different things. When forgiving others, we are releasing our claim to hold on to grudges or to seek revenge. Forgiving does not depend on the one who hurt us, but reconciliation requires the active participation of the two parties. Both must be willing not only to restore but also to rebuild the relationship and change their behaviors.

The Bible acknowledges that it is not always possible to be at peace with everyone (Romans 12:7). Unfortunately, even if we try our best, some relationships just do not work out. In those cases, it's best to just move on.

Forgiveness is a Blessing but Unforgiveness Does Not Undo Our Salvation

To truly forgive is supernatural and one of the Great Potter's blessings for us. A promising sign for knowing that you have forgiven somebody is when you no longer seek to hurt him or her. "But I tell you, love your enemies and pray for those who persecute you" (Matthew 5:44 NIV).[46]

The Great Potter taught us to pray: "Forgive us our sins, for we also forgive everyone who sins against us" (Luke 11:4 NIV). We ask Him to forgive us here-and-now while we are in the middle of the process of forgiving others. This is continuous forgiveness taking place vertically between the Great Potter and us, and horizontally between us and those who broke our clay potteries.[88]

---

[46] See also Luke 6:28.

For clay potteries burdened by a legalistic church community, it is crucial to understand that to forgive or not to forgive those who broke our potteries is *not a condition* for the Great Potter forgiving us. *It is not a condition for our salvation* because our justification is *unconditional* and based solely on His unmerited grace (Ephesians 2:8–9). Our ability to forgive others does *not* affect our salvation and permanent position as the Great Potter's children.[89]

Nonetheless, although unforgiveness will not strip away our salvation, it may have consequences for our lives and our relationships with other potteries. It may also affect our subjective experiences to emotionally feel the Great Potter's grace, peace, and joy, and impact our healing process.

Forgiveness is a precious blessing for your broken pottery. "He saved us, not because of righteous things we had done, but because of his mercy" (Titus 3:5 NIV). Similarly, we can bless others with our forgiveness. "Blessed are the merciful, for they will be shown mercy" (Matthew 5:7 NIV).

CHAPTER 55

TEARING DOWN THE FALSE GODS—DISTORTED IMAGES OF THE GREAT POTTER

*Although they claimed to be wise,
they became fools
and exchanged the glory of the immortal God
for images made to look like a mortal human being…*

Romans 1:22-23 (NIV)

Heidi McKendrick

Growing up in a legalistic church environment distorted my image of the Great Potter for three decades. By the time I finally grasped the Great Potter's *actual* characteristics, I was thoroughly burned out. But to my amazement, my broken pieces fell into the Great Potter's loving hands, which launched my healing process. During this time, I gradually internalized His unconditional love and the other secrets of broken potteries I have introduced in this book. Today, I can declare with no hesitation that I no longer believe in the same god I did in my entire childhood and youth. My God is *entirely different* from that vindictive character introduced to me back then. Immersing myself in the Great Potter's unfailing love and never-ending grace was *life-altering*, and my only regret is that I wish I had been able to get to know Him much earlier!

What we teach children about the Great Potter with our words and actions is crucial. "Let the little children come to me, and *do not hinder them*, for the kingdom of God belongs to such as these" (Luke 18:16 NIV), says the Great Potter. "Do not hinder them" is a severe warning with severe consequences: "If anyone causes one of these little ones—those who believe in me—to *stumble*, it would be better for them to have a large millstone hung around their neck and to be drowned in the depths of the sea" (Matthew 18:6 NIV). Furthermore, whatever we do to the children, we do to the Great Potter (25:40)—their angels in Heaven always see His face (18:10).

In my childhood church, I was not taught about the Great Potter truthfully. Instead, a god of wrath and fury was planted within, filling my heart with fear and dread, hindering my coming to the Great Potter and trusting in Him. Although none of these well-meaning church folks meant to make me stumble, they broke my pottery and stole my peace, joy, and security. Their view of the Great Potter prevented me from coming to Him as my shelter and refuge.

One example of the distorted teaching I received in my childhood is from a children's book that filled my mind with fear, mistrust, anxiety, and neurotic self-scrutiny. It completely distorted my idea of the Great Potter and made me feel unsafe.

While my "worldly" friends had coloring books of Disney characters, my coloring book was about the rapture. The story was about a little girl who becomes a believer, thus launching her journey on the narrow path to heaven. She looked a lot like me with two pigtails. Naturally, I colored her hair yellow to match my blond hair.

The many dangers of that narrow path are visualized in the book. I colored the traffic signs, thinking how easy it would be for this girl to slip off the road and never arrive in heaven. Indeed, she will need to be overly cautious to keep from falling into the fiery lake!

The story describes the fatal day when the girl borrows her mother's silver spoon and takes it outside to the sandbox. She forgets about it and leaves it there. First stealing and then lying by not confessing to her mother she had taken it. My five-year-old self knew that this story would not end well.

And it does not. The next page of the coloring book illustrates the girl waking up on her bed to the sound of several heavenly trumpets (I color them yellow). The rapture of the believers is taking place!

"Oh, Jesus is coming to take me to heaven!" The girl rejoices, hurrying to her parents' bedroom (I color her nightgown pink). However, the room is empty. The next page illustrates her mother and grandmother being raptured to the heavens to meet the angels. In the picture, the girl is reaching her little hands toward heaven so that she, too, would be raptured.

But she is not.

Her foot is chained to the ground by an enormous silver spoon, bigger than the girl. (I color the silver spoon and the chains gray.)

And there I am, five-year-old sitting at the kitchen table, coloring the chain and the giant spoon, coloring the trumpets, and the raptured grandmother and mother.

The image of this giant silver spoon carved itself into my soul and haunted me every night. It did not matter how much I tried to measure up to the rules and regulations, it was never enough. *I was never enough.* Every night I felt incredibly insecure, scrutinizing my over-sensitive conscience and reflecting on whether I was holding any tiny sinful secret thoughts. I had been taught that if my heart was not entirely pure, no resurrection power could lift me to the heavenly wedding during the rapture. I would be blatantly told that "I don't know you" and be turned away from the pearly gates. As a little girl, being left behind to experience the horrors of the mark of the Beast and a torturous martyrdom caused me severe nightmares.

Take time to reflect on and answer these questions:

- What kind of teaching (books, sermons, Sunday school lessons, etc.) do you remember receiving about the Great Potter in your childhood?
- How did they make you feel?
- How did they impact your idea of the Great Potter?
- Who was your most important role model in your childhood?
- How did they impact your image of the Great Potter?

The Devil's Image Presented as the Great Potter's Image

The most ingenious way for the devil to mislead us clay potteries away from the Great Potter is *to traumatize us early in life* and to damage our emotions and souls, rendering us incapable of comprehending, much less receiving, the Great Potter's unfailing love, never-ending grace, and everlasting faithfulness. We become so wounded and frightened that we have *no reason to trust Him* or surrender to Him.

If our image of the Great Potter is falsified in childhood, perhaps we will never give Him a chance to show His real self and have a relationship with us. We may never bother getting to know Him.

As a therapist, I've encountered hundreds of potteries broken because of spiritually abusive, legalistic teaching. While conducting therapeutic workshops on the false images of the Great Potter, I've heard many heartbreaking stories.

I recall after one of these workshops, a middle-aged woman came to me during the break. Her eyes wide and her voice shaking, she told of something revolutionary that had happened to her. During the workshop, she suddenly realized that all her life, since childhood, her image of the Great Potter has been identical to her image of the devil. They were alike: horrible and mean. Understanding this finally liberated her and birthed in her the correct image of the Great Potter.

Of course, the devil's particular plot is to plant in us a distorted image of the Great Potter that resembles the devil himself: accusatory, malicious, deceiving, punitive, judgmental.

Doesn't that sound like the devil?

You Shall Not Make an Image...

Of course, for us clay potteries, it is natural to create mental images to help us understand the world surrounding us. When we read a book, we form an image of the characters. We create images of other clay potteries even if we have only heard about them. When my friend tells me that she has fallen in love with a macho, tall dark-haired man, I immediately create a mental image of a Clark Gable–type.

All of our mental images are products of our imaginations, yet they may be based on past experiences, which are stored in the limbic system of the brain by the hippocampus. This is where our emotions are stored as well, so it is easy to create all kinds of emotionally associated images linked with our past experiences.

According to the second commandment Moses received from the Great Potter while on Mount Sinai, the Great Potter forbids any images to be built to represent Him. He also means that He does not like those false images that we so easily construct in our minds about Him. "You shall not make for yourself an image *in the form of anything* in Heaven above or on the earth beneath or in the waters below" (Deuteronomy 5:8 NIV). We should not bear false wittness against Him!

Although the Great Potter gave us creativity and imagination, He does not want us to create any false images about Himself. Similarly, although the Great Potter made us in *His* image (Genesis 1:26–27), we should never in our minds try to make the Great Potter in *our* image. That is, we clay potteries should never project the characteristics of ours, or others' clay pottery, onto the Great Potter. We should not "turn things upside down, *as if the potter were thought to be like the clay!*" (Isaiah 29:16 NIV)—as if a pottery could ever mold the Potter!

Our primitive capacity to love is incomparable to His unfailing and unconditional love.

Our greatest effort of forgiveness is not comparable to Him choosing not to even remember.

Our most authentic generosity is not comparable with His never-ending grace and mercy.

Our best loyalty is not comparable with His everlasting faithfulness.

We have no right to substitute any part of this broken world to enter into our concept of the Great Potter. Yet this is precisely what we often do. We create an image of the Great Potter that is neither truthful nor the full representation of Him.

Life experiences shadow our present and affect our experiences with the Great Potter as well. For example, if you had extremely strict, demanding, and unpleasant parents who always criticized you, you might quickly transfer this experience onto your image of the Great Potter, thus see Him as judgmental. Or if your parents were cold, distant, and absent, you might transfer this experience onto your image of the Great Potter and think that He does not care about you either. If your father abused you, you might unconsciously see the Great Potter, your heavenly Father, as cruel and punitive.

Do Not Transfer or Project Any Images...

This concept in which we transfer *the characteristics of the important relationships* from our past into our present relationships is a typical psychotherapy concept called *transference*. It means that we unconsciously transfer both positive and negative characteristics of our past relationships into our current relationships. Whatever we have experienced in our past relationships with significant clay potteries can easily be transferred onto our image of the Great Potter and affect our perceived relationship with Him. If we unconsciously link the Great Potter with our parents', teachers', or pastors' characteristics, we may easily create a distorted image of Him.

Another typical psychotherapy concept in which we project *our* characteristics, thoughts, and emotions onto someone else is called *projection*. Another way to see the Great Potter in a wrong light is to project onto Him our self-image, the traits of our personalities, or bits and pieces of our emotions, such as our limitations, fears, fantasies, motivations, ambitions, weaknesses, and insecurities. If *we* are scared of the Great Potter, we may unconsciously project this emotion onto Him and then feel that He indeed *is* scary. If we fear punishment, we see the Great Potter as punitive. It is typical for us clay potteries to project our conditional way of loving one another onto the Great Potter's characteristics as well as our unmerciful and unfaithful features.

It is important to realize that we should *not* have an image of the Great Potter that reflects our fears or fantasies. If we do, it does not represent Him but only *our* fears and fantasies. Our idea of the Great Potter should never be *just* a projection of some fatherly figure in heaven like Mr. Freud claimed He is.

Both transference and projections are unconscious, and we often have no idea something like that has taken place. Therefore, it is beneficial to learn what lens we use when we think about the Great Potter. Are we seeing Him through the lens of what others say about Him, what we have conjured about Him, or what *He* says about Himself in the Bible?

We should *not* have an image that projects our characteristics or personality traits onto the Great Potter, or an image that transfers our relationships with our significant people onto His attributes. *Our image of the Great Potter should never be a transference of our past relationships or a projection of our current emotions.* If it is, it is merely a false image of the Great Potter and will never do Him justice.

The way we see the Great Potter impacts our relationship with Him as it also affects our ideas of *what we think He thinks* about us. Although the distorted images are merely *false assumptions* of how we think the Great Potter sees us or acts toward us, they affect *our expectations* of Him and determine *how we act* toward Him.

If you think of the Great Potter as a punisher, you will expect nothing but punishment from Him. You may also believe that the Great Potter sends difficulties that happen to you. If you have an image of the Great Potter as an accusing judge, you will expect His displeasure with you whenever you are not perfect. Of course, this is similar in any relationship. If we have false images of any situation, this will misguide our expectations of this situation. Also, because of being broken too many times, we may have a distorted self-image and believe we are lesser than others or that we don't deserve to be treated well. Then we are more likely to expect others not to accept us and thus repeat our trauma. The following figure illustrates the process of transference and projection and how it may impact our relationships.

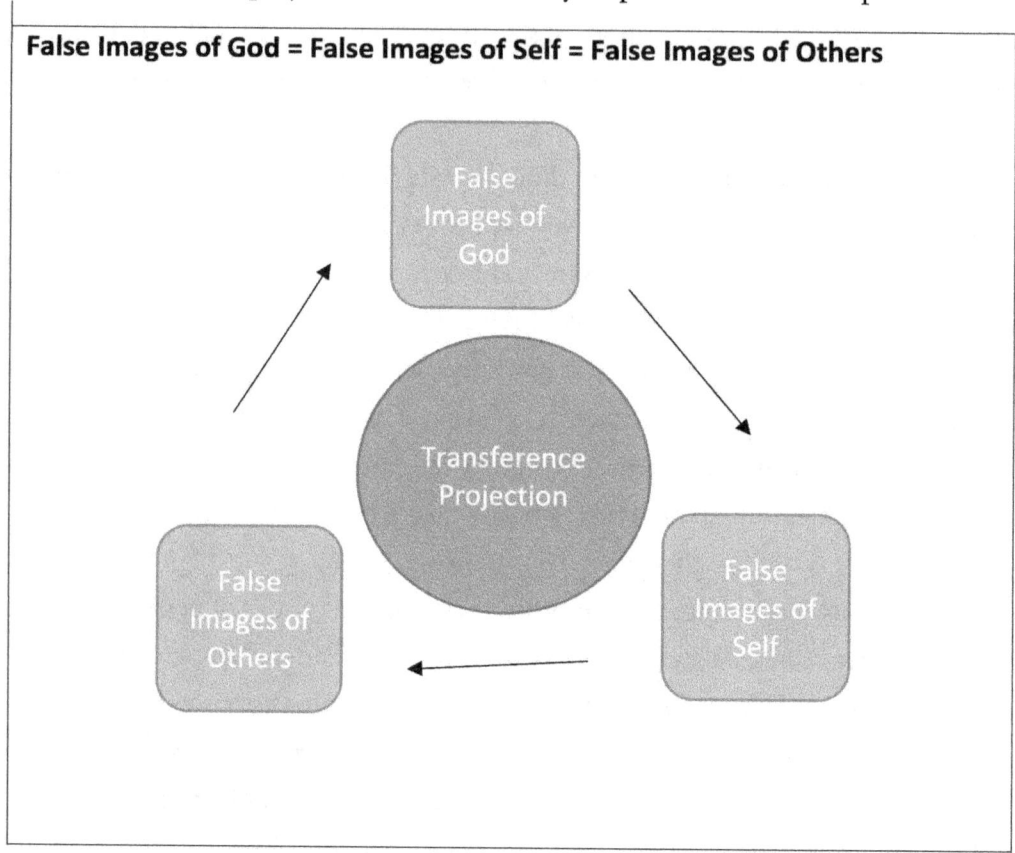

Figure 1. This figure illustrates the vicious cycle of how our distorted images of the Great Potter affect distorted self-images and distorted images of others, thus affecting our relationships with both the Great Potter and others.

Sadly, just as our distorted self-image affects our relationships with others, it affects our relationship with the Great Potter. It is challenging to be in an authentic relationship or surrender with anyone we cannot trust. This is a vicious cycle. *I cannot accept the Great Potter's unconditional love towards myself if I cannot love myself. I don't know how to love myself if I have not experienced love from others.* To stop this cycle, we need the Great Potter's unfailing love as a correcting and compensating experience for our damaged souls.

Rid Yourself of Idols…

As the second commandment holds us clay potteries responsible for any false image(s) we claim to represent the Great Potter, it is crucial to understand that our images can be nothing but deceptive, false concepts about Him. Any image we create about the Great Potter with our clay brains only diminishes Him into a small box of *our* creation, comprehensible with us. "Do not make any image of Me," the Great Potter warns because He wants to protect us from our limited imaginations. *We are simply not creative enough to imagine the Creator.*

Just as the Great Potter required Jacob's family to get rid of all their idols and go back to their beginnings and fix His altar, anyone who is infected by false images of the Great Potter must also rid themselves of them. The second commandment unmistakably commands us to get rid of any distorted images and false concepts of the Great Potter. "But ye shall destroy their altars, *break their images*, and *cut down their groves*: For thou shall worship no other god: for the LORD, whose name is Jealous, is a jealous God" (Exodus 34:13–14 KJV).

It is understandable why the Great Potter, our heavenly Father is jealous when His potteries develop distorted images of Himself and begin to relate with Him fearfully or aloofly. That's why we are to destroy the false images so that they will no longer interfere with our relationship with Him. If you have false images of the Great Potter, something perhaps you've sheltered in your mind since your childhood, *break them, cut down their groves, throw them away* and *start fresh*! Immerse yourself into the Great Potter's covenant of redemption at the Cross.

Remember, we do *not* need to create an image of the Creator! We need not project or transfer anything onto the Great Potter because He *is* the Great *I Am*. The One who is and has always been. The Creator who created us. Since Jesus is the exact representation of God, He is all we need to see when we try to "picture" God.

Examples of Distorted Images of the Great Potter

For the last twenty years, I have conducted numerous therapeutic workshops for pastors and seminary students, helping them explore their distorted images of the

Great Potter. I asked them to remember their early images of the Great Potter. "Back then, when you thought about Him, what would come to your mind?"

- How did you feel about Him?
- How did you think He saw you?
- How did you think He thought about you?
- What did you think He felt about you?
- What would He say to you?
- What did you say to Him?

I asked them to freely associate, write, or draw any images, even cartoons with speaking and thinking bubbles, that came to their minds, thoughts, feelings, and even bodily sensations. Then I asked them to explore their *current* image of the Great Potter and put their responses on a separate piece of paper. "Right now, think about the Great Potter and write or draw anything that comes to your mind. Any images, feelings, thoughts, body sensations."

- How do you think He sees you now?
- How do you think He thinks about you right now?
- How does He feel about you?
- What does He say to you?
- What do you say to Him?

After this, I asked participants to reflect on the eye-opening turning point in their lives, their Damascus Road. We then shared the different ways the distorted image impacted their lives and explored the best ways to help others restore their distorted images and meet the Great Potter as He is.

The following categories capture some examples of false ideas of the Great Potter that hundreds of participants attending my classes and workshops have shared with me over the years.[90] Perhaps you will find some of these images familiar with your past or present images. Some of these metaphors could also become collective, false images of a legalistic, spiritually abusive Christian community or cult.

A Snooper, a peeping spy, a prying private investigator, or an extremely intelligent (and scary) secret agent, covertly following our every action. He not only listens to your private discussions (planting microphones in our rooms) but also reads your mind, your most secret thoughts, motivations, dreams, and fears. He takes snapshots to coerce you back into line or as evidence to project on a screen at that final humiliating judgement in front of everyone. Like a Santa Claus with his overly excited elves, keeping a list of nasty and nice. Having this false image of the Great Potter paralyzes you with anxieties and efficiently traps you into an achievement-oriented relationship with Him.

A Meticulous Bookkeeper keeps a detailed record of every wrongdoing, wrong word, and wrong thought, always increasing his demands and setting the bar higher. If you don't measure up, there will be fatal consequences. Indeed, this false image will lead to tight-haloed performances and exhaustion sooner or later. If the entire Christian community holds this false image of the Great Potter, there are several written and unwritten rules to follow. Obeying the various behavior codes and avoiding the sin-lists become the gate-keeping measure to heaven and the way to please the Great Potter. Many potteries with a polished external façade and keeping appearances are in these church communities.

A Flash of Angry Lightning in the form of a disciplinary authority has zero-tolerance for any imperfection. He eagerly drops a hot stone from the sky on you if you even think to do something wrong. He hits you with his lightning only because he can. He enjoys his power trips like a cat playing with a mouse. He is merely waiting a moment to catch and smash your pottery. This false image contributes to insecurity and profound mistrust and is typical for legalistic and spiritually abusive communities.

A Fierce Prosecutor, punitive judge, or prison warden, he fastidiously interprets the rule of law and always nails you for some reason. He waits and watches for you to make the fatal mistake so that he can arrest you. For sure, you always do something wrong or did something imperfectly. Secret thoughts and unconscious desires, if nothing else. An authoritarian dictator, he orders humiliating punishments if the rules are not obeyed. No independent thinking or questions are allowed. This false image may lead to despair and a sense of hopelessness. Everything you do is from fear, not love.

A Spoiler of Joy, he is a party pooper whose main aim is to ensure you no longer have fun or do anything you enjoy. Even his plans for your future include things you are not interested in. If it is something you love or are excited about it cannot be God's will. *If you're happy and you know it, it's a sin…*

A Frugal Pharmacist, he cautiously measures the splashes of grace and mercy drop by drop, extremely thrifty. Eventually, he declares you've had enough, no more grace for you. Too bad if you wasted your prescription renewals. This false image will quickly contribute to spiritual burnout and spur you to give up.

An Energy Force, a distant God, withdrawn and cold, existing out there somewhere, on the other side. Even if you would like to be closer to him, it is not possible. A bit similar to the Grand Designer and Architect of the Universe but too busy running the stars, galaxies, and seas to have any concern for you. This false image can cause a sense of emptiness, loneliness, and isolation.

The Old Testament Lord Sabaoth sits on his heavenly throne in his full glory and holiness. As the General of his heavenly armies, Lord Sabaoth destroys the sinners with a breath from his mouth. As his sanctified followers, you may become his soldier crusading for him to kill sin, the unholy, unbelievers, and dissidents.[91] Of course, this is a wrong idea of the Great Potter and lacks his characteristics of love, grace, and faithfulness. However, looking at the paintings in Medieval churches in Europe, this image is often reflected in them.

A Divine Breast, an omnipotent contributor, comparable with the mother-newborn relationship, conveying a symbiotic bliss-experience of boobie-babies, fulfilling their every wish and need instantly, moving mountains for them, and creating a paradise, nurturing and wiping away all their tears.

But will they live happily ever after, healthy and prosperous, as promised…? Because this false image of the Great Potter does not allow you to become independent, the relationship may soon begin to feel suffocating, swallowing you into a black hole or a spiderweb that requires you to sacrifice everything for the cause.

A spiritually abusive, religious community may start with the bliss of finally-a-group-where-I-can-belong-and-feel-loved, but after the honeymoon, the floundering member is trapped. Brainwashing and fearmongering causes him to believe that there is no life or love outside the web. Everybody else is going to hell; they are demonic or filthy; and only want to lead astray.[92]

The false concept of promising prosperity may result in deep disappointments, serious doubts, a sense of helplessness, and anger after a broken-pottery experience. As a result, hopelessness, even depression may develop, along with the false impression of a detached Great Potter who is non-caring, hidden, silent, or non-existent.

Dangerous Concepts

Our difficulty in receiving the Great Potter in an accurate and healthy view can be due to many factors: dysfunctional family background, spiritually abusive church community, too many well-meaning yet toxic people in our lives, or a distorted Christian education and incorrect theology. It is also possible the false image of the Great Potter is a result of transgenerational trauma.

Of course, any of these distorted and false concepts of the Great Potter are damaging. They can be the source of many mental health issues such as anxiety, pathological perfectionism, neurotic disorders, false guilt, and unhealthy self-images. On a spiritual level, they cause legalism, difficulties to receive the Great Potter's love and grace, and inability to *feel* forgiven even though we *are* freely forgiven.

Just as it is unhealthy to immerse ourselves into the legalistic false images of the Great Potter as they lead us to spiritual blindness, burnout and exhaustion, it is likewise harmful to immerse ourselves in 'prosperity promising ideals' of Christian walk. If our faith is based on unrealistic images that the Great Potter is always fulfilling all our prayers the way we desire, we will be disappointed eventually and this can lead to depression.

Fortunately, we are not locked into false images of the Great Potter. He reveals Himself in the Bible and through the life of Jesus Christ.

He is easy to find!

CHAPTER 56

THE MYSTERY FULL OF GRACE —IMMANUEL—GOD WITH US

Jesus said to him, "*I am the way, the truth, and the life.
No one comes to the Father except through Me.*
"*If you had known Me, you would have known My Father also;
and from now on you know Him and have seen Him.*"
Philip said to Him, "Lord, show us the Father, and it is sufficient for us."
Jesus said to him, "*Have I been with you so long, and yet you have not known Me*, Philip?

He who has seen Me has seen the Father; so how can you say, 'Show us the Father'? Do you not believe that I am in the Father, and the Father in Me? The words that I speak to you I do not speak on My own authority; but the Father who dwells in Me does the works.

JOHN 14: 6–10 (NKJV)

The apostle Paul, who had corrected his distorted image of the Great Potter, now explores the truthful image of Him, *the mystery* of all times, the Christ:

To me, who am less than the least of all the saints, this grace was given, that I should preach among the Gentiles the unsearchable riches of Christ, and to make all see what *is* the *fellowship of the mystery, which from the beginning of the ages has been hidden in God who created all things through Jesus Christ*; to the intent that now the manifold wisdom of God might be made known by the church to the principalities and powers in the heavenly places, according to the eternal purpose *which He accomplished in Christ Jesus our Lord.* (Ephesians 3:8–11 NKJV)

He has delivered us from the power of darkness and conveyed us into the kingdom of *the Son of His love*, in whom we have redemption through His blood, the forgiveness of sins. *He is the image of the invisible God*, the firstborn over all creation. For by Him all things were created that are in Heaven and that are on earth, visible and invisible, whether thrones or dominions or principalities or powers. *All things were created through Him and for Him. And He is before all things, and in Him all things consist.* (Colossians 1:13–17 NKJV)

The apostle John also reveals the mystery of the Great Potter's ultimate plan to redeem His potteries as His expression of love—Jesus Christ, God, who came to earth to save us, forever:

In the beginning was *the Word,* and *the Word was with God,* and *the Word was God.* He was in the beginning with God. All things were made through Him, and without Him nothing was made that was made. In Him was life, and the life was the light of men. And the light shines in the darkness, and the darkness did not comprehend it. (John 1:1–5 NKJV)

The Word became flesh and made *his dwelling among us.* We have seen his glory, the glory of the one and only Son, who came from the Father, *full of grace and truth.* (v. 14 NIV)

No one has ever seen God, but the *one and only Son, who is himself God* and is in closest relationship with the Father, has made him known. (v.18)

The Son is *the image of the invisible God,* the firstborn over all creation. (Colossians 1:15)

According to Matthew Henry, *"The plainest reason why the Son of God is called the Word, seems to be, that as our words explain our minds to others, so was the Son of God sent to reveal his Father's mind to the world."*[93]

Immanuel—God With Us

It was not enough that the Great Potter revealed Himself through words. The Word also had to become *one with us,* flesh and clay, *God with a body,* giving us clay potteries the accurate picture of Him, *Immanuel, God with us* (Matthew 1:23), the essence of the Great Potter. "Therefore, when Christ came into the world, he said: 'Sacrifice and offering you did not desire, but *a body* you prepared for me'" (Hebrews 10:5 NIV).

Whenever your clay pottery is brutally smashed on the floor, and you are hurting and bleeding, you will never be forsaken as the Great Potter Himself is with you.

Immanuel, the Great Potter with you, in your suffering. The Great Potter is with you in your brokenness, the storm, the dark valley, the cave, the desert. Even if your clay pottery has sunken into a trash yard of broken potteries, He comes, finds your broken pieces, lifts them, and places them on His table. He wants to restore His relationship with His potteries.

"For to us a child is born, to us a son is given, and the government will be on his shoulders. And he will be called Wonderful Counselor, Mighty God, Everlasting Father, Prince of Peace" (Isaiah 9:6 NIV).

- The *Wonderful Counselor* will comfort you in your brokenness.
- The *Mighty God* will protect you, and whatever happens to your clay pottery is under His control.
- The *Everlasting Father* will pour His unfailing love, never-ending grace, and everlasting faithfulness over you.
- The *Prince of Peace* will guard your heart, and no matter the circumstances, you still have His supernatural peace.

John 3:16

John 3:16 encapsulates the *gospel*, but it also refers to the Great Potter's features: unconditional love, never-ending grace, and everlasting faithfulness. As in the parable of Mark 12:1–9, after the owner of the vineyard's several servants were beaten or killed by the farmers, he then sent His son, whom the workers also kill, similarly, the Great Potter sent *His* Son, the *image of Himself,* to die for us (Romans 8:32).

A Father sending His Son to suffer a cruel punishment and die on behalf of some crook tells me something about love that is difficult even to begin to comprehend. Could there possibly be any greater sacrifice than a Father sacrificing His only Son, the exact image of Himself? Could there be any more profound proof of the Great Potter's love for His potteries?

The Son, the image of the invisible God—The suffering God who takes our sin, feels our pain, and suffers with us …

Although difficult to comprehend with our limited brainpower, if we don't *begin* to grasp the depth of this sacrifice and ransom, it is impossible for us to see the Great Potter's characteristics. Furthermore, if we cannot see Him in this light, *full of grace and self-sacrificing love*, it is as if we *do not see Him at all*, which means we cannot fully comprehend His message, the gospel. "He who has the Son has life" (1 John 5:12 NIV).[47]

> God, who at various times and in various ways spoke in time past to the fathers by the prophets, has *in these last days spoken to us by His Son*, whom He has appointed heir of all things, *through whom also He made the worlds; who being the brightness of His glory and the express image of His person*, and upholding all things by the word of His power, when He had by Himself purged our sins, sat down at the right hand of the Majesty on high, having become so much better than the angels, as He has by inheritance obtained a more excellent name than they. (Hebrews 1:1–4 NKJV)

> Who is a liar but he who denies that Jesus is the Christ? He is antichrist who denies the Father and the Son. *Whoever denies the Son does not have the Father either; he who acknowledges the Son has the Father also.* (1 John 2:22–23 NKJV)

The Great Potter revealed Himself to us clay potteries, according to His eternal plan, to reconcile the world to Himself and to redeem His clay potteries. Therefore, Christ is *the exact image, the exact representation of the Father*, His characteristics, and His nature. Any image I hold of the Great Potter that differs from this image revealed in Jesus is a false image.

The Great I Am

The Great Potter spoke to Moses from the burning bush and identified Himself as: "*I am who I am*. This is what you are to say to the Israelites: '*I am* has sent me to you'"

---

[47] See also John 20:31, Acts 10:43.

(Exodus 3:14 NIV). Similarly, Jesus self-designated Himself as *I am*: "...before Abraham was born, *I am*" (John 8:58 NIV).[48] [94] "'*I am*,' said Jesus. 'And you will see the Son of Man sitting at the right hand of the Mighty One and coming on the clouds of heaven'" (Mark 14:62 NIV). Jesus *is* "'the stone [the] builders rejected, which has become the cornerstone.' Salvation is found in no one else, for *there is no other name under heaven given to mankind by which we must be saved*'" (Acts 4:11-12 NIV). Jesus, the Great *I Am*, declares of Himself the following:

I am...

- "*...the way* and *the truth* and *the life*. No one comes to the Father except through me" (John 14:6 NIV).
- "*...the gate*; whoever enters through me will be saved" (10:9).
- "*...the good shepherd*. The good shepherd lays down his life for the sheep" (v. 11).
- "*...the light of the world*. Whoever follows me will never walk in darkness, but will have the light of life" (8:12).
- "*...the bread of life*. Whoever comes to me will never go hungry, and whoever believes in me will never be thirsty" (6:35). "Let anyone who is thirsty come to me and drink" (7:37). "*...the resurrection and the life*. The one who believes in me will live, even though they die; and whoever lives by believing in me will never die. Do you believe this?" (11:25–26).
- "*...the Alpha and the Omega, the First and the Last, the Beginning and the End*" (Revelation 22:13 NIV).

Wounded Healer

The true image of the Great Potter includes the idea of *the Wounded Healer*, who experienced our pain and, therefore, can *feel with us*, even when our feelings are

---

[48] Compare with Hebrew: *Ehyeh Asher Ehyeh Asher*, meaning "I am That I am." This refers to eternally alive God who always *is*. The letters YHWH were pronounced as Yahweh. However, Rabbinical Judaism taught that it is too sacred to pronounce this name, therefore in prayers it was often replaced by the word *Adonai*, meaning the Lord, and when discussed, by *HaShem*, meaning The Name. [94]

numbed and we are too weary to cry. "For we do *not* have a high priest who is unable to empathize with our weaknesses" (Hebrews 4:15 NIV). It is from His brokenness that we can receive His compassion for our brokenness. "He was beaten so we could be whole" (Isaiah 53:5 NLT). He was broken so that our broken pottery could be healed. "By his wounds you have been healed" (1 Peter 2:24 NIV).

Despite any distorted images we may have about the Great Potter because of our experiences with other clay potteries, He planned for us to be *in a relationship with Him* from the beginning of time. Therefore, He pours over us His unfailing love, never-ending mercy, and everlasting faithfulness. This is the corrective and compensative experience necessary for our emotional wounds.

Opposite to the distorted images, the Great Potter is not disappointed but *pleased* with you. He is pleased to save you (Psalm 40:13) and restore your broken pottery. In every step of the therapeutic process on the Great Potter's table, He is pleased with your process. In His mind, you have *always* been wonderfully made, the most beautiful and the most precious child.

He is proud of you, just like any parent would be of her child.

He is excited to follow your growth, your first steps.

As the Great Potter molds you, He delights in what you will become, making good plans for your future, as any good parent does. "Dear friends, *now* we are children of God, and *what we will be* has not yet been made known. But we know that when Christ appears, *we shall be like him*, for we shall see him as he is" (1 John 3:2 NIV).

When our distorted image of the Great Potter heals, we allow Him to launch His work with us on the Potter's table, on His wheel, on His shelves, in His firing oven. This is when we also enter an authentic relationship with Him.

What do you want me to do for you? (Mark 10:51; Matthew 20:32; Luke 18:41), He asks us today on His table.

Do you want to become healthy?

Yes, I do!

Please, launch my healing process, mend my broken heart, and fill my pottery with your comforting presence.

Please, set me free from any captivity or oppression I may experience because of my brokenness.

Please, open my eyes so that I can see you in real light and immerse into your unfailing love and never-ending grace.

Please, begin the "good work" in me and finish it whenever it is ready.

... *Thank you!*

CHAPTER 57

BROKEN VESSEL IN THE GREAT POTTER'S SERVICE BUILDING A HEALTHY CHRISTIAN CHURCH

No one, when he has lit a lamp,
covers it with a vessel or puts it under a bed,
but sets it on a lampstand,
that those who enter may see the light…

LUKE 8:16 (NKJV)

As the many stories of broken potteries reveal to us, clay potteries are not exempt from brokenness. We all suffer the consequences of living in this broken world. We go through many hardships (Acts 14:22). The Great Potter uses our broken pieces as the material for the new pottery, making it stronger, and bringing us *hope* (Romans 5:3–4). Our brokenness may also become His ministry—shining His light through our cracks.

A Christian church should *always* be a therapeutic and caring fellowship of clay potteries where the love of the Great Potter is concretely known and felt in practice. It should also be a safe place for broken potteries that left spiritually abusive communities to join and recover.

Healthy Church vs. Spiritually Abusive Community

Spiritual and religious abuse refers to *misuse of spiritual authority in the name of the Great Potter.*[95] It is an old phenomenon, recognized in Biblical times, and something Jesus fierce- ly attacked. In many modern Christian communities, it flourishes because of the well-meaning leadership's false image of the Great Potter. However, there are other communities in which it is nothing but a purposeful abuse of power. It is possible that in some communities the members are so accustomed to the spiritual abuse that they fail to even recognize it.

Spiritual abuse is extremely traumatizing for the victim as it may completely destroy their trust and relationship with the Great Potter. It always involves emotional abuse but can often also include financial abuse. In some situations, it may include various forms of physical and/or sexual abuse. Whereas a victim of other types of abuses may retain their relationship with the Great Potter as a comfort and shield enabling them to survive, with spiritual abuse this is torn from them. The victims of spiritual abuse often feel alone, isolated, shunned, and banned. Cast out for Satan. The Great Potter is no longer on their side.

Spiritual abuse always smashes our pottery.

Anybody may end up a victim of spiritual abuse. The abuser may be the religious community at large, the leadership, small-groups, or relatives. A pastor or church volunteer may experience spiritual abuse from their peers, overseers, church sub-groups, or individual members of the congregation. Growing up in a neurotic and legalistic atmosphere, some victims may have experienced spiritual abuse since childhood. Those with a prior abuse history are especially sensitive to spiritual abuse. Their consciousness may already be oversensitive and burdened by shame and false guilt. Sadly, this will become a breeding ground for spiritual abuse, making it difficult to even leave the group.

Spiritual abuse wounds our potteries to its very core. It destroys our mental health and spiritual growth, stealing our sense of self-worth, dignity, and empowerment. Paralyzing us so that we become incapable of making own decisions. After leaving a spiritually abusive community, the therapeutic rehabilitation can last for years. The damaging impact of spiritual abuse has been equated with the impact of incest.

It is important to recognize the characteristics of spiritual abuse so that the new church community can help the victims to restore their damaged relationship with the Great Potter and not be further traumatized.

Although not all-encompassing, I have composed some warning signs of a spiritually abusive community, as well as positive attributes of a safe and healthy Christian community in the following table.[96] While it is impossible to compile a list without providing a context, a healthy and safe community would *not* want to have *any* characteristics of a spiritually abusive community. *Be aware* and always remember that even though spiritual abuse is practiced in the name of the Great Potter, He has nothing to do with it. Furthermore, it is not possible to worship and love Him yet hate His potteries.

SPIRTUALLY ABUSIVE COMMUNITY	HEALTHY & SAFE COMMUNITY
LEADERSHIP	
• Authoritarian & Dictatorship • Total Autonomy & Power Abuse • Narcissistic Tendencies • "One-Man-Show" • Superior & Untouchable • Lack of Accountability Structure • Defining themselves as 'God's anointed' • Declaring their 'priesthood' • Surrounded by 'YES'-men (and women) • *Bad Shepherd* re: *Hesekiel 34:2–6* • Nepotism & Bias *"The leadership is always right (even if they are wrong)!"*	• Servant-Leadership; Servant's heart according to Christ's example • *Good Shepherd*; Taking care of the members; Protecting against spiritual abuse • Team-Work • Job-Descriptions & Distinct Positions • Clearly defined roles for elders, board, pastors, staff, volunteers... • Trained Pastoral Care Staff • Membership elected Board of Directors, elders, pastors & other staff • Terms of Service defined • Transparent & Mutual Accountability Structure • Continuing Education & Regular Supervision • Emphasizing all believers' priesthood *1 Peter 2:5, 9; 1 Tim 3: 2–3; 3,5,6; 2 Tim 2:14–16; 23–26; Titus 2:7–8*
TRUTH	
• Twisted Truth • Leadership defines the truth; They claim receiving their wisdom from God • Forbidden to evaluate the leadership, doctrine, teaching, practices, prophecies, visions... • Time 'goldening' the history of the group • All pioneers worshipped on a pedestal. *"Do not touch God's anointed!"*	• Transparency: History of the group openly discussed & reflected; Not avoiding sensitive topics for reputations sake • Acknowledging harm for victims of abuse • A culture that encourages the members to evaluate the leadership, doctrine, teaching, practices, prophecies, visions... *"Do not treat prophecies with contempt but test them all; hold on to what is good"* (1 Thessalonikians 5: 20–21 NIV)
RULES & PROCEDURES	
• Leadership Dictated Rules & Procedures • Leadership determines ministries & practices • Hypocrisy: Leadership does not follow its own rules; No consequences/legal investigations of leadership & inner circle failings. *"All is allowed in the Holy War"*	• Transparent By-Laws & Policies • Clear Ethical Code of Conduct • Security/Safety Guidelines & Procedures • Protocol & Policies (i.e. conflicts, medical/mental health issues, crimes, emergencies...) • Trained Security Team & Incident Protocol

• Written & Un-written rules, practices, traditions, procedures, rituals … • Sin-lists; Holiness-lists; Achievement/Performance-lists... • Controlling the members' relationships, participation, time, clothing, hobbies, tithing, emotions, opinions, decisions, relationships, plans, calling, voting… • Interfering with members' choice of work, spouse, studying, career, housing, finances, political opinions…	• Child/Youth/Vulnerable Population Safety & Protection Template • Requiring background checks for all staff/volunteers • Strategic Protocols, Prevention plan & Investigative procedures for harm reduction/reporting suspected abuse/ harassment *Mark 12:30–31; John 13:35; Col 3:14–16; 1 Cor 13:1–13*
FINANCES	
• Leadership makes all financial decisions • Church building/land title under the leader's name • Lack of transparency in financial accounting • Leadership uses donations for their personal benefit • Secretive bank accounts • Secretive salaries & renumerations • Messy accounting • Manipulative demands & promises re: tithing • Financial Abuse	• Wise Stewardship & Genuine Generosity • Transparency & Accountability • Donations according to Charitable Law • Membership approved Annual Budget & Financial Statements • Appointment of Treasurer & Auditors for the Fiscal Year • Membership approved financial decisions: Purchasing, selling, transferring, mortgaging, pledging of land/buildings/dissolving the church… • Accounts audited & available for the members' review
MEMBERSHIP	
• Multi-Level Membership & Inside Circle • Unquestioned submission to leadership • Questioning stigmatized as 'rebellious' & disturbing harmony & unity • Revoking & excommunication of 'disagreeable' members & opposition • Direct & Indirect Discrimination: Racial, Gender, Sexual Orientation … • Women oppressed & not allowed to utilize their full talents • Spousal rapes • Children physically abused • Members targeted for sexual abuse & harassment • Only 'trusted' members allowed to participate ministry	• Written definition of membership (qualifications, requirements, procedures, privileges, responsibilities, termination…) • All members equal in the body of Christ (1 Corinthian 12) • Joint vision & mission • Building & Equipping each other • Encouraging spiritual growth • Praying for each others • All members have a role • Mobilizing every member for ministry • Everyone encouraged to serve *1 Cor 1:10–17; 8:9; 12:10–31; 14:26; Rom 12:4–8; 12:5; 15:1; 14:19; Eph 4: 1–6, 11–13, 15–16; 1 Thess 5:14; Hebrew 12:12; Acts 2:42–44, 47; 20:35; Col 2:18–19*

• Pushing certain members' to the sidelines; Diminishing & obstructing their ministry • Taking advantage of volunteers' servitude; Obligations to work for leadership/church's business • Members ostracised, shunned, banned	
COMMUNICATION	
• No dialogue/discussion with members • Silencing & Shaming • Attacking & Threatening • Breaching Confidentiality & Pastoral Gossiping • Brainwashing & Manipulating; Using manipulative prophecies & visions to support decisions • Forbidding to question & disagree with the leadership • Twisting opponent's words • Mischaracterizing opponents • Character Assassination • Excommunication of opposition • Covering Up Crimes; Sweeping issues under the carpets • When caught, use excuses & rationalization to thwart criticism • When crimes revealed, seeing media coverage as a 'trial'/ 'end time attack by the enemy' • Weaponizing their apology to silence the abuse victim; The victim blamed for embellishing, unforgiveness & bitterness; Victim accused of provoking the abuser • Spreading conspiracy theories	• Lawfully organized membership meetings • Transparency • Reporting & discussing of decisions • Studying the Bible together • Learning from each other • Open dialogue & discussion • Safe to ponder different perspectives, ask questions & raise doubts • Honesty & Integrity • Confidentiality • Humbly apologizing for shortcomings • Identifying problems • Planning how to prevent similar future errors • Reaching out ex-members • Small-group ministry to promote relationships • Age/needs specific teaching & leadership training
RELATIONSHIPS	
• Religious Elitism & Arrogance: *"Only our group holds the truth!"* • Judgemental attitude against members, other denominations, local community • Fear & Paranoia against 'the world,' 'un-believers', government, health care professionals, law enforcement... • Crusading against 'sinners' • Hateful Rhetoric • Keeping Appearances / Polished Facade	• Seeing oneself in a realistic light, saved by grace, not perfect • Not seeing 'our' group as superior • Willingness to learn from other groups • Mutual Respect • Networking with the Body of Christ • Seeing all relationships as precious • Loving each others & our neighbours • Understanding the impact of trauma in peoples' lives

• Divided World View: 'us' & 'them'-mentality. *'Those' people are not to be associated with* except for evangelism • Complete separation from 'the world' • Severing relationship to shunned members	• Carrying each other's burdens • Empathetic to the needs of others • Psychosocial work locally & internationally *Gal 6:2; 1 John 3:16; James 3:17; Luke 19:10; Romans 12:10, 18; 14:1; Jacob 4:11; Titus 3:9; Gal 5:22–23; 1 Cor 13: 1–13; Phil 1:14–2:16; Hebrew 12:14; 1 Tim 2:8*
DOCTRINE	
• Secretive & Shifting • Based on revelations, visions & prophecies • Tradition Formulated • Manipulative Biblical Interpretations • Legalism & Work-based salvation • Performance-Oriented Christian walk • Holiness Measurements • Teaching a distorted image of God • Fear based teaching of the end times • Overtly Spiritual: All areas of life seen in spiritual/demonic context. • Reproaching & Shaming members who are sick, suffering mental health issues, not prosperous, struggling…	• Clear Statement of Faith justified with Biblical teachings; Changes approved by the elders & membership • Christ-Centered, Grace-Focused, Spirit-Filled, God-Empowered • Biblical expression of God: His faithfulness, unconditional love, grace & mercy. • *Jesus, Immanuel, God with us.* • Emphasis on John 3:16 gospel *"Whosoever believes…"* • No fearmongering: *Luke 21:9* • Grounded teaching re: spiritual warfare, suffering & blessing • True worship (John 4:23)
ATHMOSPHERE	
• Fearmongering & Bible-Banging • Guilt trips & False Guilt • Shaming & Silencing • Demanding & Measuring Performances • Forcing & Controlling • Freezing & Enabling • Manipulative & Threatening • Nosiness, Snooping & Reporting	• Nurturing, Warm & Loving Fellowship • Compassionate & Empathetic • Accepting & Caring • Trustworthy & Confidential • Open & Transparent • Supporting & Helping each other • Mourning with those who mourn • Celebrating each other's successes

Broken Pottery Inn

The parable of the Good Samaritan (Luke 10:25–37) tells of a man who is violently beaten and unable to continue his journey. Not unlike the victims of spiritual abuse, he was left bleeding and alone. The story also introduces two characters representing the religious community—but we can only speculate their good reasons for not helping the abused fellow. As a therapist constantly dealing with victims of spiritual abuse, I have observed too often the difficulties victims encounter finding a safe Christian community after being deeply traumatized by a church.

Too often the church leadership closes their eyes and ears for a victim of spiritual abuse. They may feel loyalty to the abuser or abusive community (a fellow pastor or someone well-known and respected), preventing them from intervening. They may be scared to interfere because they don't want to be attacked themselves. They may doubt the victim's trauma-story, deny, or belittle. They may rationalize and excuse the abuser's actions. They may stigmatize the victim and blame them for causing their abuse. They may fear that the trauma may be contagious and cause others' festering wounds to open. They may lack trauma-informed training and fear doing more harm by helping. Unfortunately, the victim is all too often left bleeding or with more grievous injury after suffering new blows!

The good Samaritan gives a practical example of pastoral care that a victim of spiritual abuse should receive in their new, therapeutic church community. The first step towards healing of this broken pottery is for the helper to stop and identify the need, without excuses or blaming the victim. The second step is to help and take responsibility. The wounds need to be properly cleaned. There may be a need for a healing ointment, and the wounds must be bound. In a therapeutic church community nobody is left bleeding thinking that 'time will heal'! The Good Samaritan lifted the wounded fellow on his donkey, took him to the safety of the Inn to receive further care, and even paid for the rehabilitation.

I cannot emphasize enough the importance of having professional counselors and therapists in the Church community and establishing a good relationship with the local mental health community. After receiving first-aid from the church, the victim needs to be supported to continue with a professional therapist. No, I'm not minimizing the power of prayer—we are called to carry each other's burdens and sometimes our role is to help carrying the wounded to the professional therapist. For some broken potteries, the restoration process will be quite long and painful, and it is crucial they feel that their church community is supporting them in the different phases of their journey. Supporting, not stigmatizing!

Sometimes for the sake of truth and reconciliation it is therapeutic for the victims of spiritual abuse to hear the church leadership apologize publicly for the crimes of the past—abuse that occurred in their Christian communities in the name of God. Initiatives such as these have precipitated the release of shame and guilt contained often for decades by some potteries.

I like the idea of the church community and its small-groups as Inns for Broken Pottery—*a Broken Pottery Inn*. It is a refuge, a safe place to be seen, heard, cared, and protected. To rest, reflect, and recover; take shelter from the storm; experience relief—The Great Potter's table.

Containers

As clay potteries, we are called to carry one another's burdens (Galatians 6:2) and mourn with those who mourn (Romans 12:15). We are called to strengthen each others' potteries. "Therefore encourage one another and *build each other up*, just as in fact you are doing" (1 Thessalonians 5:11). "…encourage the disheartened, help the weak, be patient with everyone (v. 14).

This means that we use our potteries as *containers* for other potteries to dump into and store *their* lives' struggles and emotional pressures. Some clay potteries that help others, as the apostle Paul put it: "have become the scum of the earth, the garbage of the world—right up to this moment" (1 Corinthian 4:13 NIV).

Of course, during this process of carrying and containing one another's burdens, it is essential to realize that to avoid a total overflow of *our* storage, we must have a healthy way of emptying our containers first. If it is already full of our life burdens, there is no room to contain anything else.

For our lights to flare, we need to regularly empty our containers in the Great Potter's presence and then allow Him to fill us with the new oil. None of us clay potteries can make it if we only keep *receiving* others' burdens. We *also* need to receive from the Great Potter for ourselves and allow Him to take care of us.

Heidi McKendrick

Self-Care of Compassionate Potteries

Empathy is to emotionally tune into another's pottery and experience *their* experiences and identify with *their* emotions—being *simultaneously* on the same wavelength, but at the same time separate. It allows us to *know* what the other pottery is speaking, what they are *experiencing,* and what does it *mean* for them. Our own broken pottery experience may help us to feel compassion and empathy for other broken potteries.

Think about the Great Potter. All the stories of Him in the Bible. He felt emotions, grief, sorrow, disappointment, frustration, betrayal, rejection, pain, agony, even anger.

But most of all He felt compassion and empathy.

Storing other potteries' difficult emotions and painful experiences makes us vulnerable to compassion fatigue and vicarious (secondary) traumatization.[97] *Compassion fatigue* is often defined as the cost of caring that helpers pay when feeling deep compassion.[98] *Vicarious trauma* is the transformation of the helper's pottery as a result of empathy with other pottery's brokenness experience. As empathy is always needed to heal trauma, we may immerse ourselves in vicarious traumatization every time we help another clay pottery and receive their trauma material.

When we listen to other potteries' trauma-stories, we simultaneously witness their experiences and empathetically attune with their sense of disconnection, disempowerment, and loneliness. Feeling their feelings and containing their grief, anger, horror, anxiety, helplessness…, is like *experiencing* their dark and insecure world *with* them. As empathetic helpers, we are *always* open emotionally—every time we listen from a position of compassion it makes us vulnerable, and our inner experiences may be transformed due to empathic engagement with others' experiences.[99] If not acknowledged, and if there is not enough self-care, our clay potteries may end up exhausted, even burned out.

For example, as a therapist, when I listen to trauma survivors' detailed descriptions, if I'm not aware, their traumas may become mine as well. In those situations, I might find myself experiencing odd traumatic thoughts, feelings, and nightmares related to *somebody else's* horrible experience. I have sometimes experienced this when listening refugee women's experiences—so evil and cruel it was hard to comprehend.

Self-care for our clay potteries in the Great Potter's service is *essential* so that our lights can continue to blaze. If other clay potteries' trauma becomes ours, it may produce a distorted view of self, world, others, and the Great Potter, ultimately affecting our meaning of life. It may not only disrupt our sense of trust but also generate unusual reactions to everyday situations, tearfulness, vulnerability to over-stimulation of anything emotional, odd panic reactions, numbing of emotions, and short-tempers, for example.

We may feel overwhelmed both emotionally and physically, suffer insomnia, and even begin to experience intrusive thoughts or images of trauma stories we have heard from others, even nightmares. We may start withdrawing from regular social interactions, creativity, and formerly enjoyed activities. We may begin to experience irrational fears of the future and become cynical, even hopeless. In this situation, we may diminish healthy boundaries when rescuing other broken potteries. However, as a symptom of vicarious traumatization, compassion fatigue, or burnout, we may also set overly rigid boundaries in relationships.[100]

Over the last couple of decades, I have conducted vicarious trauma workshops all over the world for 'helpers helping others', also for pastors and church volunteers. During those workshops, I have asked them to reflect on their potteries' contents as *they* store *other's* contents. I've learned that even though this is a common phenomenon among helpers, it is not taught nor discussed enough. Lack of training and understanding of trauma and loss, the grieving process, trauma recovery, etc., contributes to vicarious traumatization among the clay potteries helping others, either as part of their jobs or voluntarily. Also, lacking is supervision and peer support that would allow validation of experiences and ventilation of feelings. Of course, those of us with a history of our brokenness are more likely to experience the impact.

Trauma Therapy Process

After writing over 450 pages about broken potteries I think it is appropriate to say few words for Pastoral counselors and Christian therapists helping broken potteries. This may also be helpful for those considering seeking counseling or therapy.

It is crucial that we take care of ourselves and seek help when we need it. The pastoral staff in any church community should be trained to conduct a risk-assessment, recognize PTSD, depression or other symptoms, and then support the suffering clay potteries to seek appropriate professional therapy and medical help.[101] Helping each other to carry our burdens is the role for Christian potteries. There is *no shame* or need to feel embarrassed if sometimes we also need to seek out the advice of a professional counselor or therapist.

Trauma *is "the result of exposure to an inescapably stressful event that overwhelms a person's coping mechanisms."* [102]

When a clay pottery undergoes trauma, there are often three experiential elements present: A devastating physical and/or emotional pain, a horrifying experience of total helplessness, and a lack of empathy, just like there was in Job's trauma experience.[103]

Being *traumatized* means something excruciatingly bad has happened, alongside feelings of helplessness—this is something many broken potteries have experienced. They were smashed on the floor and there was *nothing* they could have done to help themselves.

Being *deprived* means that at some critical time, good enough care *was not received*—the pottery was neglected or abandoned and then it broke. In both of these cases, not enough empathy was provided. Many broken potteries disclose that it was *not only* the blow they experienced, but the *lack of empathy* shown by *other* potteries during the time when these bad things happened, that injured them. In a way, *"trauma is the absence of healing responses, what did not happen afterwards."* [104]

Similarly, many broken potteries report how the empathy received *during* the most horrible events was *lessening* the damage. Looking back, many broken potteries, including myself, remember 'angels' who came to us during those critical times. They comforted us—saying the *right* words or giving that *right* book to read—something we needed to go on. Empathetic emotional resonance and containing provided by these 'human-angels,' sent by the Great Potter, brought the corrective and compensating experience that made the difference in our lives and stopped the harmful repetition of trauma. Often these angels were broken potteries themselves.

The trauma-focused helping, such as professional therapy or counseling, *always* starts by establishing the sense of *safety and grounding*. This is to be visited every session, sometimes several times, by using comforting and empowering images, thoughts, phrases, pictures, songs, praying, etc. to help self-regulating breathing, and gaining control over any disturbing images or flashbacks.

It is only after a sufficient grounding that the actual trauma-story processing can launch. Remembering and sharing our broken pottery experiences with therapist, counselors, and trusted friends decreases our fears. It is important to understand that memories themselves are not dangerous but they may sometimes *feel* dangerous. Continuously avoiding difficult memories is not a good idea as it steals our energy and may increase flashbacks, with all their associated emotions, pain, fear, rage, shame, and self-blame.

Remembering *safely* is an empowering experience; yet the process often includes a painful reactive phase with variety of feelings of anger or grief. In my practice for trauma-processing, I utilize a chronological 'life-line' or 'river of life' drawing, including the factual life-events pre-during-post-trauma, different sensations and emotions felt during the different episodes, (before-during-after), significant turning points or 'gates' that became before-after episodes.[105]

The idea is to explore the life from a *new* perspective—seeing the bigger picture—gaining new understanding, finding new empathy toward oneself, claiming ownership to one's gifts and talents, and perhaps even noticing the Great Potter's presence during the different episodes. An intellectual insight alone, for example acknowledging the broken pottery episodes, is not enough to *fully* work through a traumatizing experience. The painful emotions, whether anger, grief, shame, or guilt, must *also* be expressed—*safely*. Paradoxically, in therapy or counseling, the pottery must *feel safe* in order to *feel unsafe*.

Trauma recovery is like rebuilding a shattered house.[106] During the first stages, the ruins and the lot must be secured as safe as possible— safety fences around the construction site, ensuring necessary security, resources, and tools, drawing plans, and pulling permits for the project. It is only after the site is safe for everyone involved that the demolition and repairing of the damage can launch. The next phases include rebuilding or repairing the foundation, exterior walls, and the roof. The interior design will take place afterwards. Eventually, the walls are painted, new flooring installed, the window treatments applied; the house will have new lighting, and new life.

In my therapy/counseling practice I follow the dynamic yet not always linear phases of trauma therapeutic process:

(1) Establishing grounding, stabilization, safety, and empowering the broken pottery.
(2) Telling and witnessing the trauma/survivor-story.
(3) Experiencing and expressing trauma/survivor-story related emotions.
(4) Processing and grieving the trauma and its consequences.
(5) Restructuring the assumptive world that was damaged during the trauma, finding new meanings.
(6) Restoring trust and the sense of reality, which was also damaged during the trauma.
(7) Reconnecting and reintegrating the personality so that it is no longer defined by the trauma, and launching the future dreams.[107]

All trauma therapy, including Christian counseling with broken potteries, *must* start with stabilization and grounding that continues throughout the process. There must be a necessary safety for a particular content, next phase of processing, or particular emotions. Moving *gracefully* between the different phases and reinforcing the safety is *a sign of a safe and ethical* work environment. There should never be sense of hurry. The aim is to *empower* the trauma survivor so that their symptoms no longer rule their lives.[108] The survivors must become authors of their own recovery.[109] The counselor's role is to lead the broken pottery to have the divine appointment with the Great Counselor.

There are certain *NO's* that I want to emphasize in this chapter because, sadly, these are often violated in some churches and Christian counseling settings. As a result, the counseling may end up being a re-traumatizing experience for the already broken pottery.

- It is *not* the counselor's role to 'tell' the other pottery what to do but rather to help *them* clarify *their* thinking; what is it that *they* feel they need to do, and why. If you tell others what they should do it means *you* are now taking responsibility for their lives—and that is not realistic.
- In a therapeutic setting with broken potteries there is *no* room for any punitive attitude—absolutely no judging, shaming, Bible-banging, or fear mongering! Think about the Good Shepherd as your role-model. He never used His rod to beat the sheep but the wolves that threatened the sheep (Psalm 23:4).
- There should be zero 'pastoral gossiping.' Sharing another pottery's personal difficulties when asking for prayer support is unacceptable. Confidentiality and trust are crucial!
- A counselor should *never* suggest that a person stops any medication prescribed by their medical doctor.
- Unless they are psychiatrists or medical doctors *qualified* to diagnose, the counselor should *never* diagnose any other person.
- No broken pottery should ever be pushed, manipulated, or forced to disclose or confess any of their experiences; neither forgive and forget.
- No trauma victim should ever be silenced, stigmatized, or diagnosed 'guilty' for their traumatizing experience.
- The counselor should *never* interpret another pottery's dreams, visions, or images—these are *always* personal. The counselor should only ask questions that assist their client to explore possible meanings.
- There should be no hurry. Instead of short couple of minutes 'counselings' at the altar, or in the prayer line, there should be a designated room and time for counseling. Safe boundaries are crucial. It is also important to realize that

a recovery is always a process.
- The counselor should not ask the person 'imagine' Jesus in the room etc. Thanks to the Great Potter, we do *not* have to 'imagine' Him. He is *real*, and He *is* there. According to His promise, where two or three gathers in His name, there He *is* with them (Matthew 18:20). He is not our imaginary-friend but He is *real*. Therefore, although typical in some Christian counseling practices, it would not be appropriate to ask anybody to 'imagine' His presence.
- The counselor should not offer their own distorted image of the Great Potter to the pottery they help.
- There should be *no* spiritual abuse in any counseling setting.

The therapeutic discussion should always aim to diminish shame and isolation, and facilitate sharing, validation and witnessing. The ultimate purpose of any Christian therapeutic encounter is to provide empathy, enhance self-healing, personal post-traumatic growth, instill trust and hope, and promote healthier personality integration so that the trauma no longer overshadows how the pottery sees themselves, others, the world, their future, and the Great Potter.

It is normal for any trauma survivor to *avoid* recalling the trauma related emotions such as shame, humiliation, and helplessness—and protect themselves from pain and re-traumatization. Although professional trauma therapy involves telling trauma-stories, the *first rule,* in order to keep the process safe, is to respect the defences the victim may have, and *not* to force any trauma memories. The defences should always be treated as our God-given best friends, resources, and coping mechanisms. If we do not have enough inner resources, sense of safety, grounding, and stabilization to cope with our memories, a cathartic recollection of trauma events, and re-experiencing the associated emotions would *only* be re-traumatizing. Remembering, even if in the presence of someone empathetic, is *not* same as recovering and healing the memories. However, it may be a good start.

When listening and helping other broken potteries, it is essential to understand that *it takes time* to build a trust that was damaged because of our brokenness—and none of our potteries will be 'completely healed' until in Heaven. Until then we simply alternate between different phases at the Great Potter's table, shelves, wheel, or oven. However, even as unfinished or fractured we can serve the Great Potter and shine His light in the suffering world.

The trauma-stories shared during any therapeutic discussion are *also* survivor-stories— the victims are also *survivors*. Similarly, each trauma-story also includes their wisdom, insights, and new revelations of the *meaning* of their most difficult experiences. Finding a meaning for our trauma and purpose for our pottery is crucial for the recovery process.[110] According to Viktor Frankl, *"In some ways suffering ceases to be suffering at the moment it finds a meaning, […] We may also find meaning in life even when confronted with a hopeless situation, when facing a fate that cannot be changed."* [111]

If we only focus on the *tragic event*s in a trauma-story but neglect to discuss it's meaning, we may not be able to see anything else; the self-healing *may* have already started, or the blessing may already be visible—we may miss the big picture. In the Japanese Kintsugi art of fixing fractured pottery the goal is *not* to hide the cracks but rather re-joining the broken pottery pieces with gold, platinum, or silver. The restored pottery looks gorgeous yet it owns its broken history.

We all wear scars—but so does the Great Potter.

I always feel deeply humbled and honored when allowed to step onto another broken pottery's world, walk a mile with them, learn from them, hear their survivor-story, and celebrate the Great Potter who never forsakes.

The Great Potter Knew the Risks

As wounded healers helping others who are wounded, we continuously need to allow the Wounded Healer to continue the healing process of *our* wounds as well. As we are called to carry one another's burdens, we are also called to empty our burdens onto the Great Potter. The last thing we want is to be a helper who serves others but does not let anybody help us. "Cast all your anxiety on him because he cares for you" (1 Peter 5:7 NIV).

The Great Potter's invitation to come to Him and rest (Matthew 11:28) is also for the clay potteries who help other potteries to carry their burdens. The self-care and resting periods on the Great Potter's table and shelves are essential.

The Great Potter did not use cast iron or stainless steel as a material to contain His treasure. When He chose clay pottery to shine His light, *He knew the risks*. He knew how easily we clay potteries break. However, He also knew the *resiliency* of new clay and the *durability* of a once-fired piece, although broken. To be a lump of clay in His hands means we surrender to the different phases at the Potter's house, to be kneaded and molded and placed in His firing ovens to become the vessels that shine His blessings in this broken world. The broken clay pieces on the Great Potter's table are to be used to make the pottery exactly what He desires in His plan, "shaping it as seemed best for him" (Jeremiah 18:4 NIV).

Yes, as clay potteries, we many break even while we help others. It is important we allow the self-care and seek help when needed.

CHAPTER 58

FINAL WORDS
THE CRACKED POTTERY AND FLOWERS

Writing this book was a process of immersing myself into the secrets of broken pottery. Looking back on the history and life journey of my broken pottery, I cannot but feel the Great Potter's unfailing love, never-ending grace, and everlasting faithfulness.

Life is sun and shadows, peace and storms, dark gorges and green pastures, dry deserts and refreshing rivers, mountains and valleys. There is time for everything—we cry and laugh, weep and celebrate, hate and love, break and dance, labor and rest, give up and start up, fall and rise up.

Journeying with the Great Potter means remaining safe even if we may not always feel safe. It means we can trust Him in every situation. Quoting Corrie Ten Boom: *"When the train goes through a tunnel and the world gets dark, do you jump out? Of course not. You sit still and trust the engineer to get you through."* [112]

And the Great Potter is with us all along—He holds the whole world in His hands—He holds our cracked, broken pottery tenderly—even our tiniest clay crumbles are safely collected in His hands.

Remember the secrets for *your* broken pottery, hold them close—*nothing* can separate you from the Great Potter's unfailing love, never-ending grace, and everlasting faithfulness.

There is a blessing in our brokenness, but it does not always look that way in the midst of it. As we have discovered, the Great Potter can beautifully use even our cracks for His divine purposes; His plans are full of surprises. Therefore, we should never think that we are too broken to serve as His vessels.

For every broken pottery, I want to leave this old and touching story I first heard over twenty years ago… *The Cracked Pot.* [113]

Heidi McKendrick

The Cracked Pot

Once upon a time, there was an older man, a faithful servant whose main job was to carry water from the river to his master's house on the top of the hill. The man carried the water from the river in two clay potteries. The pots hung on either side of a rod, which he carried across his shoulders to and from the river several times a day.

One of the clay potteries was perfect in every way for carrying water. The other pottery was similar, but it had a crack in it, and it leaked.

When the old servant carrying the water reached his master's house, the perfect pottery was always full, but the broken pottery was only half full.

The perfect pottery was proud of its endeavors, and it bragged loudly. It criticized the cracked pottery for its failures and reminded it that despite its hard work, the old servant could deliver only half a pot of water due to its cracks. The broken pottery was ashamed of its deficiencies and felt horrible that it could achieve only half of what it was supposed to do.

One day the broken pottery spoke to the old servant, "I want to apologize to you. Because of my cracked side, I've been able to provide only half of the water to your master's house, and you don't get the full value from your hard work."

The old servant smiled at the broken pottery, and in his compassion, he replied, "As we return to the master's house, I want you to see the beautiful flowers along the path from the river."

Indeed, as they climbed the path from the river to the master's house, the broken pottery noticed the beautiful flowers along one side of the path, and it made it feel a bit better. But when they reached the master's house and the water in the half-empty pottery was poured out, his sadness resumed. "Thank you for trying to cheer me up with the beautiful flowers," the broken pottery said. "But again, I still must apologize for my failure."

The old servant said, "Dear clay pottery, you haven't understood what I was trying to show you. Did you notice that the flowers only grew on *your* side of the path? That's because of your crack. I planted flower seeds on *your* side of the path, and every day as we walked from the river to the house, the water that leaks from your pottery watered them. I could have found myself new clay pottery without any cracks, but I preferred to grow these flowers, and with them to bless many people."

Be Blessed and Be a Blessing!

ABOUT THE AUTHOR'S POTTERY

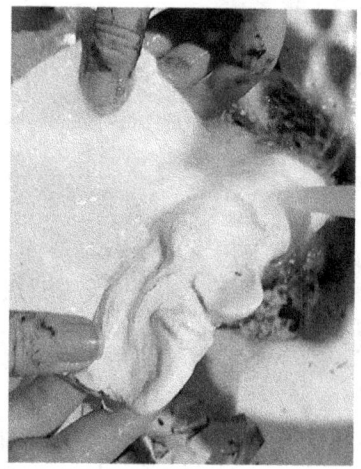

Friends have called my book *Heidi Potter's Adventures*. A fitting title as in a way birthing this book has been a long process that indeed includes, if not 'adventures,' certainly a long *journey* —the good and bad experiences, my learning process with the Great Potter. On His table, seeing, and being seen.

So a few words about my pottery's adventure.

The journey began a long time ago in the snowy north. I had met the Great Potter in my early childhood but had to go through various phases of immersing myself in the secrets of broken potteries before ridding myself of the distorted images of Him.

I finished my PhD in 1998 and I have been a full-time university professor since 1991. I hold an advanced level of psychotherapy–training, and extensive experience in working with potteries suffering psychological trauma and PTSD.

I have conducted innumerable workshops and seminars on grace-filled topics and brokenness around the world to NGO organizations, churches, seminaries, and universities.

My favourite topics include:

- Helping Helpers to Help
- Vicarious Traumatization, Compassion Fatigue, and Burn-out of Helpers
- Counselling Challenges when Working with People Suffering Psychological Trauma, PTSD, or Depression
- Refugee Trauma 101
- Spiritual Abuse
- Therapeutic Pastoral Counseling
- Healing Distorted Images of God.

… and of course: "Secrets of Broken Pottery" and "Broken Pottery Inn." My messages always include the truth that the Great Potter will never throw away our broken pieces!

I am married with two adult children. My pottery enjoys music, art, cooking, gardening, and traveling.

Workshops & Contact

If you are interested in learning more about my workshops or how you can incorporate Secrets of Broken Pottery into your small-group settings, go to www.secretsofbrokenpottery.com.

If you wish to write a review of the book, please send it to editor@katamerismou.com.

THANK-YOU!

This book combines the topics of many pastoral counseling seminars and workshops I have taught over the last couple of decades. During these years I have been inspired by many other potteries and their messages. In this book, I have tried my best to acknowledge them as much as I can recall the sources that inspired me to birth certain ideas. I apologize if I missed anyone.

I want to thank all these sources of inspiration. The other potteries who authored amazing books, researchers who investigated important topics, Bible commentaries, original language scholars, and my many friends who have honestly discussed these topics with me over the years. I want to thank all the broken potteries who have shared their stories. It has been an honor to be allowed to walk with them.

Special thanks to many editors and proof-readers during different phases of my writing process; especially to Erin K. Brown during the first draft. Thank you so much! My warmest thanks for Marie Muravski for your inspiring and talented artwork on the cover and inside the book! Thank you, Daiana Marchessi for your lovely interior design! Thank you for all of those who helped with the many phases of book production process. It was an inspiration to work with creative potteries like yourself!

Extra special thanks to my daughter for the photography and my son for helping with many publishing-related issues. Thank you for my beta-readers with your words of encouragement!

Thanks for my husband for your devoted support, hours of editing, and countless discussions on the topics of this book.

May the Great Potter fill your potteries with His eternal blessings!

And—thank you Great Potter, for always believing in me. Thank you for Your secrets that you revealed to my pottery. Thank you for making me this way!

HEIDI MCKENDRICK

NOTES

Part 1: Introduction

1   Donald W. Winnicott, *Holding and Interpretation: Fragment of an Analysis* (New York: Grove Press, 1986), 243.

2   Linda T. Sanford, *Strong at the Broken Places* (New York: Random House, 1990), 22; Irene Harwood and Malcolm Pines, *Self-Experiences in Group: Intersubjective and Self-Psychological Pathways to Human Understanding* (London: Jessica Kingsley Publisher, 1998), 165.

Chapter 5

3   Horatio G. Spafford, "It Is Well with My Soul." *Gospel Hymns No. 2*, 1876.

Chapter 7

4   I have taken several pottery making courses to learn this process but found the following websites informative about the process: Kaplan, Jonathan, "Recycling Clay: Tips for Collecting, Storing, Reclaiming and Reprocessing Your Clay Scraps. Simple Tips for Recycling Clay," Ceramic Arts Network, January 13, 2021, https://ceramicartsnetwork.org/daily/ceramic-supplies/pottery-clay/recycling-clay-tips-for-collecting-storing-reclaiming-and-reprocessing-your-clay-scraps/; O'Connor Marie, "What Will Happen If There Is an Air Pocket That Goes into The Kiln?" Pottery Crafters, accessed August 1, 2020, https://potterycrafters.com/what-will-happen-if-there-is-an-air-pocket-that-goes-into-the-kiln/; "Quick Answer: What is Kneading of Clay?" Expandus Ceramics, accessed August 1, 2020, https://expandusceramics.com/qa/what-is-kneading-of-clay-2.html; Beth Peterson, "The Firing Process for Making Ceramics. Turning Soft Clay into Rock-Hard Pottery," The Spruce Crafts, October 27, 2019. https://www.thesprucecrafts.com/an-overview-of-the-firing-process-2746250; "Potter's Wheel," Wikipedia, accessed August 1, 2020, https://en.wikipedia.org/wiki/Potter%27s_wheel

5   "Porcelain," How Products are Made, Volume 1, accessed August 1, 2020, http://www.madehow.com/Volume-1/Porcelain.html

Chapter 8

6   Ronnie Janoff-Bulman, *Shattered Assumptions: Towards a New Psychology of Trauma* (New York: Free Press, 1992).

⁷   Viktor E. Frankl, *Man's Search for Meaning* (New York: Pocket Books, 1985), 93.

Chapter 9

⁸   Rachel Yehuda and Amy Lehrner, "Intergenerational Transmission of Trauma Effects: Putative Role of Epigenetic Mechanisms," *World Psychiatry* 17, no. 3 (2018): 243–257; Linda O'Neill, Tina Fraser, Andrew Kitchenham, and Verna McDonald, "Hidden Burdens: A Review of Intergenerational, Historical and Complex Trauma, Implications for Indigenous Families," *Journal of Child & Adolescent Trauma* 11, no. 2 (June 2018): 173–186.

⁹   Bill Gaither and Gloria Gaither, *Because He Lives* (William J. Gaither, Inc., 1971).

¹⁰   Van der Veer Guus, *Counselling and Therapy with Refugees and Victims of Trauma. Psychological Problems of Victims of War, Torture and Repression* (Chichester, New York: John Wiley,1998); Richard F. Mollica, *Healing Invisible Wounds. Paths to Hope and Recovery in a Violent World* (Nashville: Vanderbilt University Press. 2006).

Chapter 10

¹¹   I combined the typical grief/trauma processes from the following sources: Elisabeth Kubler-Ross, *On Death and Dying* (New York: Macmillan, 1969); Colin M. Parkes and Robert S. Weiss, *Recovery from Bereavement* (New York: Basic Books, 1983); John Bowlby, "Process of Mourning," *International Journal of Psycho-Analysis* 42 (1961): 217–340; Catherine M. Sanders, *Grief: The Mourning After* (New York: John Wiley & Sons, 1989); Judith Herman, *Trauma and Recovery. The Aftermath of Violence* (New York: Basic Books, 1992); J. W. Worden, *Grief Counseling and Grief Therapy: A Handbook for the Mental Health Practitioner*, 3rd ed. (New York: Springer Publishing Company, 2002).

¹²   *A flashback* means that something in the environment (e.g. a certain smell, visual, sound, sensation) *triggers* the traumatic memory. Because trauma memories are stored as sensations and emotional memory, it means that *similar* ones can trigger them. When confronted with trauma reminders, by activating the adrenaline of the body, the amygdala (the fear response/emotion processing center in the Limbic System of the brain) also activates *the emergency response*. As a result the body goes into the same mode as during the original trauma, i.e. freeze, flight, fight, fright, flag or faint. In the case of PTSD (Post Traumatic Stress Disorder), the *amygdala* does not wait around for the cortex and conscious mind to examine if a threat is real or not— it simply reacts, and we may become overwhelmed by the same feelings we experienced during the original event, e.g. fear, helplessness, or horror. We will also experience the same physical symptoms, e.g.

increased heart rate and blood pressure, shallow and rapid breathing, tensing muscles, increased visual acuity and auditory sounds, sweating, trembling, and hot or cold flashes. In a way, a flashback is a 'trick' that happens on the brain. It makes the victim feel they are in danger although they are perfectly safe. The body and mind has been turned on like a light switch. *The nightmares* are like *delayed* flashbacks and can be triggered by sensory perception, either from the dream or from something that took place during the previous day. Trauma survivors often have repeating traumatic nightmares that wake them in a panic, not allowing them to go back to sleep again. References: Mollica, *Healing Invisible Wounds*; Maggie Schauer, Margarete Schauer, Frank Neuner, and Thomas Elbert. *Narrative Exposure Therapy. A Short-Term Treatment for Traumatic Stress Disorder* (Cambridge, MA: Hogrefe Publishing, 2011); Bessel Van der Kolk, *Psychological Trauma*. Washington, DC: American Psychiatric Press, 1997); Van der Kolk, *The Body Keeps the Score: Brain, Mind, and Body in the Healing of Trauma* (London: Penguin Books, 2015).

[13]   Mollica, *Healing Invisible Wounds*; Schauer et al., *Narrative Exposure Therapy*.

[14]   Ann Cattanach, *Play Therapy with Abused Children* (London: Jessica Kingsley Publishers, 1992), 147.

Chapter 15

[15]   Philip Yancey, *What's So Amazing about Grace?* (Grand Rapids, MI: Zondervan, 1997), 70. This was an essential read for my broken pottery recovering from legalism. It helped me to understand God's grace and love. I highly recommend this book and: Yancey, *The Jesus I Never Knew* (Grand Rapids, MI: Zondervan, 1995).

Chapter 16

[16]   Mollica, *Healing Invisible Wounds*, 66.

[17]   Mollica, 8.

[18]   Mollica, 72.

[19]   Mollica, 66.

[20]   "Perpetrators of Sexual Violence: Statistics," Rape, Abuse & Incest National Network, accessed March 25, 2021, https://www.rainn.org/statistics/perpetrators-sexual-violence

[21]   "NISVS Summary Report- Sexual Violence by any Perpetrator," National Sexual Violence Resource Center, accessed March 25, 2021, https://www.nsvrc.org/statistics

22   "Revelation 2:17." Commentaries of Elliot, MacLaren, Meyer, Barnes, Matthew, Gill, Jamieson Fausset-Brown. 2004-2021. Accessed February 8, 2021, https://biblehub.com/commentaries/revelation/2-17.htm; Max Lucado, *When God Whispers your Name* (Dallas, TX: Word Publishing, 1994), 199. This was an important book for my broken pottery's recovery and it was here I first encountered the idea of the white stones. I recommend this for everyone doubting God's love and grace.

Chapter 17

23   Beth Moore, *Get Out of That Pit* (Nashville, TN: Thomas Nelson Inc., 2007), "Introduction," Kindle Loc 129, Chapter 1: "Life in the Pit," Kindle Loc 242. In this book Beth Moore presents three reasons people may end up *stuck in a pit: Being thrown into a pit, slipping into a pit,* and *jumping into a pit*. Reading this book inspired me to further develop my idea of different reasons our clay potteries may break. I recommend this book for anyone experiencing "being stuck" in any 'pit.'

Chapter 18

24   Dietrich Bonhoeffer, *Von guten Mächten treu und still umgeben,* trans. Hilmar H. Werner (1945; BerlinerTourGuide, 2010), 1st verse, http://www.berlinertourguide.com/dietrich-bonhoeffer-von-guten-maechten-translation-by-loving-forces.htm.

25   Bonhoeffer, Last verse.

Chapter 19

26   Mary Gallagher, *Ancient Jewish Lullaby,* Contributed by Bernart Bartleby, Antiwar Songs, April 16, 2015, 11:22, https://www.antiwarsongs.org/canzone.php?lang=en&id=49411

Chapter 21

27   Rabbi Diana Villa and Rabbi Monique Susskind Goldberg, *The Distancing of Menstruants from the Synagogue and Sacred Rites,* To Learn and to Teach, Study Bookleds Regarding Women in Jewish Law # 5 (Jerusalem, Israel: The Schechter Institute of Jewish Studies, 2008), 12.

28   Richard N. Longenecker, *The New International Greek Testament Commentary: The Epistle to the Romans,* A Commentary on the Greek Text. On Rom. 8:15 (Grand Rapids,

MI: William B. Eerdmans Publishing Company, 2016); Charles H. Welch, *Just and the Justifier* (London: Yhe Berean Publishing Trust, 1948), 212.

29   Lucado, *When God Whispers*, 2. In this book, I first encountered the idea of our names carved in God's palms, and that they were there when he was crucified.

Chapter 24

30   Mollica, *Healing Invisible Wounds*; Schauer et al., *Narrative Exposure Therapy*; Judith R. Baskin, "Infertile Wife in Rabbinic Judaism," *The Encyplopedia of Jewish Women*, Jewish Women's Archive, February 27, 2009, https://jwa.org/encyclopedia/article/infertile-wife-in-rabbinic-judaism

Chapter 25

31   25 Greek word *Agapao*, 14921 *Oida*, 1097 *Ginoskeis*, 5468 *Phileo*. Strong's Concordance & Lexical Aids to New Testament, in *Key Word Study Bible*, Spiros Zothiates, ed. (Chattanooga, TN: AMG Publishers, 1990), 7, 20, 25, 75, 1817, 1796, 1828, 1885.

32   Merriam Webster, "Definition of Betrayal," in *Merriam-Webster's Collegiate Dictionary*, accessed February 8, 2021, https://www.merriamwebster.com/dictionary/betray%20on%20Feb%208

Chapter 26

33   William Klassen, *Judas: Betrayer or Friend of Jesus?* (Minneapolis, MN: Fortress, 1996); N. T. Wright, *Judas and the Gospel of Jesus* (Grand Rapids, Michigan: Baker Books, 2006); Mark J. Mijangos and Stephenson Humbries-Brook, "The Innocence of Judas In Film," *The Celluloid Savior Religious Studies* 407 (Spring 1997), https://academics.hamilton.edu/religious_studies/home/mijangos.html

34   Daniel Nylund, "Muistokirjoitus Juudaksesta" [Judas Memorial], Teoblogi, April 20, 2009, https://teoblogi.fi/2009/04/7212-muistokirjoitus-juudaksesta/?highlight=-Juudas, Chapter: "Kirkkohistorian Juudas" [Judas of the Church History] last paragraph and "Varoittava esimerkki" [Warning Example], first paragraph, [translated by the author].

35   Gaither and Gaither, *Because He Lives*.

Chapter 27

36   Mendy Hecht, "The 613 Commandments (Mitzvot)," Chabad-Lubavitch, Jewish Practice, accessed October 2, 2020, https://www.chabad.org/library/article_cdo/aid/756399/jewish/The-613-Commandments-Mitzvot.htm

Chapter 28

37   Leonard Cohen, "Leonard Cohen Lyrics: 'Anthem,'" accessed March 2, 2021, https://www.azlyrics.com/lyrics/leonardcohen/anthem.html

Chapter 29

38   Yancey, *What's So Amazing about Grace?* 70.

Chapter 30

39   5485 Greek word *xáris*, Strong's Concordance," accessed October 2, 2020, https://biblehub.com/greek/5485.htm; Zothiates, ed. *Key Word Study Bible*, 77, 1886.

Chapter 33

40   "Martin Luther's Quotation," accessed February 23, 2021, https://www.goodreads.com/quotes/3182271-faith-is-a-living-daring-confidence-in-god-s-grace-so

41   Joseph Thayer, "Thayer's Greek-English Lexicon of the New Testament: Coded with the Numbering System from Strong's Exhausive Concordance of the Bible, #5206, s.v. huiothesia," in *Greek-English Lexicon of the New Testament: Based on Semantic Domains*, Eugene Nida and Johannes P. Louw, eds., Bible Tools, accessed October 2, 2020, https://www.bibletools.org/index.cfm/fuseaction/Lexicon.show/ID/G5206/huiothesia.htm; "Adoption - Vine's Expository Dictionary of New Testament Words," Study Bible, accessed September 15, 2020, https://studybible.info/vines/Adoption; 5206 Greek word *Huitothesia*. Zothiates, ed. *Key Word Study Bible*, 73, 1882.

42   "Ephesians 1:5 Commentary," REV Bible, paragraph 10. accessed October 2, 2020, https://www.revisedenglishversion.com/Ephesians/chapter1/5

43   William M. Ramsay, *A Historical Commentary on St. Paul's Epistle to the Galatians* (Grand Rapids, MI: Baker Book House,1979), 352–353; "Ephesians 1:5 Commentary," paragraph 11.

44   Ramsay, *A Historical Commentary*, 352–353; Welch, *Just and the Justifier*, 212.

Chapter 34

45   Charles Spurgeon, "Charles Spurgeon's Quotation," A-Z Quotes, accessed July 5, 2020, https://www.azquotes.com/quote/877467

46   Daniel Nylund, "Velvoittava Anteeksianto" [The Obligating Forgiveness], TeoBlogi, March 3, 2010, https://teoblogi.fi/2010/03/7-17-3-antakaa-anteeksi/

Chapter 35

47   "Spiritual Life and Man's Three Dimensions," in *Basic Christianity* – Lesson 2, p. 1. Net Bible Study, accessed October 15, 2020, http://www.netbiblestudy.com/00_cartimages/Basic%20Christianity%20-%202.pdf

48   "Spiritual Life" 1.

49   "Spiritual Life" 1.

50   "Spiritual Life" 1.

Chapter 36

51   Charles, C. Spurgeon, "Good Cheer From Grace Received. No. 3020." A sermon published on Thursday, Dec. 27, 1906. *Spurgeon's Sermons* (V53), accessed March 25, 2021. https://ccel.org/ccel/spurgeon/sermons53/sermons53.i.html

52   Mauri Viksten declares we are 100% reconciled. Viksten, *Terveen Opin Paapiirteet* [Basics of the Healthy Doctrine] (Ristinvoitto: Tikkurila, 1980), 72.

53   Edward Mote. "My Hope Is Built on Nothing Less." 1834. Hymn #370, accessed March 19 2021. The Lutheran Hymnal. (St. Louis: Concordia Publishing House, 1941). http://www.projectwittenberg.org/etext/hymnals/tlh/built.txt

Chapter 38

54   Winnicott, *Holding and Interpretation*; Winnicott, *The Child, the Family and the Outside World* (London: Penguin Books, 1947/1964); Winnicott, "Ego Distortion in Terms of True and False Self," in *The Maturational Processes and the Facilitating Environment: Studies in the Theory of Emotional Development*, ed. Donald W. Winnicott (New York: International Universities Press, 1965); Winnicott, *Playing and Reality* (1951; repr., London: Routledge, 1971).

55   Malcolm Pines, *Circular Reflections. Selected Papers on Group Analysis and Psychoanalysis* (London: Jessica Kingsley Publishers, 1998), 47; See also: Donald W. Winnicott, "Mirror Role of Mother in Child Development," in *Playing and Reality*, 113.

Chapter 39

56   Judson W. Van DeVenter, "I Surrender All", in *Gospel Songs of Grace and Glory* (New York: Sebring Publishing Co, 1896).

Chapter 40

57   Corrie Ten Boom, "Quotation." Quotefancy.com, accessed April 8, 2021, https://quotefancy.com/quote/786982/Corrie-ten-Boom-Although-the-threads-of-my-life-have-often-seemed-knotted-I-know-by-faith

58   Corrie Ten Boom, "40 Powerful Quotations from Corrie Ten Boom." Crosswalk.com, accessed April 2, 2021, https://www.crosswalk.com/faith/spiritual-life/inspiring-quotes/40-powerful-quotes-from-corrie-ten-boom.html

Chapter 41

59   Bonhoeffer, *Von guten Mächten treu*.

Chapter 44

60   "Parable of the Talents or Minas," Wikipedia, accessed March 19, 2021, https://en.wikipedia.org/wiki/Parable_of_the_talents_or_minas

Chapter 45

61   Herman, *Trauma and Recovery*, 133.

62   Herman, 51.

63   Herman.

64   C. Jess Groesbeck, "The Archetypal Image of the Wounded Healer," *Journal of Analytical Psychology* 20, no. 2 (1975): 122–145; Noga Zerubavel and Margaret O'Dougherty Wright, "The Dilemma of the Wounded Healer," *Psychotherapy* 49, no. 4 (2012): 482–491; Claire Dunne, *Carl Jung: Wounded Healer of the Soul. An Illustrated Biography* (New York: Watkins/Shelley & Donald Rubin Foundation, 2000); Grant D. Miller and Dewitt C. Baldwin, Jr., "The Implications of the Wounded Healer Paradigm for the Use of Self in Therapy," in *The Use of Self in Therapy*, ed. Michele Baldwin, 2nd ed. (New York: Haworth Press, 2000), 243–261; Henri Nouwen, *The Wounded Healer: Ministry in Contemporary Society* (New York: Doubleday, 1972).

65   Charles J. Gelso and Jeffrey Hayes, *Countertransference and the Therapist's Inner Experience: Perils and Possibilities* (Mahwah, NJ: Erlbaum, 2007).

Part 4: Introduction

66   7495 Hebrew word *Raphah*, Zothiates, ed. *Key Word Study Bible*, 110.

Chapter 48

67   "Lexicon: Luke 4:18," Bible Hub, accessed March 24, 2021, https://biblehub.com/lexicon/isaiah/61-1.htm; 4434 Greek word *Ptōchois*, Zothiates, ed. *Key Word Study Bible*, 62,1873; 6035 Hebrew word *Anavim*, Zothiates. *Key Word Study Bible*, 90.

68   John Newton. "Amazing Grace." *Hymnal*. Public Domain, 1779.

Chapter 49

69   "Lexicon: Isaiah 61:1," Bible Hub, accessed March 24, 2021, https://biblehub.com/lexicon/isaiah/61-1.htm; 2280 Hebrew word Chabash, 7665 Chabar. Isaiah 61:1. Zothiates, ed. *Key Word Study Bible*, 37, 112, 1723, 1780.

70   Charles Spurgeon, "Christ's Hospital, Psalms 147:3," in *Sermons* (The Spurgeon Center for Biblical Preaching at Midwestern Seminary, Metropolitan Tabernacle Pulpit, Volume 38, March 9, 1890), paragraph 5, accessed February 20, 2021, https://www.spurgeon.org/resource-library/sermons/christs-hospital/#flipbook/

71   Spurgeon.

Chapter 50

72   Interesting read about distorted doctrines: J. Lee Grady's *10 Lies the Church Tells Women* (Lake Mary, Florida: Charisma House, 2000).

73   Miriam Adderholdt-Elliott, *Perfectionism: What's Bad About Being Too Good* (Minneapolis, MN: Free Spirit Publishing Company, 1987), 48. Adderholdt-Elliott, "Perfectionism & Underachievement," *Gifted Child Today Magazine* 12, no. 1 (1989): 19–21.

74   Winnicott, "Ego Distortion," 140–57.

Chapter 51

75   "Distorted Vision," American Academy of Ophthalmology, edited February 2, 2021, https://www.aao.org/eye-health/symptoms/distorted-vision

76   Newton, "Amazing Grace."

77   Sanford, *Strong at the Broken Places*, 37.

Chapter 52

78   "Those who are oppressed" / *tethrausmenous* ("Strong's Dictionary 2352. thrauó," Bible Hub, accessed March 24, 2021, https://biblehub.com/greek/2352.htm); 2352 Greek word *tethrausmenous*, Zothiates, ed. *Key Word Study Bible*, 36.

79   Yancey, *What's So Amazing about Grace?* 70.

Chapter 54

80   Daniel Nylund, "Kristityn salatut kiusaukset" [Secret Temptations of a Christian], in *Luova uskollisuus*, Daniel Nylund, ed. (Hyvinkaa, Finland: Kristityn Kasvu. 1985), 222. [adapted & translated by the author].

81 Corrie Ten Boom, "Quotes." Quotefancy, accessed April 5, 2021. https://quotefancy.com/quote/789887/Corrie-ten-Boom-God-buries-our-sins-in-the-depths-of-the-sea-and-then-puts-up-a-sign-that

82 Keren Gueta, "Self-Forgiveness in the Recovery of Israeli Drug-Addicted Mothers: A Qualitative Exploration," *Journal of Drug Issues* 43, no. 4 (2013): 450–467; Breanna J. McGaffin, Geoffrey CB Lyons, and Frank P. Deane, "Self-Forgiveness, Shame, and Guilt in Recovery from Drug and Alcohol Problems," *Substance Abuse* 34, no. 4 (2013): 396–404; Sarah J. Peterson et al., "The Benefits of Self-Forgiveness on Mental Health: Evidence from Correlational and Experimental Research," *The Journal of Positive Psychology* 12 (2017), 159–168; Loren Toussaint et al., "Restore: The Journey toward Self-Forgiveness: A Randomized Trial of Patient Education on Self-Forgiveness in Cancer Patients and Caregivers," *Journal of Health Care Chaplaincy* 20, no. 2 (2014): 54–74; AnnaBelle O. Bryan, Jacqueline L. Theriault, and Craig J. Bryan, "Self-Forgiveness, Posttraumatic Stress, and Suicide Attempts among Military Personnel and Veterans," *Traumatology* 21, no. (2015): 40–46; Everett L. Worthington, Jr., and Diane Langberg, "Religious Considerations and Self-Forgiveness in Treating Complex Trauma and Moral Injury in Present and Former Soldiers," *Journal of Psychology and Theology* 40, no. 2 (2012): 274–288.

83 Everett L. Worthington, Jr., *Forgiving and Reconciling: Bridges to Wholeness and Hope* (Downers Grove, IL: Intervarsity Press, 2003); Worthington, *Forgiveness and Reconciliation: Theory and Practice* (New York: Brunner-Routledge, 2006); Worthington, *Moving Forward: Six Steps to Forgiving Yourself and Breaking Free from the Past* (Colorado Springs, CO: WaterBrook/Multnomah, 2013); Everett L. Worthington, Jr., and Steven J. Sandage, *Forgiveness and Spirituality in Psychotherapy: Relational Approach* (Washington, DC: APA, 2015); Nathaniel G. Wade, Everett L. Worthington, and Julia E. Meyer, "But Do They Work? A Meta-Analysis of Group Interventions to Promote Forgiveness," In *Handbook of Forgiveness*, ed. Everett L. Worthington (New York: Brunner-Routledge, 2007), 423–439; Everett L. Worthington, Jr., et al., "Religion and Spirituality," in *Psychotherapy Relationships that Work: Evidence-Based Responsiveness*, ed. John C. Norcross (New York: Oxford University Press, 2010); Douglas K. Snyder, Donald H. Baucom, and Kristina C. Gordon, "An Integrative Approach to Treating Infidelity," *The Family Journal* 16, no. 4 (2008): 300–307; Loren Toussaint, Everett Worthington, and David R. Williams, eds., *Forgiveness and Health: Scientific Evidence and Theories Relating Forgiveness to Better Health* (Springer Science & Business Media, 2015), https://doi.org/10.1007/978-94-017-9993-5; Robert D. Enright and Richard P. Fitzgibbons, *Forgiveness Therapy* (Washington, DC: APA, 2015).

84 Karen Swartz, "Forgiveness: Your Health Depends on It," Johns Hopkins Medicine, accessed September 20, 2020, https://www.hopkinsmedicine.org/health/wellness-and-prevention/forgiveness-your-health-depends-on-it.

85   Worthington et al., *Forgiveness and Spirituality in Psychotherapy.*

86   What forgiveness is a widely researched topic. I've used the following references: Worthington, *Forgiving and Reconciling;* Worthington, *Forgiveness and Reconciliation;* Worthington, *Moving Forward;* Worthington, *Handbook of Forgiveness.*

87   J. W. Worden, *Grief Counseling and Grief Therapy;* Herman, *Trauma and Recovery.*

88   Robert Tillman Kendall, *Total Forgiveness: Achieving God's Greatest Challenge* (London: Hodder & Stoughton, 2002), 68–70.

89   Kendall, 68–70.

Chapter 55

90   Martti Hyrck, *Mielen Kuvat Jumalasta: psykoanalyyttisen objektisuhdeteorian näkökulma jumaasuhteen mielikuvamaailmaan Suomen ev.lut. kirkon v. 1948 Kristinopin tarjoaman aineiston valossa* [Images of God and Unconscious Mind's Images of God…] (Therapeia Saatio: Helsinki, 1995).

91   Hyrck, *Mielen Kuvat Jumalasta.* It was the late '90s when I first read about the concept of false images of God from Hyrck's book. This study was eye-opening for me and profoundly contributed to my process of learning to see the Great Potter in a new, healthier light.

92   Hyrck.

Chapter 56

93   Matthew Henry, "Matthew Henry's Commentary on the Whole Bible, s.v. John 1:1," Bible Study Tools, accessed December 3, 2020, https://www.biblestudytools.com/commentaries/matthew-henry-concise/john/1.html

94   "Exodus 3:14 Commentaries," Bible Hub, accessed October 15, 2020, https://biblehub.com/commentaries/exodus/3-14.htm; 1961 Hebrew word *Havvah*, Zothiates, ed. *Key Word Study Bible,* 32, 1721

Chapter 57

95   *Spiritual Abuse* concept was first introduced by Jeff Vonderen in the 1990's: David Johnson and Jeff VanVonderen, *The Subtle Power of Spiritual Abuse: Recognizing and es-*

caping spiritual manipulation and false spiritual authority within the church (Minneapolis: Bethany House Publishers, 1991); Jeff Van Vonderen, *When God's People Le You Down: How to Rise Above Hurts that Often Occur Within the Church* (Minneapolis: Bethany House Publishers, 1995). Since that time there have been countless books and articles written on the topic, describing it's characteristics and dangers. Stephen Arterburn and Jack Felton, *Toxic Faith* (Nashville: Thomas Nelson, 1991); Ken Blue, *Healing Spiritual Abuse: how to break free from bad church experience?* (ILL: IV Press, 1993); Ronald Enroth, *Churches That Abuse.* (Grand Rapids: Zondervan, 1992); Ronald Enroth, *Recovering from Churches that abuse* (Grand Rapids: Zondervan, 1994); Hank Hanegraaff, *Christianity in Crisis* (Harvest House, 1993); Jeff VanVonderen, Dale Ryan, and Juanita Ryan, *Soul Repair. Rebuilding Your Spiritual Life* (Illinois: IVP Books, 2008).

96 *Healthy Church* is a widely researched topic. For example, Rick Warren, "Rick Warren shares 8 characteristics of a Healthy Church," accessed April 7, 2021, https://www.visionroom.com/rick-warren-shares-8-characteristics-healthy-church/

97 Charles R. Figley, ed., *Treating Compassion Fatigue* (New York: Brunner/Routledge, 2002); Franoise Mathieu, *The Compassion Fatigue Workbook: Creative Tools for Transforming Compassion Fatigue and Vicarious Traumatization* (New York: Routledge, 2012).

98 Figley, *Treating Compassion Fatigue.*

99 I. Lisa McCann and Laurie Anne Pearlman, "Vicarious Traumatization: A Framework for Understanding the Psychological Effects of Working with Victims," *Journal of Traumatic Stress* 3 (1990): 131–149.

100 McCann and Pearlman.

101 Broken potteries may have experienced two types of trauma (Terr 1994): *Type I- trauma* is a single event, catastrophic, and unanticipated experience (i.e. a serious car crash, a natural disaster, an sudden loss of loved one). *Type II trauma* includes early traumatization, continuous trauma, or psychological trauma that makes person vulnerable for the Type I trauma. *Psychological trauma* includes also *strain trauma*, a "long-continued, stressful circumstance, which has traumatic effects" (Van del Kolk, 1997, 47) and *delayed trauma,* "an event distant in time which originally was without traumatic effect but which achieved a new and traumatic meaning at a later developmental period" (48). According to APA (2013) *Post Traumatic Stress Disorder (PTSD)* "includes a certain combination of the following symptoms: *A:* The person was exposed to death, threatened death, actual or threatened serious injury, or actual or threatened sexual violence, in the following way(s): Direct exposure, witnessing the trauma, learning that a relative or close friend was exposed to a trauma, indirect exposure to aversive details of

the trauma, usually in the course of professional duties (e.g., first responders, medics). *B:* The traumatic event is persistently re-experienced, in the following way(s): Intrusive thoughts, nightmares, flashbacks, emotional distress, or physical reactivity after exposure to traumatic reminders. *C:* Avoidance of trauma-related stimuli after the trauma, in the following way(s): Trauma-related thoughts, feelings, or reminders. *D:* Negative thoughts or feelings that began or worsened after the trauma, in the following way(s): Inability to recall key features of the trauma, overly negative thoughts and assumptions about oneself or the world, exaggerated blame of self or others for causing the trauma negative affect, decreased interest in activities." (274.) *The complex PTSD* (C-PTSD) refers to multiple, chronic, prolonged, developmentally adverse traumatic events that took place during childhood. *Depression* "is s more than just sadness. People with depression may experience a lack of interest and pleasure in daily activities, significant weight loss or gain, insomnia or excessive sleeping, lack of energy, inability to concentrate, feelings of worthlessness or excessive guilt and recurrent thoughts of death or suicide. Depression is the most common mental disorder. Fortunately, depression is treatable. A combination of therapy and antidepressant medication can help ensure recovery." (APA, 2021, para 1). <u>References:</u> "Depression," American Psychological Association, 2021, accessed March 2, 2021, https://www.apa.org/topics/depression; I. Lisa McCann and Laurie Anne Pearlman, *Psychological Trauma and the Adult Survivor. Theory, Therapy and Transformation* (New York: Brunner & Mazel, 1990); Lenore C. Terr. *Unchained Memories: True Stories of Traumatic Memories, Lost and Found* (New York: HarperCollins Publishers, 1994); American Psychiatric Association, *Diagnostic and Statistical Manual of Mental Disorders*, 5th ed. (Washington, DC: APA, 2013), 274; Van der Kolk, *Psychological Trauma*, 47–48.

102   Van der Kolk, *Psychological Trauma,* 47.

103   Harwood and Pines. *Self-Experiences in Group*; Winnicott, *Holding and Interpretation.*

104   Sanford, *Strong at the Broken Places*, 22.

105   It is not always easy to recall traumatic memories. While the declarative memory system stores *some* details of the traumatic event as *facts* (e.g. date, time, place, people involved), the *intense emotions* associated with the event are stored as sensations, emotional memory, or bodily memory. The trauma victim may have intense recollections of sensory details (e.g. smell of blood, loud sounds, feeling of cold), but at the same time, the traumatic experience may feel *timeless*, without having any beginning or end. As a result, the victim may not be able to differentiate between past and present threats, they remain continuously alert, feeling as if the trauma event is still going on. Even though the victim may see, feel, or hear the various sensory elements of their traumatic experi-

ence, they may not be able to verbalize them, at least not in a chronological order. This also means that similar sensations, such as a sound that someone experienced during the original trauma, can trigger flashbacks of the trauma memories, and the person may not have conscious control over their reactions. A chronological trauma-story telling is one of the therapeutic tools helping to overcome the impacts of trauma and fear, and to gain empowerment over the flashbacks. Telling the story again, step by step, in every detail, in a chronological order, while at the same time processing the related emotions allows the brain to organize the fragmented memory and store it properly into the right area of the brain. References: Van der Kolk. *Psychological Trauma*, 53; Schauer et al., *Narrative Exposure Therapy*; Mollica, *Healing Invisible Wounds*.

[106] James A. Chu, *Rebuilding Shattered Lives: Treating Complex PTSD and Dissociative Disorders* (Hoboken, NJ: Wiley, 2011).

[107] I linked Herman's three phases and Klein and Schermer's healing factors of the trauma group with Mollica's trauma-storytelling elements. See more: Herman, *Trauma and Recovery*; Mollica, *Healing Invisible Wounds*; Herman, *Trauma Story Assessment and Therapy. Therapists Journal for Field and Clinic* (Cambridge: The Harvard Program in Refugee Trauma. Harvard Medical School – Department of Continuing Education, 2006); Robert H. Klein and Victor L. Schermer, *Group Psychotherapy for Psychological Trauma* (New York: The Gilford Press, 2000). I also recommend the following trauma psychotherapy literature: Christine A. Courtois and Julian D. Ford, *Treatment of Complex Trauma. A Sequenced, Relationship-Based Approach* (New York: Guilford Press, 2016); Courtois and Ford, ed., *Treating complex traumatic stress disorders. Scientific foundations and therapeutic models* (New York: Guilford Press, 2014); Peter A. Levine, *Trauma and Memory. Brain and Body in a Search for the Living past* (Berkeley: North Atlantic Books, 2015); Babette Rothschild, *The Body Remembers: The Psychophysiology of Trauma and Trauma Treatment* (New York: W. W. Norton and Company, 2000); McCann and Pearlman, *Psychological Trauma and the Adult Survivor*; Schauer et al., *Narrative Exposure Therapy*; Van der Kolk, *Psychological Trauma*; Van der Kolk, *The Body Keeps the Score*.

[108] During a stressful situation, the brain releases stress hormones, such as adrenaline and cortisol that automatically trigger the body to react. Some traumatic events are so disturbing that the stress response never shuts off. The *Amygdala*, the fear response/emotion processing center in the *Limbic System*, simply keeps on replaying the emotional memories like a broken record. With people who have PTSD, the amygdala is so overresponsive that its size has increased and it cannot properly regulate the fears nor process the emotions any longer. Too much stress hormones in our body can cause numerous issues. One problem is that the *Anterior Cingulate Cortex*, which is involved in rational decision-making, will decrease in size. This is why people with PTSD often have problems concentrating and focusing. Very high doses of stress hormones may also cause a

decrease in size of Hippocampus, a part of the Midbrain that stores our memories. Many studies show that the Hippocampus is smaller in individuals with PTSD, thus explaining why they suffer memory loss, have difficulty recalling certain parts of their traumatic event, or have vivid memories that are always present. It is encouraging to note that therapeutic interventions can normalize the size of Hippocampus and Amygdala. For example, Karlsson's (2011) review indicates that any change in our psychological processes is reflected by changes in the functions or structures of the brain. <u>References:</u> Robert M. Sapolsky et al., "Hippocampal Damage Associated with Prolonged Glucocorticoid Exposure in Primates," *Journal of Neuroscience* 10 (1990): 2897-2902; Tamara V. Gurvits et al., "Magnetic Resonance Imaging Study of Hippocampal Volume in Chronic, Combat-Related Posttraumatic Stress Disorder," *Biological Psychiatry 40*, no. 11 (1996): 1091–1099, http://doi.org/10.1016/S0006-3223(96)00229-6; Mark W. Gilbertson et al., "Smaller Hippocampal Volume Predicts Pathologic Vulnerability to Psychological Trauma," *Nature of Neuroscience* 5 (2002):1242-1247, https://doi.org/10.1016/S0006-3223(96)00229-6; J. Douglas Bremner et al., "MRI- Based Measurements of Hippocampal Volume in Combat-Related Post-Traumatic Stress Disorder," *American Journal of Psychiatry* 152 (1995): 973-978; J. Douglas Bremner, "Hypotheses and Controversies Related to Effects of Stress on the Hippocampus: An Argument for Stress-Induced Damage to the Hippocampus in Patients with Post-Traumatic Stress Disorder," *Hippocampus* 11 (2001): 75–81, https://doi.org/10.1002/hipo.1023; Iris-Tatjana Kolassa and Thomas Elbert, "Structural and Functional Neuroplasticity in Relation to Traumatic Stress," *Current Directions in Psychological Science* 16, no. 6 (2007): 321–325; Roger K. Pitman, "Hippocampal Diminution in PTSD: More (or Less?) Than Meets the Eye," *Hippocampus* 11, no. 2 (2001): 73–74; Rachel Yehuda, "Are Glucocortoids Responsible for Putative Hippocampal Damage in PTSD? How and When to Decide," *Hippocampus* 11 (2001): 85–89; Hasse Karlsson, "How Psychotherapy Changes the Brain: Understanding the Mechanisms," *Psychiatric Times* 28, no. 8 (2011): 21–21.

109 Herman, *Trauma and Recovery*, 133.

110 Mollica, *Healing Invisible Wounds*, 48.

111 Frankl. *Man's Search for Meaning*, 135.

Chapter 58

112 Corrie Ten Boom, "Quotes." Goodreads.com, accessed April 2, 2021, https://www.goodreads.com/quotes/583815-when-a-train-goes-through-a-tunnel-and-it-gets

113 Win Bradley, "The Cracked Pot," English Editing Express, accessed November 7, 2020, https://www.english-editing-express.com/the-cracked-pot.html [Adapted by Author].

BIBLIOGRAPHY

Adderholt-Elliott, Miriam. "Perfectionism & Underachievement." *Gifted Child Today Magazine* 12, no. 1 (1989): 19–21.

Perfectionism: What's Bad About Being Too Good. Minneapolis, MN: Free Spirit Publishing Company, 1987.

American Academy of Ophthalmology. "Distorted Vision." Edited February 2, 2021. https://www.aao.org/eye-health/symptoms/distorted-vision

American Psychiatric Association. *Diagnostic and Statistical Manual of Mental Disorders*, 5th ed. Washington, DC: APA, 2013.

American Psychological Association. "Depression." 2021. Accessed March 2, 2021. https://www.apa.org/topics/depression

Arterburn, Stephen, and Jack Felton. *Toxic Faith.* Nashville: Thomas Nelson, 1991.

Baskin, Judith Reesa. "Infertile Wife in Rabbinic Judaism." In *Jewish Women: A Comprehensive Historical Encyclopedia.* Jewish Women's Archive, February 27, 2009. https://jwa.org/encyclopedia/article/infertile-wife-in-rabbinic-judaism

Bible Hub. "5485 Greek word *xáris*, Strong's Concordance." Accessed October 2, 2020. https://biblehub.com/greek/5485.htm

———. "Exodus 3:14 Commentaries." Accessed October 15, 2020. https://biblehub.com/commentaries/exodus/3-14.htm

———. "Lexicon: Isaiah 61:1." Accessed March 24, 2021. https://biblehub.com/lexicon/isaiah/61-1.htm

———. "Lexicon: Luke 4:18." Accessed March 24, 2021. https://biblehub.com/lexicon/isaiah/61-1.htm

———. "Revelation 2:17." Commentaries of Elliot, MacLaren, Meyer, Barnes, Matthew, Gill, Jamieson-Fausset-Brown. 2004-2021. Accessed February 8, 2021, https://biblehub.com/commentaries/revelation/2-17.htm

———. "Strong's Dictionary 2352. Thrauó." Accessed March 24, 2021. https://biblehub.com/greek/2352.htm

Blue, Ken. *Healing Spiritual Abuse: how to break free from bad church experience?* Illinois: IV Press, 1993.

Bonhoeffer, Dietrich. *Von guten Mächten treu und still umgeben*, translated by Hilmar H. Werner. 1945. BerlinerTourGuide, 2010. http://www.berlinertourguide.com/dietrich-bonhoeffer-von-guten-maechten-translation-by-loving-forces.htm.

Bowlby, John. "Process of Mourning." *International Journal of Psycho-Analysis* 42 (1961): 217–340.

Bradley, Win. "The Cracked Pot." English Editing Express. Accessed November 7, 2020. https://www.english-editing-express.com/the-cracked-pot.html

Bremner, J. Douglas, P. Randall, T. M. Scott, R. A. Brnen, J. P. Seibyl, S. M. Southwick, R. C. Delaney, G. McCarthy, D. S. Charney, and R. B. Innis. "MRI- Based Measurements of Hippocampal Volume in Combat-Related Post-Traumatic Stress Disorder." *American Journal of Psychiatry* 152 (1995): 973–978.

Bremner J. Douglas. "Hypotheses and Controversies Related to Effects of Stress on the Hippocampus: An Argument for Stress-Induced Damage to the Hippocampus in Patients with Post-Traumatic Stress Disorder." *Hippocampus* 11 (2001): 75–81. https://doi.org/10.1002/hipo.1023

Bryan, AnnaBelle O., Jacqueline L. Theriault, and Craig J. Bryan. "Self-Forgiveness, Posttraumatic Stress, and Suicide Attempts among Military Personnel and Veterans." *Traumatology* 21, no. (2015): 40–46

Cattanach, Ann. *Play Therapy with Abused Children*. London: Jessica Kingsley Publishers, 1992.

Chu, James A. *Rebuilding Shattered Lives: Treating Complex PTSD and Dissociative Disorders*. Hoboken, NJ: Wiley, 2011.

Cohen, Leonard. "Leonard Cohen Lyrics: 'Anthem.'" Accessed March 2, 2021. https://www.azlyrics.com/lyrics/leonardcohen/anthem.html.

Courtois, Christine A., and Julian D. Ford. *Treating Complex Traumatic Stress Disorders. Scientific Foundations and Therapeutic Models*. New York: Guilford Press, 2014.

———. *Treatment of Complex Trauma. A Sequenced, Relationship-Based Approach*. New York: Guilford Press, 2016.

Dunne, Claire. *Carl Jung: Wounded Healer of the Soul. An Illustrated Biography*. New York: Watkins/Shelley & Donald Rubin Foundation, 2000.

Ronald Enroth. *Churches That Abuse*. Grand Rapids: Zondervan, 1992.

———. *Recovering from Churches that abuse*. Grand Rapids: Zondervan, 1994.

Enright, Robert D., and Richard P. Fitzgibbons. *Forgiveness Therapy*. Washington, DC: APA Books, 2015.

Expandus Ceramics. "Quick Answer: What is Kneading of Clay?" Accessed August 1, 2020. https://expandusceramics.com/qa/what-is-kneading-of-clay-2.html

Figley, Charles R., ed. *Treating Compassion Fatigue*. New York: Brunner/Routledge, 2002.

Frankl, Viktor E. *Man's Search for Meaning*. New York: Pocket Books, 1985.

Gaither, Gloria, and Bill Gaither. *Because He Lives*. William J. Gaither, Inc, 1971.

Gallagher, Mary. *Ancient Jewish Lullaby*. Contributed by Bernart Bartleby. Antiwar Songs, April 16, 2015, 11:22. https://www.antiwarsongs.org/canzone.php?lang=en&id=49411.

Gelso, Charles J., and Jeffrey Hayes. *Countertransference and the Therapist's Inner Experience: Perils and Possibilities*. Mahwah, NJ: Erlbaum, 2007.

Gilbertson, Mark W., Martha E. Shenton, Aleksandra Ciszewski, Kiyoto Kasai, Natasha B. Lasko, Scott P. Orr, and Roger K. Pitman. "Smaller Hippocampal Volume Predicts Pathologic Vulnerability to Psychological Trauma." *Nature of Neuroscience* 5 (2002):1242-1247. https://doi.org/10.1016/S0006-3223(96)00229-6

Grady, J. Lee. *10 Lies the Church Tells Women*. Lake Mary, Florida: Charisma Media, 2006.

Groesbeck, C. Jess. "The Archetypal Image of the Wounded Healer." *Journal of Analytical Psychology* 20, no. 2 (1975): 122–145.

Gueta, Keren. "Self-Forgiveness in the Recovery of Israeli Drug-Addicted Mothers: A Qualitative Exploration." *Journal of Drug Issues* 43, no. 4 (2013): 450–467.

Gurvits, Tamara V., Martha E. Shenton, Hiroto Hokama, Hirokazu Ohta, Natasha B. Lasko, Mark W. Gilbertson, Scott P. Orr et al. "Magnetic Resonance Imaging Study of Hippocampal Volume in Chronic, Combat-Related Posttraumatic Stress Disorder." *Biological Psychiatry 40*, no. 11 (1996): 1091–1099. http://doi.org/10.1016/S0006-3223(96)00229-6

Hanegraaff, Hank. *Christianity in Crisis*. Eugene: Harvest House, 1993.

Harwood, Irene, and Malcolm Pines. *Self-Experiences in Group: Intersubjective and Self-Psychological Pathways to Human Understanding*. London: Jessica Kingsley Publisher, 1998.

Hecht, Mendy. "The 613 Commandments (Mitzvot)." Chabad-Lubavitch, Jewish Practice. Accessed October 2, 2020. https://www.chabad.org/library/article_cdo/aid/756399/jewish/The-613-Commandments-Mitzvot.htm.

Henry, Matthew. "Matthew Henry's Commentary on the Whole Bible, s.v. John 1:1." Bible Study Tools, Accessed December 3, 2020. https://www.biblestudytools.com/commentaries/matthew-henry-concise/john/1.html.

Herman, Judith. *Trauma and Recovery. The Aftermath of Violence*. New York: Basic Books, 1992.

How Products are Made. "Porcelain." Volume 1. Accessed August 1, 2020. http://www.madehow.com/Volume-1/Porcelain.html

Hyrck, Martti. *Mielen Kuvat Jumalasta: psykoanalyyttisen objektisuhdeteorian näkökulma jumaasuhteen mielikuvamaailmaan Suomen ev.lut. kirkon v. 1948 Kristinopin tarjoaman aineiston valossa* [Images of God and Unconscious Mind's Images of God…]. Helsinki: Therapeia Foundation, 1995.

Janoff-Bulman, Ronnie. *Shattered Assumptions: Towards a New Psychology of Trauma*. New York: Free Press, 1992.

Johnson, David, and Jeff VanVonderen. *The Subtle Power of Spiritual Abuse: Recognizing and escaping spiritual manipulation and false spiritual authority within the church*. Minneapolis: Bethany House Publishers, 2005.

Kaplan, Jonathan. "Recycling Clay: Tips for Collecting, Storing, Reclaiming and Reprocessing Your Clay Scraps. Simple Tips for Recycling Clay." Ceramic Arts Network. January 13, 2021. Accessed January 13, 2021. https://ceramicartsnetwork.org/daily/ceramic-supplies/pottery-clay/recycling-clay-tips-for-collecting-storing-reclaiming-and-reprocessing-your-clay-scraps/.

Karlsson, Hasse. "How Psychotherapy Changes the Brain: Understanding the Mechanisms." *Psychiatric Times* 28, no. 8 (2011): 21–21.

———. "How Psychotherapy Changes the Brain: Understanding the Mechanisms." *Psychiatric Times* 28, no. 8 (2011): 21-21.

Kendall, Robert Tillman. *Total Forgiveness: Achieving God's Greatest Challenge*. London: Hodder & Stoughton, 2002.

Klassen, William. *Judas: Betrayer or Friend of Jesus*. Minneapolis, MN: Fortress, 1996.

Klein, Robert H., and Victor L. Schermer, V. R. *Group Psychotherapy for Psychological Trauma*. New York: The Gilford Press, 2000.

Kolassa, Iris-Tatjana, and Thomas Elbert. "Structural and Functional Neuroplasticity in Relation to Traumatic Stress." *Current Directions in Psychological Science* 16, no. 6 (2007): 321–325

Kubler-Ross, Elisabeth. *On Death and Dying.* New York: Macmillan, 1969.

Levine, Peter A. *Trauma and Memory. Brain and Body in a Search for the Living past.* Berkeley: North Atlantic Books, 2015.

Longenecker, Richard N. *The New International Greek Testament Commentary: The Epistle to the Romans.* A Commentary on the Greek Text. On Rom. 8:15. Grand Rapids, MI: William B. Eerdmans Publishing Company, 2016.

Lucado, Max. *When God Whispers your name.* Dallas: Word Publishing, 1994.

Luther, Martin. Quotation. Accessed Feb 23, 2021. https://www.goodreads.com/quotes/3182271-faith-is-a-living-daring-confidence-in-god-s-grace-so.

Mathieu, Franoise. *The Compassion Fatigue Workbook: Creative Tools for Transforming Compassion Fatigue and Vicarious Traumatization.* New York: Routledge, 2012.

McCann, I. Lisa, and Laurie Anne Pearlman. "Vicarious Traumatization: A Framework for Understanding the Psychological Effects of Working with Victims." *Journal of Traumatic Stress* 3 (1990): 131–149.

———. *Psychological trauma and the adult survivor. Theory, therapy and transformation.* New York: Brunner & Mazel, 1990.

McGaffin, Breanna J., Geoffrey CB Lyons, and Frank P. Deane. "Self-Forgiveness, Shame, and Guilt in Recovery from Drug and Alcohol Problems." *Substance Abuse* 34, no. 4 (2013): 396–404.

Merriam Webster. "Definition of Betrayal." In *Merriam-Webster's Collegiate Dictionary.* Accessed February 8, 2021. https://www.merriam-webster.com/dictionary/betray%20on%20Feb%208.

Mijangos, Mark J., and Stephenson Humbries-Brook. "The Innocence of Judas In Film." *The Celluloid Savior Religious Studies* 407 (Spring 1997). https://academics.hamilton.edu/religious_studies/home/mijangos.html

Miller, Grant D., and Dewitt C. Baldwin, Jr. "The Implications of the Wounded Healer Paradigm for the Use of Self in Therapy." *The Use of Self in Therapy,* edited by Michele Baldwin, 2nd ed., 243–261. New York: Haworth Press, 2000.

Mollica, Richard F. *Healing Invisible Wounds: Paths to Hope and Recovery in a Violent World.* Nashville, TN: Vanderbilt University Press, 2006.

———. *Trauma story assessment and therapy. Therapists journal for field and clinic.* Cambridge: The Harvard Program in Refugee Trauma. Harvard Medical School – Dept. of Cont. Ed., 2006.

Moore, Beth. *Get Out of That Pit.* Nashville, TN: Thomas Nelson Inc., 2007.

Mote, Edward. "My Hope Is Built on Nothing Less." 1834. Hymn #370. *The Lutheran Hymnal* (St. Louis: Concordia Publishing House, 1941). http://www.projectwittenberg.org/etext/hymnals/tlh/built.txt

National Sexual Violence Resource Center. "NISVS Summary Report- Sexual Violence by any Perpetrator." Accessed March 25, 2021. https://www.nsvrc.org/statistics.

Net Bible Study. "Spiritual Life and Man's Three Dimensions." In *Basic Christianity – Lesson 2*. Accessed Oct 15, 2020. http://www.netbiblestudy.com/00_cartimages/Basic%20Christianity%20-%202.pdf.

Newton, John. "Amazing Grace." *Hymnal.* Public Domain, 1779.

Nouwen, Henri. *The Wounded Healer: Ministry in Contemporary Society.* New York: Doubleday, 1972.

Nylund, Daniel. "Kristityn salatut kiusaukset" [Secret Temptations of a Christian]. In *Luova uskollisuus* [Creative Faithfullness], edited by Daniel Nylund. Hyvinkaa, Finland: Kristityn Kasvu, 1985.

———. "Muistokirjoitus Juudaksesta" [Judas's Memorial]. Teoblogi, April 20, 2009. https://teoblogi.fi/2009/04/7212-muistokirjoitus-juudaksesta/?highlight=Juudas.

———. "Velvoittava Anteeksianto" [The Obligating Forgiveness]. TeoBlogi, March 3, 2010. https://teoblogi.fi/2010/03/7-17-3-antakaa-anteeksi/.

O'Connor Marie. "What Will Happen If There Is an Air Pocket That Goes into the Kiln?" Pottery Crafters. Accessed August 1, 2020. https://potterycrafters.com/what-will-happen-if-there-is-an-air-pocket-that-goes-into-the-kiln/

O'Neill, Linda, Tina Fraser, Andrew Kitchenham, and Verna McDonald. "Hidden Burdens: A Review of Intergenerational, Historical and Complex Trauma, Implications for Indigenous Families." *Journal of Child & Adolescent Trauma* 11, no. 2 (June 2018): 173–186.

Parkes, Colin M., and Robert S. Weiss. *Recovery from Bereavement.* New York: Basic Books, 1983.

Peterson, B. "The Firing Process for Making Ceramics. Turning Soft Clay into Rock-Hard Pottery." The Spruce Crafts, October 27, 2019. Accessed October 15, 2020. https://www.thesprucecrafts.com/an-overview-of-the-firing-process-2746250.

Peterson, Sarah J., Daryl R. Van Tongeren, Stephanie D. Womack, Joshua N. Hook, Don E. Davis, and Brandon J. Griffin. "The Benefits of Self-Forgiveness on Mental

Health: Evidence from Correlational and Experimental Research." *The Journal of Positive Psych* 2017, 12, 159–168.

Pines, Malcolm. *Circular Reflections. Selected Papers on Group Analysis and Psychoanalysis.* London: Jessica Kingsley Publishers, 1998.

Pitman, Roger K. "Hippocampal Diminution in PTSD: More (or Less?) Than Meets the Eye." *Hippocampus* 11, no. 2 (2001): 73–74.

Ramsay, William M. *A Historical Commentary on St. Paul's Epistle to the Galatians.* Grand Rapids, MI: Baker Book House,1979, 352–53.

Rape, Abuse & Incest National Network. "Perpetrators of Sexual Violence: Statistics." Accessed March 25, 2021. https://www.rainn.org/statistics/perpetrators-sexual-violence.

REV Bible. "Ephesians 1:5 Commentary." Accessed October 2, 2020. https://www.revisedenglishversion.com/Ephesians/chapter1/5

Rothschild, Babette. *The Body Remembers: The Psychophysiology of Trauma and Trauma Treatment.* New York: W. W. Norton and Company, 2000.

Sanders, Catherine M. *Grief: The Mourning After.* New York: John Wiley & Sons, 1989.

Sanford, Linda T. *Strong at the Broken Places.* New York: Random House, 1990.

Sangalang, Cindy C., and Cindy Vang. "Intergenerational Trauma in Refugee Families: A Systematic Review." *Journal of Immigrant and Minority Health* 19, no. 3 (September 22, 2016): 745–54. https://doi.org/10.1007/s10903-016-0499-7.

Sapolsky, Robert M., Hideo Uno, Charles S. Rebert, and Caleb E. Finch. "Hippocampal Damage Associated with Prolonged Glucocorticoid Exposure in Primates." *Journal of Neuroscience* 10 (1990): 2897-2902.

Schauer, Maggie, Margarete Schauer, Frank Neuner, and Thomas Elbert. *Narrative Exposure Therapy. A Short-Term Treatment for Traumatic Stress Disorder.* Cambridge, MA: Hogrefe Publ, 2011.

Snyder, Douglas K., Donald H. Baucom, and Kristina C. Gordon. "An Integrative Approach to Treating Infidelity." *The Family Journal* 16, no. 4 (2008): 300–307.

Spafford, Horatio G. "It Is Well with My Soul." *Gospel Hymns No. 2*, 1876.

Spurgeon, Charles. "Charles Spurgeon's Quotation." A-Z Quotes. Accessed July 5, 2020. https://www.azquotes.com/quote/877467.

———. "Christ's Hospital, Psalms 147:3." in *Sermons*. The Spurgeon Center for Biblical Preaching at Midwestern Seminary, Metropolitan Tabernacle Pulpit Volume 38, March 9, 1890. Accessed Feb 20, 2021. https://www.spurgeon.org/resource-library/sermons/christs-hospital/#flipbook/

———. "Good Cheer From Grace Received." (No. 3020) in *Spurgeon Sermons*. Dec 27, 1906. DECEMBER 27, 1906. Spurgeon's Sermons (V53). Accessed March 25, 2021. https://ccel.org/ccel/spurgeon/sermons53/sermons53.i.html.

Study Bible. "Adoption - Vine's Expository Dictionary of New Testament Words." Accessed September 15, 2020. https://studybible.info/vines/Adoption.

Swartz, Karen. "Forgiveness: Your Health Depends on It." Johns Hopkins Medicine. Accessed September 20, 2020. https://www.hopkinsmedicine.org/health/wellness-and-prevention/forgiveness-your-health-depends-on-it.

Ten Boom, C. *Tramp for the Lord: The Story that Begins Where The Hiding Place Ends*. Fort Washington, PA: CLC Publications, 1974.

———. "40 Powerful Quotations from Corrie Ten Boom." Crosswalk.com, accessed April 2, 2021, https://www.crosswalk.com/faith/spiritual-life/inspiring-quotes/40-powerful-quotes-from-corrie-ten-boom.html

———. "Quotes." Goodreads.com, accessed April 2, 2021, https://www.goodreads.com/quotes/583815-when-a-train-goes-through-a-tunnel-and-it-gets

———. "Quotes." Quotefancy, accessed April 5, 2021. https://quotefancy.com/quote/789887/Corrie-ten-Boom-God-buries-our-sins-in-the-depths-of-the-sea-and-then-puts-up-a-sign-that

———. "Quotation." Quotefancy, accessed April 8, 2021, https://quotefancy.com/quote/786982/Corrie-ten-Boom-Although-the-threads-of-my-life-have-often-seemed-knotted-I-know-by-faith

Terr, Lenore C. *Unchained Memories: True Stories of Traumatic Memories, Lost and Found*. New York: HarperCollins Publishers, 1994.

Thayer, Joseph. "Thayer's Greek-English Lexicon of the New Testament: Coded with the Numbering System from Strong's Exhaustive Concordance of the Bible", #5206, s.v. *huiothesia*. In *Greek-English Lexicon of the New Testament: Based on Semantic Domains*. Edited by Eugene Nida, Johannes P. Louw. Bible Tools. Accessed October 2, 2020. https://www.bibletools.org/index.cfm/fuseaction/Lexicon.show/ID/G5206/huiothesia.htm

Toussaint, Loren, Everett Worthington, and David R. Williams, eds. *Forgiveness and Health: Scientific Evidence and Theories Relating Forgiveness to Better Health.* Springer Science + Business Media, 2015. https://doi.org/10.1007/978-94-017-9993-5.

Toussaint, Loren, Michael Barry, Lynn Bornfriend, and Maurie Markman. "Restore: The Journey toward Self-Forgiveness: A Randomized Trial of Patient Education on Self-Forgiveness in Cancer Patients and Caregivers." *Journal of Health Care Chaplaincy* 20, no. 2 (2014): 54–74.

Van der Kolk, Bessel. *Psychological Trauma.* Washington, DC: American Psychiatric Press, 1997.

———. *The Body Keeps the Score: Brain, Mind, and Body in the Healing of Trauma.* London: Penguin Books, 2015.

Van der Veer, Guus. *Counselling and Therapy with Refugees and Victims of Trauma. Psychological Problems of Victims of War, Torture and Repression.* Chichester, New York: John Wiley, 1998.

Van DeVenter, Judson W. "I Surrender All", in *Gospel Songs of Grace and Glory.* NY: Sebring Publishing Co, 1896.

VanVonderen, Jeff, Ryan, Dale, and Juanita Ryan. *Soul Repair. Rebuilding Your Spiritual Life.* Illinois: IVP Books, 2008.

Viksten, Mauri. *Terveen opin paapiirteet* [Basics of Healthy Doctrine]. Ristinvoitto: Tikkurila, 1980.

Villa, Rabbi Diana, and Rabbi Monique Susskind Goldberg. *The distancing of menstruants from the Synagogue and Sacred Rites. To Learn and To Teach.* Study Booklets Regarding Women in Jewish Law. # 5. Jerusalem, Israel: The Schechter Institute of Jewish Studies, 2008.

Wade, Nathaniel G., Everett L. Worthington, and Julia E. Meyer. "But Do They Work? A Meta-Analysis of Group Interventions to Promote Forgiveness." In Worthington, *Handbook of Forgiveness,* 423-439.

Warren, Rick. "Rick Warren shares 8 characteristics of a Healthy Church," accessed April 7, 2021, https://www.visionroom.com/rick-warren-shares-8-characteristics-healthy-church/

Weinberg, Melissa K., and Robert A. Cummins. "Intergenerational Effects of the Holocaust: Subjective Well-Being in the Offspring of Survivors." *Journal of Intergen Rel* 11, no. 2 (2013): 148-161.

Weir, Kirsten. "Forgiveness Can Improve Mental and Physical Health." *Monitor on Psychology* 48, no. 1 (2017): 30. https://www.apa.org/monitor/2017/01/ce-corner

Welch, Charles H. *Just and the Justifier.* London: Yhe Berean Publishing Trust, 1948.

Wikipedia. "Parable of the Talents or Minas." Accessed March 19, 2021. https://en.wikipedia.org/wiki/Parable_of_the_talents_or_minas

———. "Potter's Wheel." Accessed August 1, 2020. https://en.wikipedia.org/wiki/Potter%27s_wheel

Winnicott, Donald W. *Holding and Interpretation: Fragment of an Analysis.* NY: Grove Press, 1986.

———. *Playing and Reality.* 1951. Reprinted, London: Routledge, 1971.

———. "Ego distortion in terms of true and false self." In *The Maturational Processes and the Facilitating Environment: Studies in the Theory of Emotional Development*, edited by Donald W. Winnicott, 140-152. New York: International Universities Press, 1960.

———. *The Child, the Family and the Outside World.* 1947. Reprinted, London: Penguin Books, 1964.

Worden, J. W. *Grief Counseling and Grief Therapy: A Handbook for the Mental Health Practitioner.* New York: Springer Publishing Company, 2002.

Worthington, Everett L., Jr. *Forgiveness and Reconciliation: Theory and Practice.* New York: Brunner-Routledge, 2006.

———. *Forgiving and Reconciling: Bridges to Wholeness and Hope.* Downers Grove, IL: Intervarsity Press, 2003.

———. *Moving Forward: Six Steps to Forgiving Yourself and Breaking Free from the Past.* Colorado Springs, CO: WaterBrook/Multnomah, 2013.

———, ed. *Handbook of Forgiveness.* New York: Brunner-Routledge, 2007.

Worthington, Everett L., Jr., and Diane Langberg. "Religious Considerations and Self-Forgiveness in Treating Complex Trauma and Moral Injury in Present and Former Soldiers." *Journal of Psychology and Theology* 40, no. 2 (2012): 274–288.

Worthington, Everett L., Jr., and Steven J. Sandage. *Forgiveness and Spirituality in Psychotherapy: A Relational Approach.* Washington, DC: APA, 2016.

Worthington, Everett L., Jr., J. N. Hook, D. E. Davis, and M. A. McDaniel. "Religion and spirituality." In *Psychotherapy Relationships that Work: Evidence-Based Responsiveness*, edited by John C. Norcross. New York: Oxford University Press, 2010.

Wright. N. T. *Judas and the Gospel of Jesus*. Grand Rapids, Michigan: Baker Books, 2006.

Yancey, Philip. *The Jesus I Never Knew*. Grand Rapids, MI: Zondervan, 1995.

———. *What's So Amazing about Grace?* Grand Rapids, MI: Zondervan, 1997.

Yehuda, Rachel, and Amy Lehrner. "Intergenerational Transmission of Trauma Effects: Putative Role of Epigenetic Mechanisms." *World Psychiatry* 17, no. 3 (2018): 243–257.

———. "Are Glucocortoids Responsible for Putative Hippocampal Damage in PTSD? How and When to Decide." *Hippocampus* 11 (2001): 85–89.

Zerubavel, Noga, and Margaret O'Dougherty Wright. "The Dilemma of the Wounded Healer." *Psychotherapy* 49, no. 4 (2012): 482–491.

Zothiates, Spiros, Ed. *Key Word Study Bible*. Chattanooga, TN: AMG Publishers, 1990.

www.ingramcontent.com/pod-product-compliance
Lightning Source LLC
Chambersburg PA
CBHW081404080526
44589CB00016B/2473